Walking with Strangers

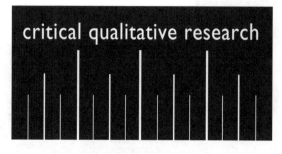

critical qualitative research

Shirley R. Steinberg
Series Editor

Vol. 29

The Critical Qualitative Research series is part of the Peter Lang Education list.
Every volume is peer reviewed and meets the highest
quality standards for content and production.

PETER LANG
New York • Bern • Berlin
Brussels • Vienna • Oxford • Warsaw

Barbara Dennis

Walking with Strangers

Critical Ethnography and Educational Promise

PETER LANG
New York • Bern • Berlin
Brussels • Vienna • Oxford • Warsaw

Library of Congress Cataloging-in-Publication Data

Names: Dennis, Barbara, author.
Title: Walking with strangers: critical ethnography and educational
promise / Barbara Dennis.
Description: New York: Peter Lang, 2020.
Series: Critical qualitative research; Vol. 29 | ISSN 1947-5993
Includes bibliographical references.
Identifiers: LCCN 2020024514 (print) | LCCN 2020024515 (ebook)
ISBN 978-1-4331-8023-1 (hardback) | ISBN 978-1-4331-1047-4 (paperback)
ISBN 978-1-4331-8024-8 (ebook pdf)
ISBN 978-1-4331-8025-5 (epub) | ISBN 978-1-4331-8026-2 (mobi)
Subjects: LCSH: Educational anthropology—Research—Methodology—
United States. | Social justice and education—United States. |
Educational change—Social aspects—United States. |
Theater and society—United States.
Classification: LCC LB45 .D45 2020 (print) | LCC LB45 (ebook)
DDC 306.430973—dc23
LC record available at https://lccn.loc.gov/2020024514
LC ebook record available at https://lccn.loc.gov/2020024515
DOI 10.3726/b16927

Bibliographic information published by **Die Deutsche Nationalbibliothek.**
Die Deutsche Nationalbibliothek lists this publication in the "Deutsche
Nationalbibliografie"; detailed bibliographic data are available
on the Internet at http://dnb.d-nb.de/.

© 2020 Peter Lang Publishing, Inc., New York
29 Broadway, 18th floor, New York, NY 10006
www.peterlang.com

This book is dedicated to Dreamers.
And to those who fight to make public schools a
site of social justice, equity, and promise.

Contents

Figures

Tables

Preface

The "position of the stranger stands out more sharply if, instead of leaving the places of his activity, he settles down there."

(Simmel, 1908 in Lemmert, 1993, p. 201)

Sometimes we end up in the middle of something we never quite knew we were getting into. Sometimes we find ourselves in foreign territory, bewildered and lonesome, doing our best to figure out what is going on around us while also trying to figure out ourselves. Sometimes we look in the mirror and see something new. These were the kinds of experiences I had in Unityville.[1]

This "years later" context now includes the U.S. Government, under the administration of President Donald Trump, separating children from their parents at the border, promoting attitudes of criminalization toward border crossers, and seeking the funds to build, maintain and militarize a wall on the U.S. southern border. I feel walled in by the starkly expanding contradictions between these policies and the epitaph "Give us your tired, your poor, your huddled masses yearning to breathe free." The unacceptable murder of Black people by state force and the further destruction of native land evidence the persistent and pervasive reach of white supremacy with its unequal treatment of Black and Brown peoples. This current moment offers a particularly poignant vantage point for returning to the methodological story of our ethnographic work with "newcomers" in Unityville.

Unityville is a suburban town in the Midwest United States where trans-national and immigrant youth were enrolling in the schools at expanding rates. Many educators in Unityville felt unprepared to succeed with the new students. I was invited into Unityville schools because the educators wanted help. I am a critical participatory ethnographer and I facilitated what we eventually called the "IU-Unityville Outreach Project"—a critical collaborative participatory ethnographic endeavor through which inquiry, methodology, and educational project activities were inseparable. This book is a story about strangers, ordinary strangers, trying to understand one another through the contexts of inquiry and schooling. As one of many tales that could be told about our experiences with the project, this is a methodological one.

People in Unityville thought of their town and their schools as monocultural. When "newcomers" moved in, things seemingly began to change. Of course, they did. Though change itself might be resisted, it is an unavoidable characteristic of human life. Into the schools walked middle-class students from Japan whose fathers had assumed temporary positions in their corporations' nearby offices. Flanking them on all sides were students from Mexico who had migrated with their families for a variety of reasons including opportunities for work and educa-tion. Mingled with the students from Mexico were youngsters from other Central and South American countries. Spanish-speakers comprised the largest group of "newcomers," wielding the smallest amount of economic, political, and cultural U.S. capital. In addition to these groups, there were families arriving from a vari-ety of countries. There was a Palestinian-Israeli family, a Taiwanese family, and a Russian family, for example. The ethnic, national, linguistic diversity of Unityville has continued to blossom through the years, family by family and group by group. Though it might seem obvious that the migrating students and their families were strangers to Unityville schools, we should also note that I, too, was an outsider there. For whites in Unityville, African Americans had been outsiders in earlier days. And, Unityville sits on the historical land of Kiikaapoi, Miami, and Adena Native peoples for whom Euro-Americans had been strangers.

Early ethnographers were considered outsiders. In fact, ethnographers of the nineteenth and early twentieth century were largely progeny of the reigning European colonial ambitions and mindsets. The difference between ethnographer and "native" was unacknowledged fodder for ethnographic judgments and discov-eries. Contemporary ethnographers have to take seriously what it means to enter and leave communities to which one does not belong. Researchers both magnify and traverse their tenuous connection to insiders by establishing relationships with their participants and joining in the life activities through which their participants are simultaneously engaged. That was my position in Unityville. I didn't even know where Unityville was on a map before this project began. I brought with me a team of graduate students, all of whom were unfamiliar with both Unityville and one another. Though we came from the same university, we were from different departments, different countries, different language groups, different religious upbringings, and with different interests.

The strangeness doesn't end there. Community members themselves can co-exist without really knowing or understanding one another. People in Unityville assumed that without the "newcomers" their town was monocultural and homogeneous. Perhaps their presumed similarities ended up hiding things they did not know about each other and erasing things they didn't know how to see. There was newness to be found even in the most familiar of relationships and contexts. "The stranger is an element of the group itself" as we discover that "a trace of strangeness ... easily enters even the most intimate relationships" (Simmel, 1908, in Lemmert, 1993, pp. 200, 202). As Ahmed (2000) has argued, "The stranger is somebody we know as not knowing, rather than somebody we simply do not know" (p. 55). According to Ahmed (2000) our knowledge of ourselves is intimately linked to how we understand the boundaries of our self-knowledge by marking strangers as outsiders to that self-knowledge. In a deep way, then, border-crossers, transmigrant youth, strangers are already both disruptive of the center and part of its very definition.

The IU-Unityville Outreach Project developed into an opportunity for diverse groups of people to come together in an attempt to face resistance, fears, dreams, struggles, triumphs, community, and relationships. When we began, people were barely speaking with one another about the "newcomer" "situation." Critical participatory ethnography became our path to caring about, understanding, and expressing our shared and disparate life trajectories. Somehow, day-by-day, we forged this complicated nest of research and educational engagements. We began *walking* together.

I was primarily responsible for the research effort which was seamlessly intertwined with the overall project aimed at reaping the social and educational benefits of this newly diversified school population. This book is about the methodological practices, theories and experiences that constituted the project. The research was critical because we drew on critical metatheory and methodology and because we cared about fostering more just and equitable social circumstances, where people could listen to one another, speak freely of their experiences and their needs, and foster mutual understanding and respect. We studied white privilege/supremacy, language oppression, and other damaging forces involved in the maintenance of the status quo in order to resist those forces. We harbored special concerns for Untiyville's strong and articulate transnational youth caught in conditions set to disempower them and leave their lives under-articulated. This special concern both united and distanced us from people in Unityville, though it was a steady feature of our encounters across the life of the project. This story brings to the foreground the methodological practices, decisions, creativities, and challenges while backgrounding the substantive stories. Thus the book offers a reversal on the more typical ethnographic tales that background methodology in order to foreground participants, fields and communities.

The book enters the scholarly conversation at a time when post-qualitative approaches challenge the very tradition of qualitative methodologies like ethnography and give reason to question the doing of social research.

> Someone suggested I begin a new qualitative study, and I entertained that possibility for about thirty seconds. I hadn't done a "qualitative" study since 1997, two years after I graduated with my doctorate, and that study had been an impossibility for many reasons. Whenever I thought about doing qualitative research in the ensuing years, I froze up and went to the movies instead. It's not that I hadn't been reading, writing, thinking, and inquiring relentlessly. I just couldn't do qualitative research. It was unthinkable, so undoable. (St. Pierre 2014, p. 9)

What does it mean to produce a methodological text in this moment? What does such a text have to offer? Part of the answer to these questions depend on how one conceptualizes research. For me the most ideal image of research is an egalitarian and equitable conversation. A conversation *with* people that seriously honors and defers to the wisdom, value, and ethics of those at the metaphorical table. It is purposeful and dialogic, fallible and action-oriented, ethical and open. It takes into account the perspectives of all who would be affected by its work to the extent possible, recognizing that this will always be partial. At a presentation during the International Congress on Qualitative Inquiry 2016, an audience member asked the esteemed group of scholars comprising the panel, "Why should we continue to do qualitative inquiry?" One of the panelists had an answer for himself. Norm Denzin said that as a veteran of the Vietnam war, he must still actively do things to try to make the world a better place. He still believes this is possible. He still believes research has a place in this goal. So do I. And, as hate crimes are on the rise, anti-immigrant propaganda is being spewed, whiteness persists as a rallying cry for racial brutality, and blatant anti-factualism is publicly tolerated, it is important to speak into the conversation with careful methodological exploration of what it is research can offer the world, not just in the realm of findings, but in the realm of doings. Using my image of research as a conversation, "findings" are not to be thought of as FOUND or as FINAL. Instead, the findings themselves are conceived as only an aspect of the iterations of knowledge and methodology.

There are a few publications reporting the findings of IU-Unityville Outreach Project (see Brantmeier, 2007; Korth, Martin, & Sotoo, 2007), but this book is unique because it speaks of the research process itself. The methodological focus of this book is very different from other critical ethnographies, including those that look specifically at the situation of marginalized youth in schools. Laurie Olsen's (1997) *Made in America* is a splendid ethnography of immigrant students and teachers in a diverse school community. She cared about many of the same substantive issues we confronted in Unityville. Lourdes Diaz Soto (1997) critically examines how bilingual students and families struggle in the context of public schooling in one particular industrial community (see *Language, Culture, and Power: Bilingual Families and the Struggle for Quality Education* published in 1997). Loukia Sarroub's *All American Yemeni Girls: Being Muslim in a Public School*, 2005, focuses on the experiences of Muslim girls in a public school in the Midwest as "othered." A study by Enrique Sepúlveda III (2011) introduces a pedagogical approach (acompañamiento) he used with Mexican transmigrant youth in California. Acompañamiento is an orientation toward *walking with* which tightly corresponds to the methodological orientation I present in this book. Such critical studies in educational ethnography make compelling arguments and provide rich descriptive accounts. They help us understand the diverse opportunities heeded and missed with students of color in our U.S. schools.[2]

As a complement to the substantive publications, this book provides a detailed analysis of the critical inquiry process itself, including innovations to both theory and practice. The book should benefit researchers who want a firsthand account of what it means to be in the field critically. By foregrounding the methodological tale, I do not ignore the substantive interests and concerns, but rather tightly link their emergence to the fieldwork and analysis through which they are contextualized. Students often ask me to talk about the aspects of research that are not easily made visible: How were decisions made in the field? How were problems confronted? What kinds of innovations were employed? How were the data analyzed? What kinds of relationships were developed? Were there ethical issues? I want to take readers into the heart of my research practices—its challenges, surprises, and insights, through my experiences in Unityville schools.

This collaborative and participatory critical ethnography emphasizes a *withness*. Researchers did not enter the field with research questions and a plan for collecting data. Instead, we created ways to interact, explore, draw out, and express that which we were both experiencing and desiring as individual members of an integrated project. The collaborative and participatory character of the study constitutes the interstitial tissue of our work together. Similar to the description of acompañamiento by Sepúlveda (2011), we took an attitude of *walking with* as strangers to one another, learning side by side. Acompañamiento is described by Sepúlveda (2011) as being

> borne out of a deep sense of empathy, a place where people can come together to dialogue on their most pressing concerns and to support each other as they made their way in their new school and country. It emerged because fellow human beings were in need ... acompañamiento represents the creative acts of a people making space, creating place, and building community in an increasingly fragmented global world. (p. 568)

We used a variety of data collection and analytic techniques producing a rich constellation of methodologies. For example, we used Baol's *Theatre of the Oppressed* (1979) with teachers as a way to explore bullying experiences of "newcomer" students (Chapter 6). Using drama with participants blurred the line between data collection and data analysis. It also introduced analytic challenges—bringing the ethnographer face-to-face with "acting as if" structures of meaning and the juxtaposition between the way things seem and the way things could be. Such methodologies do not stand as a recipe for how others should conduct ethnography, but rather exemplify the ways in which researchers might respond to the context in the process of conducting research. Being responsive to the site requires researchers to weave together opportunities for data generation that are appropriate to the situation with the potential to transform, create, and adopt analysis procedures that are intersubjectively attuned to interactive and relational aspects of the site.

Another interesting feature of this particular ethnography was its active focus on change. The IU-Unityville Outreach Project was aimed toward transformation. Thus, it was necessary to pay attention to what changed and what didn't, mechanisms for maintaining the status quo, and various ways in which change could be noticed through differing conceptions of time. Of course, progress in Unityville was multifaceted and uneven. Depicting and understanding such transformations required the development of subtle analytic techniques. I drew on Wood's (1989/2000) philosophy of time to generate analyses and demonstrate both the process and the outcome of that methodological effort (Chapter 7). You will see these and other unique aspects of the study highlighted in the chapters that follow.

Being a stranger is not, in and of itself, extraordinary, but for us, it ushered in a precious opportunity, seemingly beyond any one person's vision or effort, any single group's monopoly. It was having the strangeness within that energized and made possible all manner of critical and hopeful potentials both methodologically and practically. What ensues is a methodological dialogue that inseparably unfolded through a concern for the educational opportunities available to transmigrant students, strangers amongst strangers in an inevitably turbulent and exciting time in the life of Unityville schools. "One of the radical promises of critical research is the possibility that we can tell a different story" (Fine, 2018, p. 11).

Notes

1. Unityville is a pseudonym. I was a stranger to the place and I was not the only one. Years later, when memories are reshaped by fresh readings and reinvigorated by white nationalist politics, I find there is still something to learn and share from our critical ethnographic work there.
2. See Appendix A for a brief review of the substantive ethnographic literature. Such efforts should be lauded and encouraged.

References

Ahmed, S. (2000). *Strange encounters: Embodied others in postcoloniality.* New York, NY: Routledge.

Boal, A. (1979). *Theatre of the oppressed.* New York, NY: Theatre Communications Group.

Brantmeier, E. (2007). Everyday understandings of peace and non-peace: Peacekeeping and peace building at a U.S. Midwestern high school. *Journal of Peace Education, 4*(2), 127–148.

Fine, M. (2018). *Just research in contentious times: Widening the methodological imagination.* New York, NY: Teachers College Press.

Korth, B., Martin, Y., & Sotoo, N. (2007). Little things that make a big difference: Trust and empathy on the path to multiculturalism. *Scholarlypartnershipsedu, 2*(1), 25–44.

Olsen, L. (1997). *Made in America: Immigrant students in our public schools.* New York, NY: New Press.

Sepulveda III, E. (2011). Toward a pedagogy of acompañamiento: Mexican migrant youth writing from the underside of modernity. *Harvard Educational Review, 8*(3), 550–572.

Simmel, G. (1908). The stranger. In C. Lemmert (Ed.) (1993), *Social theory: The multicultural and classic readings* (pp. 200–204). Boulder, CO and San Francisco, CA: Westview Press.

Soto, L.D. (1997). *Language, culture, and power: Bilingual families and the struggle for quality education.* Albany: State University of New York Press.

St. Pierre, E. (2014). A brief and personal history of post qualitative research: Toward "post inquiry." *Journal of Curriculum Theorizing, 30*(2), 1–19.

Wood, D. (2001). *The deconstruction of time.* Evanston, IL: Northwestern University Press. (Original work published 1989)

Acknowledgments

This book reflects the methodological story of the IU-Unityville Outreach Project. I recall brainstorming this idea for a book as I sat beside my friend Joan Parker Webster on a bus travelling between Oxford and London. Joan enthusiastically and intellectually encouraged me then as she often has.

The project involved a lot of people. Some of those I cannot name—the wonderful educators and Dreamers of Unityville, whose dedication to transformation should fill us all with inspiration. Contemporary U.S. politics remind us that the struggles to openly include transnational, im/migrant members of our communities is a life and death one. Unityville schools supported the project with their professional, financial, socio-emotional, and intellectual means. They invested.

Indiana University supported the project by awarding me grants. More importantly, graduate students from IU were deeply involved in the project. You will get to know them through the text, but I want to specifically acknowledge them here. I learned from each of them. Chris Frey was our initial project coordinator. He was easy to trust and his commitment to the project was contagious. Naomi Sotoo was a fierce advocate. When I first met her, she impressed me right away with her gender and ethnic awareness and sensitivities. Yu-Ting Su worked closely with the Taiwanese students, helping them navigate cultural changes and disjunctures with their family members back home. She became the students' personal confidante for years. Monica Hasbun, fighting her own challenges as an international student, sacrificed to participate in our work. Maura Pereira de Leon's heartfelt connection to the students benefitted from her being mama to Latinx immigrant kids of similar ages. Her commitment to use research for good characterizes her work then and now. Yoko Nakamichi Martin ended up dedicating several years of her life to Unityville as an English-as-a-New-Language (ENL) aide. She also participated in the Japanese Saturday school in Indianapolis. Her deep compassion made an important mark in the schools. She began studying Spanish in order to foster her efforts with the ENL students. She worked tirelessly and carried the longest presence in Unityville of any of our IU team members. The work was emotionally difficult, and she stayed with it. Nelson Soto and Ana Baratta Soto both completed dissertations in Unityville, where they worked with educators' stories in efforts to increase caring and empathy. The schools expressed deep appreciation for them both. Felipe Vargas, Latinx activist, mentored me in community-based activism particular to Dreamers ("Deferred Action Child Arrivals" college aspirants). His indefatigable commitment to political action included making documentaries with Latinx youth testimonios, walking across the country in protest, and engaging in many other non-violent actions that have helped to shape the political landscape of resistance. Ed Brantmeier, a recognized peace scholar, shepherded a cadre of Unityville educators through the development of an interdisciplinary intercultural peace curriculum at the high school. He spent hours at the school, on the road, and with me debriefing and thinking carefully about how to develop intercultural peace. His work is subtle and revolutionary and you will see his name a lot in this book. I offer a special introduction to Dini Metro-Roland, who contributed a chapter to the book. During the project, he took on the job of examining the history of Unityville. His historical analysis, Chapter 4, reminds us that every situation is threaded with an historical context. His sense of humor and critical mind contributed to the project in intangible ways. He conducted interviews and observations related to the implementation of the peace curriculum at the high school and was deeply embedded in the project's activities there. Each of these wonderful people have continued their courageous and excellent work in the world through a variety of academic and non-academic pursuits. I will be forever grateful that our paths intersected. I encourage you to look them up.

I have had other important collaborations with student friends/colleagues that certainly inspired the writing of this book. I am involved in what will be a lifelong collaboration with Pengfei Zhao, Karen Ross, and Peiwei Li. Together we share unbounded affection, trust, intellectual curiosity, and ethical commitments. Our collaborative work is the most sustained scholarly partnering I have experienced to date. In another collaborative effort, I have been active with an LGBTQIA+ youth-led community organization. The youth in this group are powerful. If the future is theirs, we are in good hands. The adults are dedicated accomplices, always ready to follow youth leadership and stay at their side. I have worked particularly closely with youth members of the organization's teaching committee, Brie Blauvelt, Spencer Biery, Piper Lacy, Rae Victor, and adult volunteer Suraj Uttamchandani, who completed his Ph.D. degree at IU in 2020. He's a creative and energetic thinker and researcher. I am, also, deeply involved with a Feminist Research Collective, whose members are radically changing the way we pursue scholarly life. This evolving group presently includes Suparna Bose, Lucy Carspecken, Alycia Elfreich, Dajanae Palmer, Pooja Saxena, Samantha Silberstein, Sylvia Washington, and Pengfei Zhao. Watch for great things from these women!

My sister, friend, colleague, Chalmer Thompson, has blessed me with enduring love and bold racial and social justice wisdom. Just by being who she is, she compels me to be a wiser, better person. Her writing and thinking challenge white supremacy and bring rebellious justice and freshness to every conversation. My personhood has benefitted from her in ways that go so deep they are not easily expressed. And, she introduced me to Uganda and our colleagues there. They have embraced me with the strength of their character, the warmth of their welcome, the sharpness of their ideas, and the social connectedness of their commitments: The late Mr. Okumu (who is deeply missed), Dr. Nathaniel Mayengo, Dr. James Kagaari, Dr. Jane Namusoke, Kirabo Nakasiita, Gastone Byamugisha, Richard Atuhairwe, Edward Ntare, Winifred Kysoba, Sarah Bunoti, Sister Mary Goretti, Dr. Ali Baguwemu, Dr. Henry Kibedi, Dr. David Olema, Paul Sebukalu, and our many other friends and their families.

Meagan Call-Cummings relentlessly pushes on the meaning of participation in participatory research efforts. Her dissertation was among the more uniquely written of any I have seen. She is great at coloring outside the lines, with grace, creativity, meaning, and integrity. I know she will inspire others as she has inspired me to reach through boundaries.

Being in the field is wrought with complications. No one lives out these complications better, in my opinion, than Elizabethe Payne. Her work to change the educational contexts of LGBTQIA+ youth has led to important policy implementations in New York. Her scholarship has global impact and her commitment to the social justice needs of those oppressed by patriarchy and its stranglehold on gender and sexual politics has been at great personal sacrifice. Her research institute, QuERI, and ongoing collaboration with Melissa Smith are a perpetual beacon of critical scholarship.

Many scholars have motivated me. I cannot name them all, but you will see evidence of their inspiration in the citations and pages that follow. I am specifically moved by the work of Michelle Fine and her colleagues at the Public Science

Project, the fearless Patti Lather, and the Oxford Ethnography and Education conference community. My friend Christina Huf challenges my thinking through meaningful and sustained dialogue.

Just a few more personal acknowledgments. I am grateful to Peter Lang who was patient with me as I found new reasons to write this book. My parents, Burris and Barbara Dennis, always travelled. Always invited people into our home. Always conversed about what they believed. And they taught me how to value people who are different from me. My interest in projects like this one makes sense given the trajectory of my upbringing. I have a large family who sustains me in important ways, including my nephew Chandler who was living with me during the time I was writing this book.

My life, and therefore, this work has also benefited from long relationships with Helen Gore Laird and her family, Glenn, Tanya, Elizabeth, Adam, and Kadin. For decades now Helen has been the wiser, funnier partner in our parallel play. She still keeps my teacup in her kitchen though we live states apart.

Phil Carspecken, a dear friend and brother in the pursuit of all things good, served as worthy listening post during the years I was involved in this project. I am grateful for his continued and deeply trustworthy companionship in life. We have shared so many ideas and experiences that I could never fully acknowledge his influence on me, intellectually, spiritually, and emotionally. Lucy Carspecken has, also, been a long, trusted friend. I admire her and her scholarship. She orients herself in work and life through love. Their sons, Sunil and Roly, will always be important to me.

My partner, Cicada, became part of the project through the writing of this book. He gave up morning time with me so I could sit at the computer. He handled the formatting directions from Peter Lang. He offered feedback and editing support across the book. He even checked references. He deeply understands the value of demolishing white privilege, racism, and patriarchy. He sees the *me* I want to be. I can't imagine finishing the book without him sitting beside me on the couch.

When I was involved with the Unityville project my kids were in middle and high school. They gave up time with me, encouraged me politically, and opened themselves up to learning about what was happening in a distant town. My son Jordan Korth is a music teacher, now teaching at an international school in Malaysia. He is funny, creative, trustworthy, kindhearted, and sees things in the world that many miss. He and his family remind me to be bold and not give up. His partner, Chelsea, holds a Ph.D. in Educational Policy and is a strong advocate for democratized schooling. Both of them are contributing to bettering the world through education. My daughter Kabara Korth Praskavich is my model for social justice advocacy. She has always been a fighter for what's right and a willing student of justice. She speaks out and I have learned from her. Her partner, Michael Praskavich, keeps things real. He can see multiple sides of any issue and he is great at identifying paths toward understanding. His enthusiasm is contagious. All four of them have encouraged me and supported me across my various endeavors.

My grandchildren, Burris, Ignatius, and Ovilee, keep me imagining, playing, and laughing. It is in their names that I persist in fighting for just causes of the day. Each of us in our own ways must figure out who we are *to be* in the political movements of our times and we must answer to those who come after us.

CHAPTER ONE

Theory, Practices and Politics in Using the Label *Critical*: Naming Matters

According to a factsheet on the rights of *all* children to enroll in school produced by the United States Department of Justice and the United States Department of Education (2014):

> All children in the United States are entitled to equal access to a basic public elementary and secondary education regardless of their actual or perceived race, color, national origin, citizenship, immigration status, or the status of their parents/guardians. School districts that either prohibit or discourage, or maintain policies that have the effect of prohibiting or discouraging children from enrolling in schools because they or their parents/guardians are not U.S. citizens or are undocumented may be in violation of Federal law. (p. 1)

During the time of our study, school districts were not legally allowed to ask parents about their or their child's citizenship or immigration status when determining if the child resides in the district. This act of civil justice protected the generation of youth whose presence in Unityville schools became the impetus for our work. Many of those students are now DREAMERS according to the U.S. DREAM Act (Development, Relief, and Education for Alien Minors Act) which never passed. The DACA (Deferred Action for Childhood Arrivals) program began in 2012 since the DREAM act (versions of which have been presented to the U.S. congress since 2001) had not yet been passed. DACA does not provide a

path to citizenship for childhood arrivals, but it does defer their potential deporta-
tion. The political debates and actions were part of the lives of young transnational
students in U.S. schools during the time of this study and this has continued. The
political context is an important one for both schooling and research. As Carol
Hanisch (1969) pointed out, the personal is political.

As one might always expect, the language around terms like "alien," "illegal alien," and "undocumented immigrant" are contested. Von Spakovsky (2018)
claimed on The Heritage Foundation webpage that "'Undocumented immigrant' is a politically correct made-up term used to obscure that fact that such
aliens have violated U.S. immigration law." In July 2018, under the direction
of Attorney General Sessions, the Department of Justice released an email
instructing Offices of the U.S. Attorneys to use the phrase "illegal alien" and not
"undocumented immigrant" because this later phrase is not used in U.S. code.
The purpose of this directive email was "to clear up confusion." While it is the
case that the phrase "undocumented immigrant" is not used in U.S. legal code,
it is preferred by the media. In 2013 the Associated Press changed its policy so
that it no longer referred to people as illegal, indicating that only actions would
be labeled "illegal." CNN and other broadcasters only use the term "alien" when
quoting legal code. The Library of Congress wants to remove the phrase "illegal
alien" from its subject headings. In 2009, Supreme Court Justice Sotomayor used
the phrase "undocumented immigrant" in a decision for the first time. In a 2012
immigration decision, the Supreme Court did not use the phrase "illegal alien"
or "illegal immigrant" except when citing documents that used those phrases.
According to Hiltner (2017), "undocumented immigrant" is preferred by the
people to whom it refers. This matters. Names count. Beginning in the George
W. Bush presidency, public schools were asked to *not* inquire into the documentation status of its students. School officials still presumed some of its students
were in the country without documentation, but they could not gather evidence
to establish whether or not this was the case. These possibly-undocumented
"strangers" to the schools were called "newcomers" and they were contrasted
with what Unityville educators called "traditional students." Again, names matter. There was a Trad Youth student organization at Indiana University (IU) that
spouted hate in the name of white pride and nationalism. It was difficult for me
not to interpret the use of the word "traditional" in Unityville through the context of a nostalgic call to white authority and a blatant rally for white supremacy
(Wildeman, 2013) as it was being used by the Trad Youth student organization.
Thus, as we stumbled into this project together, we wrestled with the ongoing
negation of naming and its implications, including the need for names such as
"traditional" and "newcomer."

It was the presence of "newcomer" students in Unityville that sparked my eventual involvement. Unityville educators struggled to make sense of their professional and ethical responsibilities to educate all children, regardless of what assumptions were made about who they were or where they were from. An opportunity opened up in this confluence of *not knowing* even how to refer to the transnational students against a backdrop of having to distinguish them from students who had been in the community a long time. Having to name the stranger in order to unify the *at-home* community was just one of the many indicators that educators were not sure what to do. This opportunity morphed into our eventual IU-Unityville Outreach Project.

Being Called

One weekday morning in the fall, 2003, I arrived at my office to a beeping phone message that ended with a provocative request: "Can you help these students? They don't know how to be students in American schools." I had never met the person whose voice lingered in my machine, nor had I heard of the school district from which she called. I re-listened to the message before deciding how to respond. Roberta,[1] the caller, mentioned that she worked at Unityville High School which in recent years had been enrolling increasing numbers of new students who did not speak English. She had heard that it might be possible to connect these "newcomer" non-English-speaking students with university personnel using distance education technology. The goal, from her point of view, would be to have someone who spoke the home languages of the students provide those students with information about how the school works, what the school expected and how to follow the school rules. She had hoped that it would be possible for such informational exchanges to "fix" the students so that they would be able to meet school expectations and thereby have a more successful schooling experience.

I returned Roberta's call. I was attracted to the prospect of helping the "newcomer" students and the school, but I was uneasy with the agenda of fixing students. I indicated that if she and others were more broadly concerned about fixing their school, then I would be inclined toward joining them in the effort. A small cadre of educators, including an administrator, responded positively to my open proposal. That initial contact was the start of our IU-Unityville Outreach Project, a project that, in the end, is best described as *critical ethnographic participatory action research*. But, of course, at this point in the story, none of us really knew what we were getting into, what it would be called, and much less how it might best be described in the end. We had a starting place—a concern for addressing the educational complexities of a diversified student community. The eventual name of the project indicated that we, as a group, intended to reach OUT to students/families who were clearly not IN—not included.

Humble Becomings

Our first task was to learn more *from* and *with* the people of Unityville, despite Roberta's hope that I might just have ready answers for their "problems." I didn't. We needed to know more about the community and the people's experiences as a basis for facilitating and understanding any change efforts. Context is important to me and I was sure that any plausible possibilities for altering the schools would need to be anchored in the experiences and knowledges of the Unityville community.

There has been an intransigent gap between educational research and practice owed in some part to a persistent lack of cooperation and mutual engagement (Venderlinde & von Baak, 2010). Amongst Unityville educators, even at the outset, there was a complicated combination of attitudes towards our university team (particularly towards me) and towards the "newcomer" students. This mix of feelings predominantly included *distrust* of outsiders, (including a distrust of those from an "ivory tower") AND YET a *hope* that someone (from the outside) would come in and remedy the problems without disturbing the scene too much. Contrary to their expectations, we university folks entered as learners trying to understand the particularities of their situation (Lincoln & Guba, 1985). We, also, entered with an open and positive mind toward the transnational students themselves, which contrasted with the suspicion toward them that we encountered at the schools. The cadre of educators with whom we[2] spent much of our first year was as excited as I was about this idea of taking time to engage with the Unityville school community in order to learn more about what was going on there. Together, we set a date to conduct focus group interviews. I provided Roberta with a basic structure for the focus groups (for example, I wanted about six participants in each group and I wanted the groups homogenous by role [teacher, student, and so on] and primary language and then by gender if there were sufficient numbers of people in any particular role and language group). Roberta organized a focus group schedule and arranged both the space and times for our interactions with interviewees. I enlisted the support of interested and variously skilled graduate students.

On my end, I sent out an email message that described the circumstances and invited graduate students to respond if they were interested in the situation, and most specifically if they had some experience with qualitative research coupled with expertise in the specialized language/cultural knowledge befitting Unityville's needs. I didn't know enough about what might evolve to be very precise. The largest groups of "newcomer" students at that time were Spanish-speaking, Japanese-speaking, and Mandarin-speaking and thus it was important to secure speakers of those languages. The first person I heard from was an Educational Foundations student named Chris Frey. I had not met Chris before this, but I was excited by the additional enthusiasm and energy that complemented his expertise. He had a keen interest in Japanese culture and language, plus policy expertise. Chris became our group coordinator and served as the initial Project Director for the university side of things. He garnered commitments from other students and organized our work together. Ultimately, we ended up with an impressive original team. We met several times to create focus group interview protocols for the various constituencies with whom we would be meeting: students, parents, administrators, community leaders, and teachers. It is important to the story to know that our university contingent went into these focus group interviews with *openness*. None of us knew what to expect nor did we have any clear idea about where this humble beginning might take us.

Unityville was hours away from IU. One early morning in November, as budding friends and colleagues, we clamored into a couple of cars and caravanned away from a dark, lonely campus with maps and coffee, apprehension and enthusiasm. We arrived in daylight, meeting Roberta face-to-face for the first time. Of course, we met many other people that day, many of whom became vital participants in the project, but our affection and bond with Roberta remained uniquely strong and important for us, particularly for me.

Roberta had scheduled focus groups throughout the morning, the afternoon, into the evening. She had arranged space for us to do the various focus group interviews and she had orchestrated a schedule for participants so they were coming and going all day long with the exception of a small lunch break. At noon our university team retreated together at a local restaurant in order to check-in with each other about how things were going. We managed breaks during the day to keep our energies fresh. Chris and I were responsible for holding focus group discussions with teachers, administrators, community members, and white high school students. Yoko and Naomi conducted focus groups with Japanese speakers. Yu-Ting facilitated focus groups with Mandarin speakers. Nelson, Maura, and Monica facilitated focus groups with Spanish speakers. As I walked into rooms where Spanish, Mandarin, and Japanese were being spoken, I saw kids smiling and expressing themselves in ways their teachers had never had the chance to witness. I was encouraged at the thought of schools that welcomed linguistic and cultural diversity rather than limiting itself to controlling or managing that diversity.

I began to imagine schools where students and teachers engaged in conversations with one another and with their respective communities using a variety of languages. This was a vision of schools where linguistic diversity flourished and was considered an important component to a strong education. This image of linguistic diversity became the example through which my own understanding of diversity evolved and through which budding transformations began.

There were five aspects of "becoming" that marked my engagement in the early efforts of the project. First of all, the project came to me and I was open to it. Letting projects find me and develop slowly has been a characteristic of my long-term ethnographies. The project belonged to Unityville in the first place. That is, they invited me to join them and they had their own ideas about what they needed and what they hoped to accomplish. My ideas about the project emerged alongside theirs. I helped to hone the focus of the work (shifting the original question from "Can you fix these students?" to "How can we create schools that support the success of 'newcomer' students?" for example). I saw myself as a facilitator with research skills. Secondly, I did have ideas about research and the social world that made this project appealing to me. I wanted to participate because I valued the minoritized students and I appreciated the willingness of the school staff to confront its own challenges and possibilities in the interest of the students. Thirdly, I care about doing research that contributes to making the world a better place for all of us. This project had that kind of potential. Fourthly, the design was flexible and emergent from the start. We launched into a project without having it totally mapped out. Lastly, despite the ambiguity that characterized much of the project's beginnings, I must point out that my own ongoing *critical commitments* were not as uncertain.

This chapter focuses on the meaning of the label "critical" both in its general sense and with respect to the particular practices of this project. The chapter discusses what it means to name one's own work *critical*, identifying with the theory, practice, and politics of both the name and naming. The chapter is long compared with other chapters in the book: I hope you will approach it with the egalitarian, dialogic intent with which it was written—skim, read slow, argue with it, and visit the included appendices for more theoretical engagement at your own discretion. Originally it was composed as two chapters separating methodological theory and methodological practice, but this seemed counter to the point I was trying to make about their deep integration and co-existence.

Connecting Theory, Practice, and Politics

Have you ever been asked, "What is your theoretical framework?" Have you read ethnographies in which the researchers say that they are using a particular "theoretical lens?" Have you tried to situate your own research into a specific paradigm vis-à-vis Lincoln and Guba (1994)? Have you located your research into one of the five approaches described by Creswell (2006)? All these questions reflect attempts to characterize how theory, research practice, and politics intersect in any given particular study. In disagreement with de Munck's argument (2000) that ethnographic studies are usually non-theoretical (p. 281), I want to make quite explicit the way theory was involved in our ethnographic practices and I want to clarify the value of naming one's work.

Making Theories and Positions Visible

There has been a long-standing slight-of-hand in educational research—namely, a conventional and enduring belief that knowledge is (and should be) neutral and that there are neutral means to its production. In this way of thinking, the researcher must do her best to be neutral (a synonym for unbiased or objective) in order to produce valid findings through the research process. Accordingly, the greater the personal involvement of the researcher, the greater the likelihood for bias. Drawing on the successful work of the natural sciences, the observer/researcher was largely considered wholly separate or other than the phenomena of interest. Such researchers were deemed capable of using methodological tools to discover the truth about the world. For example, let's say the researcher was interested in knowing more about the human heart, the scientific method would enable the neutral study of the human heart regardless of the scientist's own feelings, life story and so on. Such beliefs about neutrality have perpetuated a sharp distinction between objectivity and subjectivity where objectivity is associated with truth certainty and subjectivity is associated with bias and uncertainty as an inevitable compromise to objectivity. In this way of thinking, research falls into the category of objectivity. This orientation toward truth and research does not demand that the researcher articulate either her theoretical perspectives on knowledge and truth OR her positionality. The slight-of-hand hides a researcher behind a veil. Often that veil is made up of methods. For example, one might operationally define particular variables without ever, first, mentioning *the one* who did the operationalizing or, second, identifying the conversations *for which* the operationalizing is relevant.

Let's take one of several possible approaches to critiquing this slight-of-hand: Clarifying the relationship between facts and values. Drawing on values is by its nature not neutral. Yet, we typically do not operate without our values. Thus, we must understand how it is we can engage our values and investigate objective facts while also acknowledging that we hold relevant values. Former U.S. President Obama (2018) proclaimed, "We have to actually believe in an objective reality ...."

You have to believe in facts. Without facts there's no basis for cooperation …. I can't find common ground if somebody says, 'Climate change is just not happening.' I don't know where to start talking with you. If someone says it's an elaborate hoax, where do we start? …. As with the denial of rights, the denial of facts runs counter to democracy." The denial of rights is an argument of values and the denial of facts is an argument of objectivity. We must be able to deliberate both. This critical point was, also, raised by Paulo Freire (2000) who argued that oppression is both objectively verifiable and morally unacceptable. Politically charged anti-factualism draws to the foreground a need to once again confront the relationship of facts and values through public scholarship. While we recognize that facts are claimed in and through a field of values, the facts and values are debated in different ways and can be recognized and distinguished in language.

Ethnography is well-positioned to understand this relationship through participants' ordinary practices and lifeworld understandings. Critical ethnography additionally aims to raise for dialogue any critiques and contradictions that those practices, routines, and logics bury through the way the fact/values relationship is established in popular culture and lived experience. Ethnographic research can contribute to the creation of conversational opportunities within cultural moments that can help ethnographers *speak with* people whose lives are complicated through the smearing of facts and the misappropriation of values (Korth, 2005). The intertwining of the theoretical, the practical, and the political is not a denial of our ability to claim facts, it is rather a rich way of thinking about truth that makes it possible for us to converse about the coordination of social life through factual claims understood within their contexts.

If we assume that knowledge is not neutral, then we hold ourselves accountable to an expanded repertoire of responsibilities (Kuntz, 2015), not the least of which is claiming our personal starting place—theoretically, practically, and politically. The rest of this section exemplifies such claiming for those of us who were involved with the IU-Unityville Outreach Project.

Ivory Tower Theory and Real World Practice. All research projects draw on theory in multiple ways. Theory might serve the project by explaining an approach to substantive questions. For example, with this project, we could have drawn on theories of second language acquisition (SLA) to guide how we approached our research questions. Theory might function to explain why particular methodologies are especially well-suited for exploring specific questions. For example, people who ascribe to a sociocognitive theory of SLA argue that qualitative methods are best suited to the study of SLA because the methods take the context into account and context is crucial to sociocognitive SLA theory (Atkinson, 2002). Theory might provide concepts, assumptions, and definitions that researchers can draw on throughout the research process. For example, the sociocognitive theory specifies definitions for "language," "cognition," and "interaction" which researchers could use in their studies (Atkinson, 2002). Each of the above examples demonstrates that theory can be linked to inquiry in unambiguous ways. These linkages all sound very academic. It will come as no surprise that to non-academics (like the teachers in Unityville) theory and research are thought of as emanating from the "ivory tower" where they remain isolated from the real world of practice—and therefore not very relevant to what goes on in ordinary life (Biesta, 2007; Vanderlinde & van Maak, 2010). This fissure between theory and practice aligns with a belief: theory is intellectual (and therefore the work of intellectuals) and practice is what we do in our everyday lives (and therefore the work of practitioners).

In their book *Transforming Social Inquiry/Transforming Social Action*, the editors Francine Sherman and William Torbert (2000) argued for a complimentary path through this specific academic/practical divide. Their argument supposed that expertise from both sides would provide reciprocally valuable knowledge to any relevant conversation. Sounds like common sense. Sherman and Torbert could have been describing the IU-Unityville Outreach Project at the start. We began with a rough complimentary arrangement—that is, those from the university had certain linguistic and cultural, research and theoretical knowledge that the educators in Unityville (with a few exceptions) *seemed* to lack. On the other hand, educators at Unityville had classroom teaching and contextual expertise that (for the most part) was deficient amongst the university participants. Moreover, the transnational/transmigrant students brought experiences that were (generally speaking) not shared by others in Unityville (nor was this expertise consistently valued by the schools or community in the beginning). Thus, this functional relationship provided us with a structure for engaging in dialogues that included and respected the various kinds of expertise we each brought to the conversations. This was our starting place.

If the relations had not progressed beyond being complimentary and respectful, the project would not have been as transformative as it was. Theory and practice functioning as co-informers in the life/work of a project is not satisfying in the end because it leaves other important connections between theory and practice unaddressed. In our experience, things got blurry: theory wasn't just connected to the practice of research according to the various functions it might have served.

Many social science researchers have argued that theory and practice co-constitute each other (Fraser, 1987; Harding, 1987b; Lather, 2007 to name just a few feminists who make this argument). In this view, the two are not distinct complimentary forces, but two aspects of the same phenomena. The connections between theories and practices are neither observable nor measurable in the strictest sense. Theories are, instead, *implied logically* through practice. One strand of qualitative research has made distinct use of this view. Grounded theorists Strauss and Corbin (1997) developed an entire methodological approach that aimed to put into discourse the implicit theories of people's linguistic, cultural, and material practices. Pragmatists also make use of this point in a central way. For example, Dewey (1989) famously suggested that all humans are theoreticians as they actively engage in their lives, in their practices. Pragmatists suggest that precisely because theory is implicit in practice, it can be reconstructed from practice. As a reconstruction, a theory can be distinctly articulated, critiqued, even re-applied reflexively to new practices. From the theoretical side of things, a social science theory is expected to demonstrate its merit on three levels, in terms of its metatheoretical principles, in terms of its methodological implications, and in terms of its fit with findings (the empirical world of social practices). We engaged in methodological decisions that benefitted from thinking theory-practice as two ways of orienting toward the same phenomena. We used the name *critical* to describe our particular theory-practice.

Naming

Let's return to the questions I posed at the start of this section: What is your theoretical framework? Your lens? I prefer to use the word "metatheory" (instead of "lens" or "framework") when I describe the connection between theory and practice as well as when I describe the body of assumptions that explain how the theory works as practice. Simply put, metatheory is the theory that supplies principles that researchers might, at least implicitly, employ in testing, deliberating, constituting, reading, and justifying theories themselves. With respect to methodology, metatheory supplies the theoretical assumptions that make sense of a theory of practice as well as the theoretical assumptions of practices associated with the conduct of a particular study. According to Willis Overton (1998), "A **metatheory** is a set of interlocking rules, principles, or a story (narrative), that both describes and prescribes what is acceptable and unacceptable as theory." Overton continued on to say that metatheory and methodology are intertwined as metatheory produces a vision of the nature of the world and its subjects/objects and methodology produces a vision of the tools one might use to study that world. For this study, both the theory and the methodology (as a set of practices) were "critical." Jürgen Habermas's (1985, 1987) Theory of Communicative Action (a critical social theory) served my work as metatheory. Phil Carspecken's (1996) critical methodological theory guided the conduct of the study. Neither of these was used exclusively, but both were used centrally and importantly.

Why Metatheory? The reason the term "metatheory" fits our work better than "lens" or "framework" is because it emphasizes the following three aspects in its description of theory-practice. First of all, it emphasizes the idea that there is something at work in addition to the substantive theories themselves, which guides even the choice of substantive theory. I think of this metatheory as a theory of meaning and understanding—a theory that is inclusively broader than any one specific substantive knowledge base (like SLA). Secondly, it suggests reciprocity—we expect that the theory both impacts and is impacted by all aspects of the study. The terms lens and framework are, more fundamentally, static metaphors that suggest theory is something external to an object of inquiry, but through which or on which that object of inquiry is perceived or built. In contrast the word "metatheory" implies relations: something beyond, with, adjacent to, and relative to the theory. Thirdly, the term metatheory supplies the criteria through which its own merits can be assessed, whereas "frameworks" and "lenses" must be justified by reasons external to their own claims. That is, metatheories should be reflexively able to apply their own principles to judge and explain their own work. Critical theory was metatheory for us.

According to Habermas (1985), every study has the potential to contribute to the social world through its findings, its methodology, *and its metatheory*. I love this. It suggests that metatheory is not an unquestioned set of assumptions, but rather an initiating piece of a dialogue. Such an approach counters the "tendency of ethnographers to neglect the theoretical relevance and potential for research" (Snow et al., 2003, p. 182). If we think of research as a dialogue rather than a monologue, then perspectives rather than lenses and starting assumptions rather than frameworks serve as better phraseology to describe the work of metatheory in inquiry. Without a dialogic perspective, it would be easy to conceptualize the theoretical principles in a fixed, unidirectional, unquestioned way which would make the findings relevant primarily to those who are already able to assent to the same set of theoretical principles from the outset. Furthermore, we know that fixed unidirectional, unquestioned ways of approaching a study have been successfully critiqued by post-modernists (Scheurich, 1997), post-structuralists (Kuntz, 2015), and new materialists (Barad, 2012). Certainly, with criticalism there are starting assumptions which serve as a ground for how the inquiry is conceptualized. Certainly, with criticalism there are commitments at the outset. However, these assumptions and commitments are brought under examination in the process of conducting the research itself. The word "critique" is meant to signify the centrality of calling knowledge into question through an inferred dialogue. This applies to our metatheory, our theories, and our practices because it is basic to its own theory of meaning (Habermas, 1985).

What Are the "Grounds" and "Foundations"? At this point, it is possible you are wondering if the word "metatheory" is simply a replacement for the word "ground." Grounds are multilayered. Grounds are implied across multitudes of communicative achievements—from specific arguments to metatheories. Metatheories have a more precise function than grounds, and they, too, have grounds. Metatheories describe the relationship of theories to practice and theories to their own justifications. The term "ground" is used to describe the principles of justification that underlie any given set of knowledge or truth claims.

In post-modern social science, the concepts of grounds and foundations have fallen into disrepute, replaced by a strong relativism that argues for multiple and unstable "grounds" (which can be iteratively deconstructed) and "foundations" (which can be permanently destabilized). Yet, the "grounds" for such deconstructions and the "foundations" of such destabilizing moments are often themselves ignored in arguments opposing the idea of grounds. Norm Denzin and Yvonna Lincoln (2008) suggested that foundations are multipled and that truth is partial. Regarding the argument that there are multiple foundations, they wrote that there are many competing foundations/grounds such that the traditional goal of holding fast to ONE ultimate mega-truth or metatheory which would attempt to account for all possible theories must be abandoned (Denzin & Lincoln, 2008). This is itself a form of metatheoretical truth claim. The point that truth is partial is a deep insight that must not be discarded no matter what one attributes to the status of "grounds." In fact, it might be easier to acknowledge the partialness of truth when grounds are expressly engaged. Denzin and Lincoln (2008) did not suggest, as a matter of fact, that researchers do not refer to grounds or foundations in their work, but that these grounds, no matter what they are, are insecure and cannot be unified. It is easy enough to see the multiple references to foundations, including the foundations of anti-foundations perspectives. The theory associated with anti or multiple-foundational stances and practices of claiming those stances are incongruent. You see, in order to make such statements, one necessarily invokes a set of foundational claims. Denzin and Lincoln (2008) would not contest this. In fact, they probably would not be too uncomfortable with the incongruency between arguing against foundations while invoking some. It seems unavoidable. Patti Lather (2007) dove into this murky swamp and got "lost." She advocated for staying in the discomfort, incongruity, and loss. She asked, "[W]hat opens up in the face of the loss of absolute knowledge?" (p. 3). She chose to explore the limits and intersections of methodology and the loss of knowledge. This is where the incongruency led her and it seems the incongruency was necessary, perhaps desirable. Others agree (see e.g., Chang 2005).

Though, not all scholars would agree. Horace Fairlamb (1994) wrote that the incongruency results from a false dichotomy between (a) assuming there might be a FOUNDATION of foundations as a form of knowledge that *informs* the knowledge itself and (b) being able to reject necessity clauses regarding knowledge. He argued that we do not have to choose between these and, thus, we do not have to rest content with the incongruency. In other words, he thinks that we can have notions of a foundation, like those we find in Habermas's (1985, 1987) Theory of Communicative Action, and simultaneously understand that as a foundation the theory also co-exists with a partial and contingent notion of truth claims—even with respect to its own underpinnings. Like Fairlamb, I am not satisfied with interpreting theoretical incongruencies as the end of the story, in part, because it leaves the conversation of foundations splintered and without reconciliation as if that is the best one can hope for and as if allowing irreconcilable differences preserves something precious in the splintering that would be lost were dialogue on foundations to persist. Certainly, it avoids foreclosure on dialogue which has happened when disagreements are merely covered over or when differences are obfuscated through power. One's explanation and description of the differences is never without underpinnings. In my view, the incongruencies can be best understood as a reflection of the partiality of truth so insightfully brought to our attention by the work of Jacques Derrida (1974), Sandra Harding (1990), and others.

Jack Donnelly (2007) defined foundations as the end to all possible "why" questions. And it is this idea that most anti-foundationalists oppose—acceptance of an unquestioned stock of beliefs or claims. Yet, in a quirky way, this is the current state of the anti-foundational perspective—it no longer seems legitimate to ask "why" of their own foundational claims to anti-foundationalism. Donnelly's (2007) definition of foundations, however, does not fit with a Habermasian view of "grounds." "It is the very foundationalist ideal of closing off philosophical and hermeneutic[3] questionability—either with some theoretical structure or some methodological security—that the hermeneutic revolution [which informed Habermas's TCA] seeks to challenge" (Fairlamb, 1994, p. 7). This is *partly* the case because of the partialness of truth claims themselves.

Habermas argued that grounds are "claims that can be criticized and argued for" (Habermas, 1985, p. 9). This suggests that grounds are communicative achievements. Fairlamb (1994) put it like this: "For precisely at the foundational moment, the moment when empirical and formal theories lay claim to the heart of truth, hermeneutics steps in and discovers the questionability of *all* epistemic assumptions [assumptions through which knowledge would be judged as valid] … Hermeneutic universality does not appeal to privileged grounds, but to the instability of all grounds" (p. 8) … for "it is clear that the structure of the question is implicit in all experience" (Gadamer, 1988, p. 325). It is, perhaps, insightful to translate what Denzin and Lincoln (2008) and others called "foundations" to "conditions" because this allows us to talk about the critical and hermeneutic conditions of knowledge where questionability, for example, would be a condition (Fairlamb, 1994). This and other such conditions, for example the intersubjective conditions of understanding or meaning, are discussed below. Following Habermas, specifically, all possible interpretations for the word "grounds" will connote their own questionability. Furthermore, we find in Habermas's work, the particular possibility of not dichotomizing theory and practice even with respect to the grounds one theoretically invokes. There is a need to talk distinctly about theory and practice, but their link is articulated as reason and dialogue and not as an inherent dichotomy.

What Are the Grounds and Conditions of Critical Theory? There is a broad swath of diversity amongst critical qualitative researchers. According to Joe Kincheloe and Peter McLaren (2007), "Critical theory should not be treated as a universal grammar of revolutionary thought objectified and reduced to discrete formulaic pronouncements or strategies" (p. 404)—a very nicely worded way of saying we don't want to produce ONE TRUE critical theory with ONE SET of specified methods. They noted that numerous critical traditions have been inspired by a myriad of theorists including Hegel, Foucault, Derrida, and Habermas. Of course, we can add to that list Fraser, Crenshaw, Deleuze and Guattari, Freire, Spivak, Minh-ha, Barad, and a host of other theorists who have called into question some aspect of the status quo. Because Kincheloe and McLaren (2007) had an important impact on criticalism, they were often asked to provide some precision to the messy array of work that has called itself critical. In responding to such requests, they concerned themselves with trying to keep the critical dialogue and disagreement alive (p. 403). In my view, this is a key characteristic of *critical* research: the metatheoretical capacity and demand to call its own claims to truth into question. Kincheloe and McLaren's (2007) paper served to keep the dialogue amongst criticalists open and alive. Their view of criticalism didn't end up as a free-for-all, anything-goes, version of truth because the conditions through which they found merit in the critical process transcended and uncovered the more provisional and unstable grounds associated with particular truth claims themselves. In other words, the claims we find in our metatheory are those that support the basic processes of calling truth claims into question, including those metatheoretical claims of its own making. There is a lovely synergy here that means that we as researchers can use metatheories recursively, reflexively, and reflectively—hence theory and practice are conjoined. In other words, the same provisional grounds we invoke in our methodological practices, in our substantive practices, and in the theories that are entailed in those practices DOUBLE as the conditions within which the metatheory is also practiced methodologically and substantively. Rather than invoking these as closed assumptions toward a forced façade of coherency, we can entertain them as open conversation pieces that move us toward understanding.

If I engage in critical inquiry, I must entertain critical theory on a number of levels. I must understand and at least not reject its basic principles at the outset, I must be able to use the theory to examine practices of interests, and I must be able to justify the methods and methodological theories in terms of their capacities to afford us access to the phenomena of interest. As a researcher, I must do all of this at least provisionally on the terms afforded by the metatheory with a willingness to recognize their fallibility and see them change. It is metatheory that facilitates a researcher's ability to discuss the extent of consistency that seems to exist between relevant substantive theories, the methodological theory, and the method. *Being clear on the grounds and ways through which we are accepting the theory does not preclude us from interrogating it.* In my experience, taking care to be clear promotes me taking a questioning attitude toward all three: substantive theory/practice (findings); methodological theory/practice (methods); and metatheory. On this point, Elizabeth St. Pierre (2014) argued that a critical approach would encourage researchers to think through theory rather than through methods.

It might seem that I am suggesting that one picks and chooses metatheories contingent to the substantive theory or substantive question one is asking (Naples, 2003). I am not. I have had many students say something like this to me, "I am interested in studying how participants talk about their own experiences with X [a particular phenomenon]. This seems to fit the goals of phenomenology[4] because phenomenologists are interested in understanding experience. So, I am going to do a phenomenological study." The student identified a substantive interest [experiences with X] and then adopted a methodological and theoretical perspective commonly associated with that interest. Statements like this rely on a very strategic view of explaining how practice and theory are integrated. When a researcher takes this attitude toward her work, she limits her view of the relationship between theory and practice to a functional one. It is better to begin with some ability to argue for the theory/practice on a metatheoretical level.

When I said at the beginning of this chapter that I entered the Unityville scene with critical commitments already in place, I was, in part, referring to how I was orienting my work through critical theory—as the theory of meaning and understanding I find most plausible. Across all specific practices and theories it makes the most sense to me. It is the ground from which I enter my work/practice; ground that will be questioned and informed by the work itself. I could not go into the project with phenomenology or post-positivism as metatheoretical ground for the study because I do not find those metatheoretical principles as compelling. This does not mean that I will totally reject the methods associated with those traditions. Instead, I can relocate those methods by exploring their fit with criticalism on a metatheoretical level. As a quick example: I was interested in the lived experience of transnational students in Unityville and I found that the interview techniques commonly practiced through phenomenology were helpful. To pursue the possibility of using phenomenological interview strategies, I examined the metatheoretical assumptions of phenomenological methods—particularly as they pertained to interviews on lived experience. I put those metatheoretical assumptions into dialogue with critical metatheoretical assumptions. I used this dialogue to inform my methodological decisions. As it turns out, Habermas (1985) drew insights from phenomenology without inheriting the conundrums which have prevailed against phenomenology as a theory (see Derrida 1974, 1975). Sparing you the particular details of this (which you can find in other places, e.g., Tugendhat, 1989) suffice to say my use of phenomenological methods required careful exploration of both critical and phenomenological metatheories. This was a far more engaged process than simply choosing phenomenology as my metatheory because I was interested in studying lived experiences.

Consequently, I would not have chosen to participate in the IU-Unityville Outreach Project from a critical perspective while opting to participate in another study from a phenomenological perspective and yet another study from a post-positivist perspective. This theoretical consistency and commitment does not mean that I fail to query the propositions and practices of critical theory as part of my work or draw on other theoretical insights and challenges. In fact, the best way to encourage such queries is to articulate one's metatheoretical propositions in the first place. It happens often enough in social science that metatheoretical principles are left unacknowledged to do their work intuitively rather than deliberately. Qualitative researchers, particularly in education and sociology, have been called to task because their work was not easily understood through the metatheoretical principles quietly at work in the more traditional, quantitative research of those fields. Qualitative researchers were asked to explain their methodologies, which meant explaining metatheory: the principles justifying methodological decisions as well as their views of knowledge, subjects, objects, meaning, and validity—all which seemed on the face of it to diverge from the practices of quantitative social science (Foley & Valenzuela, 2008). If one uses mainstream approaches, less explication of metatheory is required. However, it would not be bad practice for all social scientists to locate themselves explicitly with respect to their working metatheoretical assumptions. In the second half of this chapter, I do that by articulating some of the basic metatheoretical principles I drew from Habermas's (1985, 1987) Theory of Communicative Action.

The Politics of Naming

Metatheories are not neutral. They do not escape the burden of political awareness and its ramifications or the sociocultural context of their assumptions. One of the common aspects of critical theories is that they hold scholars accountable for naming and articulating the effects of their metatheories on the research. The politics of doing/thinking more generally are pervasive to doing/thinking research more specifically. Politics here refers to authority and political relations. Within fields and within methodological traditions, there is power in naming (Lynch, 2015), power in choosing names. The proliferation of POSTs (post-positivism, postmodernism, post-structuralism, post-qualitative, and so on) in the naming practices of social science give evidence of this. Names are not merely ways of associating one's self with a category. Names enact ways of doing/being/becoming that have consequences and that matter. Names can never fully account for or describe something to which they might refer. There is no 1:1 correspondence between a name and a thing. Derrida's (1975) deconstruction of the sign makes this point philosophically, but we can each come to it on our own by noticing both the partialness and the necessity for naming ourselves. Certainly, there are politics to particular names and there are politics in the naming process. Who has the right to name? What baggage does the name carry? What does the name highlight or hide? In this chapter we are specifically focused on naming the traditions within which my methodological decisions take up ongoing conversations.

As you read, right up front, I am locating my work through the ideas, assumptions and questions of Critical Theory. The name has consequences.

Critical Theory as Metatheory

The word critical is a common descriptor in the qualitative research literature. For this reason, and because it is fundamental to understanding the IU-Unityville Outreach Project, it is worth exploring in detail. Once the meaning of criticalism is clarified, then it becomes easier to tell the methodological story to follow. It has been my experience that some common misinterpretations of critical research contribute to an incomplete understanding of its practices. For example, I have had students tell me that they can't use a critical approach because it would not be acceptable in the social or cultural situation to lodge criticism at their impending participants or to focus specifically on power. These comments reflect a misinterpretation of critical theory when posited from the Theory of Communicative Action (Habermas, 1985, 1987). One of those misinterpretations is that the word critical is interpreted to mean that critical researchers are overly negative and ONLY point out what's wrong. Thus, researchers think that they would inevitably end up criticizing *the people* involved in the study as well as taking an "I know better than the participants" stance. While critical methods afford critiques of practices and conditions, they do so by radically insisting on understanding and engaging participants in the first place. Many critiques surface precisely because they articulate something at work in the lives of participants. Moreover, this connotation of the word "criticism" is too narrowly construed to account for what it is critical researchers do in the name of critique. Doing critical inquiry involves facilitating both the questioning and the understanding of tacit assumptions entailed in one's meaningful activity. This questioning and understanding is best accomplished *with* people rather than *for, to,* or *on* people.

A second misunderstanding associated with the use of the word "critical" involves the assumption that criticalists are solely and explicitly focused on power and inequity. This is a misunderstanding because it limits the way power and inequity are conceptualized—critical theorists work toward quite subtle understandings of power and inequity which do not just come down to having an explicit research question about inequality or oppression. As Carspecken (1996) suggested, "critical qualitative research is meant to be quite universal in the topics [and cultural situations] it can investigate. This is because all acts of inquiry beg the same set of core questions, and critical theory has addressed these questions in the most promising ways" (p. 3).

More Than One. There is not just one critical theory nor one origin/history of critical theories. Consequently, it has become necessary for scholars to devote a sentence or two articulating their critical perspective and affiliating that perspective with a few major writers in the field so as to clarify being this or that kind of a criticalist. I have done this myself—thus far, aligning my criticalism with Habermas (as I will continue to do here) and feminist writers that include Patti Lather (2007) and Michelle Fine (2018). Sometimes researchers devote a paragraph to identifying the core metatheoretical principles involved in the *particular* critical theory they are using, but most often writers resort to articulating elements of the study that most criticalists would have in common. For example, in many of my own publications, I used the following quote by Kincheloe and McLaren (2007) to describe the intentions of my research:

> Inquiry which aspires to the name 'critical' must be connected to an attempt to confront the injustice of a particular society or public sphere within the society. Research thus becomes a transformative endeavor unembarrassed by the label 'political' and unafraid to consummate a relationship with emancipatory consciousness. (p. 406)

Max Horkheimer (1972) argued that criticalists would not be satisfied with merely adding to world's knowledge. Most critical theorists concern themselves with research that promises to make the world a better place. This is an ethical stance that carries with it a set of values. Criticalists tend to express an interest in the well-being of "others," including, in the first place, those who are participating in their research. Criticalists tend to share an interest in dismantling power relations that result in inequality and injustice—though as mentioned earlier this does not have to be explicitly identified as a question and often, instead, takes a very subtle form in the findings. Criticalists, also, tend to share a view of meaning and/or knowledge as socially constituted and non-neutral. They take seriously the call to reflect on and investigate their own claims to knowledge, power, and truth. These very general descriptions tend to find agreement amongst critical researchers. Many researchers, regardless of metatheoretical premises, might argue that their work is intended to make the world a better place. The refined way in which this includes questioning core claims to knowledge, power and truth distinguishes critical efforts from those whose primary form of change involves adding to knowledge or discarding knowledge for something that works better in solely objective terms.

Beginning with Habermas. I used Habermas's (1985, 1987) Theory of Communicative Action (TCA) as metatheoretical guide and resource. By introducing readers to TCA and its metatheoretical principles, I hope to provide a better understanding of my starting place in the IU-Unityville Outreach Project and across the overall unfolding of the project. Remember that for readers just being introduced to Habermas, the ideas might seem overwhelming, in which case, this part of the chapter is probably best thought of as a touchstone one can return to as needed. I introduce new concepts and ideas in a naturalistic way and we re-find them throughout the text. This means that your understanding of these ideas and concepts will probably develop through your reading of the book. Also, refer to Appendix A if you would just like a little more than what you find here.

Habermas developed the TCA as a social theory. He drew on a variety of philosophical traditions converging in some respects on the critical thought of the Frankfurt School. Habermas was born in Germany in 1929. What a time to be a young German. As a former member of the Hitler Youth Program, he experienced what he has often described as "the first rupture, which still gapes." As a result of the Nürenberg trials where the shocking atrocities of German activities were made public, Habermas was confronted with a deeply disturbing account of a Germany he thought he knew. The indelible lessons of this experience have been inextricably linked to his scholarly work.

Choosing Habermas has an impact. The choice rankles feminists with whom I have an affinity. Its emphasis on rational deliberation is criticized by those who have worked against the gendered history of rationalization in western philosophy (Spivak, 1999). It fails to lift women philosophers into a primary position of authority. Even in Habermas's earlier writings, he used male pronouns exclusively. My own engagement with TCA has not been one of simple adherence, as I nuanced and tempered my understanding of the theory by reading through it with other voices and ideas (see Dennis 2018a as an example). By choosing to name this work as informed by Habermas's TCA, I set myself up to be accountable to the impact and ramifications of that choice.

Habermas's Theory of Communicative Action as Critical Metatheory

Habermas explicitly said that TCA is not a metatheory (see 1985, p. xli)—it is not a theory of theories and is, instead, a theory of society. Nevertheless, Habermas delivered the metatheoretical principles underlying the theory which makes it easy to draw on the TCA for metatheoretical purposes. TCA put forward a distinct set of claims and stands as one of several possible critical theories to which contemporary criticalists are likely to refer. Thomas McCarthy (1994), who prodigiously wrote about and translated Habermas's work, has said that "Habermas's basic intention in developing the theory of communicative competence was to provide normative theoretical foundations for social inquiry" (p. 333). Thus, my engagement with TCA does not contradict the hopes Habermas had, since I will be describing its metatheoretical status for critical social studies. There is no way to adequately summarize the full metatheoretical influence of TCA on my research, so a brief outline will have to suffice. But, one important point to make here is that I am not using TCA in either a static or understudied way. I am a student of Habermas's work as I both respectfully and critically engage with it. In this section, the metatheoretical principles are presented according to tiers. The tiers are my way of showing how I imagine the metatheoretical principles are related to one another. I do not think of these as a flat set of principles aligned linearly, but rather as a nested and interlocking set of principles that are co-related to one another.

Underlying Metatheoretical Principles of TCA

It makes sense for me to think of the principles in three concentric nests: Primary principles on which all other metatheoretical principles rest; principles on truth and validity; and principles of basic distinctions. This organization is my interpretation of Habermas's work. While others may disagree with the ways in which

I have labeled and organized the principles, few would disagree that these principles reflect TCA.

Primary Principles. The two principles on which other TCA principles rely are: (1) Intersubjectivity is the basis for meaning, understanding, and truth. (2) Truth is internally linked to validity.

Intersubjectivity Is the Basis for Meaning, Understanding, and Truth. Intersubjectivity refers to the potential for two or more people to take each other's position in the process of understanding. If we orient ourselves toward understanding, we are able to understand one another because we are able to see how utterances, interpretations or actions make sense from one another's perspectives. Often times, when we interact, our assumptions about the potential to reach understanding are left implicit. Intersubjectivity is not, from Habermas's point of view, an idea that suggests we perfectly understand another's perspective nor that anyone's perspective is transparent. Rather, it is a communicative proposition that suggests that our communicative acts presume a potential for understanding (even in misunderstanding) which we are in turn able to make explicit with more or less success.

Truth Is Internally Linked to Validity. Habermas argued that communicative actions imply assumptions of truth. Those assumptions are quickly and implicitly understood as validity claims—that is, underlying claims that validate what is being enacted as true. It is these validity claims that surface when we disagree or question the meaning of an action. For example, if someone tells me that there are a lot of "newcomers in a school who do not speak English," I might interpret this to be true if I understand the meaning of "newcomer," I assume the school needs students to speak English, I have a sense of what it means for students not to speak English in the judgment of the school, I can accurately count the students, and so forth. If I am not sure what the statement means, I could ask, "Do you mean that they do not speak English at all?" or "Do you mean that their lack of English is a problem for the school?" The test for truthfulness is a matter of validity and not solely a matter of match between the claim and the external world, as is often the way the concept "truth" is applied to research (Carspecken, 2003). For Habermas (1985), "A *validity* claim is equivalent to the assertion that the *conditions for the validity* of an utterance are fulfilled" (p. 38).

Principles on Truth and Validity. These first two primary principles help us understand TCA's principles on truth and validity. Firstly, we must assume that *meaning is uncertain.* We can never know for sure, what another person means. Secondly, *truth is conditional.* What this implies is that the meaning of communicative acts are conditioned by the assumptions of validity entailed in them. They are considered true or criticizable or examinable relative to the conditions of their validity claims. This is one aspect of the way Habermas conceptualizes truth as socially constituted. Thirdly, *truth is consensual*, at least tacitly. What this means is that truth is itself socially and communicatively achieved—it does not sit outside communicative acts as if the communication DELIVERS the truth of something outside of itself entirely. The consensual nature of truth does not mean that people reach consensus on all claims, but that when something is established as true, it is because there has been some level of consensus. Fourthly, *truth is fallible*. Because we can never secure ultimate consensus, we must acknowledge that there is always some sense in which the fallibility of our truth claims might be just beyond the consensus we have been able to achieve or just beyond our awareness and understanding in the moment. Fifthly, *there is a distinction between the claim one makes and the content to which that claim points*, an insight that was well-developed by Derrida (1975) and Michel Foucault (1988). Claiming is a speech act that always points beyond itself—to, for example, an objective reality, or a subjective state of affairs, or norms/values guiding how we might behave with one another. Lastly, *epistemological orientations will presuppose ontological assumptions*. That is, claims about how we know will carry assumptions about the nature of the thing we are claiming to know. These two go hand in hand: doing/claiming implies being.

Principles of Basic Distinctions. I take up three fundamental distinctions proposed by Habermas. These distinctions are between (a) objectivity, subjectivity, and normativity; (b) acts oriented toward understanding and acts oriented toward success; and (c) lifeworld and system. I will briefly describe each of these.

All theories make ontological and epistemological assumptions. Ontological assumptions involve suppositions about the nature of existing. Epistemological assumptions involve suppositions about the nature of knowing. Some recent thinkers even use the term "onto-epistemological" to indicate the concomitant and co-emergent nature of the two. The ontological and epistemological assumptions associated with TCA were clarified through important distinctions between *objectivity, subjectivity, and normativity* as categories of validity. "[T]he idea is not that there are three ways in which things exist but rather that communication requires *existence* claims pertaining to three categories" (Carspecken, 2003, p. 1018). This distinction brings much needed critique and precision to social science. Objective validity implies that a world of things exist external to those subjects who might know about, talk about, study or otherwise engage with the things. Consequently, the world of things is primarily knowable through the senses. These claims indicate the status of things in the external world. The validity of these claims depends on the principle of multiple access and involves testing out "what is" and "what works" using specified procedures and definitions. This world of objects existing external to subjects constitutes an ontological supposition. Such suppositions are linguistically necessary.

Subjective validity implies the existence of an internal world comprised of my feelings, intentions, desires, states of mind, and so on as well as an objective world into which that internal world can be projected. Subjective claims indicate "what is" about experiences internal to me. The validity of these claims involves assumptions about my honesty and sincerity. Subjective claims work off of the principle of privileged access (rather than multiple access). Here, Habermas has suggested that communication requires a supposition about the ontological nature of subjects as having feelings, desires, intentions, mental states and so on not accessible to others in the same way they are to the individual subject who claims them for her own.

Normative validity implies a social world for which there is a mutually agreed upon, shared set of norms and values. This social world is structured via communication. Normative validity does not refer to something that exists outside of communication as we find presupposed in objectivity and subjectivity. Normative validity claims indicate what should be consented to as good/bad AND right/wrong within a community. Norms and values are validated by examining whether or not they should be consented to, based on both the system of norms and values within which they make sense as well as the extent to which they facilitate the best good for those affected by the claim. Validity is achieved by examining the network of claims within which the questioned claim emerges. Again, Habermas suggested that communication depends on supposing a social ontology.

The distinction Habermas articulated between objectivity, subjectivity, and normativity is a reconstruction of the way people understand meaningful acts as evidenced in the way they resolve misunderstandings and query disagreements. In everyday life, these types of validity are tethered in their content to specific communities. That is, we cannot separate the validity of the any of the three types of claims from the specific communities within which those claims makes sense. This is most obvious with normative claims and least obvious with subjective claims, but holds across all three. Thus, all validity claims are contextual (which is an argument against the idea that researchers should not claim/hold positions relevant to their research). His work critiques objectivism as the only ontological premise through which to make truth claims. (He is not alone in critiquing this problem.) Moreover, he argued that communication depends on all three forms of ontological presuppositions. This is an important insight for social science.

Habermas distinguished between *acts oriented toward understanding and acts oriented toward success.* He wrote that, "social actions can be distinguished according to whether the participants adopt either a success-oriented attitude toward one another or one oriented to reaching understanding. And, under suitable conditions, these attitudes should be identifiable on the basis of the intuitive knowledge of the participants themselves" (Habermas, 1985, p. 286). When a person is engaged in actions oriented toward success, she has minimal interest in winning the assent of others beyond what is necessary to secure the success of the goal. However, "in communicative action participants are not primarily oriented to their own individual successes; they pursue their individual goals under the condition that they can harmonize their plans of action on the basis of common situation definitions [understandings]" (Habermas, 1985, p. 286). This communicative condition of harmony involves acts oriented toward understanding. For Habermas (1985), understanding is always in play, even in acts oriented toward success because acts oriented toward reaching understanding are the original mode of language use (p. 288). Imagine trying to achieve success with little interest in others agreeing with you. You just want them to do what you want them to do, regardless of whether they assent with your goal or means. Even in this case, there must be some level of communicative understanding through which the other people can be expected to acquiesce to your demands. Maybe they are able to understand negative consequences that would result if they do not do what you want them to do or perhaps they care about you or are invested in you as a person and they are willing to sacrifice in order to help you reach your goals.

Habermas made a distinction between *Lifeworld and System*. Lifeworld, according to Habermas, can most simply be thought of as the sociocultural milieu through which people come to understand one another. "Subjects acting communicatively always come to an understanding in the horizon of a lifeworld. Their lifeworld is formed from more or less diffuse, always unproblematic, background convictions" (Habermas, 1985, p. 70). As we know, it would be impossible to reach understanding in every instance in which we are coordinating our activities with others. For example, I cannot negotiate with farmers for the price of crops I buy in the grocery store, but this is not unimaginable in some sociocultural contexts. System is the concept Habermas used to describe how meaning gets systematized so that it does not have be negotiated at every turn. As a consumer, I do not have to negotiate the fair trade for goods of my labor with the goods of someone else's labor because money stands in for that negotiation.

Making Commitments in the Field: Toward a Critical Participatory Ethnography

Paul Willis (1981) conducted a study of working-class boy culture which is widely considered inspiration for critical ethnographers. It wasn't that he was following something called a critical method which resulted in the ethnography, but rather that his Marxist intuitions and expansions, interests and concerns, converged through the study as a commitment to understanding working-class lads with whom he explored critical questions. Willis's book foregrounds his findings and field practices, while developing theory in the background.[5] Many critical educational ethnographers aspire to achieve what Willis's book achieved in scope and depth. In fact, a multitude of critical ethnographies have been published in the decades that have followed the printing of Willis's study. One such ethnography is Carspecken's (1991) *Community Schooling and the Nature of Power: The Battle for Croxteth Comprehensive School*. His study was similarly set in an English working class secondary school, this time in the 1980s. Carspecken's study examined the nature of power involved when a working-class community illegally occupied and ran its local secondary school in the wake of national school closings. Carspecken was one of the activist-teachers involved in the battle to keep the local school running. His theoretical, political, and critical interests of the time came together in the project. Like Willis, Carspecken did not enter the field with a "critical" methodological strategy or design to guide him, but rather with intuitions, concerns, commitments, and sensibilities which were informed by the substantive social theory with which he was engaging. Both Carspecken and Willis learned things through their fieldwork that were reciprocally informed by and returned to theory. Both went on to write more explicitly about critical theory and methodology. Their stories are not totally uncommon (see works by Everhart, Lather, Weiss, Fine and others). The field of educational ethnography brings together people who might have a well-studied approach to ethnography, but who just as well might not. Some people find themselves in a field of opportunity, and endeavor to do their best by it—exploring ideas, experiences, theories and methods as they go. By telling the methodological story of the IU-Unityville Outreach Project, I aim to demonstrate both aspects of doing ethnography: the way in which one's theoretical and methodological background can benefit and complicate fieldwork; and the way in which characteristics associated with intuition, creativity, openness, fluidity, and genuine exploration (which are evoked precisely because of the context) all contribute to the lived trajectory of doing ethnography. It is with this kind of double-sidedness that I put Carspecken's (1996) *Critical Ethnography* into practice.

Introducing Critical Methodology

There are numerous good sources that have reviewed varying histories of critical ethnographic practices in education in order to provide impressive overviews (e.g., Anderson, 1989; Carspecken, 1999b; Kincheloe and McLaren, 2007; Yon, 2003), so I do not intend to reproduce those efforts here. According to Daniel Yon (2003),

Margaret Mead "foreshadowed" a swing in anthropology from an ethnographer as "detached observer" to an ethnographer as "champion [of] the rights and interests of marginalized groups" (p. 413). Thus, her work "evoked" a new engaged and activist research (p. 414). Additionally, the Spindlers, well-known anthropologists of the twentieth century, encouraged a transformation in educational ethnography from the business-as-usual anthropology to an approach that was mindful of the "social responsibility of the researchers and the ethical implications of the research" (Yon, 2003, p. 414). In the 1970s, Ray Rist (1973) published an ethnography of urban education in the United States which produced ethnographic "demystifications" of schooling in order to critique "dominant ideologies of social mobility by calling attention to the role of schools in normalizing social inequality" (Yon, 2003, pp. 417–418). There were a number of ethnographies (in addition to Willis's and Carspecken's) which became touchstones in the development of critical ethnography (e.g., Anyon, 1980; Everhart, 1983; McRobbie, 1978). These studies did not emerge from one particular methodology or theoretical perspective, but did break, in some important ways, from social science as it was being practiced and theorized. According to Anderson (1989),

> Critical ethnography in the field of education is the result of the following dialectic: On the one hand, critical ethnography has grown out of the dissatisfaction of social accounts of "structures" like class, patriarchy, and racism in which real human actors never appear. On the other hand, it has grown out of a dissatisfaction with cultural accounts of human actors in which broad structural constraints like class, patriarchy, and racism never appear. (p. 249)

This tension is central to the dialogues that characterize critical methodological theory and in the methodological decisions that researchers encounter and produce. We can see both aspects of this tension in contemporary practice: "Research in the critical tradition takes the form of self-conscious criticism—self-conscious in the sense that researchers try to become aware of the ideological imperatives and epistemological presuppositions that inform their research *as well as* their own subjective, intersubjective, and normative reference claims" (Kincheloe & McLaren, 2007, p. 406, emphasis added). See Appendix B for a rough comparison of different critical orientations.

Understanding Critical Theory as Methodological Practice

Throughout this book, readers will see the theory at work in the methodology. One specific starting place is Carspecken's 1996 book on Critical Ethnography. At this juncture, I want to highlight six of the many key methodological ideas that I drew from this text:

- Reconstruction is different than representation;
- Typification, a recognition of how to act in a particular social setting, is a way of describing how we come to understand situations;
- Praxis, as developed from Marxist theory, links productive activity with recognition and the capacity for humans to see themselves as worthwhile and understood in the lives of others;
- The Habermasian distinction between system and lifeworld (as described above) has methodological impact;
- Egalitarianism is necessary when doing research WITH others and is central to understanding one another; and
- Facts and values can and should be distinguished from one another, though certainly they are intertwined.

Each of the above points are explored below, but are discussed in further detail in Appendix C.

Reconstructive Sciences and Reconstructive Analysis. Reconstruction involves making tacit knowledge and assumptions explicit. Reconstructive sciences do not emphasize sense-perception or representational correspondences. Instead, researchers would put the implicit practices and meanings into words given the contexts of the activities. For example, when we understood how Unityville educators were using the word "newcomers" we understood it not by relying on our senses nor by solely making a one-to-one correspondence as if identifying who does or does not fit the category. Instead, we reconstructed the use of the term "newcomer" in its context in order to articulate the insider/outsider assumptions, the racial implications, the pejorative nature of the community's use of the word, and so on.

Typification. When you walk into a room and you see someone you know, you are aware of a situation in which you know what to do, you know how to act meaningfully. If the social setting of the room is a party, a class, a memorial service and if the room is crowded, empty, filled with desks and so on you recognize the opportunities for acting that are available to you. This broad, but bounded, potential for meaningful action is what Carspecken called a social "typification" (see Carspecken, 2003, pp. 1018–1021). Typifications are social setting possibilities for acting. Even if we act in opposition to what would be socially appropriate, we do so by recognizing what would be socially appropriate. Typifications are not social scripts, but they are implicated by social scripts. They are culturally shared and can be reconstructed from interactions. They do not exist in space and time, but are referenced by what does happen in space and time. When I walked in the high school office at Unityville, I greeted the secretaries, signed into the visitor's book, and gathered my visitor pass name tag. The typification could be described as a polite albeit formal entrance through a gatekeeping system. I recognized the secretaries' responsibilities for greeting visitors and ensuring that they followed they protocol. I understood the need for gatekeeping. I accepted what was asked of me because I appreciated the rules. I also experienced this greeting ritual as an opportunity to express appreciation for the secretaries and my warm feelings toward them.

Praxis. Carspecken (2003) reworked the concept praxis toward its most intrinsic meaning—that actions oriented toward understanding at root put forward the possibility that the self will be understood by others. As people are understood, their selves are recognized through that understanding. He goes on to make the point that being recognized (ultimately by the self) is a core motivational structure to praxis theory (Carspecken, 2003, p. 1036). Being recognized through one's claims to truth is powerful. When we feel our claims are being misunderstood, we feel our selves, also, being misunderstood (Dennis, 2018b). This point is important for claims researchers might make about others, but, also, for the way in which participants may or may not be understanding one another. Certainly in Unityville, we were starting off with a serious fissure in the abilities of teachers and transnational students to understand one another.

System and Lifeworld. Carspecken (1996) made use of Habermas's distinction between system and lifeworld. In his five stage critical ethnography, the first three stages are designed for making explicit the implicit aspects of sociocultural milieu through which participants come to understand one another (the lifeworld). The last two stages are devoted to spelling out systemic relations and the intersection of lifeworld and system in the everyday routines of participants (p. 189). Analyzing system phenomena extends beyond reconstructive analysis, to describe the systematic or structural elements conditioning the coordination of actions across cultural/lifeworld contexts. "Epistemologically, systems analysis foregrounds universalizing claims to multiple access [remember these are associated with objectivity]. These claims approach ... a position that any anonymous person could occupy" (p. 189). Thus, methods associated with stage four and five of Carspecken's critical ethnographic approach involve taking a relative outsider's view toward the more objective patterns visible through routines, outcomes, and functions of lifeworld activities across time and space as well as connecting those patterns with a broader world/literature of findings.

Egalitarianism. "No research *on* us, *without* us." When we conduct research, we do so WITH people who are agents of their own lives. We respect that. Engaging in research with people requires egalitarianism coupled with caring. Knowledge is not neutral and research has effects. Knowledge is always a complicated prism of multiple perspectives. Egalitarianism is the best way to insure that the multiplicity of perspectives are claimed, voiced, nourished, and examined.

Facts and Values. If someone says to me, "Those kids don't speak English" they are foregrounding a fact-based claim, but if they say "Kids in this school should speak English" they are bringing forward a normative claim that implies the value of the English language for the certain context. Distinguishing between facts and values is important for a critical methodology. A fact would be something like a claim that such-and-such IS a particular way—a claim about the way things ARE and the way things WORK. Facts are objective claims in Habermas's terminology. Facts are falsifiable or supportable through primarily objective means and thereby operate through the principle of multiple access. If we say that a kid doesn't speak English, we should be able to objectively verify their level of English speaking in ways allowing for multiple access (operationally defining what it means to "speak English" and so on). Justifying the claim that kids in Unityville should speak English requires something different—it appeals to social values and norms that are contextual. It requires that we reach agreement about how we should act—what we ought to do. Facts and values are justified differently and this distinction will have impacts on how we justify the varying claims our research produces. Critical power will involve being able to describe, for example, the objectively verifiable conditions of inequality while also being able to espouse socially-anchored values and norms against inequity (Freire, 2000).

Critical Theory as Lived Practice

In this final section of the chapter I want to return to talking directly about the Unityville project. A hodge-podge of people including IU student-researchers and Unityville educators and students set into motion a project whose ends were not in sight and whose details were not, at the outset, known. Thus, our research had to be flexible and open. Dialogue was essential. Goals had to be negotiated and plans had to be responsive to multiple needs and perspectives. Throughout the life of the project we conducted "hundreds of hours of observations, interviews, focus groups, as well as a variety of alternative data collection strategies. For example, at the high school, we constituted a teacher inquiry group who collaboratively created and implemented a multi-disciplinary intercultural peace unit. We obtained IRB approval from both the university and the Corporation's school board. We examined data on all such project activities" (Dennis, 2009, p. 69). We used a variety of analytic approaches (Carspecken, 1996; Dennis, 2009; Korth, Martin, & Sotoo, 2007) which will be discussed in upcoming chapters. And, we employed a variety of validity strategies to insure a high quality of data and interpretations. These strategies included peer debriefing, member checks, strip analysis, negative case analysis, the use of recording devices, the use of key informants, and interviews to check out observational interpretations (Carspecken, 1996).

A year or so into the research it was possible to see what threads seemed to stitch the various aspects of the project together over time and across specific activities. It also became possible to describe the emergence of a design and the recursive nature of naming what it was that we were doing.

Characteristic Threads

The following threads were the living fabric of enacting critical theory through research practice. The threads included: (a) programmatic interventions; (b) relationships; (c) priorities—project first, research second; (d) complexity of views; (e) loyalty to students; and (f) insider/outsider dynamics. The threads implicated the critical theory I have been outlining—but they were not produced by the theory. That is, the theory did not cause these threads. Other similarly-oriented critical research projects would likely identify different threads.

Programmatic Interventions. The IU-Unityville Outreach Project intended to make changes. Transformation was desired. Researchers and participants collaboratively planned, implemented, and assessed interventions which altered what was going on at the schools. Interventions included such things as an interdisciplinary peace curriculum, weekly video-conferences with focus groups of students and graduate student researchers, teacher professional development seminars, structural changes in the English-as-a-New-Language (ENL) program, use of modification plans in teaching, and so on. Those volunteers who participated actively were collaboratively and democratically engaged in the modification decisions. The interventions were not the brain-child of our university team and instead depended upon the inspiration, motivations, and agreements amongst our Unityville collaborators. This democratic engagement of participants in making changes matches key characteristics of Participatory Action Research. In Participatory Action Research (PAR), researchers *work with* participants toward transformation, liberation, and revolution, *entering explicitly* into a situation where their engagement with participants intervenes purposefully in the life of the community (Savin-Baden & Wimpenny, 2007). "There exist relatively few occasions, in the course of a lifetime, which provide the opportunity to confront processes of radical social transformation" (Fals-Borda, 1979). The IU-Unityville project was that kind of occasion; first and foremost for the people of Unityville. Programmatic interventions were the explicit junctures through which our critical ethnography and the desires of the school were simultaneously energized.

Relationships. Those of us from IU were invited guests. We were in Unityville schools at the administrators' behest, the teachers' goodwill, and the students' bidding/friendship. Being guests produced both facilitative and debilitative effects, but most importantly it spoke to the intentions of those who invited us—they wanted change and support. Across the various categories of participants (administrators, teachers, students, parents, and so on) the relationships were different. For example, we were confidants for administrators, held a gamut of relationships with teachers, and were advocates with and for students. To engage in these ongoing relationships, we had to be open, willing, and self-reflective. Caring for our relationships and engaging care as a feature of our research was central to being authentic and sincere in our interactions (Korth, 2003; Korth, Martin, & Sotoo, 2007). We did not approach these relationships as experts, but rather as co-equals in concern.

Project First, Research Second. After our first six months in the field, I made a long-term commitment to the Project. We did not ever think of our research as in any way contrary to or in competition with the Project itself. Putting the Project first meant making a commitment to stay in the field serving the schools for as long as we were needed. It also meant offering stability to the Project in terms of University participation. It meant writing for their needs first—not publishing or presenting scholarship to an academic community as the first priority. The point is that we were involved because we cared about the Project and our scholarship was always a by-product of that investment. We were project participants in the first place.

Complexity of Views. Perspectives in the field were widely varied and contentious. Research actually drew this complexity out into the open. Prior to the start of the research/project there was little articulation of views and an absence of dialogue, even amongst teachers. In fact, one of the biggest needs at the outset of the project was getting basic conversations started. There were obvious reasons why educators did not understand the perspectives of the students/parents and vice versa, but the educators were not even communicating their positions with one another. Once people started talking with us, the complexity was revealed and this created a space for dialogue and for the development of visions.

Loyalty to the Students. We did not enter or stay in the field with ambivalence in terms of loyalties. After our first few months we made an explicitly collective decision to remain in the field BECAUSE we had gotten to know the ENL students and we did not want to abandon them. Neither did we want to abandon those educators who shared our concerns. We knew that some of our work would be analogous to putting Band-Aids on wounds, but we believed somehow that Band-Aids were better than nothing. Our IU team members easily agreed on a couple of things. First of all, we had an expressed concern for the immediate situation of the students. As Felipe (a Latino IU researcher) put it, "They don't get these days back. Every day that is miserable is a day they cannot re-live. And it is a day that moves them in either a positive or negative life direction." Despite the complexities of attitudes and experiences, it is important to note that our IU loyalty to students was in alignment with some insiders who were similarly dedicated. Loyalty to the students was a clear indication of the critical values shared by those of us actively aligned with the research goals.

Insider/Outsider Dynamics. Of all the ethnographic projects I have been involved with, this is the one in which I experienced the strongest insider/outsider dynamics. These dynamics did not only mark researcher relations with participants, but also participant relations with one another. The "newcomer" students were considered "outsiders" by even the most dedicated educators. Teachers themselves were known as insiders or outsiders based on their longevity and history in Unityville. A dialectic and dialogic methodology was important to working within and through the insider/outsider dynamics that positioned each of us in relation to one another. Such insider/outsider dynamics were best navigated and negotiated through a long-term commitment such as is afforded by an ethnographic approach. Even the pseudonym UNITYVILLE speaks into the internal insider/outsider dynamics which became even more clearly and critically articulated through the project/research itself. Chapter 2 is devoted entirely to exploring these dynamics.

The Emergence of a Design: Establishing Commitments in the Field

To conclude this chapter, I present broad-level design descriptions. The basic characteristics of the study included:

- A focus on organically established local problems and promises (a characteristic of participatory action research);
- A long-term commitment (a characteristic of ethnography);
- An interest in both the face-to-face engagements that resulted in educational outcomes/experiences and the systemic and structural forces at work in the delivery of educational opportunities (a characteristic of critical inquiry and participatory action research and, often enough, ethnography);
- A commitment to understanding multiple and diverse perspectives (a characteristic of all three);
- Collaborative, democratic, fluid relationships between participants and researchers (a characteristic of all three);
- Commitments to self-reflective educational and research practices (a characteristic of critical and participatory action research);
- Respect for cultural and linguistic diversity (a characteristic of critical inquiry and contemporary ethnography);
- Respect for the ordinary expertise of the participants (a characteristic of all three); and
- Critical openness to dialogue and understanding as a basis for our interactions (a characteristic of critical inquiry and participatory studies, especially critical participatory action research).

Naming, by Design. These characteristics fit some research designs better than others. Certainly, I drew heavily on Carspecken's Critical Ethnography, but perhaps the IU-Unityville Outreach Project is best described as Critical Participatory Action Ethnography. Donna Haraway (1997) used the term "ethnographic attitude" to indicate employing "a method of being a researcher in the face of practices and discourses into which one inquires … an ethnographic attitude is a mode of practical and theoretical attention, a way of remaining mindful and accountable" (Haraway, 1997, p. 190). At the outset, I was confronted with a request for help with a problem. This request invited the action orientation. I brought with me an appreciation for critical theory and its explanation of both meaning and inquiry. Once our research team was actually engaged with people in Unityville, the ethnographic nature of the project was visible. Remember that we all entered the effort (before it coalesced into a "project" or "study") with questions, concerns, openness, and willingness. We did not enter the field with a design spelled out. We did not enter with an articulated research question. These all emerged. The basic contours of the IU-Unityville Project became apparent within months. For example, our overall research question was developed over the course of 3 months. It was:

> Given the history and circumstances of Unityville schools, how might positive educational experiences be forged for newcomer, non-English speaking students?

This broad research question was articulated by a cadre of Unityville educa-tors once our research team produced its report of initial findings. The research question reflected a large umbrella interest, capable of inviting numerous inter-nal investigations and sub-interests. For example, we had a group of teachers at the high school (facilitated by Ed Brantmeier) developing and implementing an interdisciplinary intercultural peace curriculum in order to better understand how to foster positive relationships among students. At the middle school, there was a study of teachers' attitudes toward Latinos (Nelson Soto was focused on this). At one of the elementary schools, there was inquiry into transnational, non-English speaking parental views of the school and of educational aspirations for their chil-dren (Naomi Sotoo was focused on this). Such research efforts transpired organi-cally from within the larger IU-Unityville Outreach Project. They always surfaced either at the instigation of Unityvillers or in collaborative dialogue that included both IU and Unityville representatives.

The IU-Unityville Outreach Project. This is how it happened. In November 2003, a group of seven graduate students and myself journeyed to Unityville and conducted focus group meetings as described earlier. Each IU person tran-scribed (and translated to English where necessary) the focus group sessions they specifically facilitated. We uploaded those transcriptions to secure files. Unityville paid the graduate students for their work developing, conducting, and transcribing the focus group sessions. I did an analysis of the data and then debriefed that analysis with my IU colleagues. We produced a report of this work in the form of a 72-page, single-spaced document that was offered to the cadre of educators who had inspired the project. We then met as a group (IU and Unityville participants) to discuss the report and decide if anyone was interested in doing more.

In overarching terms, that initial report indicated that by-and-large teachers and administrators did not feel a sense of engagement or empathy regarding their transnational/transmigrant students. There was a paucity of cultural and linguistic expertise/preparation/confidence among educators regarding their ability to work with their new students. Parents of these students were pleased with the schools and seemed to believe the schools were providing their children with incomparable educational opportunities. The transnational students' experiences, without excep-tion, were devastatingly depressing. Their voices compelled our IU team to stay with the project and moved a cadre of Unityville educators to broaden their con-cerns and advance their queries. More of these findings will be presented in later chapters, but I think you will see how these focus groups influenced the design of the study if, at this juncture, you are provided with some of the findings that were made available through that initial report.

With respect to the Unityville educators and townspeople, we learned:

1. "People in [Unityville] believe, almost without exception, that the success of the newcomer ENL student is dependent upon the development of fluency in English. English is considered the primary indicator of assimilation, attitude, family support, and integration.
2. Schooling is believed to be a business, skill-oriented proposition where newcomer ENL students are largely talked about in terms of value added, value depleted, skill deficit/asset terms.
3. Newcomer ENL students present the schools and the community with a [pereceived] new situation, one that most people believe take some new skills, attitudes, and dispositions" (Korth et al., 2004, unpublished Unityville Report).

The "newcomer" students reported harsh experiences with very few bright spots. Their experiences provided excruciating detail of how they felt excluded, disrespected, invisible, and unhappy. They reported being regularly bullied and harassed. They felt caught between the dream that had brought their families to Unityville and the experiences they were having there. They did not want their parents to know how unhappy they felt. This was the case regardless of language group or country of origin. The teachers were disconnected from the students and the students experienced this as alienation.

There was not as much diversity within subgroups as we might have expected at the outset in terms of perspectives articulated through the focus groups. This can probably best explained as a function of three things. First of all, our IU team was basically unknown so it could have been difficult for participants to deeply explore their experiences and attitudes (which almost always brings diversity to the surface). Secondly, the people at the site seemed to lack experiences talking about race, language, and diversity and so there were a lot of "truisms" used that might have just been because people lacked the kinds of skills that come with experience in such conversations. Thirdly, these data were gathered in short order on one day. They were not the sort of findings taken alone that one would publish, but they provided us all with a conversational starting place.

From this starting place, through the medium of videoconference, a group of dedicated educators and a group of university scholars looked each other in the face and decided to embark on a project with a broad goal. In a month we had secured Institutional Review Board (IRB) approval for the project. Later, we secured approval from the Unityville School District Board. A grant was obtained to help fund some of the Project's efforts. And our team of participants, both at the university and in Unityville, expanded. From this point, research questions, methods, designs, involvement, commitments, understanding, knowledge, and outputs proceeded. This book is a story of that process.

> [C]ritical researchers enter into an investigation with their assumptions on the table, so no one is confused concerning the epistemological [assumptions about the nature of knowledge] and political baggage [even as attributes] they bring with them to the research site. (Kincheloe & McLaren, 2007, p. 406)

As our motley crew drove into Unityville for the very first time that November morning in 2003, we had only talked about metatheory in the most practical of ways. We had acknowledged the situation of the schools and the transnational students and we had imagined our potential role in contributing to some kind of progress there. We had worked openly and in an egalitarian manner to establish how we would proceed with the focus groups. We had started sharing our own migration stories with one another as well as our own stories as workers in schools. Each of these conversations and the processes of our dialogic engagement carried within them the principles of Habermas's TCA without us pointing this out or setting this up as an intentional goal. Nevertheless, the insightful benefits of Habermas's work on my own ways of thinking about research, social life, problem resolution, and so on were brought along, as it were, in the way I approached the project. Sheffer (2007) argued that there is "a productive role of theories and concepts for exploratory [ethnographic] studies" where theories "are not used as prescriptions or templates" but enter a dialogue where change happens (p. 170).

St. Pierre (2014) has now famously suggested that it has become impossible for her to conduct qualitative research doing business as usual—that is, going out and finding subjects to observe and interview so as to learn about this or that. All of the basic concepts involved in doing research in more conventional ways did not make sense to her any more. She originated the phrase "post-qualitative" as a way of moving past the standard ways of thinking about research to start a fresh. She primarily drew metatheoretically on Foucault (1988) and Deleuze and Guattari (1987) and she advocated thinking through theory as a way to raise questions of interest. She might have recommended to a student interested in second language learners in Unityville schools that the student read everything Foucault has written and then begin to ask the questions Foucault might ask. Perhaps the student would come up with questions like "How do schools create second language learners?" or "What affordances or constraints are deployed through the category of second language learners?" or "What markers are rendered invisible through the category of second language learners?" A post-qualitative orientation provides a challenge to doing business as usual and can be contrasted with the ways in which I was also oriented toward doing research critically. What we call ourselves matters. How we name ourselves become ways in which we enter conversations. They carry accountability. And when we enter, expecting we will be changed by the conversation, our names are always provisional and contested.

Notes

1. All names are pseudonyms.
2. I will describe later who participated on the team, but I use the phrase "we" here to indicate those of us from the university—myself and a team of seven graduate students.
3. Hermeneutics is a branch of philosophy interested in the contextual interpretation of meaning. It is used here and throughout the text to describe an orientation toward interpretation that takes context deeply into account, always assuming that understanding involves being able to grasp meaning as it would be grasped in context.
4. Phenomenology is an entire field of philosophical study that includes original thinkers like Hegel and Heidegger. It is briefly described as a focus on phenomena—experience and consciousness as objects are always apprehended or understood through experience and consciousness.
5. For example, we find an important reworking of the Marxist notion of "praxis" (Carspecken, 1999, see pp. 40–44 specifically, and the second essay more generally) and a practical understanding of reproduction theories which have since invigorated the way social scientists think about agency in relation to social outcomes. I understand that contemporary materialist philosophy, for example in the work of Barad (2008), challenge these notions of agency.

References

Anderson, G. (1989). Critical ethnography in education: Origins, current status, and new directions. *Review of Educational Research, 59*(3), 249–270.

Anyon, J. (1980). Social class and the hidden curriculum of work. *Journal of Education, 162*, 67–92.

Atkinson, D. (2002). Toward a sociocognitive approach to second language acquisition. *The Modern Language Journal, 86*(4), 525–545.

Barad, K. (2012). Matter feels, converses, suffers, desires, yearns and remembers: Interview with Karen Barad. In Dolphijn, R., & Van Der Tuin, I., *New materialism: Interviews and cartographies* (pp. 48–70). Ann Arbor, MI: Open Humanities Press.

Biesta, G. (2007). Bridging the gap between educational research and educational practice: The need for critical distance. *Educational Research and Evaluation: An International Journal on Theory and Practice, 13*(3), 295–301.

Carspecken, P. (1991). *Community schooling and the nature of power: The battle for croxteth comprehensive school.* New York, NY and London, England: Routledge.

Carspecken, P. (1996). *Critical ethnography in educational research: A theoretical and practical guide.* New York, NY and London, England: Routledge.

Carspecken, P. (1999b). There is no such thing as "Critical Ethnography": A historical discussion and an outline of one critical methodological theory. *Studies in Educational Ethnography*, *2*, 29–55. Oxford, England: JAI Press.

Carspecken, P. (2003). Ocularcentrism, phonocentrism, and the counter enlightenment problematic: Clarifying contested terrain in our schools of education. *Teacher's College Record*, *105*(6), 978–1047.

Chang, Y.-K. (2005). Through queers' eyes: Critical educational ethnography in queer studies. *The Review of Education, Pedagogy, and Cultural Studies*, *27*, 171–208.

Creswell, J. (2006). *Qualitative inquiry and research design: Choosing among five approaches* (2nd ed.). Thousand Oaks, CA: Sage.

Deleuze, G., & Guattari, F. (1987). Introduction: Rhizome. In *A thousand plateaus: Capitalism and schizophrenia* (B. Massumi, Trans., pp. 3–25). Minneapolis: University of Minnesota Press. (Original work published 1980)

de Munck, V. (2000). Units for describing and analyzing culture and society [Special issues: Comparative research and cultural unity]. *Ethnology*, *39*(4), 279–292.

Dennis, B. (2009). What does it mean when an ethnographer intervenes? *Ethnography and Education*, *4*(2) 131–146.

Dennis, B. (2018a). Working without/against a compass: Ethical dilemmas in educational ethnography. In D. Beach, C. Bagley, & S. Marques da Silva (Eds.), *Handbook on ethnography of education* (pp. 51–70). Hoboken, NJ: Wiley Press.

Dennis, B. (2018b). Validity as research praxis. *Qualitative Inquiry*, *24*(2), 109–118.

Denzin, N., & Lincoln, Y. (2007). Introduction: The discipline and practice of qualitative research. In N. Denzin & Y. Lincoln (Eds.), *The landscape of qualitative research* (3rd ed., pp. 1–44). Los Angeles, CA: Sage.

Denzin, N. (2008). The new paradigm dialogs and qualitative inquiry. *International Journal of Qualitative Studies in Education*, *21*(4), 315–325.

Derrida, J. (1974). *Of grammatology*. Baltimore, MD: John Hopkins University Press.

Derrida, J. (1975). *Speech and phenomena: And other essays on Husserl's theory of signs*. Chicago, IL: Northwestern University Press.

Dewey, J. (1989). *The philosophy of John Dewey: Two volumes in one* (J. McDermott, Ed.). Chicago, IL: University of Chicago Press.

Donnelly, J. (2007). The relative universality of human rights. *Human Rights Quarterly*, *29*(2), 281–306.

Everhart, R. (1983). *Reading, writing, and resistance: Adolescence and labor in a junior high school*. London, England: Routledge & Kegan Paul.

Fairlamb, H. (1994). *Critical conditions: Postmodernity and the question of foundations*. Cambridge, England: Cambridge University Press.

Fals-Borda, O. (1979). Investigating reality in order to transform it: The Colombian experience. *Dialectical Anthropology*, *4*(1), 33–55.

Fine, M. (2018). *Just research in contentious times: Widening the methodological imagination*. New York, NY: Teacher's College Press.

Foley, D., & Valenzuela, A. (2008). The politics of collaboration. In N.K. Denzin & Y.S. Lincoln (Eds.), *Handbook of qualitative research* (pp. 217–234). Thousand Oaks, CA: Sage.

Foucault, M. (1988). *Michel Foucault: Politics, philosophy and culture.* New York, NY: Routledge.

Fraser, N. (1987). What's critical about critical theory: The case of Habermas and gender. In S. Benhabib & D. Cornell (Eds.), *Feminism as critique* (pp. 31–55). Minneapolis: University of Minnesota Press.

Freire, P. (2000). *Pedagogy of the oppressed* (30th anniversary ed.). New York, NY: Continuum. (Original work published 1970)

Gadamer, H. (1988). *Truth and method.* New York, NY: Crossroad.

Habermas, J. (1985). *The theory of communicative action, volume 1: Reason and the rationalization of society* (T. McCarthy, Trans.). Boston, MA: Beacon Press.

Habermas, J. (1987). *The theory of communicative action, volume 2: Lifeworld and system: A critique of functionalist reason* (T. McCarthy, Trans.). Boston, MA: Beacon Press.

Haraway, D. (1997). *Modest_Witness@Second_Millenium. FemaleMan©_Meets_Oncomouse™. Feminism&Technoscience.* New York, NY: Routledge.

Harding, S. (1987). Conclusion: Epistemological questions. In S. Harding (Ed.), *Feminism & methodology* (pp. 181–190). Bloomington: Indiana University Press.

Harding, S. (1990). Feminism, science, and the anti-enlightenment critiques. In L. Nicholson (Ed.), *Feminism/postmodernism* (pp. 83–106). New York, NY and London, England: Routledge.

Hitner, S. (2017, March 10). Illegal, undocumented, unauthorized: The terms of immigration reporting. *The New York Times* (Section A, p. 2).

Horkheimer, M. (1972). *Critical theory.* New York, NY: Seabury.

Kincheloe, J., & McLaren, P. (2007). Rethinking critical theory and qualitative research. In N. Denzin & Y. Lincoln (Eds.), *The landscape of qualitative research* (3rd ed., pp. 403–456). Los Angeles, CA: Sage.

Korth, B. (2003). A critical reconstruction of care-in-action: A contribution to care theory and research. *The Qualitative Report, 8*(3), 487–512.

Korth, B. (2005). Choice, necessity, or narcissism. A feminist does feminist ethnography. In G. Troman, et al. (Eds.), *Methodological issues and practices in ethnography. Studies in educational ethnography, volume 11* (pp. 131–167). Oxford and London, England: Elsevier.

Korth, B., Frey, C., Hasbun, M., Nakamichi, Y., Pereira, M., Soto, N., Sotoo, N., & Su, Y. (2004). *Report of IU-Unityville Outreach Project.* Unpublished report to school corporation.

Korth, B., Martin, Y., & Sotoo, N. (2007). Little things that make a big difference: Trust and empathy on the path to multiculturalism. *Scholarlypartnershipsedu, 1*(2), 25–44.

Kuntz, A. (2015). *The responsible methodologist: Inquiry, truth-telling, and social justice.* Walnut Grove, CA: Leftcoast Press.

Lather, P. (2007). *Getting lost: Feminist efforts toward a double(d) science* (Suny series in the philosophy of the social sciences & Suny series: Second thoughts: New theoretical formations). Albany: State University of New York Press.

Lincoln, Y., & Guba, E. (1985). *Naturalistic inquiry.* Beverly Hills, CA: Sage.

Lincoln, Y., & Guba, E, (1994).*Competing paradigms in qualitative research.* In N. K. Denzin & Y. S. Lincoln (Eds.), *Handbook of qualitative research* (pp. 105–117). Thousand Oaks, CA: Sage.

Lynch, G. (2015). What's in a name? The politics of naming ethnic groups in Kenya's Cherangany Hills. *Journal of Eastern African Studies, 10*(1), 208–227.

McCarthy, T. (1994). *The critical theory of Jürgen Habermas.* Cambridge, MA and London, England: MIT Press.

McRobbie, A. (1978). Working class girls and the culture of femininity. In Women's Study Group (Ed.), *Women take issue: Aspects of women's subordination* (pp. 96–108). London, England: Hutchinson.

Naples, N. (2003). *Feminism and method. Ethnography, discourse analysis, and activist research.* New York, NY and London, England: Routledge.

Obama, B. (2018, July 17). *Nelson Mandela Annual Lecture* [Video]. Retrieved November 10, 2019, from https://www.nelsonmandela.org/content/page/annual-lecture-2018

Overton, W.F. (1998). *Metatheory and methodology in developmental psychology.* Retrieved November 10, 2019, from https://astro.temple.edu/~overton/metatheory.html.

Rist, R. (1973). *The urban school: A factory of failure.* Cambridge, MA: MIT Press.

St. Pierre, E. (2014). A brief and personal history of post qualitative research: Toward "post inquiry." *Journal of Curriculum Theorizing, 30*(2), 1–19.

Savin-Baden, M., & Wimpenny, K. (2007, May). Exploring and implementing participatory action research. *Journal of Geography in Higher Education, 31*(2), 331–343.

Scheurich, J. (1997). *Research method in the postmodern.* London, England: Routledge Falmer.

Sheffer, T. (2007). Event and process: An exercise in analytical ethnography. *Human Studies, 30*(3), 167–197.

Sherman, F., & Torbert, W. (Eds.). (2000). *Transforming social theory/transforming social action: New paradigms for crossing the theory/practice divide in universities and communities* (2nd ed., Outreach Scholarship Series). New York, NY: Springer.

Snow, D., Morrill, C., & Anderson, L. (2003). Elaborating analytic ethnography: Linking fieldwork and theory. *Ethnography, 4*(2), 181–200.

Spivak, G. (1999). *A critique of postcolonial reason: Toward a history of the vanishing present.* Boston, MA: Harvard University Press.

Strauss, A., & Corbin, J. (1997). *Grounded theory in practice* (1st ed.). Los Angeles, CA: Sage.

Tugendhat, E. (1989). *Self-consciousness and self-determination (Studies in contemporary German thought)* (P. Stern, Trans.). Boston, MA: MIT Press.

United States Department of Justice & United States Department of Education. (2014). *Fact sheet: Information on the rights of all children to enroll in school.* Retrieved July 19, 2018, from https://www.justice.gov/sites/default/files/crt/legacy/2014/05/08/plylerfact.pdf

Vanderlinde, R., & van Braak, J. (2010). The gap between educational researchers and practice: Views of teachers, school leaders, intermediaries and researchers. *British Educational Research Journal, 36*(2), 299–316.

von Spakovsky, H.A. (2018, July 30). 'Undocumented immigrant' is a made up term that ignores the law [Commentary]. Retrieved September 9, 2018, from https://www.heritage.org/immigration/commentary/undocumented-immigrant-made-term-ignores-the-law

Wildeman, M. (2013, November 8). Student activist promotes 'traditionalism.' *Indiana Daily Student*. Retrieved November 12, 2019, from https://www.idsnews.com/article/2013/11/student-activist-promotes-traditionalism

Willis, P. (1981). *Learning to labor: How working class kids get working class jobs.* New York, NY: Columbia University Press. Morningside Edition.

Yon, D. (2003). Highlights and overview of the history of educational ethnography. *Annual Review of Anthropology, 32*, 411–429.

CHAPTER TWO

We: Complex Relationships at the Slash of Insider/Outsider Dynamics

[W]e are complicit in the world we study. Being in this world, we need to remake ourselves as well as offer up research understandings that could lead to a better world.

(Clandinin & Connelly, 2000, p. 61)

Lather and Smithies (1997) introduced their book *Troubling the Angels* by claiming that the book was, in part, about "researchers both getting out of the way and getting in the way" (p. xiv). They continued on to say "Telling of a loss beyond our knowing, this book, then, is about the limits of what can be said and known about the lives of others" (xiv). Then they concluded the paragraph with this insightful and compelling sentence:

> Doing this work is both a service and a learning, our challenge has been to risk the necessary invasions and misuses of telling other people's stories in order to bear witness with fierce but unsentimental conviction that such stories can transfix, overwhelm, linger, and compel in taking readers to the place where this research has brought us, a place where we can see all the "truth" that we can handle and be grateful for it. (p. xiv)

This purpose is a far cry from the exotic anthropologist's manuscripts of the nineteenth and early twentieth centuries. Inevitably, at the very heart of any research process are insider/outsider relations, but those relations are excruciatingly foregrounded in the work of critical ethnography because researchers are self-consciously aware of their own presence in the field and what that presence might mean for participants, including for the democratization of the research process. Our goal was a realistic form of doing research *with* one another, without knowing who we were together at the start. Barbara Rogoff (2003) described *insiders* as those who actively engage in the shared practices of understanding with one another at a particular research site and she defined *outsiders a*s those who do not regularly and meaningfully participate in those shared meanings and activities. Though in a practical and anthropological way this distinction serves a discursive function, I agree with the many who argued that this binary does not adequately acknowledge the complexities of researcher/participant relationships. Yet, to be honest, we strongly experienced an insider/outsider binary as a feature of our work together. We endeavored to "trouble" (as Lather and Smithies, 1997, would say) this distinction in ways that were authentic, ethical, and productive.

When we first visited Unityville as a research team, we were immediately introduced to the insider/outsider dynamics within the community—we ourselves were positioned as invited outsiders. Others more inside than us thought of themselves as outsiders because they were not born in the community, despite having raised their own kids there. Some white folks told us that Black folks in the area had been considered outsiders in days past but were now thought of as "just like us"—as insiders (this is examined more closely in Chapters 4 and 5). Several community members reported the efforts that were taken to welcome the "newcomer" Japanese families to the community such as hosting a "welcome banquet" when the new executives arrived in town. The Mexican workers and their families were not treated to the same welcome. Such differences constituted layers of outsiderness amongst the transnational students. The process of traversing insider/outsider dynamics involved navigating the various borders that persisted within the community itself and not just those that enmeshed the researcher in the community. Within the layers of what it meant to be an insider, lurked the markers for inclusion and exclusion which indicated values that were enforced, contested, and implicated through those same distinctions.

Moreover, the insider/outsider contrast was interpretively meaningful because it had inferential consequences and because people construed the meaning of similar activities differently across the contrast. For example, people who were interpreted as insiders had more cultural power in the school. This meant that white students who were "assertive" were interpreted as "leaders" while Latinx students who were "assertive" were considered troublemakers. Cultural capital played a role in establishing insiderness as well. There was a Mexican American student who moved from California to Unityville. That student was immediately interpreted/treated as an outsider because they had an Hispanic surname and spoke Spanish.

Though the student was bilingual with English and Spanish, he was automatically placed in the ENL class. But the student's ability to speak English and their competence in soccer gave them a higher status with the whites at Junction High. The whites at Junction "liked" this guy well enough not to slur him as much as they did other Latinx students. In focus group interviews, the white students agreed that he "tried" more than others "to get along." Though they still considered him an outsider—not one of them (in those early days) realized he had been born in the United States and therefore was a citizen of the U.S. in the exact same way that they themselves were.

Historically speaking, U.S. social scientists had long practiced a form of objectivity through which it was assumed that researchers had to be outsiders in order to conduct valid and worthwhile studies. This is linked with the idea that the researcher is/should be completely different than/other than the phenomenon being studied. Taking an insider perspective was considered biased. Foucault himself, critic of objectivist knowledge (1995), was skeptical of the insider position. He suggested that it would be difficult to "know what was really going on" if one were mired in the sociocultural and subjective contexts, beliefs, and attitudes of an insider position because such positions limited what one could "see." Foucault identified an important risk to insider knowledge, however, I am interested in a both/and position. An external perspective can raise questions that are not easily posed from internal perspectives while internal perspectives can, also, engage with important problematics and subversions from within the lived experiences that could be easily misunderstood from the outside. What an external perspective can bring to the dialogue is important for critical endeavors. External perspectives can locate the consequences of interpretations, the unintended outcomes, while also refraining from taking things for granted in the ways insiders might do. An internal perspective is important when we think of research as oriented toward understanding. An outsider perspective that is not tethered to an orientation toward understanding assumes a perspective of power and risks privileging their own knowledge over the perspectives of insiders. An internal critique can, also, foster a critique that benefits from comprehending the vulnerabilities, the disjunctures, the silences, and the contradictions that riddle the experiences in participants own words/actions. When we can grasp these internal dynamics from a WE position,[1] as researchers, we are closer to insider perspectives. In this chapter, I write about working the insider/outsider slash so that critical endeavors are dialogically engaged. The slash between insider and outside is a sociopolitical ground of difference: The gray, transmutable area of existence.

I became friends with Roberta. She was the person with whom I first had contact in Unityville and she was the person with whom I organized most of our project activities. It was crucial to have a relative insider with whom to share ideas, talk over interpretations, and learn about local dynamics. In those early days, particularly, she provided our team with direction and stability. She invited us all to dinner, met me for coffee, and regularly debriefed with us following our visits to the town. Roberta raised her children in Unityville, but reported feeling like an outsider still, after several decades. She described a dynamic that centered on how many generations of one's family had been raised in Unityville. People with longevity were the *real* insiders. Because Roberta had raised her children in Unityville she was more of an insider than people who worked at the schools, but did not live in Unityville. The way longevity structured insider/outsider dynamics piqued our interest in the history of the town (more on this in Chapter 4). The basic descriptors that people used in conversation, such as the division between "traditional" and "newcomer" students, recanted the longevity aspect of the slash between insiders and outsiders.

Outsiders Coming In

We literally drove for hours from outside Unityville to arrive at the schools. We had to obtain special permission, ultimately from the School Board, to regularly enter the schools. At first, we university people were connected with Unityville people through phone calls and email. Then, in person through meetings and focus groups—all of which took place in Unityville. Then, we met regularly with the transnational "newcomer" students through distance education connections. After several years, one of our team members was hired by the district to work at Junction High School. Entering Unityville was a careful, deliberate, negotiated, and long process, but also a haphazard and lucky one. We did not fully appreciate the subtlety of the process until we had stepped aside. In the 2020 nationalist context of the United States, I *feel* the marks of the insiders within me and I know that as I have moved away from Unityville, being with people there changed me. We came to belong to one another.

We Were Outsiders from IU

Who we were changed over time—that is, we as individuals changed, as did the members of our university contingent. Remember that Chris Frey, a graduate student at the time, was our coordinator. His interests in intercultural education had been a prominent characteristic of his scholarship. He was the first to answer my email call-out inviting graduate students to join the team. We built a multilingual, multidisciplinary team. Shortly after receiving Chris's response, we were contacted by others and we were able to stitch together a marvelous group. Naomi Sotoo was a Japanese student in the school psychology program. Yoko Nakamichi Martin was a Japanese student enrolled in the language education program. Yu-Ting Su was a counseling student from Taiwan. Monica Hasbun, a master's student from Colombia, joined us only for the early days. Maura Pereira de Leon was a Venezuelan student of instructional system's technology. Students who joined us along the way included Nelson Soto, a bi-racial, Spanish-speaking American team member studying in the higher education and student affairs program. Ana Baratta Soto was an El Salvadorean school psychology student with a minor in counseling focused on the work of Martin Baró. We were also joined by Ed Brantmeier, a white U.S. student of peace education in the educational policy studies program and Dini Metro-Roland, a white U.S. Hungarian-American Curriculum and Instruction student. Felipe Vargas, Latinx activist, joined us for specific events. Most of the team was fluent in more than one language, and the rest of us were able to use a second or third language for simple communication. The project needed every single one of us.

We Were Skilled/Prepared. None of us had ever been into the Unityville schools. We were outsiders coming in. We had a special status from the beginning—a status that had consequences. We had been invited in. On our very first day, when we were shepherded into a large distance education classroom, where Roberta was the teacher, we organized our plans under Roberta's guidance. Of course, we had come prepared. We had focus group interview protocol for transnational student groups prepared in Japanese, Spanish, and Mandarin. We worked in coordinated teams of two. We, also, had English interview protocol for white students, teachers, administrators, and community members. Chris and I conducted those focus groups. We audio recorded the interviews and took field notes. We left the school for lunch so that we could debrief midday. We would do all of our work that day at Junction High School, though the district had arranged to bring people to us from other schools and from within the communities (e.g., civic leaders). In subsequent visits we also met with guardians of the transnational students. We invited other university students to participate when specific needs arose—for example, Felipe Vargas, joined us to deliver professional development on gang awareness given his expertise working with Latinx gangs in Indianapolis.

We Were Hopeful Resisters. I remembered that at one point that first morning in Unityville, I walked into a large room where our team members were facilitating various focus group sessions with the transnational students in their home languages. I felt an instant ray of hope for our society as I witnessed animated groups of students talking in small groups, different languages ringing out from different corners of the space. Right away our presence that day began a resistance to policies that seemed to harm the "newcomer" students—policies like "English Only." This policy was specifically adopted as a response to the transnational students and it was especially harmful to them. The "language barrier" was a main topic of interest in the teacher focus groups. Teachers had strong, but not well-informed, opinions about the need for that English Only policy. Our linguistic resistance to this policy grew during our time in Unityville. It was one of the characteristics that marked our initial outsiderness. We could get away with breaking the policy and we were even able to broker the use of languages other than English into our school-funded activities. For example, the weekly focus group meetings with small groups of students using distance education technology were conducted in languages other than English on school time and using school monies. Students were organized into linguistic groups of less than six. Middle school students were brought to the high school for their weekly sessions. The students were allowed to meet as a group with one of our teammates using their home languages to talk about whatever they needed/wanted to talk about. We did this for a whole school year and the district paid our university students for this work. Much later in the project Yoko spent two years as a paid aide in the ENL classroom—connecting daily with the transnational students and using both her first language Japanese and the Spanish she was developing in that context as well as English. Eventually, a multilingual attitude developed *within* Unityville, rooting itself as part of a transformational process (more on this in Chapters 6 and 7).

We Were Advocates. We made an important distinction between allies and advocates (Uttamchandani et al., 2019)—allies supported members of marginalized communities and made themselves available to stand up for and speak out on behalf of individuals. We certainly did plenty of this during our ethnographic work. Allyship was crucial for children/youth who were functioning at the margins of school life. However, advocates were those who were involved in working alongside members of marginalized communities to change the power dynamics and structures of the status quo toward social justice equity, including supporting leadership amongst the transnational students. Our use of students' home languages in the school and as the basis of our work with them and their families despite the English Only policy was an example of our advocacy. Ed considered himself a regular advocate in the high school. For example, he advocated with a teacher for one of the Latino students to be given more time to complete an assignment when that student had specifically requested Ed's help.[2] Ongoing advocacy built stronger networks within the Unityville schools themselves as we were joined by Unityville insiders who advocated with us for the students.

We Were Committed Researchers/Educators. And, we were recognized as such by the Unityville community. We were able to talk the language of the schools, but we were also able to ask dumb (albeit sincere) questions about the particulars of schooling in Unityville. We had credibility with teachers as professional educators and experienced researchers, but we had a different kind of credibility with kids— they told us things that they were not telling others, they trusted us to be their advocates in the schools and they appreciated our knowledge of schools when it came to answering questions they had or describing things they might do within the school context. Many of our own transnational team members had migrated to the United States from other countries and had transitioned into U.S. schools. Students found this helpful.

We Had Reasons for Being There

Over the years, it should be noted that three of our IU students conducted dissertations through this project, several others completed early inquiry projects, and there have been some publications. As one would expect, there were many reasons we were in Unityville individually and those reasons changed over time, but one of the things that bonded us, was our commitment to diversity and social justice and their value for schools. With varying sets of background experiences and commitments we *shared a love for the students and a desire to serve their best interests.*

As individuals, we were generally and variously committed to promoting equity in schools. We wanted to promote equity and affirmation of diversity within institutions. We shared a passion for doing social justice work. Some of us were long-time activists for social justice and others were finding their way to more public equity work. We sought justice. For many of us, our long-term commitments to peace and social justice taught us to be passionate about our own transformations and conscientização or critical consciousness (Freire, 2000). Those commitments neither materialized nor disappeared as bookends to our work in Unityville. In fact, negative sociopolitical attitudes that we witnessed toward im/migrant families and youth at the time has become familiar national politics through the election of Donald Trump. Unityville, at the time, was a microcosm of the larger-scale complexities that have festered into a national fight for/against a full-scale assault on our transnational communities. So, the work, broadly speaking, continues.

Values as Connection

At the outset, our IU contingent met several times a week to prepare for our first set of focus group interviews. Those interviews galvanized our commitments. As we transcribed and began to analyze those interviews, our conversations with one another deepened. We prepared a report for the school district with recommendations and conversation points. Our small cadre of Unityville and IU educators developed a plan of action which Chris Frey, Ed Brantmeier, and I presented to the School Board. After receiving support for myriad of proposed activities, we found our commitments could be put further into action. This shared starting place created a synergy amongst us that would see us through some challenging times in the life of the project.

Each team member had slightly different roles, strengths, and responsibilities in the project. For the IU members this meant different forms of engagement and differing amounts of time on the project. For example, Naomi met with Japanese students once a week using distance education technology. Ed was not involved with the online student focus group meetings, but instead met biweekly with a group of teacher inquirers who would create the peace curriculum at the high school. Nelson worked with students and teachers at Cambio middle school. Yoko was immersed over the years in the ENL classroom, serving as an aide and informal advocate for the transnational students at the high school. Our IU team had weekly meetings, often on Sundays at my home, to share insights and experiences, discuss readings, as well as offer support to one another. We enjoyed informal time together in car rides on the trek from Bloomington to/from Unityville. These were times that forged personal opportunities for relationship building and for learning to understand the various experiences that we came to think of as "insider perspectives."

We struggled quite a lot at various points in the life of the project. There were things happening at the schools that were problematic for us. We had to carve out a path that remained hopeful and educative while also advocating for our transnational youth. Our weekly meetings became an opportunity for us to engage in self-care. In fact, at one point, my colleague Dr. Chalmer Thompson, whose expertise includes liberation psychology (see Thompson, 2019), spent a Sunday afternoon helping us process the trauma of witnessing and being a part of systemic racism as it took its particular form in Unityville. We learned together, encouraged one another, and provided critical feedback. We oriented ourselves toward conscientização, Freire's (2000) idea of critical consciousness-raising (Korth, 2002) and held each other accountable to the goals of equity and social justice. Our connections outside of Unityville (but in relation with Unityville) depended in part on our outsiderness, while also benefitting our relationships inside.

Insider Complexity

"There isn't a whole lot of diversity in Unityville. I mean when you look at our population of students, I mean we have like 16 African Americans, you know I mean a very, like I said there, just isn't a whole lot of difference."[3] Yet, we knew going into the project that Unityville was complicated with differences that were somewhat blurred through their focus on assimilation and homogeneity. It was interesting to learn about both the internal variation in the Unityville community and the mechanisms through which that variation was managed. At a Teacher Inquiry focus group[4] meeting in December, 2004, Pam identified an issue that she thought the peace curriculum should address.

> Just as each one of us are in this group, even though we belong to the same group here we're all very different and have different (stresses) views about things. So, you can't say I would agree with what Roberta (stresses) says or what Susan (stresses) says. But then I might (stresses), so you can't assume anything about any individual person just because they're within that group. ... Or just because they come from a certain place.[5]

There was diversity amongst educators in terms of attitudes and interpretations of the transnational students. Table 2.1 displays some of those crucial differences. In the beginning, transnational-positive attitudes were expressed by only a handful of people, while the mainstream attitudes were vociferously articulated. Unityville members of the Project noted the significant lack of empathy amongst their colleagues and the white student population at Junction High. The extent to which a lack of empathy was widespread changed over time, but empathy for the transnational students or lack thereof continued to mark differences within the insider community.

Transnational students were inside as outsiders: inside-outsiders. With respect to the transnational students, the Unityville community treated Latino/a/x students worse than Japanese students (the next largest group in the transnational student community). Japanese students came with their fathers who had executive positions in Japanese corporations. They were only in the United States for a few years. These kids were not conceptualized as migrants. There was a privately organized Japanese Saturday school in Indianapolis for parents and students around the state. Also, Japanese students used technology to stay in touch with friends and family in Japan. When the Japanese families moved to town, the city would throw a welcome banquet. Despite this more positive orientation, Japanese transnational students and families were not really insiders. They were just "less of a problem" than other transnational students.

Additionally, Black students were largely missing in the discourse about students in general. The talk primarily suggested that Black students were so

Table 2.1 Some Examples of Differences in White Educators' Beliefs and Attitudes Toward Transnational Students: A Sampler

Topic	Mainstream Attitude or Belief	Transnational-Positive Attitude or Belief
Spanish-speaking skills	"They can't even speak Spanish for that matter." "Students don't even know their own language. They fuse it with *our* language." – as if saying "how dare they do that."	"And unfortunately some of our Spanish students don't do very well in Spanish class. Which, um, I don't really find surprising, because one-it would be like us going to take a first grade English class I think, probably, learning vocabulary that we've known all of our lives."
Assimilation	"Japanese students are honorary whites." "We're all the same."	"If we made the effort here to learn [their language – Spanish], they would respect us too for trying to communicate—they would be more involved in our classes— we wouldn't seem so unapproachable."
Privileging their home language and culture	"They separate themselves."	"I don't want them to lose their culture"
Hispanic students sitting together in the cafeteria	"I mean I've noticed, then again these are probably similar things that you've noticed yourselves in your observation, but like in the cafeteria, you know the students, the Spanish speaking students they tend to hang out together." "They separate themselves." "They all congregate together – it's a problem."	"What makes me sad is walking into the cafeteria and seeing them [the Hispanic students at the high school] all sit together. Cuz, I mean I understand the camaraderie among them, but I just wish some other— some of the min—or majority kids would come over and sit with them or just try un—I don't know, get them involved in some way. It's just, uh, I just think it's sad. Cuz they're sort of like their own little island, you know."
Inclusive curriculum and pedagogy	"Don't make different lessons for Hispanic students" "that's not fair"	I want "students who aren't in the majority have representation within the curriculum, and are made to feel that their culture is respected."

Table 2.1 *Continued*

Topic	Mainstream Attitude or Belief	Transnational-Positive Attitude or Belief
	"Um. I mean you have to really be able to reach out to those students. But at the same time it can't be so much that, ok, *everyone* is getting hurt by it as well." (italics added for emphasis)	
Empathizing with transnational students	"They need to just learn English"	"But it was neat for me, because, I mean I speak some Spanish, but I'm not by any means fluent. And for me being there with all these Hispanic students, they were just going on and on in Spanish and I'm thinking oh my goodness, you know I can't understand half of what they're saying and then when I would try to communicate with them in Spanish I would feel silly, thinking am I saying the right thing, do I sound really stupid? You know, so it was kind of a neat experience"
Discrimination	"I don't see a big discrimination thing here at all—"	"Hispanics get a lot of harassment."
	"I think they bend over backwards to make them feel welcome."	"Hispanics are the new group for American students to put down. ... There is a lot of prejudice."
	"The community has embraced the Latino population."	"Hispanics face a lot of challenges."

assimilated that they were not really different from the white students. Yet, labels like "traditional" students did not seem to apply to Black students and mostly the staff described the Black students as "not a problem," "largely nonexistent," "totally the same, no different," and "invisible" while retaining the not-so-subtle language of white supremacy (more on this in Chapter 5). The erasure of the relevance of being black in the Unityville schools was another medium through which students were differentiated.

Demographic Descriptions from 2004

As previously reported (Dennis, 2009), Latino/a/x, Japanese, Taiwanese, and Palestinian students comprised the largest subgroups in the transnational Unityville school community.

> Until 2000 there was no special program for ENL learners. In 2000 one of the English teachers who knew some Spanish was partially reassigned to teach the newcomer students for two class periods a day. This teacher was not provided with training to support her reassignment. From 2000 to 2002 the White student population rate decreased from 95% to 90% in inverse relation to the rise in newcomer students. Asian student enrollment increased from .5% to 1%; Hispanic student enrollment increased from 1.4% to 3.7%. There was a steady African American population during these years of less than 1%. The rest of the population comprised newcomer students who fell outside the categories of Asian and Hispanic. (Dennis, 2009, p. 67)

As of 2019, the school enrollment had continued to rise for Latino/a/x groups (more than quadrupling since 2004—with students predominately migrating from Mexico) while the white population in the county declined to around 80 percent. Black student enrollment had nearly doubled by 2017 when compared with 2004, though this was still a very small number of students and significantly lower than the state average. Meanwhile, the number of multi-racial students increased significantly. The teaching staff continued to be predominantly white (over 98 percent). The total number of students in 2017 was between 4,000 and 5,000.[6] Over half of the students, in 2017, received free or reduced lunch.

The increasing diversity of the student community coupled with the retention of a white teaching staff makes the lessons of this project still relevant.

"They've invaded." Outsiders Within

Several teachers conflated the school with the town and argued that outsiders had "invaded" their town. Some teachers even complained about the aesthetics, reporting that "Hispanics" were painting homes and buildings in "bright colors," which seemed distasteful and strange (almost as if such "bright colors" are un-American). One of the teachers was quite clear that he did not want the "newcomer" students in his school or his town. This unabashed entitlement to the town meant that conceptually someone could be physically *inside* the school, but socially and materially *outside*. Of course, this is not a unique story in United States school history. It is part of the contradiction of public schooling as yet to be totally worked out, but, also, not without some small successes. In Unityville, the transnational students and their families were part of the slash that constituted the insider/outsider dynamics. More on this below.

The community's claim to be a homogeneous social collective (we, us, our) in some denial of its own diversity, functioned as one of the conditions for the oppression of transnational and Black students within that community. The district officially reported on its demographic diversity, but the talk of privileged members of the community (those in power through money, authority, and cultural privilege) made use of a "we" that didn't reference the whole. Privileged people in the schools, used "we" as if they were talking about the whole community, even though that so-called "we" only referred to themselves and others like them. This "we" erased and actively silenced the diversity within. Moreover, teachers and administrators complained about the use of hyphenated statuses in the United States (African-American, for example). Even using the category name "Hispanic" suppressed diversity. Many Latinx students reported that the mainstream kids would assume that all Latinx youth came from Mexico. This took a while to undo. Reporting on an Aha! moment, years into the project, one of the counselors told Dini,

> I grouped them [all of the Hispanic kids] together [as] Hispanic, but it was neat, because when they introduced each other to other people they'd be like "This is my Dominican friend," "this is my Mexican friend," you know, they'd go by country, which we don't normally do [for] them. Um, so within—they are very diverse and we—I mean we do, sort of group the Hispanic students together. But they are a very diverse group within themselves, because we've got—trying to think, I think we've got kids from Puerto Rico, Mexico, Dominican Republic, I can't remember where all from, but—.

Many of the teachers distinguished insiders from outsiders by lumping the following insider characteristics together: English-as-one's language, identification as Christian, being in the United States legitimately by birth, and whiteness. Insiders with those characteristics were implicitly attributed with particular entitlements—chief among those the power of naming the *outsiders within*. For example, educators used the term "newcomers[7]" (instead of "transnational" or "transmigrant") to indicate the migrated students were new to being in Unityville. This language reinforced an orientation of *THEM* coming to *US*. The language of invasion, take-over and negative change were commonly associated with how the teachers/administrators related with the students. Had the name "transnational" been used, the orientation could have offered a resituation of Unityville conceptually as becoming part of a global community precisely through the migration of students—bringing the town into a global network. The political language of "invasion" present in Unityville at the time, was heightened nationally through the election of Donald Trump to the presidency. From the contemporary vantage point, it is easy to see a link between the language Unityville educators used at the time of the study, and the rhetoric of Donald Trump and his supporters with respect to the need for a wall at the southern U.S. border. According to an August 2019 Washington Post article,

> President Trump has relentlessly used his bully pulpit to decry Latino migration as "an invasion of our country." … And he has warned that without a wall to prevent people from crossing the border from Mexico, America would no longer be America. "How do you stop these people? You can't," Trump lamented at a May rally in Panama City Beach, Fla. Someone in the crowd yelled back one idea: "Shoot them." The audience of thousands cheered and Trump smiled. Shrugging off the suggestion, he quipped, "Only in the Panhandle can you get away with that statement." (Rucker, 2019)

The point that the transnational students were inside against the will of the *real* insiders was important to the dynamics of exclusion at the school. For example, longtime Unityville educators were not really expected to comply with policies that required teachers to make accommodations for the transnational students because those teachers were entitled to think of the new students as unwelcomed invaders. Teachers involved in the Project described these colleagues as unwilling to change, which those teachers themselves acknowledged. "We didn't ask for this. Why is it our problem?" "I'm not changing for them [the transnational students]." "I don't want them [the transnational and im/migrant community] in *my* town. Period." This attitude was treated as if it was both immutable and acceptable by other Unityville colleagues.

Fine (2018) described such insiders as being "exiles within" (p. 11). One of our Latino students said what many of them also articulated and felt: "We don't belong." The politics of exclusion specifically reproduce(d) systems of marginalization, damage, and injustice. These politics of exclusion animated the very educational souls of our transnational students in the sense that it was at the heart of what it meant to be educated in the United States.

Working the Slash[8]: Insider-Outsider Dynamics

In the section above, I described the dynamic aspects of the two sides of our project's slash, exploring it deliberately and directly. It was important for us insiders and outsiders to work the slash together, to use Fine's (1994) insightful "working the hyphens" idea. That is, we had to engage in the liminal space of the slash—liminality as an uncertain time between what was and what's to come.[9] Liminality literally means threshold. I used it in this context in order to note that the insider and outsider contrast did not function as a binary in Unityville. The slash represented a gray space of liminality that was directional (that is, outsiders moving toward the inside), progressive (one could be more or less an insider or outsider), and gatekeeping (not everyone could become an insider and some ended up invisible while others ended up trapped as exiles in the space between outsider and insider—a third culture space[10]). The aspects of the slash I describe below include: longevity, race, and the impossibility of becoming the same. Following that, I describe primary mechanisms for maintaining the status quo with respect to insider hierarchies: power, getting along, fear mongering, erasure, and aloofness (lack of empathy). Certainly, those mechanisms formed homologous relations with one another and were systematically engaged.

Structures of the Slash

The liminal space of the slash between insiders and outsiders was configured through sociocultural constructs that included longevity, race, the impossibility of becoming the same, and erasure. These constructs riddled our IU relationships with Unityville educators as well, but not to the same degree as it did for transnational students because we IU folks were allowed "inside" more easily even if just temporarily. As we grew to understand and articulate the structures entailed in this in-between zone, we were better equipped to engage together with our Unityville counterparts and move toward a complicated sense of WE.

Longevity as Clout. There was one especially poignant example of the way longevity structured the liminality of this in-between in Unityville. One of our transnational students, Ms. Tu, from Taiwan was struggling at the high school in one of her classes. The teacher persistently called on her before she was ready to respond. She was slower to understand the questions and slower to compose a response than her English-as-their-only-language students, in large part because she was still mentally translating. In addition, she felt aggravated amounts of shame in the class for not being able to respond proudly. She talked with the ENL teacher and with Yu-Ting, our IU graduate student who worked with the Taiwanese high schoolers. Together the team suggested that Ms. Tu compose a letter to the teacher that expressed her desire and willingness to participate in the class, while also explaining that her level of competence with English and with the class material made it difficult for her to easily and correctly answer on the spot. The team worked with her to propose an alternative scenario: she could indicate to the teacher in a subtle way that she was prepared to answer a particular question in a given moment. She delivered this note to the teacher. To our dismay, the teacher rejected the idea. The teacher told Ms. Tu that he could call on her whenever he wanted and that he was not going to lower his expectations for her. He insisted on treating all kids "the same." It was only fair. I met with him following this incident and he expressed his displeasure with his town having been invaded. He was not interested in Ms. Tu's success at, what he considered, the expense of his own teaching style. He believed that accommodating her in such a way would be a disservice to his other students. There were other incidents of him singling out Ms. Tu in ways that contributed to her feeling isolated and depressed. He believed the responsibility for her fitting in to the school rested on her shoulders entirely. To do anything special for "them"/ her would be unfair to the "traditional" students. He wanted "those kids" to move on, to leave his town. I spoke with one of the administrators about his attitude. He had clout. He had longevity. The solution: We moved Ms. Tu out that class and did not assign any other transnational students to his teaching load. The teacher was happy and our transnational students were out of harm's way. His longevity gave him the informal power to choose who he taught and who he didn't teach. Obviously, not everyone in the school could have such power because the public school's mission is to teach *all* kids. This particular solution was neither sustainable nor desirable on a large scale, and it simultaneously reproduced Unityville's own version of exceptionalism and elitism. Nevertheless, it was an important Band-Aid in the slash.

Doing ethnographic work meant that our IU contingent fundamentally made long-term commitments to the field (relative to most research in schools), and this advantaged our relationships in Unityville. My age, recognizability through the characteristics of insiderness (white, Christian, born in the United States, longtime educator) meant I was "accepted" more easily than others. In my early interviews with teachers and community members, this status afforded some level of trust evidenced by the kinds of things educators said. Because our work as ethnographers in the schools was change-oriented, we were not fully embraced by those who resisted change, however, it was clearly assumed that I would somehow understand the "traditional" positions as an insider might have also understood them.

A handful of white Unityville educators expressed disagreement with the practices that rewarded longevity and punished "newcomers." Those, like Roberta, who participated in the Teacher Inquiry group, lamented their longtimer, Unityville colleagues' unwillingness to change. Teacher inquirers contrasted their own progressive attitudes with those who wanted to keep things the way they had always been.

Race as Right or Wrong. As has been true for some time in the United States, "others" were identified in the school through racial terms, while whiteness was tucked into the language of what it meant to be "traditional," "right," and "one of us." One of the Unityville team members, with a slip of the tongue, described what they hoped would change at Junction High through our work. They said, "Um, and I don't know if those students will have also branched out from the social aspect of, you know, um, *black versus right* (corrects herself) white, Hispanics, Native Americans, whatever."[11] Perceptions of Hispanic students reduced language to race. Hispanic[12] was the term used in Unityville to describe all Latino transnational students, befitting most of them as speakers of Spanish. However, the language and racial aspects of the students were largely conflated. While an overwhelming number of educators said they believed that learning English was a skill which was possible for "newcomers" to acquire, they also used racialized ways of thinking about the transnational students that indicated there was more to traverse than language. Earlier in the chapter, I mentioned the student who moved to Unityville from California. Having brown skin, fluency in Spanish, and a Latinx surname insured that he was not an insider despite is fluency in English and his status as a natural born U.S. citizen. So, while English language proficiency was described by teachers as the biggest barrier to being successful as a transnational student, speaking Spanish, or Japanese, or Arabic was tightly conjoined with racial suppositions.

When students did not speak English, they were explicitly described as doing something wrong. This wrongness was linked to a web of interpretations that included thinking of the students, especially the Latinx students, as bad. White high school students told us that if the "newcomer" students didn't speak English it was because they had a "bad attitude." Teachers distrusted students who were not speaking English at school so they felt compelled to police language usage. Teachers told us that if students spoke Spanish in the class that they were probably "cheating," "making fun of the teacher," "plotting" or "being disrespectful." The assumption was that the transnational students were engaged in bad behavior that the their white, English-speaking students were not involved with. Moreover, teachers associated students speaking languages other than English at school as an increased responsibility for surveilling the kids. The interpretation of badness was made clearer when teachers sought to solve the problem by eliminating the right to speak a language other than English at school (as if it was *bad* to speak those languages) rather than taking the responsibility to learn Spanish in order to better monitor the "bad" behavior. One of the high school teachers told Ed,[13] "I wonder if they are putting up a front and using the language as their excuse for ignorance. And, ah, because sometimes I'll talk with (a colleague) and say 'What about so and so?' 'What?' 'What?' You know, and she'll say 'Oh, he or she knows more than what they are saying.' Their English is pretty good. You know, blah, blah. So they are kind of pullin' your leg from time to time, to think that they don't understand what I'm saying but they really truly do understand what I'm saying so ... (implying that the student cannot be trusted)."

In this racialized liminal space, with language and skin color as operational markers, our IU research team was able to create opportunities that "insiders" themselves eschewed. For example, we used languages other than English to speak with the students and their families. School personnel drew on our linguistic and cultural expertise from the beginning (which helped to locate us at the slash with Unityville's transnational students), even while they themselves refrained from making linguistic connections in the students' home languages. As another example, we university team members called out and advocated for students when we witnessed racist actions/talk in the schools. We had a special outsider status that afforded us an opportunity to speak into the racial violence in ways our collaborators did not always find possible for themselves. For example, Ed told a story of witnessing the school security guard give repeatedly negative attention to a Black male kid in the high school. Ed did his best to disrupt those interactions in the moment, while we worked together to try to make more sustainable, systemic changes. Though our Unityville collaborators basically agreed with Ed's actions, they had a hard time engaging in such advocacy themselves—at least at the beginning.

There were a few teachers who resisted the racial ostracizing. In a December Teacher Inquiry group meeting, one of the teachers argued that the racial discrimination needed to stop. She claimed the school would be better if, it were free of

-isms. You know like racism, prejudice, sexism, elitism, homophobia, all of those. (Pauses) I think.. You know sort of (sighs) helping to facilitate a little self-reflection (stresses) on everybody's part. Sort of figure out, OK, first be really honest about, you know, everyone's individual views and attitudes. And then reflection on that (stresses) and then take it somewhere further.[14]

Another teacher dreamed outloud,

I think it would be kind of neat if people in the community knew that whenever they were talking to a student from our school district that you don't talk about discriminatory things, you don't say racial slurs because these are students who don't appreciate it and they're not going to stand for it. And I thought that would be something really special.

In contrast with more typical Unityville talk, these perspectives were transformative because they did not erase the racism, and they attributed it and its benefits to white people.

The Impossibility of Becoming the Same. There was no clear path for moving through the inchoate liminal space at the slash of the insider/outsider dynamic. It seemed that moving was unidirectional (moving from outsider to insider), though it was impossible to fully become an insider because of what it meant to be an insider in the Unityville context. The educators did not verbalize this as an impossibility, but it seemed to those of us on the team that the insiderness needed to be transformed if outsiders were to be more fully included, to more fully belong to the school community. Transforming the structures of insider exclusivity required describing those structures at the outset.

Educators and mainstream students in Unityville almost unanimously endorsed a belief in the power of assimilation. Assimilation meant work on the part of the outsiders. It meant entering the school community on terms already established relative to insiders only (i.e., they existed prior to any clear knowledge of the transnational students). Assimilation meant being perceived as the same by the educators and by long-standing members of the Unityville community (more on this is Chapter 5). For example, many educators said that, we "are all the same" here. They referred to the assimilation of Black students as resulting in them being "no different" from "us." "They are just like us [meaning just like whites]." However, the students of color experienced it differently. One of the Mexican American students told Nelson (an IU member of the team), "They [the whites] think they are better than us—when I tried to make friends with them, I had to change my look—in LA I dressed a certain way, here I had to completely change—and they still don't accept me." The transational students were convinced both that they were not wanted by most people in Unityville and that there was no way to traverse the rejection. Our transnational students were not seeking sameness, they were seeking a minimal form of acceptance. However, many (not all) Unityville educators imagined sameness as the assimilationist version of the American dream. It was their ideal. An ideal they wrongly assumed *should be/was* shared.

U.S. politicians took up an aspect of the liminality when they created opportunities for child im/migrants, regardless of their paperwork, to attend U.S. public schools and eventually to attend U.S. colleges as residents if they had successfully graduated from an accredited U.S. high school. A path to citizenship for these youngsters (including those in our study) has continued to be debated.

Through our ethnographic practices, we urged a multicultural peace orientation that moved beyond tolerance, inclusion, and acceptance toward belonging through a complex WE-ness (Brantmeier, 2008). From our earliest days in Unityville, we were struck by the way people in the schools tended to refer to the transnational students as "those" kids—never "my" kids, never "my" students. We modeled an affiliation with the students that encouraged we-ness and aimed to break down the barriers educators perceived. Even with our first report, we wrote about what the kids were telling us, about their experiences with racial violence so that it could not be washed away. Similarly, we advocated for a more complicated view of belonging that did not require either sameness or assimilation. We oriented more toward the vision of a diverse community mutually engaged. We did this methodologically.

In contrast to the more mainstream view of (unattainable) sameness, one of our Unityville Project educators described her experiences with the "newcomer" Latino/a/x students like this:

> Well, I think for me, it's helped give me a passion to work with these students. Um, because I feel like it's almost two ways, because I'm not just trying to help them, but they're teaching me too. They're teaching me different things. Um, and not that I expect something—I don't expect to be reciprocal, but it's kind of neat, because I do get to learn about different cultures from them, um, and I mean I think that's where part of the whole text book issue and U.S. perspectives comes from, because I remember being in high school and learning about, um, battles between the United States and Mexico and how it was kind of like "Hooray, us, U.S.," you know what I mean, so I'm kind of torn inside thinking "Ok, is this a good thing or a bad thing, did I win or lose?"

She was a bi-racial member of the community who passed for white and largely let that happen. However, her relationships with Latinx students at the high school, were affording her opportunities to reflect on earlier life experiences where her Histpanic ethnicity was troubled.

Our IU team members resonated with ideals that did not reduce to everyone being the same, or everyone being assimilated. For example, in our initial report to the Unityville schools, we wrote:

> Unityville has a few individuals who can speak Japanese and Spanish and who have been influential in making connections with the students and in some cases with their parents. Increasing the number of adults who can interact with the ENL students in their home languages would build on this important strength. Using and extending the language competence of faculty and staff would be a worthwhile endeavor. Some specific ways this might be developed further could include:

- Provide language instruction for educators (maybe even using community leaders as teachers)
- Contract with community leaders to provide translation on notices for parents, meetings with parents, and so forth
- Use high school students who are in their second year of Japanese or Spanish as well as newcomer high school students to work with elementary or middle school students using the home language.

(Korth et al., 2004)

Mechanisms for Maintaining the Status Quo

One of the teachers I interviewed on my very first visit to Unityville warned me that "Unityville is not one for change, Junction High School is not one for change—don't take kindly to a lot of change—we like the status quo." Maintaining the status quo is the work of privilege and Unityville was, by no means, unique in this regard. In this section, I introduce just a couple of mechanisms that were specifically known amongst educators to be effective for maintaining the status quo, namely aloofness, fear mongering, power over, and getting along. These mechanisms were not merely descriptions of how things were working at Unityville. The mechanisms were, also, the context within which our ethnographic project was being carried out. I will conclude each subsection with a brief statement about what these dynamics and mechanism meant for how we engaged ethnographically with Unityville schools.

Aloofness or Lack of Empathy. In our original report to the district based on our initial focus group and individual interviews, the university team noted a significant lack of empathy for the experiences and situations of the transnational students. Julianne, one of the Unityville teacher inquirers, lamented that in the high school, there was "… a lack of understanding, or more of a lack of *wanting* [emphasized] to understand. And a lack of empathy. Yeah, definitely a huge lack of empathy."[15] Aloofness worked to keep the teachers from recognizing the humanity of the transnational students and their families. Aloof talk and relational distance restricted the teachers' abilities to take the position of the "newcomers." It was unusual to hear teachers or white students talk empathetically about the transnational students, but perhaps even more poignantly, educators did not refer to the transnational students as "our" students. "Our" was reserved for their "traditional students." Several teachers used the word "everyone" to basically refer to all other students EXCEPT the "newcomers." Such talk erased "newcomer" students, but also indicated that serving the transnational students was not worth putting the teachers *more important, traditional students* at a perceived risk. A cultivated aloofness facilitated the choice to value the mainstream Unityville students at the expense of our transnational students. The barriers for relating were even blamed on the transnational students: "it's their ignorance, their language barrier."

Our stance as ethnographic team members was to prioritize the needs of our transnational students. We emphasized the value of the "newcomers," their families, and their languages/cultures. We purposefully developed empathy with and among team members and students and we engaged in project activities that fostered empathy, nurtured relationship building, and encouraged cultural reflection. We did not take an embracing or accepting attitude toward the aloofness. Some members of the community expressed good intentions toward the students and we connected with those intentions. Together we argued that aloof, non-empathetic orientations toward the students limited the teachers' capacities to understand the students. We called into question the taken-for-granted claim that it was the language barrier that educators and traditional students blamed for the teachers' inability to connect with the students.

> I've seen with teachers and students a real lack of empathy dealing with language. Where I would hear, see, a group of Hispanic students speaking Spanish to each other, and have another student walk down the hall and say, "Don't do that here." Trying to tell them don't speak your native language here. … a total lack of empathy that there could be any reason why they would niche together [to speak Spanish] that wasn't nefarious. (Julianne)[16]

Fear Mongering. Unityville white students and educators promoted fears, particularly, but not only, with regard to their Latinx students, especially at the high school. Fear mongering began from a perspective of aloofness toward the students. Ed reflected on the following story.

> [Y]ou know I've heard various student comments um walking in the halls, going in between classes and stuff. Like one kid came out of the lunchroom one day and he was a Euro-American male. He said to his friend "Be careful". I asked him I said "What do you mean by 'Be careful?'" And he said "It's dangerous around here. This is a dangerous place" I said "Really! How is it dangerous?" And I said "Why is it dangerous?" And he looked around and saw a Latino kid and he said "Because people like him (stresses) are here."

One of the administrators retold a story of white people feeling threatened. The story itself reproduced racial and culture fear.

> Um, if a Hispanic group of boys whistles at a Caucasian girl and says things about that girl in Spanish, you know, that probably would be something a white person would

say like, you know, "hey baby," "hot mama," whatever, that would be threatening not so much to a girl but if a Caucasian man (stresses) heard and saw that. That would be uncomfortable, he would feel probably threatened that you have somebody different going after a Caucasian girl. That can create hostility.

Ed asked the administrator if this was a hypothetical situation or if this was a description of something that had happened. The administrator continued on to report that this happened to one his daughters who was with her boyfriend and the boyfriend was afraid when the Hispanic men whistled at the daughter. Apparently, there was more fear experienced and described than would have been the case if the men doing the catcalling were white.

Another person reported, "And here's the issue. I think its that Unityville has seen some crime things that they had never seen before until the Hispanic population … I mean my first year here they had a drive-by shooting. … Where somebody shot up a car and that's never happened in Unityville before, and unfortunately it was linked to a couple of Hispanic kids." Such retold stories propagated and perpetuated fear that was out of proportion to the actual risk. In this instance, a kid who was from Texas drove to Unityville to do the shooting, so the perpetrator was not from Unityville, rather the victim was. The fear mongering mechanism functioned as justification for whites to stay aloof and disconnected from the transnational students. Teachers asked things like, "Who are these people?" "Are they going to hurt us?" "Are they here to take our jobs?" Teachers claimed that the police were regularly called out to the Hispanic parts of town and in general, white people in the Unityville did not trust their new transnational students. One teacher told us what she thought about Hispanic students in the schools, "They are dark colored. They wear browns and blues. I don't trust these people." The racialization of the fear was fueled, not by facts, but by ignorance (a by product of aloofness) and lack of empathy. Roberta hoped that by developing a peace curriculum the fear and ignorance could be changed. She said, "And I had [written down that] ignorance and the lack of empathy [served as barriers to implementing a peace curriculum]. Both of those breed that lack (stresses) of understanding that creates fear, and, hatred can kind of spawn from fear."

Moreover, the fear mongering was linked conceptually with patriotism. One of the administrators received the following hand-written note from a Junction High student—a white boy we referred to as Jerry Changer. He called out the fear mongering in his note.

Received March 17, 2005 from Jerry Changer

Greetings. My name is Jerry Changer. I'm in the 10th grade and an okay student. One of my best friends is Sarah. She is an Arabic girl who is from Israel. Everyday, I hear people slander her. I hear people threaten her. They see all Arabs as "terrorist," an image created by modern society. It is my hope that we can break down these barriers, but it is increasingly difficult. I love my country, but it is hard to oppose army boys in a climate of patriotism. One used to be my friend. He never thought like that. Now, he says Sarah should die.

What exactly have they been taught? Moreover, when I see and hear my elders put up with this, it leads me to question if they are in favor of this racism or not.

With much respect

Jerry Changer

When we heard fear mongering directly, we questioned it. We probed into it. We did not just take it for granted. Then, we repeated what we heard with the Unityville partners to raise awareness. We also used the substance of the fears to create educational opportunities. For example, people in Unityville expressed their fears about the growth of Latino gangs so we invited Felipe, an Indiana Latinx gang expert, to lead workshops in the schools that equipped teachers to better understand what was going on as well as understand the roots and possibilities of working toward peace. Often enough, the fear was implicit to what was being said or done. We reconstructed its meaning (Carspecken, 1996) and shared what we learned with our Unityville colleagues in efforts to target educational opportunities to dissuade the fears. The development of the peace curriculum was one major example of work intended to transcend the fears and burst through the aloofness that was being buttressed by the fears. We, also, encouraged the expression of fear so that it could be worked through on a feeling level.

Power-Over. I daresay that in schools, in general, authoritarian modes of relating with youth are common means of control. Thus, perhaps there will be readers who believe that power over, when used for good, is a positive tool. We found throughout our fieldwork that power-over was a mechanism to resist change. Power-over students was not merely about control, it was about maintaining the status quo of authority relations. For example, the teacher I described earlier who did not want to adjust his teaching methods to accommodate Taiwanese transnational student, Ms. Tu, used his power over Ms. Tu to reproduce his authority to maintain things as they always had been in his class. This power-over mechanism was also linked to aloofness—to not "being buddy-buddy with students. Keeping *that* distance." Harkening back to Chapter 1, the power of naming was a complicated form of power-over. For example, the persistent use of the name "newcomer" student to refer to transnational/transmigrant students from a variety of different national and linguistic contexts, but not in reference to any new white students that joined the schools made it clear that the power to name reproduced the status quo. In this text, I am conscious of that power and I move uncomfortably between the names chosen, the names desired, and my associations with particular names as well as what the naming affords in terms of resisting the oppressive status quo. The status quo was not benign.

Power-over served the status quo by heightening its policing on the less advantaged, more vulnerable students in the school. Julianne had an epiphany during her work on the peace curriculum. She recognized the link between power-over and maintaining the status quo of privileges. She said, "Knowing, that to create an equal society, we [white U.S. citizens] would not (stresses) grant privileges to everyone ... And I think that's their greatest fear, is that equality means, 'I give up [something].'" Julianne claimed that, "We [white people] should not accept any of them [racial and class privileges]." As Brantmeier (2008) noted, this required not just a change in the playing field, but a whole new field. Racism, sexism, heterosexism, and other forms of oppression were tied directly into Unityville forms of privilege and power-over in a complex system that reproduced the status quo. While it might be tempting to point the finger at Unityville, they are not unique. The systemic reproduction of the status quo through power-over is endemic to U.S. institutions, despite, at times, our best intentions otherwise. The IU-Unityville Outreach Project was a hope for change.

Throughout the research process, we kept ourselves open to being "wounded in the field"—a descriptor initially used by McLaren (1992b) to describe what it means to have the experiences in a research field challenge your sense of self. Being open to those challenges wounds one's ongoing sense of being (as a kind of status quo). We IU team members felt wounded and so did many of our Unityville partners. In contradiction to the power-over and as part of our self-care, we fostered equity and inclusiveness in our ethnographic practices and we posed challenges to the power-over routines that were typical to these and most U.S. schools.

Getting Along. The phrase "getting along" was used often by school officials and white students to describe what they considered a measure of success. Ed conducted an interview with a teacher inquirer who said, "one of the things [I am] looking for in another school that's very important to look for is to know whether teachers get along." Referring to the students at Junction: "I think for the most part they get along." "Getting along" was interpreted as "no reported problems with which administrators had to deal." It was a form of keeping the peace where keeping the peace meant not rocking the boat. Getting along came at the cost of denial and erasure. Turning the other way. For example, Pam, one of the teacher inquirers, remarked that everyone knew the teachers who were unwilling to adapt or grow to accommodate the transnational students, despite policies that "required" accommodations. Nevertheless, under the banners of "getting along" and "professional respect," those unwilling teachers were left alone by their colleagues. White students were not actively encouraged to "get along" with the transnational/transmigrant students, but transnational students were interpreted as uncooperative and separatist if they congregated together. The burden to "get along" was theirs.

As an ethnographic team, we articulated what it looked like to get along, that is, how getting along worked interactively. We also had to take into account that our Unityville partners wanted us to all get along with one another. We remained friendly with our hosts. We did not pick fights or respond aggressively to aggression that was aimed at us. We did our best to get along. Yet, we experienced this as a tension, as if we had been co-opted into securing the status quo. Our most prominent mode of getting along was good listening. We sought to understand even those perspectives with which we held strong disagreements. But reaching mutual understanding is hampered when it goes only one way. We established a cadre of educators with whom we shared a mutual orientation toward understanding. Arm in arm, with this cadre, we together worked to both "get along" and resist the "getting along." For example, earlier I described the difficult situation for Ms. Tu in one of her classes. We forged a response to this oppressive situation that kept the peace with the teacher in question, but resisted the practice of oppressing youngsters through one's power as a teacher. We resisted the idea that a vulnerable student had to sit there and take such oppression. In such ways, we resisted getting along.

Conclusion: Position-Taking Beyond the Slash Through Research Activities

As a research team (including both university scholars and Unityville educators), we sought openings for people in the schools to develop some empathy and understanding with one another. Bianca hoped that students would be "forced to take on different perspectives." We knew that the chances for this would be fostered if we could create spaces where educators were able to position-take with their "newcomer" students. We collectively wanted to bring more of the school community into the circle of care for trans/migrant/transnational youth. The administrators at Junction High agreed to devote one whole professional development day to this purpose. So on one day in February we orchestrated a series of learning events carefully planned to invite educators into the experiences of "newcomer" students and their families. I will draw attention to two such activities in order to illustrate how we worked the slash toward empathy. We started off the day in the auditorium with all educators. Both of the activities that I describe below, happened during this beginning whole-group session.

During the first activity, Yoko and Naomi delivered a very simple math lesson (not longer than 8 minutes) in Japanese. This was followed by a short elementary math quiz that audience members were asked (in Japanese) to complete. In this brief activity, teachers began to express their discomfort, failed to respond to the simple quiz, and tuned out. They started talking with their peers in English (for which they were reprimanded in Japanese). This activity brought them, without warning, into the experience of being instructed in a language that most of them did not know. The few people in the audience who did know Japanese were not able to offer help or support to those around them. Teachers expressed feeling frustrated, angry, incapable, and so forth. For many of them, this was the first time to be in a position similar to that of their students and they were surprised at their own emotionally negative reaction even given the brevity of the lesson and their awareness that there was nothing really at stake because it was just an in-service "game" with no tangible consequences.

As a second activity our research team members performed a script through which we drew together the translated voices of the youth with whom we had been talking (See Appendix D). It was striking to our Project team that even the well-intentioned teachers, for the most part, had not found a way to establish empathy with their transnational students. One challenge to building empathetic relationships with the disjuncture across languages: Teachers had never heard the kinds of things we heard from the students because they were not conversing regularly with the students in the students' primary languages. We concluded the introductory session with this voiced-over script leaving the words of the students ringing in the space.

Through these two activities, Unityville teachers across all levels were given an opportunity to confront the socio-relational and interactive webs of difference, including who they were in that web. These activities were informed by fieldwork, were energized through the facilitation of researchers, and, also, contributed to the research itself. These examples demonstrate the ways in which the research process *was not* like snapping a well-placed photo of the scene in order to primarily capture in time what the scene looked like. Instead, these research activities were specifically oriented toward facilitating position-taking through and about transmigrant students' experiences. This allowed all of us (researchers and educators) to engage ethically together by coming to understand better who *we* are, together, as a web of relationalities. They illustrate ways we worked the slash.

The slash was political and had consequences. Least important among those consequences was the relationship managed between me (a white, economically advantaged, educated, woman) and the white educators of Unityville. Most important were the lives of the racially erased Black students and the undervalued transnational students, whose very existence in the school was dangerous.

Notes

1. In this chapter, I will use the capitalized "WE" to indicate an imagined WE position that is dialogic and inclusive, and I will use "we" to indicate a specific we, like we researchers or we white people in Unityville.
2. Taken from Ed's field reflections November 24, 2004.
3. Taken from Ed Brantmeier's interview transcription with an administrator at Junction High November 22, 2004.
4. The Teacher Inquiry Group was an interdisciplinary cadre of 7 educators who worked with Ed Brantmeier to create and implement a peace curriculum. They met weekly during the 2004–2005 academic year.
5. Taken from Ed Brantmeier's notes, Teacher Inquiry Group Observations September 12, 2004. Junction High School.
6. I am purposefully imprecise in order to protect the confidentiality of the district without misleading readers.
7. I primarily put the term "newcomers" in quotes throughout the text to indicate its problematic use. It was conceived of as racially benign by most educators in Unityville and was not really brought into critical dialogue in a sustained way within the schools.
8. I use this in deference to Michelle Fine's (1994) "Working the Hyphens."
9. Victor Turner (1969) introduced the use of this term is describing "coming of age" rituals in anthropological understandings of moving from one age to another. During the ritual one is no longer the child and not yet the adult. The rituals help to hold the community together and carry the child-becoming-adult through the uncertainty. He also considered liminal spaces to be cultural, shared spaces where feelings and experience united those involved in the rituals.
10. This term was introduced by Ruth Unseem (Unseem et al., undated) during the 1950s to describe children who were being raised outside the country of their passports (in this case American children being raised in India after their American parents had re-located).
11. Drawn from Ed Brantmeier's field data on a teacher inquiry meeting at Junction High school on September 12, 2004.
12. There is controversy on the whether or not the term Hispanic or Latino/a/x is most inclusive. Academically speaking, Hispanic was used to describe people who spoke Spanish, and Latino was used to describe people who came from Latin America (including Indigenous, colonized, colonizing descendants regardless of language affiliation). I have primarily used Latino/a/x except where I am intending to indicate the less precise "othering" conceptions of Unityville insiders. Practically speaking, these labels refer to the same Spanish-dominant learners in the Unityville schools.
13. High school teacher interview with Ed Brantmeier in November 2004.
14. Ed Brantmeier's fieldnotes, December 9, 2004.

15. Ed Brantmeier fieldnotes, November 17, 2004.
16. Taken from Ed Brantmeier's fieldnotes Noember 17, 2004.

References

Brantmeier, E.J. (2008). Building intercultural empathy for peace: Teacher involvement in peace curricula development at a U.S. midwestern high school. In J. Lin, E.J. Brantmeier, & C. Bruhn (Eds.), *Transforming education for peace* (pp. 67–89). Charlotte, NC: Information Age.

Carspecken, P. (1996). *Critical ethnography in educational research: A theoretical and practical guide.* New York, NY and London, England: Routledge.

Clandinin, D.J., & Connelly, F.M. (2000). *Narrative inquiry: Experience and story in qualitative research.* San Francisco, CA: Jossey-Bass.

Dennis, B. (2009). Acting up: Theatre of the oppressed as critical qualitative research. *International Journal for Qualitative Methods, 8*(2), 65–96.

Fine, M. (1994). Working the hyphens: Reinventing self and other in qualitative research. In N. K. Denzin & Y. S. Lincoln (Eds.), *Handbook of qualitative research* (pp. 70–82). Thousand Oaks, CA: Sage.

Fine, M. (2018). *Just research in contentious times: Widening the methodological imagination.* New York, NY: Teachers College Press.

Foucault, M. (1995). *Discipline and punish: The birth of the prison.* New York, NY: Vintage Books.

Korth, B. (2002). Critical qualitative research as consciousness-raising: The dialogic texts of researcher/researchee interactions. *Qualitative Inquiry, 8*(3), 381–403.

Korth, B., Frey, C., Hasbun, M., Nakamichi, Y., Pereira, M., Soto, N., Sotoo, N., & Su, Y. (2004). *Report of Unityville Outreach Project.* Unpublished report to school corporation.

Lather, P., & Smithies, C. (1997). *Troubling the angels: Women living with HIV/AIDS.* Oxford, England: Westview Press.

McLaren, P. (1992b). *Life in schools: An introduction to critical pedagogy in the foundations of education* (1st ed.). Boulder, CO: Paradigm Publishers.

Rogoff, B. (2003). *The culture of nature of human development.* Oxford, England: Oxford University Press.

Rucker, P. (2019, August 4). How do you stop these people? Trump's anti-immigration rhetoric looms over El Paso massacre. *The Washington Post.* Retrieved October 29, 2019, from https://www.washingtonpost.com/politics/how-do-you-stop-these-people-trumps-anti-immigrant-rhetoric-looms-over-el-paso-massacre/2019/08/04/62d0435a-b6ce-11e9-a091-6a96e67d9cce_story.html.

Thompson, C. (2019). *A psychology of liberation and peace.* New York, NY: Palgrave Macmillan.

Uttamchandani, S., Pfingston, I., Smith, B., & Dennis, B. (2019, June 30). ALGBTQ+ youth expertise on allyship and advocacy for educators. *The Assembly: A Journal for Public Scholarship on Education, 2.* Retrieved October 28, 2019, from https://www.colorado.edu/journal/assembly/2019/06/30/lgbtq-youth-expertise-allyship-and-advocacy-educators

CHAPTER THREE

Ethics of Being With/In

The only safe way to avoid violating principles of professional ethics is to refrain from doing social research altogether.

(Bronfenbrenner, 1952, p. 453)

Sometimes the miles it took to arrive in Unityville corresponded with the emotional distance I felt. The drive time allowed me an opportunity to "prepare" myself for what might lay ahead. The drive home afforded me an opportunity to reflect on the day's activities. I recognized that the emotional distance was largely mine to traverse. The drive became an affective bubble surrounding my time in the schools.

I walked into the teacher's lounge after signing in at Junction High School's front desk. I had greeted the school's armed security officer. I had passed students in the hall, most of them strangers to me personally. I had peeked my head in to greet Roberta. I, now, found myself seated at a rectangular table in the teacher's lounge as staffers popped in and out of the room, getting their own workdays started. There was not much more to the moment. I was gathering my thoughts for what might transpire. Preparing my notebook. Making sure all my equipment was ready, spare batteries were handy, and multiple pens were reachable. Yet, somehow I felt as if all this prep work was a form of bracing myself for the encounters to come. Bracing is perhaps too strong a word, for I was happy to be there and I was excited for the day. Yet, much like willingly and excitedly stepping onto a roller coaster, I had a feeling of tightening up as I steeled myself for the day's activities.

Back out into the hallway, I went. This time I was headed for a classroom. Students were also in the hall moving to their classes. I arrived at the place that had been designated for my focus group meeting with a group of white high school students—the "traditional" students as they were problematically called within the school community. The school never invited African American students into my meetings with the "traditional students." My time with the students was spent listening to them talk, primarily about how they disliked the "newcomer" students, why they disliked them, and their speculations on why these "foreigners" had come to their town. I was bleeding inside as I listened to them speak. I wanted to hear them, but I was sorry this was the way they were making sense of their transnational peers. I wanted these "traditional" students to have different, more accepting perspectives. I wanted their attitudes toward their cool new peers to change. After all, it was my intention to be involved in that very change process. Perhaps more to the point, it was hard to find myself in their talk. It was hard to locate who I was in this place, in these relationships, and through these interactions. Initially, I listened with a somewhat feigned openness. It was easy for me to accept and appreciate that these were their genuinely expressed attitudes, but, I had a naggingly uncomfortable feeling about *who* to be. I couldn't really accept who I was in this scene. This account roughly described my feelings in the field during the first 6 months. Though we had the beginnings of a professional advocacy team in our IU-Unityville Outreach Project, we had not, yet, found white student advocates, like Jerry Changer, whose note about his friend Sarah you might recall from Chapter 2.

One Sunday afternoon in the spring 2005, with the windows open and the sunshine beaming into the room, we (the IU teammates) were sitting together, mostly on the floor, in my living room. Yoko, Naomi, Ed, Felipe, Nelson and I. We were feeling sad. We had been encountering scenes at the high school that troubled us. One by one we shared scenes we had witnessed. We talked about what it meant to intervene or not in these scenes (Dennis, 2009b). Ed recalled seeing the school's police officer treat a Latino student more harshly than was necessary, badgering the student without provocation. We all heard white students telling Latinx kids to "go home," calling them "dirty Mexican" and "beano" through which they indicated that transnational students, especially Latinos, were not welcome in the school. And that was exactly how our transnational students interpreted the messages. They reported, "They don't want us here." "Even the teachers don't want us." The kinds of activities we witnessed and were told about involving what seemed to us to be the mistreatment of students taxed our capacities to *be with* our participants in the field. One IU student likened being in Unityville to a kind of death. The ongoing anti-immigrant, racial violence made it challenging for us to be who we wanted to be in the field, and it was hard to see how being there could be opportunities for all of use to become new.

Seemingly gone were the days when we easily thought of ethics as a well-oriented, functioning compass with ethical issues worked out through IRBs and the ethical dilemmas in the field resolved through the moral knowledge/goodness of the researcher (Dennis, 2018). Perhaps we were always wrong to think of ethics like this. Years ago, McLaren (1992), who was writing of his ethnographic work in schools, indicated that he found himself "wounded" in the field and concluded that a willingness to have his very sense of self called into question in painful and difficult ways was central to his experience as a researcher who engaged *with* others in an authentic and open fashion. In order to be personally changed, we researchers must approach our field encounters through an openness to becoming new (Brantmeier, 2016; Korth, 2002). "You must be prepared to be threatened and to change through your field work" (Carspecken, 1996, pp. 169–170). Yet, we, also, knew that our social justice commitments were right—they were transformable, but we would not abandon them (Freire, 1972). This was our collective ethical stance: an openness to changes that would deepen and strengthen our social justice commitments and how we understood them.

> A social justice position requires a constructive opening toward differences in which we as researchers are willing to learn and transform ourselves as a result of our interactions with others, in so far as we recognize the other and his or her culture, experiences, and knowledge. (Peñaranda, Vélez-Zapata, & Bloom, 2013, p. 37)

As a matter of practice, ethnographers aim to be richly involved in the everyday lives and interactive milieu through which their participants are engaged. This is a complex endeavor. Take for example, Erich Goode's (2002) account of building intimacy with ethnographic informants through sexual encounters. Reportedly, it is an untold story that ethnographers were known to engage in sexual relationships with participants (Zussman, 2002). Goode's (2002) work sparked conversation about the ethics of intimacy in the field. Another recent set of ethnographic ethical controversies arose through the work of Alice Goffman (2014, *On the Run: Fugitive Life in an American City*) where inconsistencies and fabrications in reporting were largely related to Goffman's efforts to keep her participants' identities confidential (Neyfakh, 2015). Are there general principles which can guide ethnographers in their intimate commitments and encounters in the field? In other words, how can our talk about ethical practices reach beyond, but also deeply into, the individual experiences and encounters of ethical situations?

Not all of the possible ethical entanglements of ethnographic endeavors are resolvable prior to being in the field and those entanglements cannot be authentically eclipsed by approval from IRBs (Verhallen, 2016). Most are not resolvable in separation from the ongoing nature of the field itself (Beach & Vigo Arrazola, 2019). An ethnographer's ethical activity is forged through a complicated set of relational networks coupled with reflexivity. It was this *ethical being with* of ethnographic practice that I did not totally grasp in our early days in Unityville. I have come to understand that one cannot abstain from taking an ethical position on who one was/is *with/in* one's being with others. One cannot, really, put at arms-length their own practical ethicality. In a recent chapter (Dennis, 2018), I concluded with this thought, "In my own rethinking, ethnographic ethics are practices in the imaginative possibilities of becoming *with* others, practices through which my own self is at stake and through which the instantiation of myself as *a self* is open and fallible" (Dennis, 2018, p. 63). I felt the challenge of *being with* and also *against* those in Unityville who expressed white, privileged attitudes that I found chillingly familiar. The long drive to and from Unityville gave me transition time to think through my ethical location in the complicated web to which I was committed.

In the present chapter, I explore how we might collectively think about the ethics of our ethnographic doing/being. I took a reflective perspective to do this (Verhallen, 2016). I join ethnographers who have started to write about this self-reflexive positionality as ethics (Cammarota, 2007; Peñaranda, Vélez-Zapata, & Bloom, 2013; Zhang, 2017; Tomaselli, 2016). The chapter is not an explication of rules to follow in the field or a manual for how to successfully traverse the ethical review process in order to end up with an "approved" study. Navigating the IRB and articulating general ethical principles were never as challenging for me as heading into a research site day after day as a person whose ethics were staked by my very participation in the research process. "I am not impartial, or objective ... [and this] does not prevent me from holding always a rigorously ethical position" (Freire, 1994, p. 22). However, the chapter is, also, not a sympathetic confessional (though these are certainly important for the field). I aimed to enter a dialogue of social researchers who recognize that research contributions include ethical accountabilities (Fine, 2018; Kuntz, 2015; Lather, 1986).

Thinking About and Through Ethics

Across the various modes of thinking about ethics, there has been a tendency to recapitulate an orientation that is researcher-centric. Elizabeth Murphy and Robert Dingwall (2007) suggested that ethnographers typically hold themselves responsible for both consequentialist and deontological ethics (Casteñada, 2006). Karl Hostetler (2005) admonished researchers to admit that doing no harm through our research was not the same thing as enacting ethically good research. Ethnographers seek to avoid harm and to enact benefits for the social world (including for the lives of participants) which one can associate with consequentialist ethics. Moreover, ethnographers hold themselves to a standard of respect and social equity (justice) which we can associate with deontological ethics. Researcher-centeredness was accomplished primarily by describing ethical dilemmas and activities as a vehicle for the researcher to explicate her own ethics through action or explanation. This is how I formerly oriented myself in the field (Dennis, 2009b). This orientation can be rethought by drawing a few insights from Karen Barad's (2008) new materialism. She wrote, "Ethics is not [fundamentally] about right response to the other, but about *respons*ibility and accountability for the lively relationalities of becoming of which 'we' are a part [which *involves* one's responses to others]" (italics added, p. 333)?

Ultimately of course, such an orientation does not do away with the idea that institutional representatives have legal and moral accountabilities through which certain ethical principles (such as informed consent) must be enacted in relation to one's "human subjects." The increasing litigious regulation of schools and research are at odds with critical ethnographic endeavors which are, by their very nature, flexible, intimate, and evolving (Herron, 2018). Moreover, the necessities of IRBs do not sufficiently account for the ethical "intra-actions" of an ethnographer (Beach & Vigo Arrazola, 2019; Verhallen, 2016). Barad (2008) introduced the word intra-action to replace interaction, as (what she considered) a more accurate description of how things are. That is, to her way of thinking, we are not separate ontological entities interacting with one another, but rather an entangled whole (human and material) constantly in motion intra-acting together. Aaron Kuntz (2015) encouraged scholars who aim to be socially responsible in their research to engage "in work that changes the very political relations that inform our identities … [to] risk ourselves … [to] generate new ways of becoming" (p. 29)—similar to McLaren's (1992) call to be wounded in the field. Using Barad (2008), Kuntz (2015), and St. Pierre (2014), I reworked my own thinking around ethics into a more emergent, socially instantiated, relationally established configuration. This was a move away from thinking of ethics through the paradigm of the lone ethical researcher enacting her ethics (more or less satisfactorily) according to a set of rules or principles. It was a move toward an image of ethical entanglement as collective participation in the ethnographic life of the field within which we are located. Entanglement is a concept I drew from Barad (2008) who suggested that things/non-things don't exist as separate, but instead are already always entangled.

Entanglements become visible through patterns of diffraction, or resonances and dissonances whose differences "make a difference" (Barad, 2012, p. 49). Barad compels us to ask, how we are responsible and accountable "for the lively relationalities of becoming of which 'we' are a part" (Barad, 2008, p. 333)? Because Barad wanted to abandon our regular notions of human agency, her insights into the entangled nature of ethics were provocative for me.

Katherine Irwin (2006), amongst others, argued that feminist, interpretivist, and postmodern arguments critiqued the "distance" that had been associated with the privileged researcher position in social science. She noted that researchers had begun to think of research ethics in more "intimate" terms oriented toward how the researcher both behaves and writes. Even so, the discourse on research ethics

> primarily focused scholarly attention on the individual [researcher] behaviors and choices in the field. The result has been a micro-politics of research ethics that focused our attention on a litany of minor research decisions at the expense of understanding, articulating, and pointing out the structural sources and processes of inequality and harm. (p. 157)

It seemed unavoidable to be complicit in ongoing inequities and harm in our ethnographic endeavors. Irwin argued, through the experience of her long ethnography of tattooists, that we should focus on ethical deliberations regarding how our research work is constrained by, resists, or reinforces social structure through our *doing* of it (p. 171). As educational ethnography functions, the inquiry will always co-involve researchers and participants. Moreover, the structures that constitute the research interactions will also be reproduced in their outcomes (see Anthony Giddens' concept of social structuration, Giddens, 1984). When Ed Brantmeier (2016) wrote about being wounded as an educational researcher on the Unityville project, he wrote, "Understanding a research site, from the inside-out, requires allowing one's own sense of what is right and wrong, what is good and what is true to be questioned by the logic and everyday meaning-making of participants in the research process" (p. 1). Though Brantmeier did not explicitly link that point with ethics in his paper, the implication can easily enough be made: One's sense of self as ethical, one's understanding of right/wrong, good/bad are brought into the dialogue and are open for revision in relationship with those one is ethnographically engaging. Any and all boundaries to this openness can be reflected upon by the ethnographer.

Unni Wikan (2012) was asked by her Balinese participants to do more than thickly describe their context. They asked her to create resonance. Wikan (2012) wrote that creating resonance with participants requires us as researchers to implicate "… ourselves, actively and emotionally, in the other's world" (p. 75).

This resonance inheres in dialogue. In building her argument, Wikan noted that resonance makes its demands communicatively on all participants as a willingness to engage with each other's worlds of meanings, worlds evoked through the encounters of shared experiences (2012, p. 57). Leela Prasad (2019) advanced the concept of resonance to a form of ethical resonance as being "… moved by something or somebody so much that our ways of being are altered" in an enduring way (p. 411). Such a description of ethics fits a transformative, inclusive, *we* as a reworked description of ethnographic ethics.

In this section of the chapter I outline what I found to be theoretical tensions in thinking about *we*-oriented ethics and I locate ethics as *ethical self-relation*.

Theoretical Tensions

As discussed by Tessa Verhallen (2016), "Scheper-Hughes's (1995) argument that in order for ethnographic research" to be considered ethical "it must contribute to the lives of the people being studied" is aligned with Hodge's (2013) argument "… that 'an entirely detached and passive anthropology is not an ethical one' (p. 293)" (Verhallen, 2016, p. 458). In 2018 I published a chapter for a handbook on educational ethnography through which I reflected upon and re-thought my own orientation toward research ethics. In that chapter I critiqued two previous publications (Dennis, 2009a, 2009b) that actually deliberated ethics in the context of the Unityville study. In that 2018 publication I drew on the works of St. Pierre (2000, 2008) and Kuntz (2015) to provide touchstones for my reflections. One outcome of that effort was the identification of two key tensions in how ethics are conceptualized in research literature and practice:

1. The tension between universality and absolutism
2. The tension between the subject as substance and the subject as becoming

Universality as Non-Absolute. Conflating universality with absolutism means that we are taking a universal claim like "The earth revolves around the sun" and giving it absolute unchanging certainty. When characterized as absolute, the claim is not, practically speaking, open for interrogation or questioning. In earlier times, people argued that the sun revolved around the earth, and in fact Galileo was found guilty of heresy in 1633 for promoting Copernican theory. Nowadays, *we know that* the earth revolves around the sun, not the other way around. This is a universal claim in that we expect that people all around the globe would understand this claim to be true if they were afforded similar definitions and the means scientists used to reach this conclusion. Even so, it is possible to imagine scientific challenges to the claim, including projections about how the universe is changing. The universal claims are just that: claims. Through the claims, actors are positioned and the criteria for challenging the claims are embedded in the claims themselves. While it is not likely that the claim "the earth revolves around the sun" will be successfully upended anytime soon, we are still able to recognize what it would take to counter that claim. This is what I mean by suggesting that the universal is non-absolute. We do not have to interpret universal claims as ontologically absolute and if we do, we would be denying the structure of a universal claim. Universal claims have a contingent aspect to them (Carspecken, 2003), which renders them open to potential critique.

The claim about the earth revolving around the sun is an objective claim. It is about the way things are/the way things work in a presupposed externally existing world (external to the subjects who move through it). Remember from Chapter 1, I presented Habermas's (1985) argument that our communication depends on such ontological distinctions.[1] Let's look now at ethical universal claims. Perhaps one such claim is "Thou shalt not kill." This claim could be considered universal because it is expected that most people around the globe would recognize the validity of the claim across social and material contexts. The claim even could be used to judge behavior across quite diverse cultures (Korth, 2006). If someone did not share this ethic, they would likely explain their own views by pointing to something broader to which both the speaker and hearer could agree. However, the claim itself, while interpreted as universal, is also understood as contingent. In U.S. legal code, for example, different contexts for killing affect its interpretive and judicious ramifications. And state sanctioned killing, for example use of the death penalty or police justifications for killing unarmed Black men in the United States, stand as exceptions/contradictions to the adage. Those contradictions get morally justified through different ethical suppositions assumed to supersede "thou shall not kill."

Ethical claims, whether tacit, implicit, or explicit, are communicative actions. Ethical claims point toward a social world of normative agreements and assumptions about how we should *be* with one another. Ethical claims have a universal aspect to them, which is something like, "I trust that we can agree that WE should/should not …" Here the WE is a claim for universal recognition through the ethical proposition.

When ethical claims are being deliberated and talked about with one another, the universality aspect can be critiqued by raising questions about (a) how inclusive the (implied) WE is, that is, to whom does the "we" refer (who should not kill?) and/or (b) the content of the claim is something that *we should* agree with (like whether or not it is actually wrong to kill). This ability to question, converse and dialogue about ethical claims through their universality belies absolutism as a characteristic. Further, it suggests two important points. It means that we do not have to relegate ethical deliberations to the domain of the unquestionable (where fundamentalism and reason cannot co-exist). Ethics are debatable and "we" can reach consensus. It, also, means that ethical claims assume a "we" that is name-able and parameters that are identifiable.

Being recognized by others through our ethical claims is validating. It lets us know that we are a worthwhile and good being. Our goodness and our rightness are both acknowledged. But again, not absolutely.

When universal claims are interpreted as absolute, then it is not possible to posit a dialogic, transformational, emancipatory ethics entwined relationally with others. Such an interpretation of ethics has not caught up with more contemporary reflections on ethics as dialogically constituted. *Perhaps, ethics isn't what I, as an individual do in relation with others, perhaps it is what WE do together for us through our intra-action.*

Subject as Becoming Being. Participants in our ethnographies are not objects. They are subjects—they are recognizable as having an awareness of being, feeling, wanting, and becoming, among other characteristics. Qualitative researchers have been using the word "participant" to describe those who engage with us in research, in part to promote equity in our relationships with participating "others" which, also, holds us accountable to the ways we might have "subjected" people to research. The significance of making a distinction between conceptualizing people in our studies as subjects rather than objects is that we, as researchers, want to recognize the subjectivity of our participants: That they can know, respond, express feelings and intentions about, and engage in self-awareness through our studies. And moreover, that we can see ourselves in their place and we are aware of the potential for them to do likewise.

Using words like "subject" and "participant" generally connote a human-centeredness. In tension with the humanism, some of the references I cited in this chapter have argued against the human/non-human binary and critiqued a theoretical and practical over-reliance on the human as the central figure in social/science. For example, Barad (2003) argued that agency is dynamic, it is a doing, not a trait of an independent actor. In fact, the doing (the agency) would be an entanglement of human/non-human matter. For Barad (2003) specific subjects and objects come into view so to speak, because of an agential cut. Agential cuts produce differentiations between structure and agency, subject and object. For Barad, these agential cuts are collaborative doings. Let's transpose the "we" embedded in an ethical claim into a "doing" and a "doing together." Thinking about our *being* as *doing* reminds us that we should not think of our being as a neutral blank slate from which to act, but rather as an ongoing becoming through our intra-actions which are always already entangled with or conditioned by complex social relations. My rendition here does not fully take up Barad's alter-humanist orientation. My friend, Lucy Carspecken (through personal conversation) wisely reminds me that humanism has yet to be fully realized. I agree with her. I think that abandoning humanist recognition of the subject as an actor with important autonomy relinquishes, all too soon, social justice aims. For me, these are not incompatible with ideas of expanding our senses of ethics to a collective *doing*.

People, so it seems to me, are always already becoming *being*. To emphasize that being is doing though communication makes it possible for us to distinguish between being, doing, and becoming (Carspecken & Cordeiro, 1995). This has relevance for thinking of ethics as ethical action. Our being/doing will always have an ethical aspect to it, by which I mean there is always an aspect which can be talked about through shared understandings of ethical action. This sharedness includes our responsibilities toward racism, sexism, heterosexism, and other mechanisms for marginalizing people in our communities and around the globe. It reminds us that we not free so long as others are not free.

Shared responsibilities and principles of action can be reconstructed from action itself. For example, Adam Serwer, writer for "The Atlantic," reconstructed the logic of family separation policies during the Trump era. He quoted Stephen Miller, senior adviser at the time to President Trump, as saying, separation is a "potent tool in a severely limited arsenal of strategies for stopping immigrants from flooding across the border" (quoted by Serwer, 2018). Just at a quick glance, we can reconstruct the following ethical principles: "One should protect one's borders from invaders" AND "Our ends should be sufficient to justifying our means" AND "Immigrants should be stopped from entering the country." Reconstructing the field of meaning involves putting into discourse the possible range of interpretations that would be plausible for both the audiences and authors of claims (Carspecken, 1996). By focusing on the ethical aspects of the field of meaning, I was isolating the meaning according to its particular validity type (i.e., objective, subjective or normative). Following Carspecken, 1996, I articulated the ethical claims as normative-evaluative claims which articulate what we as a social community hold each other accountable to in terms of what we consider good/bad or right/wrong in our relationships with one another.

Moreover, those shared responsibilities can take into account varying social locations. I contributed to a plenary session (Dennis, 2017) where I presented the idea of intra-sectionality as a reading of Kimberlé Crenshaw's (1989) intersectionality through Barad's (2003) concepts of intra-action and entanglement. In that talk I argued that intersectionality was a concept that applied to people caught in a web of multi-marginality (being both black and woman in a racist and sexist system), not merely to people with differing statuses or roles (like being a mom and a lawyer). Crenshaw's (1989) use of the concept of "intersectionality" called our attention to the point that a Black woman did not just experience the effects of racism coupled with the effects of sexism, but rather that her experience was a unique intersection which muddled the mistreatment as not solely racism or sexism, but as an entanglement of the two (Crenshaw, 1989). When standing in the metaphorical intersection of a road, there is no difference between the two roads that are now united at the intersection. I argued that as a straight cis white woman, intersectionality is not a term that applies to me. I am largely privileged in the world, though I do experience the oppression of sexism. Nevertheless, I wanted to understand who I am with respect to such social intersections. How am I connected and complicit with those intersections of marginality? Intra-sectionality emerged as my response. I conceived of intra-sectionality as the forces and doings that are intricately productive of intersections—the naming of the roads, the traffic enforcement, and so on. The intersections do not just exist distinctly and independently in a vacuum. I used the concept of intra-sectionality to indicate the intra-action involved in creating and maintaining minoritized intersections in our social lives. My whiteness is enmeshed with the phrase "people of color" and with positioning people of color as outsiders in the U.S. social context. To the point of this book, the status of transnational students is not disconnected from my own status. They are intra-related.

When we take the idea of intra-sectionality seriously, we take seriously the experiences of those who lives have them caught in the intersections. Such experiences re-center the margins and reveal the mainstreamed sidelines that hold the center of marginality in the intersections. Our ethical responsibility could have started from this set of conceptions. Imagining simultaneously the intersections and the structures/forces that instantiate and recapitulate them, calls forth for us an ethical responsibility *FOR* the collective undoing of the structures trapping people in the intersections and *TO* the people targeted through oppressive intersections. A social justice approach must do more than name and recognize the intersections. A social justice approach must also subvert and disrupt those intersections (Fine, 2018; Freire, 1972). I argued that people co-enact ethically with one another as an ethical WE. This perspective proposes that ethics has a communal constitution (Dennis, 2018), despite how problematic that is. Our intra-actions involve us in mutual ethicality.

As I thought of research ethics through these two tensions, I foregrounded a sense of "ethics as (1) *being with*, (2) involving the multipositionality of truth,

(3) affording challenges to/refusals of habitual ways of being/telling the truth, and (4) opening up new ways of experiencing one's self and the way one talks about one's self as valid" (Dennis, 2018, p. 62). How do we as researchers, then, locate ourselves in this we-ness? How do we work toward an inclusiveness we?

Ethics as Internal Self-Relation

When making a statement about ethics, the self is always also implicated. The claims about the self that are implicit to ethics involve claims about *being*. The internal relation of *being* as *doing* is the practical aspect of ethics. This sense of *being* comes about through *doing* and through the recognition or validation of others who are also acting with respect to our *being*. Hence, we would be constituting a rudimentary form of WE which could be nurtured, consciously developed, and sustained. Dawn Goodwin (2003) wrote about an ethical dilemma she faced doing her dissertation research and suggested that the "ethical and moral considerations are intimately tied not only to my role as a researcher but to my personal identity(ies)" (Goodwin, Pope, Mort, & Smith, 2003, p. 569).

For example, our team actively disregarded the district's English Only policy at the schools. We did this deliberately through activities using the students' home languages to communicate with them and their parents in project-specific activities. But our language use seeped into the hallways, especially with the use of Spanish. As someone who has considered herself a monolingual English speaker and a recipient of the benefits of linguistic hegemony in the globally connected world, my years of coursework in Spanish did little to move me into the meaningful world of Spanish speakers. This project was different. It was an opportunity for me to engage with Spanish/speakers in ways I had not previously taken up. It changed how I interfaced with the hegemony of English by, in my case, using my Spanish as a political act, not just in Unityville, but with respect to the hegemony of English more broadly. Alongside my work in Unityville, I imagined possibilities for a multilingual university classroom—a class more open to linguistic diversity. I used Spanish transcripts in class, making sure we had at least one Spanish speaker (albeit across differing levels of fluency) in each group. I considered how I was intra-sectionally part of the hegemonic, oppressive force that wielded injustice to university students who did not speak English as their first languages. However, the fact of the matter was that I could not enact linguistic justice in either my university classes or Unityville without the collaborative participation of others.

This idea of ethics as self-relation does not have to be interpreted through the concept of individuation if we use Barad's concept of intra-action to build up how we think of relation. Self-relation is, by its nature, intra-relational. The self and other are not binaries, but rather two aspects of "identifying as" such and such. The identifications are constituted of inherent structures of recognition and validity. That is, the self is a socially recognizable way of locating one's becoming intra-relationally. Internal to this way of thinking about the self will be assumptions of good/bad and right/wrong which involve how the self *is enacted into being*. In the example below, the self I performed was complicit in the mistreatment of a Latino student.

> *One ordinary day in the life of the Unityville ethnography, I walked into Junction High School, signed in at the office, and meandered down the hall. The loud sound of the bell chimed just when I would have expected it, and it signaled the change from second to third period at this particular moment. The hallways were suddenly a flood of students as far as the eye could see. I maintained my balance in the sea of movement and kept walking toward the teacher's lounge where I would start my day.*

> *This was not the first occasion, but on this morning, I witnessed a white student walk aggressively into a Latinx student. Give a mean stare. Keep walking. The Latinx student continued walking.*

> *The situation evaporated into the frantic pace of the moving sea. Before I could catch the next breath the moment was beyond my reach.*

> *I knew I would have an opportunity to check in with the Latinx student later. I had no idea who the white kid was.*[2]

Many educational ethnographers witness bullying. Such witnessing constitutes a dilemma because it is a situation wherein one would *want to* be able to engage in the scene in an ethically responsible way but knowing how to do that is not always clear. Some ethnographers resolved such dilemmas by intervening when possible (see Dennis, 2009b; Kuntz, 2015). Others took up the critical opportunity to reflect on their impulses withhout assuming that their own sense about the need for intervention was correct (see Kofoed and Staunæs, 2015). Many others, including myself (Dennis, 2009b), conceptualized these kinds of dilemmas as *opportunities to behave ethically*—the researcher finds herself in a moment that requires an ethical response. All meaningful actions are opportunities to act ethically, but in an ethical dilemma, the ethical aspects of the impending possibilities are in tension or are foregrounded. Examining such dilemmas has been common in writings on ethnography and ethics (Dennis, 2009b), however, the internal connection of ethics to self-relation has not been commonly explicated (Herron, 2018). Moreover, the sociality or intra-relational aspects of the ethics has not been clearly articulated (Prasad, 2019).

My own ethical orientation shifted through my experiences and work with Unityville and in the process of reflecting on the Project since that time. I am now thinking of "ethics" as a stronger version of *being with* which foregrounds an inclusive and diverse "we"—a we capable of opening up new ways of knowing and experiencing ourselves. I moved to this orientation precisely because I realized that what I recognized of the self-relation for me in these ethical dilemmas was similar to and connected with how others in the scene (the white student, the Latinx student, the other kids in the hallway, the educators in the hallway, my own graduate students) were acting in relation to one another.

> A more critical reflection on 'reflexivity' and 'ethics' not only renews our debates around binaries of the research participants/researchers, colonial/colonizer, and East/West, but also redirects our attention to the 'in-between' space and, as a consequence, allows us to explore more the creative and complex role played by affects, emotions, and everyday expressions. (Zhang, 2017, p. 28)

I asked:

- How are we responsible and accountable "for the lively relationalities of becoming of which 'we' are a part" (Barad 2008, p. 333)?
- How can we question the taken-for-granted assumptions of the readily available descriptions of life as we know it so that we can begin to refuse what we are in those descriptions to live/be/do life differently (St. Pierre 2008)?

These questions located the process of *becoming being* IN RELATION *with others* as a collaborative endeavor. How is it we should act in light of the bullying possibilities? And who am I in this very practical, situated "we?" This intra-relation, this "we" is an ethical one that refrains from setting me as ethnographer over and against a particular scene of actors within and through which I must act ethically. Instead, intra-relationality positions me as critically (taking up the St. Pierre question) involved with the ongoing activities through the ethical orientations of responsibility and accountability (taking up the Barad question) specifically with respect to *becoming being with*.

In the above scenario I was part of a whole scene in which active bullying was treated as normal. My actions were already part of that scene, even in the anticipation that there might be someone who would "catch" the bully and someone who would propose ways to support the victim. Anything I did (including seemingly not doing anything) was an intra-active interpolation of all of us together—those of us catching the bullies, those of us supporting victims, those of us not grasping a specific role in the bullying scene, and so forth. I began this chapter musing on how difficult it was to be both *with and against* white Unityville participants in their quests to find themselves in relationship with so-called "newcomer"/outsiders. A strong version of *withness* must be able to include difference without setting up a "with us" or "against us" binary.

Melinda Herron (2018) described a situation in which school administrators admonished her for "getting too close" to the high school students with which she was working as a researcher. She reflected on the situation and established a course of action with one particular student, with whom the closeness had become problematic in the administrators' eyes. Herron began talking with Sam, the high schooler, about boundaries. Herron discovered that she was not in sole control of the relationship she had with Sam. Though her training, IRBs, and other touchstones of ethical accountability had not adequately prepared her for relationship challenges, the ethical problem was consistently characterized as Herron's and yet there was not a feasibly ethical solution that did not involve Sam's participation. William James (1949) wrote that "neither the whole of truth nor the whole of good is revealed to any single observer" (p. 284). Beth Eddy (2014) linked this with what Sandra Harding (1991) called "strong objectivity"—namely, that the experiential perspectives of diverse actors produce stronger versions of objectivity than a so-called neutral point of view. Ethical claims might be similar (Eddy, 2014).

Methodological Implications of Ethical Thinking: Unityville in Motion

Have you ever wondered if one research design is inherently more ethical than another? Have you ever wondered if doing any kind of research will always involve some moral compromise? In contemporary post-qualitative dialogues, St. Pierre (2014) indicated that she does not intend to conduct research like ethnography in the future—perhaps, in part, because to do so is ethically problematic. Have you ever wondered if doing ethnography might ask too much? Perhaps it asks the researcher to take up relationships that are inherently tricky and ethically challenged. For example, as a result of the culturally anointed power dynamics between researchers and participants, it would be difficult for equity to be central to researcher-participant relationships even in situations where equity is a fundamental piece of the researcher's orientation to methods. Historically speaking, ethnography was a mechanism for exoticizing and colonializing others. Perhaps that history cannot be overcome even with critical intentions.

A methodological process of any sort, ethnography included, will present several ongoing opportunities for all of us (ethnographic participants/researchers) to explore the "lively relationalities of becoming" through which we engage together.

These possibilities surface within the intra-relational, intra-active context, not as universal standards, but as ethical moments of *being with*. In this section I imagine aspects of ethnographic activities as emergent ethical opportunities. I use specific examples from the Unityville project to illustrate five such opportunities: (1) Ethics as rupture to the insider/outsider dynamics, (2) Ethics as the accessible other/speaking truth to power, (3) Ethics as self-care/care for all of us, (4) Ethics as seeking justice in the everyday mistreatment of students, and (5) Ethics as staying.

Ethics as Rupture to the Insider/Outsider Dynamics

In my family I was taught not to be vain. It was considered wrong *to be vain*. Of course, I didn't live up to that 100 percent, but when I was vain, there was a heavy, internalized burden to justify the misalignment and acknowledge that my vanity was wrong. The link between vanity and *being* bad is not understood in the same way across different communities. The nuances of my family's way of thinking about vanity might not be grasped by people who were not in my family. Insiders and outsiders are partially divided by such distinctions in their moral and ethical orientations.

As you learned in Chapter 2, it was not possible for me, as a relative outsider in Unityville, to have quickly grasped the ethical orientations and local situations without engaging with the Unityville communities. The insider/outsider dynamics in Unityville were particularly palpable, but they were also relative. Everyone seemed aware of the categories of insider/outsider and regardless of how one was categorized, participants shared knowledges of WHO was an insider as well as WHAT the mechanisms were that maintained the insider/outsider separation and retained the oppression of students who were caught in the intersection of racial and linguistic discrimination.

Though there was a privileging of insiderness, this was complicated in a number of ways. The complications of this insider/outsider dynamic became our collaborative ethical opportunity. Remember that the school initiated our work by calling me (I had not contacted them with a particular research interest). Administrators asked Roberta to reach out to me—reaching to the outside from the inside. I came in. I brought people with me. The school wanted us to reach out to and talk with the "newcomer" students. The transnational students were there inside the school with their outside, "foreign" ways of talking. We brought those other languages in with us, too. This multilingual cacophony of engagements were an ethical opportunity of inclusion and respect. This opportunity snowballed because we were working *with one another* in the situation, always attentive to the ethical aspects of our working and being together. If we just trace this one snowball, we find something rather amazing. You already know that we facilitated weekly small language-based focus group meetings with transnational students. We also helped to create and distribute new district brochures for parents that were made available in three different languages. And, educators began using their variously developed, minimally-acknowledged language skills informally within the schools (from, perhaps, having taken Spanish in high school decades earlier, for example). All of this was going on while the district's English Only policy was in place. The ethical resistance to this policy was one that emerged from within: We drew on an insider/outsider dynamic that had largely been functioning as a constraint and turned that into a resource. Flipping the outside in.

As you now know, in the beginning, Unityville educators were not expressing much empathy or respect for their transnational students. As time went along, the ethical aspects of the insider/outsider dynamic were transformed. We saw this evidenced further in a conversation Ed had with a high school math teacher. The math teacher told Ed that he was able to "learn enough" Spanish to convey basic mathematical ideas using Spanish phrases for students whose English was limited. He learned Spanish for the purpose of teaching. We, together, had begun forging an ethical deconstruction of the "linguistic barrier" between insiders and outsiders.

The cadre of teachers working with Ed on a peace curriculum talked about using the experience of Japanese internment camps during World War II. This poignant example intuitively foregrounded extreme insider/outsider dynamics. The teachers who raised this as a curricular possibility commented:

Ed: *O.K. So we are getting a theme field here … Interdependency, conflict resolution—negotiation, mediation, and consensus, more specific Japanese internment, WWII, Hiroshima. Could we take … this event and um grasp* (pause) *what's the theme there?*

Lisa: *Um.*

Roberta: *It creates an awareness of man's inhumanity to man.*

Lisa: *Yah. Um, historical ethics*

Roberta: (talks over) *Things people are not very aware of, most don't even realize there were ever such a thing as Japanese internment camps.*

Lisa: *Right.*

The teachers acknowledged the historical fact that Japanese Americans (insiders) were treated as if they were the enemy (the ultimate other). The U.S. government refused to trust Japanese Americans to be fully American. The teachers in the inquiry group collectively considered this treatment inhumane. They also assumed that most people were not aware of this American-against-American mistreatment as a mechanism in the effort to protect the American borders. As Project collaborators, we came to understand that characterizing insiders as outsiders was an act of oppression. And we were ethically opposed to such oppression—in thought, word, and deed.

Our WE cannot fully develop, as humans, so long as we allow the deeply internal other to remain othered. One of the first ethical ruptures to be taken is to disturb the insider/outsider positioning, including the othering of insiders. The transnational students were *inside* the school, not just physically, but, also, with an interactive part to play in an ethical refusal of the reproduction of white privilege, power, and hegemony.

Ethics as the Accessible Other/Speaking Truth to Power

Gillian Rose (1996), Jewish descendant of Holocaust survivors, explored the ethics of othering (the example she wrote about the othering of Nazis in Holocaust portrayals). She used the phrase "activity beyond activity" to write of the "fallible and precarious, but risk - able" mutual self/other claims of being (p. 13), while she courageously stepped into the necessity of seeing one's self even in the "most nasty" or "deplorable" of others, and most certainly in what it means to construct an other as either deplorable or nasty.[3] It was just this kind of struggle that kept me thinking early on that I had to act *against* those in Unityville whose actions engaged racism and oppression. However, as actors, our conversation excludes the other as subject the minute we speak in ways that do not include recognizing the other as a mutually valid actor. Othering someone is an active doing, not a once-and-for-all static outcome of action. However, Rose's point goes further. She actively located herself as the perpetrators of inhumane death. Not to valorize the inhumanity. Not to re-center the powerful in her own life's story. Rather, to call attention to the interconnections that knitted their humanities together. *Doing this does not set perpetrators of violence and survivors/victims of violence as moral equivalents.* Instead, this special form of position-taking fosters clarity about the entanglements of inhumanity and humanity in order to claim ethical potential—it takes an agential cut (using Barad's concept) through which the enactments of perpetrating and victimizing people are the effects of self/other binaries. This was very important. I wanted to figure out how to acknowledge that both sides were not just different (oppressing is never merely a difference), but also stay open to the ethical possibilities for engaging oppressors.

Aligning morally with the students was easy for those of us from IU but locating ourselves through the actions of some of the educators was more of a challenge. We needed to understand the perspectives of perpetrators, particularly in terms of white privilege, without engaging in perpetrating violence and oppression and without succumbing to an implicit moral equivalency of all actors. I did this by articulating the feeling level orientations under the oppressive routines. For example, I tried to resonate with the fear that was fueled by the mongering. I engaged in active listening and I wrote interpretations from the perspectives of those who expressed attitudes that did not align with my own sense of morality. I also imagined the perpetrators as open, potential, loved ones. One of the teachers complained to Ed that four white boys in her class were speaking negatively about Hispanic students, and she felt distressed about this and, also, about how she had handled it. Ed volunteered to use the focus group structure as an opportunity to open dialogue with the white boys about their attitudes, with the hope that some understanding and transformation could happen. Sometimes such opportunities came to obvious fruition and other times they didn't. Regardless, we consistently oriented ourselves toward understanding and including everyone while calling out racism and other forms of oppression to the best of our abilities (all of us involved with the project endeavored to do this).

Leaving this as a position-taking thought experiment was not good enough. We had to speak truth to power together, including *with* those who were engaged, purposefully or not, in the mistreatment of transnational students. We acknowledged good intentions, for example, as shared amongst our WE. While at the same time, we welcomed changes in both our thinking and our behavior regarding those intentions and any fragmentation suggested by how the motivations were directed. We displayed the internal diversity that was evidenced through the ethnographic research and we took action toward our best and evolving purposes. For example, initially there were a lot of assumptions about where the Latino students came from and why they had come to Unityville specifically. White students commonly lamented that "Hispanics came to take away our jobs [the jobs of white people as if those jobs "justly" belonged to the white people]." The language of "invasion" and "take over" created the felt need for emotional and physical of protectionism. The associated assumptions contributed to an expanded distance between the white community and the Latinx transnational students. We recognized that holding such unchecked assumptions got in the way of project's ideals. However, it is important to point out that our orientation toward understanding the commonly held attitudes amongst white Unityvillers was not strategic. It was inclusive. It reflected that our interest in understanding was effectively co-existing with our social justice goals. We, also, understood that while those assumptions were prevalent, they were not totalizing. There were teachers who wanted to better understand the migration stories of the youth and there were teachers who wanted to focus on how to connect with the students. And some of those teachers were also afraid.

Ethics as Self-Care/Care for All of Us

Professional self-care has been advocated as a form of ethics (see, e.g., Bamonti et al., 2014). Their argument was that one could not take care of others well, if one was not taking care of one's self. Moreover, caring for one's self, it was argued, is as ethical as taking care of others. The advocacy for self-care was largely discussed in terms of balancing the care of the self with the ability to care for others. Irving Yalom (2005) described the successful practices of group psychotherapy in which he identified group care for the whole as inclusive of individual care—taking care of each other was a step toward taking care of the group and toward group cohesion (one of the attributes of successful groups). It was our goal to take care of each other and encourage self-care. We realized that by taking care of individuals we were contributing to well-being of all of us, and we noticed when self-care manifested as something *over and against* others. We devoted attention to individual students and teachers while also attending to school culture and systemic histories/polices/practices. This critical bifocality (Weiss & Fine, 2012) empowered us to both care for individuals as needs came up and locate those needs in the larger picture. Our responses held both the individual and the school/district goals in mind. I believe this doubled care promoted collaborative ethics.

In Chapter 6 you will read about how we approached bullying with teachers. Chapter 6 demonstrates one way through which we paid attention to the details of individual bullying events in the high school, while pressing forward for non-idiosyncratic responses to the bullying at the school level. We focused on taking care of individually bullied students as we pushed toward cultural and school-wide solutions. We, also, applied this principle to our own self-care and to the professional care of Unityville educators. As members of our IU team, we used the time of the drive and our regular Sunday afternoon meetings to care for each other and create camaraderie around our social justice goals. In collaboration with Unityville educators, our IU-Unityville Outreach team members served as listening partners for other educators in the school, constituted a teacher inquiry group at the high school (facilitated by Ed) as a space for those involved to provide care for one another, and supported the professional care and continuity of the ENL program, particular with Yoko's sustained presence in the high school and with the transnational students. The care was transformative in that the dialogue reflected conscientização and the ensuing activities gave us opportunities to act new in the changing sociocultural landscape. Moreover, the needs identified through our caring often indicated cultural vulnerabilities which were important to understanding the mechanisms of oppression (Dennis, 2013).

Ethics as Seeking Justice in the Everyday Mistreatment of Students

The intentions to be methodologically inclusive (no research on people without their participation) and critically just (injustice anywhere for any one of us is injustice everywhere for all of us) situated our engagement with the transnational students as more ethically central to our ethnographic activities (Fine, 2018). "We are caught in an inescapable network of mutuality, tied in a single garment of destiny. Whatever affects one directly, affects all indirectly" (King, 1963). This inclusive ethics required us to be advocates for transnational students, specifically against their everyday mistreatment and in support of their educational potential. Justice for our transnational students was simultaneously and intrinsically an aspect of justice for all of us.

Tessa Verhallen (2016) conducted an ethnography with single mothers within the system of child protective services. She wrote,

> My aim to unveil the asymmetries between the single mothers and the state representatives executing child protection orders … made me committed to the marginalized single mother families who were engaged in a struggle for emancipation. This meant that I took sides, but I also had to gain and maintain credibility from both sides, which frequently led to a difficult balance between advocating for the families and giving no judgmental response. (p. 457)

When we listened to the transnational students during the first year of the project, we heard the strong us/them dynamics that had also riddled the teachers' and white students' talk. "They scream at us in the halls." "Even the teachers make fun of us." "They tell us, 'Migrant, leave our town.'" Our transnational students reported feeling unhappy, "There is no time when I feel happy here." We understood that injustices, oppression and disrespect were intolerable for us as an ethical community. Limiting the good life to a defined subset of insiders was unacceptable. Inclusion was a necessary, but insufficient way of thinking about justice and equity—we moved implicitly toward a socially just, inclusive concept of belonging as an ethical ideal for our work in Unityville. This was our *with*.

Ethics as Staying

Being in and *with* the field for a long time granted us researchers ethical opportunities and responsibilities. Typically, education ethnographers are interactively engaged with participants over the long haul (Jeffrey & Troman, 2004) which would make it virtually impossible to do ethnography without taking a relational stance whether one acknowledges that relationality or not. In our Project in

Unityville, the relational aspects were built through networks of small, organized groups within the schools. These networks served as nexuses for our overall ethnographic work. We became part of the community, understanding its ethics, but also standing as relative outsiders to those ethics at times. When we witnessed white students demonizing Arabic classmates, police officers acting harshly with African American male students, or a teacher policing student behavior through homophobic taunts, our witnessing was ethical collusion unless it was ethical disruption. There was no neutrality. Our day-after-day engagement involved the ongoing, collaborative, ethicality of acting.

Long-term engagement in the field meant that we could work together to increase empathy which would also strengthen a sense of WE. As entanglements of a complicated community, we could not "other" the community. We had to recognize our own entanglements and we had to imagine what it was WE could do together to move toward justice together. Injustice for one is injustice for all. Just for all demands, justice for those treated as if they are outsiders. Long-term engagement in the field reminded us that no one is an outsider to humanity.

In Closing

Somewhere in the middle, both in time and in process, I was hanging out, ethnographically speaking, with teachers in the lounge. No recorder. No field notebook. A sandwich from home in my hand and chips from a machine. The conversation started, I am sure, in part for my benefit. Teachers were talking about the "newcomers" and their own experiences with "those" students. They were specifically hoping I would understand their experiences. Of course, I did understand how difficult it was to find that your regular ways of teaching were not being successful. I did understand what it meant to be in a teaching situation for which one felt unprepared. But thinking of the transnational students as "those" students rather than "our" students was a linguistic signal of the distance many teachers felt with respect to transnational students. That was harder for me to relate with. All of us, actively involved in the project, used those conversations as invitations to create a broader, ethical we—one that had "those" students transformed to "our" students. We were able to shift the false contest between "our" traditional students and "those" "newcomers" in order to find ethical solutions that could work for all of our students. And we were able to begin to complexify the notion of "we."

In Chapter 2, I gave an example of a teacher who held the idea that it was not fair to treat transnational students different or special. Not fair to the traditional students. This view was shared by many of the teachers, not just that one.

Teachers who espoused this view of fairness believed that it was ethically important to treat *all* students equal—this ethical claim resulted in teachers not making
accommodations to support the transnational students (even when prompted by
school leaders). This false equation pitted "newcomer" students against "traditional"
students while erasing Black students in a contest for teachers' resources and favor-
able school policies. In order to transform these differing ethical stances, we had
to raise the question of whose students these were. How can the needs of the
transnational students be considered as important as the needs of the mainstream
students? The ethical call for fairness did not actually have fair outcomes. Roberta
talked with Ed about a need for a Spanish-speaking tutor to help two of our transnational students. She said, "Teachers feel they have *an ethical responsibility to not
make concessions.* In the final analysis, these students need to be treated equally." Ed
responded, "Is fair being equal, and is equal always fair? Is the belief, that all students must be treated equally?" Roberta said, "Yes, the same standards." Ed probed
further, "Is that what is fair?" The two continued working together to figure out
how to get the transnational students the help they needed despite the reigning
attitude resisting such support. Eventually, in one of those faculty lounge lunch
conversations, we birthed an idea. We created a buddy system at the high school
through which white students were paired with transnational students. The pairs
were given three goals: (1) get to know each other, (2) explore cultural differences,
and (3) do homework. The buddy system was not merely a pedagogical strategy,
it was an ethical advancement because it moved forward diverse ethical claims
as collaborative ethical action with a response that repositioned the "newcomer"
students as "our" students.

Ultimately, a recharacterization of ethics in critical educational ethnography
as collective intra-action not only situates us as collaborators with others in a deep
way, it compels our affiliation with all the distinct and divergent sets of experiences
in an effort to engage social justice as an inclusive arrangement of difference. This
proposal doesn't erase one's individual ethical accountabilities, but rather strength-
ens them. This was the kind of *we*-ness to which we aspired.

Notes

1. In my read, this does not contradict Barad's (2008) idea that agency slices the world up into
   ways of speaking and knowing it. Such slicing actions carry their own consequences for that
   knowledge.
2. Barbara's reflective notes January 18, 2004.
3. I made reference here to the name calling that happened during the 2016 U.S. presidential election between Hillary Clinton and Donald Trump.

References

Bamonti, P., Keelan, C., Larson, N., Mentrikoski, J., Cameron, R., Sly, S., ... McNeil, D. (2014). Promoting ethical behavior by cultivating a culture of self-care during graduate training: A call to action. *Training and Education in Professional Psychology, 8*(4), 253–260.

Barad, K. (2003). Posthumanist performativity: Toward an understanding of how matter comes to matter. *Signs: Journal of Women in Culture and Society, 28*(3), 801–831.

Barad, K. (2008). Queer causation and the ethics of mattering. In N. Giffney & M. Hird (Eds.), *Queering the non/human* (pp. 311–338). Farnham, UK: Ashgate.

Barad, K. (2012). Matter feels, converses, suffers, desires, yearns and remembers: Interview with Karen Barad. In Dolphijn, R., & Van Der Tuin, I., *New materialism: Interviews and cartographies* (pp. 48–70). Ann Arbor, MI: Open Humanities Press.

Beach, D., & Vigo Arrazola, B. (2019). Ethical review boards: Constitutions, functions, tensions and blind spots. In H. Busher & A. Fox (Eds.), *Implementing ethics in educational ethnography: Regulation and practice* (pp. 32–48). New York, NY: Routledge.

Brantmeier, E.J. (2016). Wounded in the field of inquiry: Vulnerability in critical research. In P. Hinchey (Ed.), *A critical action research reader* (pp. 284–290). New York, NY: Peter Lang.

Bronfenbrenner, U. (1952). Principles of professional ethics: Cornell studies in social growth. *American Psychologist, 7*, 452–519.

Cammarota, J. (2007). A map for social change: Latino students engage a praxis of ethnography. *Children, Youth and Environments, 17*(2), 341–353.

Carspecken, P. (1996). *Critical ethnography in educational research: A theoretical and practical guide.* New York, NY: Routledge.

Carspecken, P. (2003). Ocularcentrism, phonocentrism, and the counter enlightenment problematic: Clarifying contested terrain in our schools of education. *Teacher's College Record, 105*(6), 978–1047.

Carspecken, P., & Cordeiro, P. (1995). Being, doing, and becoming: Textual interpretations of social identity and a case study. *Qualitative Inquiry, 1*(1), 87–101.

Casteñada, Q. (2006). Ethnography in the forest: An analysis of ethics in the morals of anthropology. *Cultural Anthropology, 21*(1), 121–145.

Crenshaw, K. (1989). Demarginalizing the intersection of race and sex: A black feminist critique of antidiscrimination doctrine, feminist theory, and anti-racist politics. *University of Chicago Legal Forum, 1*, Article 8.

Dennis, B. (2009a). Acting up: Theatre of the oppressed as critical qualitative research. *International Journal for Qualitative Methods, 8*(2), 65–96.

Dennis, B. (2009b). What does it mean when an ethnographer intervenes? *Ethnography and Education, 4*(2) 131–146.

Dennis, B. (2017, October). *Destabilizing power and authority: Taking intersectionality seriously.* Plenary speech at the Comparative and International Education Society Symposium, Washington, DC.

Dennis, B. (2018). Working without/against a compass: Ethical dilemmas in educational ethnography. In D. Beach, C. Bagley, & S. Marques da Silva (Eds.), *Handbook on ethnography of education* (pp. 51–70). Hoboken, NJ: Wiley Press.

Eddy, B. (2014). Learning to understand others. The pragmatic rhetoric of ethnography and religious ethics in Clifford Geertz's "Works and Lives." *Essays in the Philosophy of Humanism, 22*(2), 137–157.

Fine, M. (2018). *Just research in contentious times: Widening the methodological imagination.* New York, NY: Teachers College Press.

Freire, P. (1972). *Pedagogy of the oppressed.* New York, NY: Penguin Books.

Freire, P. (1994). *Pedagogy of hope.* New York, NY: Bloomsbury Press.

Giddens, A. (1984). *The constitution of society. Outline of the theory of structuration.* Cambridge, MA: Polity Press.

Goffman, A. (2014). *On the run: Fugitive life in an American city.* Chicago, IL: University of Chicago Press.

Goode, E. (2002). Sexual involvement and social research in fat civil rights organization. *Qualitative Sociology, 25*(4), 501–534.

Goodwin, D., Pope, C., Mort, M., & Smith, A. (2003). Ethics and ethnography. An experiential account. *Qualitative Health Research, 13*(4), 567–577.

Habermas, J. (1985). *The theory of communicative action, volume 1: Reason and the rationalization of society* (T. McCarthy, Trans.). Boston, MA: Beacon Press.

Harding, S. (1991). *Whose science? Whose knowledge?: Thinking from women's lives.* Ithaca, NY: Cornell University Press.

Herron, M. (2018). Ethnographic methods, young people, and a high school: A recipe for ethical precarity. *Anthropology & Education, 50*(1), 84–96.

Hodge, D. (2013). The problems with ethics. *PoLAR, 36*(2), 286–297.

Hostetler, K. (2005). What is "good" education research? *Educational Researcher, 34*(6), 16–21.

Irwin, K. (2006). Into the heart of ethnography. The lived ethics and inequality of intimate field relationships. *Qualitative sociology, 29*, 155–175.

James, W. (1949) *Pragmatism.* New York, NY: Longman's, Green and Company.

Jeffrey, B., & Troman, G. (2004). Time for ethnography. *British Educational Research Journal, 30*(4), 535–548.

King, M.L. (1963, August). *Letter from Birmingham jail.* Retrieved November 1, 2019, from https://web.cn.edu/kwheeler/documents/Letter_Birmingham_Jail.pdf.

Kofoed, J., & Staunæs, D. (2015). Hesitancy as ethics. *Reconceptualizing Educational Research Methodology 6*(1): 24–39.

Korth, B. (2002). Critical qualitative research as consciousness-raising: The dialogic texts of researcher/researchee interactions. *Qualitative Inquiry, 8*(3), 381–403.

Korth, B. (2006). Establishing universal human rights through war crimes trials and the need for cosmopolitan law in an age of diversity. *Liverpool Law Review, 27*(1), 97–123.

Kuntz, A. (2015). *The responsible methodologist: Inquiry, truth-telling, and social justice.* Walnut Grove, CA: Leftcoast Press.

Lather, P. (1986). Issues of validity in openly ideological research: Between a rock and a soft place. *Interchange, 17*(4), 63–84.

McLaren, P. (1992). *Life in schools: An introduction to critical pedagogy in the foundations of education* (1st ed.). Boulder, CO: Paradigm Publishers.

Murphy, E., & Dingwall, R. (2007). The ethics of ethnography. In P. Atkinson, A. Coffey, S. Delamont, J. Lofland, & L. Lofland (Eds.), *Handbook of ethnography* (pp. 339–351). Los Angeles, CA and London, England: Sage.

Neykafh, L. (2015, June 18). The ethics of ethnography. Retrieved January 31, 2017, from http://www.slate.com/articles/news_and_politics/crime/2015/06/alice_goffman_s_on_the_run_is_the_sociologist_to_blame_for_the_inconsistencies.html

Peñaranda, F., Vélez-Zapata, C., & Bloom, R. (2013). Research from a social justice perspective: The systematization of an experience. *International Review of Qualitative Research, 6*(1), 37–55.

Prasad, L. (2019). Ethical resonance: The concept, the practice, and the narration. *Journal of Religious Ethics, 47*(2), 394–415.

Rose, G. (1996). *Mourning becomes the law: Philosophy and representation.* Cambridge, England: Cambridge University Press.

St. Pierre, E. (2000). Poststructural feminism in education: An overview. *International Journal of Qualitative Studies in Education, 13*(5), 477–515.

Sr. Pierre, E. (2008). Decentering voice in qualitative inquiry. *International Review of Qualitative Research, 1*(3), 319–336.

St. Pierre, E. (2014). A brief and personal history of post qualitative research: Toward "post inquiry." *Journal of Curriculum Theorizing, 30*(2), 1–19.

Scheper-Hughes, N. (1995). The primacy of the ethical. *Current Anthropology, 36*(3), 409–440.

Serwer, A. (2018, June 20). Trumpism, realized. *The Atlantic.* Retrieved November 10, 2019, from https://www.theatlantic.com/ideas/archive/2018/06/child-separation/563252

Tomaselli, K. (2016). Research ethics in the Kalahari: Issues, contradictions, and concerns. *Critical Arts, 30*(6), 804–822.

Verhallen, T. (2016). Tuning the dance of ethnography: Ethics during situated fieldwork in single-mother child protection families. *Current Ethnography, 57*(4), 452–473.

Weiss, L., & Fine, M. (2012). Critical bifocality and circuits of privilege: Expanding critical ethnographic theory and design. *Harvard Educational Review, 82*(2), 172–201.

Wikan, U. (2012). *Resonance: Beyond the words.* Chicago, IL: University of Chicago Press.

Yalom, I. (2005). *Theory and practice of group psychotherapy* (5th ed.). New York, NY: Basic Books.

Zhang, J. (2017). The irreducible ethics in reflexivity: Rethinking reflexivity in conducting ethnography in Shangi-La in southwest China. *Tourism, Culture & Communication, 17*(1), 19–30.

Zussman, R. (2002). Editor's introduction: Sex in research. *Qualitative Sociology, 25*(4), 473–477.

CHAPTER FOUR

Same over Time? An Historical Context Written by Dini Metro-Roland

Does history repeat itself? Is it merely the same over time or can we break free from our past to create an unforeseen future? The question of our proper relationship to history is timely. Our public life is saturated with interpretations of history meant to shape our collective memory of the past, legitimate various programs and policies in the present, and frame our orientation towards the future. Slogans such as *Make America Great Again* or *Hope and Change* are tightly packed with emotionally charged symbolism designed to establish our relationship to history, often by way of blind nostalgia or willful forgetting. Not surprisingly, these clichés of history also galvanize voters in powerful ways. The recent proliferation of nativist rhetoric has intensified our fears of the unknown and further polarized the country over fundamental questions about our democratic values, the social and economic benefits of immigration, and even the humanity of our transnational migrants and their reluctant hosts. That the very same voters are susceptible at different times and in different situations to conflicting narratives is testament to our fickle and deeply contentious relationship to history. At the same time, how we make sense of the past directly impacts our present and future; the stories we tell about our shared history validate and shape our attitudes and actions toward one another and the surrounding world. By coming to better understand a particular community's various connections to history, critical ethnographers gain valuable insight into the patterned and contested value systems of its members. In this specific study, a greater awareness of Unityville's past in relation to today's *narratives of mono-culturalism* help us contextualize the explicit and implicit stories that rationalize decisions made on behalf of the "newcomer" students by Unityville administrators, teachers, and citizens alike.

In making sense of our relationship to history, we should be wary of simplistic judgments. On the one hand, it is irresponsible to view the past as a fateful reflection of the future, the same over time. History is change—certainly temporal, but also social and material. The way things were then, are not, in fact cannot be, the same in the present. On the other hand, reading our present without acknowledging the various legacies of history is reckless as well. History is a living part of the present. Many of the naturalized positions we take as researchers, teachers, students come to us from the past. Not only are there recognizable patterns and traditions that we repeat throughout our lives, but it is often quite satisfying to preserve the same over time. By doing so, we recognize the meaning-making qualities of our inherited traditions, the fruits, if you will, of those who came before us. In fact, even when we don't seek to preserve the past in the present, it is there looming in the environment.

This chapter explores how a rich appreciation of historical context can contribute to critical ethnography. After a brief discussion of the public uses of history and its application to critical ethnography, we turn to the narrative of monoculturalism and its historical roots in two periods of Unityville's past. This will provide needed context for Chapter 5, when we explore the disconnect between history and the collective stories that were told about monoculturalism as the timeless, inevitable path to becoming American.

History of the Present: A Theoretical Framework

In the late 1990s, Daniel Goldhagen's (1996) book, *Hitler's Willing Executioners*, created a maelstrom of controversy throughout newly united Germany. Rather than lay blame solely on the Nazi party and its leaders, the author argued that it was ordinary Germans who voluntarily conducted the massacres of the Jews. They did so, the author claimed, without any internal turmoil because of a unique "eliminationist anti-Semitism" that permeated German culture. Supporters of the book commended the author for his courageous, clear-eyed account and for challenging the widespread amnesia with regard to the complicity of average Germans in the Holocaust (Deák, 1997). Critics of the book argued that

the work is shoddy history, riddled with generalizations, omissions, and tautol-
ogies designed to appeal to a "young" public audience hungry for smug conclusions to an exceedingly complex topic (Deák, 1997; Körner, 2000). Habermas
(2001a), among the most prominent German intellectuals who weighed in on
the controversy, defended the work in an essay aptly titled, "The Public Use of
History."[1] Despite some reservations about the generalizability of his thesis,
Habermas praised Goldhagen for writing a quintessential work of public history.
It is Habermas' unique take on historiography—rather than the substantive arguments about the book's merits—that warrant special attention here. In particular,
Habermas underscored two aspects of history that spoke directly to the practice
of critical ethnography.

First and foremost, Habermas illuminated the intimate productive relationship between past and present (as well as future) in historical consciousness. It is
not historical facts alone, but historical facts and their interpretation that comprise
the field of public history. Our "hermeneutic ability" to view the past, he wrote,
"varies with our understanding of freedom: how we value ourselves as persons,
and how much we expect from ourselves as political actors" (p. 37). For Habermas,
the "ethical-political discourse of collective self-understanding [triggered by this
book] raises just this pre-understanding as a topic of discussion. How we see the
distribution of guilt and innocence in the past also reflects the present norms
according to which we are willing to accord one another mutual respect as citizens
of this Republic" (p. 37). What Habermas was referring to here is the temporal
structure of the horizon of understanding that accompanies all interpretation. The
relationship between past and present is dialogical; one's interpretation of history
is shaped by the present while one's present is correspondingly shaped by history
and our interpretation of it. This relationship is also unmistakably intersubjective; history is never purely mine or yours; it is always a shared history between
members of a community. It consists in a shaping of and reaction to value systems
that are collectively acknowledged. This is so on the most basic level. Consider
how dependent we are on language, an intersubjective medium, in making sense
of our past and its implications for us and others. Consider further how dependent our evaluations of the past and its implications are on collectively determined
value systems and criteria. It is for this reason too that the Goldhagen debate
was dubbed a war between generations. Younger Germans approach the subject of
the Holocaust with radically different pasts, experiences, and expectations than do
their parents and grandparents.

Secondly, Habermas claimed that good public history augments our capacity to reflect on our own traditions and self-interpretations. The true value of a
work such as *Hitler's Willing Executioners* (Goldhagen, 1996) does not reside in

its condemnation of past Germans, but in its potential to help "bring about some clarity concerning the cultural matrix of a burdened inheritance, to recognize what they themselves are collectively liable for, and what is to be continued, and what revised, of those traditions that once had formed such a disastrous motivational background" (p. 31). Shaking "any naïve trust in our own traditions" public history invites citizens to critically reflect on their own relationship to the past and to think differently about their collective identity in the present as well as in the future. As this debate about the proper interpretation of the holocaust reveals, while the past might shape our understanding of the present, the traditions we inherit from the past are always open to critical reflection and change. For those who have inherited a past that includes death camps and anti-Semitism, or chattel slavery and racism that have been endemic to the constitution of the United States, the notion that history is not destiny can be both liberating and demanding since we can only free our collective selves from aspects of the past if we take collective responsibility to deal with it constructively.

Good public history, for Habermas, entails two components. First it must illuminate the importance of our historical past and the intersubjective nature of the relationship between our interpretation of the past and its bearing on our present understanding of self and others. But this largely descriptive move is insufficient unless a second move is made. For a good public use of history, we must submit these interpretations of the past and its relation to our interpretations of self and others to critical reflection and dialogue. We must therefore hold in tension the Janus-faced nature of public history that must look back to the past while simultaneously also looking forward to the future.[2]

If we think of these two aspects of public history as understanding the implications of historical context and engaging in historical dialogue about these implications, then it is easy to see their relevance to critical ethnography. In contrast to positivist research, ethnography turns on a process that is rich in both historical depth and critical conversation, emphasizing thick description, meaningful relationships with subjects across time, and the ability to critically engage with what one finds in the field. This is especially true for critical ethnographers who draw heavily on the work of Jürgen Habermas. After all, the very concepts that form the basis of his communicative theory—intersubjectivity, validity claims, and the epistemology-first principle—have temporal structures that reward attention to context *and* invite critical analysis.[3] (See for instance Chapter 7 for a detailed examination of this temporal quality.) To take seriously the validity claims of both native and transnational members of the Unityville community requires that one first understand the horizons of validity (or value systems) from which these claims are made and evaluated. But this is only a first step. Ethnography isn't critical if it merely stops at the descriptive and doesn't also interrogate what is understood with an eye towards a more promising future. Implicit in this approach, then, is the belief that the traditions, prejudices, and conceptions of self and community that make up the worlds of the researcher and the researched are always open to analysis, dialogue, and consequently, transformation.

With this in mind, I illustrate in this chapter the role that history can play in critical ethnography by analyzing the narrative of monoculturalism, the backdrop against which insider/outsider distinctions and validity claims about the purpose and function of schooling are frequently made by native residents of Unityville. Though there are other themes from the past that arguably belong in this chapter, the repeated references to this narrative in our conversations with members of the community (see Chapter 5) warrant special attention. That this narrative permeated the very language of schooling and framed the intersubjective expectations of native residents with respect to how "newcomers" *should* adapt to community norms and *should* accept responsibilities accordingly made addressing questions about its source and implications imperative.

- From where do these insider/outsider markers and assumptions come?
- How does the narrative of monoculturalism reinforce insider/outsider distinctions and shape the approach to educating "newcomer" students?
- How does this narrative fit with the skill-based orientation favored by many teachers and administrators who are relative outsiders to the community?
- What view of history is reflected in the narrative of monoculturalism?
- What is omitted from this narrative of the past and why does it matter?
- How should this generalization of the past affect the education of "newcomers" today?
- Are there alternative interpretations of the past that promote more promising dialogue?

Historical Context: The Narrative(s) of Monoculturalism

Whether referred to as background analysis, site feasibility research, or thick description, all good ethnographies provide some understanding of historical context and identify meaningful cultural and historical aspects of the community (or communities) under study. Historical context is of course broadly conceived. Though this present chapter presents a rather traditional historical analysis, there are many different ways ethnographers contextualize and re-contextualize the common cultural world of its participants. At the same time, the quality of attention afforded to historical context can vary widely. While all ethnographers enter the field with preconceived research methodologies, ideals and commitments, some adopt a strong instrumental-strategic approach to historical context that from the start precludes serious consideration of other perspectives and possibilities. For these ethnographers, historical context is simply a matter of framing their story and conclusions before the evidence is laid out. Other ethnographers treat the process of historical analysis in a way that invites the emergence of new questions and avenues of investigation. For these ethnographers, historical context both grounds and informs their research questions and analyses. It is this latter understanding of historical context that is most characteristic of our project at Unityville. While our team of researchers felt a natural affinity with transnational students and were certainly supportive of their right to maintain cultural and personal integrity, we also sought, in principle, to take seriously the claims of those who saw the matter differently. We did not do so simply for tactical reasons—to better know your enemy—but because we genuinely sought to better understand the concerns, fears, and hopes of all participating conversation partners from the schools and community.

Being open to the claims of others is risky, time-consuming and oftentimes frustrating. It can derail ethnographers from their initial path of research, and even compel them to undergo a radical reevaluation of their motives and positions. It was in response to conversations we had in the field during our research that eventually convinced us of the need to better understand the sources of the monoculturalist narrative that helped form the town's self-image and the dominant approach to the transnational students.

The narrative of monoculturalism, like so many narratives that shape our lives, was rarely explicitly defined in our conversations with Unityville residents. Yet, the illocutionary force of this narrative was present in the everyday language of community. Shorthand references to outsider/insider distinctions and common-sense appeals to what we should expect of "newcomers" permeated discussions about the Latino/a/x students, for example, "They just don't get it," "This is just the way we do things here," or "They need to adapt to our ways of doing things in order to fit in." The shape and contents of this narrative was more fully evident in the various public histories, newspaper articles, and other official and unofficial historical sources about the town. The narrative of monoculturalism went something like this:

> Our community of Unityville goes back generations to the pioneer families who settled in the area during the early 19th century. The history of the town is replete with the heroic acts of patriotic citizens who have faith in American exceptionalism, respect for the rule of law, and embody the town's strong (Protestant) work ethic, morality, and common sense. Despite our mixed ancestry, our community has embraced the English language and (Midwestern)

American values. We are suspicious of powerful outside influences, fads and trends that chal-
lenge our traditional way of life. With few minor and fleeting exceptions, our community
comes together around these core traditional values. All religious and ethnic differences pale
in comparison to what unites us as a community. Learn our ways and you will be embraced
by us. We are one big family.

Variations of the monoculturalism narrative were clearly articulated in the local histories written by Unity county residents throughout the late nineteenth and twentieth centuries. Their stories of the Indiana frontier and pioneer life, of German immigrants who settled in the town and shed their old language and customs to become American, and of the integration of the town's African American community, painted a picture of a town that persevered in the face of many challenges to the Unityville way of life.[4] While many communities studied by ethnographers have little historical record, the stability and cohesion of this small community, and the fact that many residents of the town and county can trace their roots in the area back several generations, meant that history played a significant role in the self-interpretation of the community.[5] The rich source of local histories and narratives attested to that importance.[6]

Before I begin, a brief word on sources is necessary. While the self-interpretations of the town's histories are extremely useful, the function of these local histories is conservative, written not to provide critical reflection of the past but to reaffirm the grand narrative of the community where unity and cohesion triumph over diversity and conflict. Despite sincere attempts to be objective and accurate, it is not surprising that all the local historians fail to meet, in at least one important respect, Habermas' criteria of a good public history. While they illuminated the relationship between past and present, as well as indicated possible futures, they avoided engaging in the kind of historical dialogue that invites readers to critically reflect on the inherited culture of the past and its relationship to the present and future self-understanding of the community.[7] It is for this reason that I looked to other available resources, mainly evidence collected in interviews, school yearbooks, professional histories of the region, newspaper articles, and church records, for a better understanding of the narrative of monoculturalism as it emerged as a dominant trope in the self-understanding of the community.

My investigation of the historical context of the narrative of monoculturalism will focus on two aspects from Unityville's past, the turn of the century language and culture issues of the town's ethnic German population and the segregation and integration of the African American community during the first half of the twentieth century.[8] As my study will reveal, the integration of these two ethnic groups into the community took radically different paths and complicate the language of monoculturalism prevalent today.

Insiders Apart: German Language and Culture in Unityville

Of particular interest to the present investigation is the experience of the ethnic German population which played a prominent role in the economic and social life of Unityville during the nineteenth and early twentieth century. With the exception of today's "newcomers," they represent the only sizable non-native English-speaking population to live in Unityville. Unlike the current Spanish-speaking population, however, they enjoyed many notable advantages which secured them a unique status in the city. Not only was their percentage of the population much higher than today's "newcomers,"[9] but German families actively participated in the very establishment of the county and city as well. Moreover, the German residents of Unityville wielded tremendous social, economic and political power in the community. Made up of an assortment of farmers, owners of shops, taverns, and many of the furniture factories for which the town was well-known,[10] as well as ministers, priests, nuns, teachers, principals and politicians, the ethnic German population was an integral and, according to surviving accounts, well regarded segment of the community.[11] At the same time, the Germans' insistence on preserving a vibrant connection to the German language and German culture clearly set them apart from the English-speaking community. The story of their integration into mainstream culture speaks to the power of monoculturalism and provides insight into some of the challenges facing "newcomers" today.

Given the lack of reliable and detailed sources, there is very little that can be said for certain about the German community of Unityville. Many came during the waves of German immigration in the 1830s and following the 1848 revolutions of Europe. These immigrants and their children attended their own German ministered churches, mainly Catholic and Lutheran but also Presbyterian. Though divided in faith, evidence suggests that the various communities were nevertheless united in their concerted effort to preserve a path to American citizenship that honored the German language and essential aspects of German culture. Services in all three religious communities were conducted in the German language until the early twentieth century when English services were also made available.[12]

Introducing children to German language and culture was accomplished in various ways. Many German Catholics turned to the local Catholic school, St. Joseph, which was established in 1884 by the Sisters of St. Francis at Oldenburg, an order of German and Austrian nuns whose mission was to provide bilingual Catholic instruction to the German Catholic population throughout the Midwest.[13] The German Lutherans and Presbyterians chose instead to send their children to the more Protestant-friendly common schools. Dr. G.G. Winter, the pastor of the First German Evangelical Lutheran Church, taught foreign languages and later served as principal at the local high school. Taking advantage of the 1869 Indiana state law that *required* the provision of "efficient teachers" to teach the "German language as a branch of study" in all schools with interested parents of at least 25 students in attendance, the German community was able to assert the German language as a legitimate subject of study. The public schools routinely recruited German language teachers from Germany and elsewhere and the Unityville high school boasted a German department with a rigorous curriculum.[14]

What is known for certain is that by the time the United States entered the Great War against Germany, this once vibrant German speaking community, like other German communities throughout the country, lost their will or ability to preserve their lived connection to the German language and to many distinctive aspects of their German culture.[15] In fact, it was during this time that the German language was altogether dropped as a subject of study in the public school curriculum, never again to return. Although a quarter of today's residents still claim German ancestry, knowledge of the German language is almost nonexistent in Unityville today.[16] Given this ancestry, it is noteworthy that German was not one of the foreign language options in the high school at the time. Not surprisingly, the public histories of the town remained largely silent about this period of its history. Even the failed attempts of the German community to maintain their distinctive language and culture is rarely noted. Where rarely noted, when it is discussed the issue has been treated as a natural part of the social order of things:

> Those [German immigrants] who came to [Unityville] were criticized by the rest of the populace for being 'clannish' and especially for insisting that their children be given their schooling in the German language. Moreover, as a Temperance wave was sweeping the country in those years, the newspapers frequently vented their wrath on the 'Dutch,' many of whom were in the saloon business. True, they formed their own societies, owned a Turner Hall, which they dedicated in 1860, organized a German band and later had their own churches, in which services were conducted in their own language. Yet, the Germans, for the most part, became stalwart, prosperous citizens, adding much to the economic and social growth of the town. Their language gradually fell into disuse and the process of Americanization proceeded *normally* [emphasis mine]. (McFadden, 1968, p. 147)

In another, the authors simply noted:

> Before World War I German was a part of many high school language programs, but it was not after the war started. (Unity County Historical Society, 1992, p. 49)

And then under a section titled "Unity County Churches," a member of the church contributed the following:

> The German-American community opened up as the younger members, who had become Americanized through the years in school and business, welcomed their

friends. The German services were continued in spite of the dissatisfaction of some of the younger members who no longer were conversant in German. Dr. G.G. Winter conducted the first English service on Sept. 3rd, 1911. For several years services were held in both languages until finally the German language was dropped completely, probably due to public pressure during the first world war. (p. 206)[17]

Another contributor recounted the family history stating:

The entire family held membership in St. Zion Evangelical Church and were very active in the German community that had grown in [Unity] and Rush counties. As the children mixed with others at school, they learned to speak English and became involved with the outside community. As the years passed they took their places among their English-Speaking neighbors. The Americanization process worked steadily and the old ways gave way to the new, as is the way with all people everywhere. (p. 348)

One finds a similar story in the church records of the First German Evangelical Zion Church:

During these first years, [the church was established in 1836], all services were conducted in the native German tongue, since the original settlers were unfamiliar with the English language. However, as the children attended the schools of this new land, they lost touch with the old ways, and when they grew up and established their homes, it became apparent that changes must be made if the Church was to remain the center of their lives. Therefore on September 3, 1911, the first English service was held in the Church. For some time two services were held, one in German and the other in English. (First German Evangelical Zion Church Records, n.d.)

Catholic recollections of the switch from German to English in their community reflected the same rationale:

The German-English language muddle was still a problem at the turn of the century. Children exposed to German-speaking parents and grandparents, plus the mixture spoken by the nuns and priests, were often thoroughly confused. "Guten tag Pfarrer" (Good afternoon Father) and "Bet fur uns" (pray for us) were common German responses that had no meaning to the children. In fact, German high masses were offered at least once a month to accommodate the Deutsch-speaking segment. As could be expected, tension sometimes existed. On at least one occasion, parishioners protested to the bishop when a non-German speaking priest was assigned to their parish. They were promptly told to accept the man, that they were now Americans, not Germans! (Catholic Church Records, 1982)

These short accounts, written decades later, hid more than they revealed about the nature of the German community and language policies at the time. The truth is more complicated. While records of the German community in Unityville were scarce, there was reliable historical information about German attempts in the state and region to preserve their linguistic and cultural traditions. Not surprisingly, proponents (and critics) focused their attention on education, the right of the ethnic German population to educate their children in the German language. If we view the issue in Unityville as a microcosm of this larger problem facing German-Americans in the region, then we can see the extent to which the preservation of German culture was dependent on maintaining language rights in schools and the effect it had on future generations once those rights were rescinded.[18]

Support for German language instruction in publicly financed common schools was strong in many of the nineteenth century Midwestern frontier states. Non-German advocates of German language instruction argued that it made sense economically, socially and politically. It was economically profitable as a means to attract skilled German immigrants into the state. It was socially desirable as a way to reinforce important familial ties during the disruptive process of Americanization. It was politically important as a means of strengthening the fledgling common school network against the further expansion of an already large number of ethno-centered private schools that instruct students exclusively in the German tongue. William T. Harris, the superintendent of St. Louis schools, espoused an early version of the Melting Pot idea in support of German language and culture instruction. He saw the assimilation process of German-Americans as both necessary and *reciprocal* in nature. While ethnic Germans should be encouraged to adopt American values and language they will inevitably also contribute beneficial aspects of German culture into the American fabric.[19] Other advocates went even further than this, viewing such policies as a possible path to American citizenship that embraced biculturalism and bilingualism.

Due in part to this reasoning, and as a testament to the strong political and economic influence of the ethnic German community in the region, cities like Indianapolis, Cincinnati and St. Louis experimented with different levels of bilingual education in public schools. The 1869 Indiana state law made public instruction in German possible in any district where "twenty-five or more children in attendance at any school of a township, town or city, shall so demand."[20] Unityville was probably most affected by the policies of neighboring Indianapolis, which despite its relatively small German population compared to some Midwestern cities, such as St. Louis, Cincinnati, and Milwaukee, developed a strong, extensive German language program in the public schools from second grade through high school. While the German program initially encouraged segregation by creating separate schools for German-Americans, a preference for mixed courses began to take shape in 1874 to prevent ethnic clustering and promote the German language to non-German students (Probast, 1989, p. 164). In order to provide all interested elementary students with 25–30 minutes of daily German instruction, the district recruited teachers mainly from Germany and Cincinnati. Additional German annexes were created for six to eighth grade students who wanted half day instruction in German, including subjects such as geography and American history (Ramsey, 2009, p. 280). On the benefits of learning subjects in two languages, the *Annual Report of the Public Schools of the City of Indianapolis, 1882–1883*, reasoned that bilingual instruction taught "the pupil the very difficult lesson that a thought is independent of a form of words, and may be variously expressed. It threw the pupil perforce into the selection of words for the expression of his thought rather than into his memory for the set of words there stored" (Ellis, 1954b, p. 261).

A strikingly high percentage of students in Indianapolis took advantage of this opportunity. In the 1880s, there were about 2,000 students who studied German in district schools and high schools. At the turn of the century, that number increased to almost 7,000 students (in 34 district schools and both high schools) out of a total of just over 28,000 students. By 1916, just before its demise, the program boasted almost 10,000 students (Ellis, 1954a, p. 359). At the same time, English-speaking resistance to bilingualism was strong throughout the program's existence and it was only due to the concerted efforts of a determined German population that such reforms were even possible (Schlossman, 1983, p. 169). This resolve ground to a halt once the United States entered the war against Germany. Even the German language newspaper *Der Täglische Telegraph* became suddenly silent in fear of being branded as traitors to the war cause (Ramsey, 2002). It was no longer possible for the German population to remain both American and German in the eyes of the state and the country.[21]

On January 29, 1918, the board of trustees for Indianapolis public schools officially dismantled the German language program for all elementary schools, arguing among other things, that "public schools should teach our boys and girls the principle of one nation, one language, and one flag, and should not assist in perpetuating the language of an alien enemy in our homes and enemy viewpoints in the community ..." (Ellis, 1954a, p. 374). On February 25, 1919, the state legislature of Indiana reaffirmed this sentiment in more forceful terms with passage of the McCray Act, which stated that instruction in all schools, public and private, be conducted in only English, specifically emphasizing that the "German language shall not be taught in any such schools within this state." This *included* private schools. As if the anti-German undertones weren't clear enough, the law was amended later in the year to allow "Latin or any modern foreign language except German" to be taught in the high schools (Ellis, 1954a, p. 375).[22] Nativist attitudes that promoted a deep fear of all outsiders only increased after the War, especially with the rise of Communism and suspicions that pockets of Bolshevik cells worked to undermine American capitalism within various ethnic communities in the country.

Unfortunately, there was very little information about how these events played out in Unityville. Given the political and social climate, it was not surprising that little written record of the response of the German community was available. What we do know is that tension between retaining the community's fluency in the German language and culture and giving it up to become "American" was already evident in the region well before World War I. This tension must have been palpable to the Unityville audience of the Unity County Chautauqua Fair (1912) who after enjoying the gypsy music of the Austro-Hungarian Orchestra and Bavarian and other German folk songs sung by the Tyrolean Alpine Singers, listened to Miss Ruth Hemenway's reading of "The Melting Pot," Isreal Zangwill's "great immigration problem play," as the program described it. The play tells the story of a Russian aristocrat, Russian Jew, and German conductor who together symbolized the symphony of immigrants who gladly leave Europe behind with "her pomp and chivalry built on a morass of crime and misery" to become proud Americans. The play ends with the protagonist proclaiming in hopeful tones:

DAVID
(Jewish violinist):   It is the fires of God round His Crucible. There she lies, the great Melting Pot-listen! Can't you hear the roaring and the bubbling? There gapes her mouth [He points east] the harbour where a thousand mammoth feeders come from the ends of the world to pour in their human freight. Ah, what a stirring and a seething! Celt and Latin, Slav and Teuton, Greek and Syrian—black and yellow—

VERA
(Russian aristocrat):   —Jew and Gentile—

DAVID: Yes, East and West, and North and South, the palm and the pine, the pole and the equator, the crescent and the cross—how the great Alchemist melts and fuses them with his purging flame! Here shall they all unite to build the Republic of Man and the Kingdom of God. Ah, Vera, what is the glory of Rome and Jerusalem where all nations and races come to worship and look back, compared with the glory of America, where all races and nations come to Labor and look forward! [He raises his hands in benediction over the shining city.] Peace, peace, to all ye unborn millions, fated to fill this giant continent-the God of our children give you Peace. [An instant's solemn pause.] The sunset is swiftly fading, and the vast panorama is suffused with a more restful twilight, to which the many-gleaming lights of the town add the tender poetry of the night. Far back, like a lonely, guiding star, twinkles over the darkening water the torch of the Statue of Liberty. From below comes up the softened sound of voices and instruments joining in "My Country, 'tis of Thee." [The curtain falls slowly.] (Zangwill, 1906)

By the time the United States entered the war against Germany, the metaphor of the Melting Pot and the language of monoculturalism thoroughly shaped public sentiment in Unityville. This version of Americanization became the law of the land. Not only did German language instruction cease completely, but the silence of the German language proponents of the time was followed by the subsequent public silence of citizens and local historians concerning the half-century history of bilingualism in Unityville and Unity County.

Outsiders Within: Racial Segregation and Integration in Unityville

Writing about life in segregated Unityville in the 1940s, the biographer of the town's most famous athlete[23] described town life thusly:

> What [the black community] found in [Unityville] was an attitude best expressed by a local newspaper editor who, urging whites to contribute money for the building of [Frederick Douglas, the all black school], had written, "These people can't help being colored among us." The racial violence that plagued other Indiana communities had largely passed by [Unityville] ... Prominent black speakers such as Frederick Douglass and George Washington Carver had been well received at the city's opera house (after speaking before an integrated crowd in nearby Richmond, Douglass had barely escaped with his life.) And though the editor of the [Unity] Democrat had railed against an impending "Ebon onslaught" when a ragged group of seventeen starving men, women, and children had stumbled into town during one of the harshest winters on record, they had been fed, clothed and housed at public expense. But charity was one thing, full acceptance another. There was no mistaking the fact that [Unityville] was a segregated town. Like all the town's black children, [Don Hall] attended [Frederick Douglas]. The public swimming pool was closed to him, except on Tuesday mornings just before it was cleaned. On hot summer days, Don and his friends swam instead in Little Blue River, behind the county fairgrounds, near the spot where they hosed down the elephants when the circus came to town. Since his family would not have felt welcome at most white churches, [Don] missed most of the Church-run summer camps and enrichment programs. He could not belong to "the Rec," the town's teen center. When he could scrape up pocket change for a Saturday double feature at the Strand, [Don] and his friends had to sit in the balcony. One day a week was "Negro Day" at Kennedy Park, when [Don] and others who won footraces received ribbons with "Colored" stamped on them ... In all this, there were no signs saying "Colored" or "Whites Only." There was very little explicit enforcement, and most day-to-day interactions between blacks and whites were polite and respectful. Segregation was the crazy uncle in the attic, the unspoken code of conduct, just "the way things are." (Graham & Cody, 2006, p. 18)

The unspoken fact of racial segregation that dominated Unityville during the interwar period and beyond makes it difficult to gauge the effect it had on the African American community and inter-race relationships. There is however ample evidence that racial categorization and discrimination were both natural- ized and common. Even well-intentioned statements in the press are laden by the legacy of slavery. Most references to African Americans were charged with the racial language and stereotypes of the period, such as when the writer for *The [Unity] Republican* complimented the "new colored star, Stepin Fetchit, who plays the role of the lazy but shifty-footed Gummy" in his review of the talking movie *The Hearts in Dixie* (Sloane, 1929) or when a writer from *The National Volunteer* condescendingly remarked:

> The colored orator, Frederick Douglas, lectured at Blessing's Opera Hall on Tuesday evening last, to a large audience, many of whom expressed themselves as highly pleased with the effort. Fred is a very good speaker and usually manages to say a great many things calculated to please his audience. (The Colored Orator, 1870)[24]

At the same time, as the quote above suggested, there was little evidence of the racial tension and more violent manifestations of injustice that marked many com- munities in the region. At times the town even came to the defense of their African American community, and acts of charity—or perhaps well-meaning paternal- ism—were not uncommon. The status of outsiders within is an apt description of the way in which African American residents of the town were viewed by their white neighbors. They were family and yet separate. This was the case in many towns in Indiana.

The history of African American presence in Unityville begins in the nine- teenth century. Initially, the few African American residents came to Indiana as former slaves, and in some cases, continued to be treated as such despite Indiana's 1787 laws forbidding slavery. The *Unity National Volunteer* recounted matter-of- factly in 1871:

> He (Jacob) came to this county in 1820 from North Carolina, bringing with him Isaac (everybody knows 'Old Ike' who is now head cuisine at the Ray House), Silas and Dilly Coleman. They were always treated as members of the family, and remained with Mr. Fox until they were 21 years of age, when they were allowed to go as they pleased. (Unity County Historical Society, 1992, p. 96)

Despite this, the author of one local history wrote that "no indication exists of any real anti-Negro feeling in Unityville since only 21 Negroes lived in the county by 1860" (p. 100). Nor, no doubt, was there an open-door policy towards runaway and former slaves as there was in neighboring counties with high populations of Quakers and Wesleyans.[25] The History of Unity County (1887) mentioned the names of several Black families, the establishment of two African American churches, and the fact that Daniel M.'s family were members of "the white Methodist Episcopal Church" (p. 400). In 1869, Unityville established, in compliance with state mandate, School no. 2 (later named Frederick Douglas) for the education of its African American children (Unity County Historical Society, 1992, p. 57). Voting rights were also withheld from African American citizens until well after the 13th and 14th Amendments were passed. According to an April 13, 1870 issue of the local *Unity Republican*, "Madison Estes, the blacksmith, cast the first colored vote ever cast in [Unity] county ..." (*Unity Republican*, 1870).

By the turn of the century, a small but stable African American community had formed in Unityville. The *1892–1893 Unityville City Directory and County Gazetteer* (1893) listed about 39 Black families, two black churches and an Odd Fellows Colored Lodge. In 1904, the Black community was recorded over 600 strong. In keeping with the unwritten rules of segregation, the vast majority of the African American residents lived on one of four connecting streets. African Americans with professional ambitions were limited to the field of teaching at the all-black school or to ministering at one of a few black churches. The vast majority of women worked as "domestics" and men worked in construction or in factories, the sole exceptions being Gray Lee, the minister of the Second Baptist Church, and Jenetta Hargrove, teacher, and her husband J.H. Hargrove, the minister of the Second M.E. church. Despite the establishment of a few African Americans owned small businesses that catered to the African American community, the limited employment opportunities for African Americans did not change until well into the mid-twentieth century. Even then, very few African Americans managed to attain positions of great influence in the town. One history book, after claiming that the Civil Rights led to the emergence of equal economic opportunity for blacks, listed only servicemen and athletes, three teachers, an assistant store manager of Sears, and two local politicians (a justice of the peace and a city councilman) as notable African Americans in the town (Unity County Historical Society, 1992).

In the 1920s, a sizable percentage of white Protestant residents of Unityville and Unity County joined the Klu Klux Klan. Local histories dismissed this as a passing fad, "the 'in' thing to do" that was limited to "a couple of Klan parades in town and a few cross burnings" (p. 131) or claimed that is was the design of mostly outsiders who passed through in a "monster" procession while "disapproving but silent spectators watched" (McFadden, 1968, p. 292). This view wildly underestimated the influence of the Klan in the county. According to the data from a 1925 internal review of Klan membership, over 32 percent of the native-born white male population of Unity County were identified by the local Kleagle as KKK members, making Unity County home to the seventh highest percentage of Klan membership (out of 92 counties) in the state (Moore, 1991, p. 48). In fact, as the historian Leonard Moore pointed out, the likely percentage of white Protestant males who joined the Klan at its peak must have been significantly higher since the "native-born white male" category includes Catholics and second generation immigrants and does not take into account the estimated 30 to 40 percent decline in Klan membership that took place during the early spring of 1925 (p. 47).[26] Various issues of the *Fiery Cross*, the mouthpiece of the KKK in Indianapolis, include advertisements for several Unityville stores[27] and stories about the establishment of a KKK chapter for women, a standing room only KKK meeting at the auditorium of the city building, and even a small procession of woman dressed in KKK regalia for the funeral of a friend ("Unityville, IN has Big Meeting," 1923). The cover page of the School Organizations section of the 1923 Unityville high school yearbook contains a picture of a Klan member with a whip and gun. Klan activity was high throughout the state; Unityville was no exception.

At the same time, recent historians attributed the rise of the KKK in Indiana more to fears about modernization, anti-Catholicism, and xenophobia than specific hostilities toward African Americans, which they added, was certainly unexceptional for the time.[28] This was likely to be the case in Unityville as the only recorded act of violence in the town was the burning down of the Catholic Church in 1923. Although it was common knowledge that members of the KKK were responsible, no one was arrested. Accounts in both the [Unity] *Democrat* and [Unity] *Republican* failed to even mention the suspicion of KKK involvement.[29] The appeal of the Klan and its support for "100% pure Americanism" represented a powerful counter narrative to the Melting Pot. It was an ideology where everyone had their own place, some outside of the country. One plausible reason why so little emphasis was placed on the African American community in KKK publications like the *Fiery Cross* and in the community of Unityville was because de facto segregation effectively prevented members of the African American community from encroaching on the perceived (spiritual, material and political) domain of white Protestants. Nevertheless, given the considerable intimidation against African Americans experienced in neighboring counties, the Klan's presence in the town could only have caused fear and apprehension among the African American community.[30] The *Indianapolis Recorder*, the city's only black newspaper, certainly viewed the Klan with deep suspicion. In fact, there was evidence that suggested the Klan's close identification with the Republican Party convinced a significant percentage of African Americans in Indiana to vote, for the first time, the Democrat ticket or in many cases, to simply not vote at all (Thornbrough, 1961, p. 612).

Though KKK members won the governorship and a majority in the state legislature in 1925, the popularity of the Klan in Unityville and the rest of Indiana nosedived in 1926 following a series of scandals and high-level corruption.

The interwar period proceeded with very little structural change to segregation and few resources to maintain the separate but equal system. During the depression, the Frederick Douglas school underwent some remodeling with recovery program funds provided by the federal government (Unity County Historical Society, 1992, p. 58) and there were reports in 1940 of a city council discussion to turn an abandoned building into a recreational center for African Americans.[31] The councilmen, according to the *Unity Republican*'s account, ultimately decided that although the current center is "entirely inadequate" and "certainly no credit to the city" it was better to save park funds until a more suitable alternative was found (*Unity Republican*, 1942).[32] It does bear mentioning that since Frederick Douglas only went to sixth grade, some academically talented African Americans did attend the white high school prior to integration. But this number, according to the yearbooks of the period, was quite low. Typically, just one or two African American students graduated each year.[33] Other than a few places of employment, the two communities lived apart from each other; they attended separate schools, churches and social functions.

While de facto segregation remained intact even after the integration of schools in 1949, ideas about race in Unityville and elsewhere changed dramatically during and after the Second World War. Although school integration (as mandated by the state) lacked the heroic battles and public drama of the civil rights movement in the South, there was a noticeable sea change in the mental landscape of both Black and white Americans. For one, African Americans became increasingly more vocal about their dissatisfaction with the status quo; organizations like the NAACP and the Federation of Associated Clubs vigorously advocated for school and societal integration. As early as the 1930s some Indiana politicians, especially the few African American legislators, called for an end to segregation in hotels, theatres and public places (Thornbrough, 1987, p. 306). While this failed, the fight to secure equal access to public accommodations continued throughout the 1940s. The Second World War contributed to this movement as African American soldiers returning from the war refused to accept second class status. As a writer of the African American daily, *Chicago Defender*, put it, "Hitler is dead in Germany, but Hitlerism goes marching on in the United States. Wherever a Negro is forced to take a back seat in a bus, wherever a Black man must pay a tribute on his right to vote, wherever color is the criterion for admission to a theater or restaurant, Hitlerism is still alive" ("Hitler is Dead," 1945).

School integration in Unityville occurred with little public fanfare and largely avoided the public displays of racial tension and conflict experienced in many Indiana towns during this time. School integration did not, for instance, trigger wide-scale social protest like it did in Gary when over 600 angry white students successfully picketed on the streets against the transfer of 24 Black students to their high school.[34] Nor was there a question of establishing a separate high school for African American students as the Indianapolis board (led by Clemens Vonnegut, the man who spearheaded the fight for German instruction) had done in 1927 when it founded Crispus Attacks High School.[35] For one thing, there simply wasn't enough money or student numbers to do so. The small and non-threatening size of the African American community probably also contributed to the smooth transition. Yet it was the town's collective experience of a series of events that, perhaps more than anything else, paved the way for school integration.

While it took the Great War to dramatically change the situation for the German population, it was the road to the state high school basketball championship that epitomized the complex relationship between the Black and white community of Unityville. Before the civil rights movement had gained real traction, The Unityville coach, himself an outsider, shocked the town and state by making his team the first of any white schools in Indiana to start three Black basketball players. In the beginning of the season, the Unityville White Eagles, were ridiculed by local residents as the "Black Eagles." As the team gained notoriety and the nickname passed through the lips of angry spectators from opposing teams, the Unityville community rose to the defense of their players and, in a sense, made many of the struggles these players experienced a matter of defending town pride. These incidents, which were not confined to isolated cases of threats and insults but included the indignity of constant verbal and physical intimidation and the logistical problem of finding a hotel or restaurant that welcomed Black patrons, could no longer be ignored by the white players and the white citizens of Unityville (Graham & Cody, 2006).[36] What began as a problem only experienced by the Black community came into full view so that it was not even uncommon for white residents to complain of racist referees or advocate for the integration of college sports.

By the end of the season, the topic of segregation, an unspoken facet of life in Unityville, became at least partially exposed to public discourse as a problem to address. In a banquet honoring the team, the principal of Frederick Douglas optimistically proclaimed to a church crowd:

> I am deeply proud to be connected with the [Unityville] school system because it has proven its belief in the fundamental principles of American Democracy. Not only in

sports, but in every activity, each and every pupil, regardless of race, creed, or considerations of family influences of the lack of it, is given and encouraged to use every opportunity to develop his or her talents to the fullest. Democracy is practiced as well as taught in our [Unityville] schools. (Graham & Cody, 2006, p. 81)

Meanwhile, the local paper, the *Unity Democrat*, approvingly published an open letter in defense of integrating college sports.

An open letter to K.L. (Tug) Wilson, Commissioner, Big Nine Conference) From John Whitaker

Dear Mr. Wilson, I attended the Indiana state finals Saturday and saw [Unityville's] great team content for the state title. The outstanding starts for [Unityville] were [Don Hall, Jim Murray, and Marcel Johnson]. Three Negro boys … Virtually every coach who was in Indianapolis Saturday was agreed on two things (1) THAT [DON HALL] OF [UNITYVILLE] WAS THE CLASSIEST INDIVIDUAL PLAYER EVER TO APPEAR ON AN INDIANA HIGH SCHOOL FLOOR (2) THAT THE ATTITUDE AND CONDUCT OF THE NEGRO CONTESTANTS WERE ABOVE REPROACH AT ALL TIMES.

The point is, Mr. Wilson, we keep hearing that the Big Nine conference has an "unwritten agreement" not to use Negroes in basketball. If so, WHY? If the biggest, braggingest athletic conference in the middle of the greatest country in the world can use Negroes like Buddy Young, Ike Owen, Dallas Ward, Duke Slater, George Taliaferro and the like to draw $200,000 crowds for football … and Negroes like Jesse Owens and Eddie Tolan to win Olympic crowns … why can't it use them in basketball. (Open Letter, 1947)

Notwithstanding the higher standards implicitly held to Black players in this letter, these and other comments by the press indicated pride in the manner in which their Black players faced adversity and supported greater integration.[37] At the very least, these events prepared the mental ground for school integration when it occurred less than two years later.

At the same time, the strides made from school integration did not change the overall state of segregation. While students attended the same schools, Black children were still prohibited from playing in the white recreation centers, sitting in the white section of the theatre, or swimming in the public pool (Graham & Cody, 2006, p. 17). That would have to wait until the 1950s and 1960s civil rights movement. Unlike the case of the German population, it is difficult to point to a watershed moment when there was a concerted effort by all to integrate the African American community. Instead, integration proceeded gradually and on different levels and in some important respects inequality still exists today. Despite early attempts at gaining equal access to public accommodations, it was not until 1963 that the state legislature passed a law with teeth that equated "equal educational and employment opportunities and equal access to and use of public accommodations" with "civil rights" and granted oversight to a Civil Rights Commission (Thornbrough, 1987, p. 336). Though inequality was still evident, the white members of the community described the African American inhabitants of Unityville as having gradually achieved an insider status not granted to the transnational students in our study. Given their longtime presence and contributions to the town's history, these African American inhabitants play an integral role in the Unityville story. Even so, there are few African Americans in the schools and the percentage of the population is significantly lower (2019) than the state average.

Critical Historical Dialogue

Both the German and African American populations of Unityville experienced pressures to simultaneously conform with and separate from the mainstream community at large. Both groups jumped back and forth between insider and outsider status depending on the shifting contingencies of history. Members of both marginalized groups along with the rest of the town's population had to react to regional and national trends and challenges largely not of their choosing. Despite their distinct paths to becoming members of the Unityville community, both Germans and African Americans were caught in the narrative webs of monoculturalism and its ensuing battles between assimilation or exclusion.

These two vignettes also present a narrative of the past that can serve as a public history in the true Habermasian sense. That is, they underscore the historical context of the current collective values of the community, including its approach to recent immigrants *and* they also raise the opportunity for dialogue, by challenging arguments that history fates us to think of ourselves and others in the way that we do. Is it inevitable, for instance, that immigrants today follow the same Melting Pot pattern of the last century? For one, a closer look at the past reveal competing visions of what constitutes the Melting Pot and being American. Many leaders of the ethnic German population in Indiana believed in a path to becoming American that allowed one to maintain one's native language and strong elements of one's culture. That this vision ultimately failed to reach fruition does not mean that it shouldn't be considered in the present.

Critical ethnographers can use history as a way of taking stock and interrogating traditions. In an earlier theorization of the public's use of history, Habermas reminds the reader of a question posed by Karl Jaspers:

> Can one continue the traditions of German culture without also assuming historical liability for the form of existence in which Auschwitz was possible? … Is it possible to remain liable for the context in which such crimes had their origins and with which

one's own existence is interwoven, in any way other than through the solidarity of the memory of that which cannot be made good, in any way other than through a reflective and keenly scrutinizing attitude towards one's own identity-creating traditions? (Habermas, 1988, p. 47)

The same question can be asked of any culture with a past. Can we appeal to the culture and traditions of American democracy without also understanding it as a liability for the form of existence in which slavery is possible? Or can we appeal to the real benefits of the Melting Pot pattern without also understanding it as a liability for those who would maintain their native language and culture or for those who were the victims of the way that the Melting Pot metaphor was discriminately applied to specific ethnic groups, thereby strengthening racial segregation? These are questions that critical ethnographers can pose not only to the residents of the community under study, but to a general audience who also lives with the consequences of this shared past. The history of language policies and segregation in Unityville is not merely a local affair, but speaks to questions we all should ask, researchers included, of our inherited traditions. Critical ethnographers need history, then, to ground their work in a context of singularity and broaden it out to a more generalizable conversation about our state, regional or national values and traditions. There is no simple repetition of the same over time.

I conclude the chapter with three general points on the monoculturalist narrative which illustrate the power of history for critical projects and complicate the "same over time" adage.

On the Sources and Specific Impact of the Monoculturalist Narrative

Understanding the history of both the German and African American citizens of Unityville reveals how the dominant narrative of monoculturalism emerged in the town due to local and regional events and trends. The expectation that immigrants leave their language and culture behind has a complex and tangled history in this country as the case of the ethnic German population illustrates quite clearly. To what degree did these past experiences constitute stable patterns of behavior and interpretation? To what extent were these patterns passed down through the generations in ways that shaped the town's self-understanding and approach to the "newcomers?" To what extent was the loss of German language and culture inevitable? We viewed Harris' alternative interpretation of the Melting Pot to mean a reciprocal adaptation in which some form of bicultural and bilingual community would emerge. Is such a vision possible for current transnational communities, particularly for Latino/a/x students? Or what about the experiences of the African American community are applicable today? Could successes, like those inspired by the high school basketball team, be fostered in contemporary times in order to produce a climate of appreciation and acceptance? What could compel the district to move beyond such specific forms of appreciation to creating a climate of inclusive belonging? Is it the same over time? Does the town's current approach to "newcomers" necessarily have to reflect past trends and orientations? As you will see in Chapter 5, the story of how German-speaking immigrants became English-speaking residents was lost, leaving only the outcome of assimilation.

On the Inevitability of Monoculturalism

In an essay titled, "What is a People" Habermas (2001b) argues that "the idea of a 'spirit of the people'… always directed toward a real or imagined past, poses insurmountable difficulties for the future-oriented intentions of liberal republicanism" (p. 4). This has certainly been true with regard to the narrative of monoculturalism. There is an aura of inevitability in the very rhetoric of the monoculturalist narrative, a naturalizing effect that rendered the assimilation of Germans and other nineteenth and early twentieth century immigrants as part of the logical process of becoming Americans. One can easily see this in the matter-of-fact manner of one local historian: "As the years passed they took their places among their English-Speaking neighbors. The Americanization process worked steadily and the old ways gave way to the new, as is the way with all people everywhere" (Unity County Historical Society, 1992, p. 348). The normalization of this process makes this narrative a powerful lens through which to view "newcomers" today. Even teachers who reject the assimilative intent of this narrative often appeal to elements of the story in defense of their students. One teacher explained to me that her husband hires Mexicans because they are *hard workers* who do things that many of our white residents are too lazy to do. Another blamed the lion's share of intolerance on "white trash" students who lived on the outskirts of the town. They don't represent the people of Unityville. The relative outsiders who filled the administrative and teaching positions of the school also, ironically enough, reinforced this narrative in indirect ways. There was little attempt to critically explore the town's history, and most were reluctant to address issues of racism and intolerance in the school culture. School administrators and teachers tacitly reinforced the power of the monocultural narrative by emphasizing basic skills and vocational training as educational goals and by assuming that cultural norms and values of the "newcomer" students belong outside the school's orbit of influence.

On the Divergent Effects of the Monoculturalist Narrative

While the ethnic German population felt pressure to deemphasize their cultural distinctiveness and give up their language, the African American community faced a strong exclusionary force that resisted total acceptance of their community. The Melting Pot metaphor functioned differently for each of these cases. The manner in which "newcomers" adapt to their new surroundings and the town's willingness or refusal to accept the "newcomers" need not follow the same script. The context is certainly different. Until WWI, the German-American community enjoyed certain (white) privileges when compared to other immigrant groups, such as Chinese, South and East European Catholic and Jewish immigrants. Although they had to face anti-German sentiment, especially during the war, they never had to overcome the deep-seated racism or the legacy of slavery as did their African American neighbors. What it means to be included was and is different for each group. Contemporary transnational students are also different from one another and from other groups in history. Perhaps these differences could be better interrogated in order to understand the racialization of the assimilation tensions. When assimilation is treated as only a cultural phenomenon, the racialization remains a silent, but powerful force in the assimilationist process. In the next chapter we explore monocultural mythology of Unityville and its contemporary ramifications for how Unityville understood itself and others, some of which reflected an idealization of histories without knowledge of the actual histories. By bringing historical research into the ethnographic practice, we were able to critique the ways in which histories were retained as monocultural mythology.

Notes

1. Not only did Habermas defend the book, he also presented Goldhagen with the esteemed Democracy Prize.
2. This view of public history borrows from the ideas of neo-Marxist historians who participated in the History Workshop and Oral History Society of the 1980s. According to Spalding and Parker (2007), these historians emphasized human agency over economic structures and focused on three ideas. "Firstly, it was argued that individual and collective memories were not simple records of past events, but shaped and edited accounts. Secondly, that in the process of editing memories, individuals and communities created myths; stories whose content and emphasis underpinned the values of the individual or community. Thirdly, that such myths by shaping perceptions of the world, played a key role in determining how people would act" (p. 136).
3. For many researchers, history is a source of unending and impractical frustration: the more one investigates the past of a particular place or people, the more one realizes just how much is left to be explored. Given the tendency (particularly strong among doctoral students) to become too engrossed in theoretical digressions, one might reasonably ask why should any researcher risk entanglement in the webs of history? For those who already know what they will find before they find it, historical context and analysis falls in the same dreaded category as "theoretical framework"; a burdensome, though necessary, component of one's study that is best retro-fitted once one's conclusions are complete. I believe that this view of history misses the point. Though

intimidating and never-ending, history is a quintessentially human practice, both deeply rich and fallible. Like the subject of any good ethnography, there is always something lurking beneath the surface that begs further analysis. The inconclusiveness of history does not prevent researchers from making conclusions, but it does—if done correctly—accentuate the fact that all conclusions are fallible and open to further scrutiny.

4. It would be misleading to consider these the sole arbiters of the community self-understanding, especially since all but one was written before the 1990s and a great deal has changed in the community since then. Moreover, the narrative of monoculturalism is not unique to this town, but reflects the convictions of many throughout the state and country. Clearly the source of monoculturalism is not exclusive to this location. There are, however, good reasons why paying close attention to what the texts say and how they say it can provide valuable insight into the community and its self-understanding. First of all, the language of these texts is accessible, written in the language of the community, published by a local press that only recently closed shop in 2006. The self-referential character of many, make it appear that it was a collective affair—our town, our families of Unityville. The acknowledgments of many of the public histories indicate wide community support. In keeping with this genre of history writing, the authors depended on family members to contribute information for the large section devoted to biographical and genealogical accounts of notable families and religious communities of the town and county. Finally, most of these texts are readily accessible to the public in the public library, high school library and archives.

5. The town's population grew from around 10,000 inhabitants at the turn of the century to almost 20,000 today.

6. For a town that has never reached a population of more than 20,000 inhabitants, 50,000 in the county, the historical output is quite impressive. In addition to a number of shorter narratives written about specific communities and organizations, usually religious in character, I found eight local histories of Unity County or Unityville (Chadwick, 1977; *History of Unity County*, 1887; Karmire, 2006; McFadden, 1968; Unity County Historical Society, 1992; *Unity County, Indiana History and Families*, 1992; Wetnight, 1971).

7. "Subtle though it is," writes a member of the Unity County Historical Society in the forward of one such history, "a patriotic theme underlies this work, and makes 'Biography of a Town' incomparably better than ordinary history." McFadden, 1968, p. viii). In a forward of another history (Oliver, 1996) this sentiment is spelled out more clearly "Today it is different. Amid the social diversity and increased individualism that exists in present day [Unityville], a meaningful sense of community also persists—and it must be fostered in every generation or it will vanish. One of its components is shared American ideals; another is public awareness of the local past; a third is commitment to the future and common good" (p. 5). The same sentiment rings true of the other works on the town and region. Mostly written at the turn of the 19th century or in the latter half of the 20th century, these works treat history in a Whiggish, progressive fashion, employing a number of recognizable tropes to romantically describe the development of the community from its early frontier roots to the community it is now. See Moore (1996) for an account of how these tropes romanticize and gloss over crimes in the nation's past.

8. In a larger work, this study would include the history of the frontier and the dismissal of American Indian tribes. A community must start somewhere and all the self-descriptions of Unityville begin in the early 19th century when white man entered Indian territory and eventually settled in what is now Unity county. Unityville's most famous son, Charles Major, wrote a children's book, *Bears of Blue River,* about pioneer life in the 1820s. The town memorialized the book by erecting a statue of a boy holding two bears in the center of public square. (Originally

it was in front of the Charles Major Elementary School.) The Frontier is still very much a part of the narrative of monoculturalism, as its actors are seen to embody principles and values that are still celebrated by the community. In 1991, the historical society sponsored a Pioneer Fair, with Frontier Militia reenactments. McFadden (1968) tells the story through founding archetypes: the Indian fighter and perpetual adventurer who contributed to the founding of the territory and then quickly moved on to more exciting challenges; the prudential leader, who had the foresight to and the will to civilize, and the pioneer women, who "[f]ollowing 'her man' down the stump-pricked wilderness trail she helped him create a new home in an often hostile environment" (p. 38). While all writers mention the Delaware, Miami, and Potawatomi tribes, very few give them more than passing attention, i.e. that the Indians were pushed out, that the Potawatomi tribes were kind enough to cede their land for a road leading up to Michigan. The image that one is left with is of a wilderness tamed by pioneers of European descent. The reality is no doubt more complicated and morally problematic than this depiction suggests.

9. According to the 2017 U.S. census estimates, Hispanic Americans make up 8.4 of the city's population, up from 1.9 percent in 2000. While this percentage has certainly risen significantly in recent years, evidence suggests that the percentage of Hispanic Americans do not equal what seems to be a high percentage of German Americans living at the turn of the century.

10. Unityville was known as the "Furniture City of the Middle West" (*Unity County Interim Report*, 1992, p. xxxi).

11. Considered by the "race science" of the time to be superior to the undesirable Italian, Slovak, Hungarian, Jewish and other immigrant groups that entered the country at the turn of the century, Germans enjoyed what today we would call white privilege. This perception of Germans is still evident today. One contemporary town historian (of English descent) frequently refers to individuals of German stock as "vigorous workers," "diligent," "having sterling traits and praiseworthy characteristics" or "unimpeachable integrity and sound judgment." (Chadwick, 1977, p. 448.) Many of the prominent Germans at the time were also members of various so-called secret societies. See Chadwick, 1977; *History of Unity County*, 1887). There is also mention of a chapter of the Order of Harrugari society, a non-religious German-American singing organization established to preserve and protect German culture and German language. There was also a German Benevolent Society in 1870 (German Benevolent Society, 1870)

12. When St. Joseph Church was rebuilt, it was celebrated by a "dedicatory sermon by Rev. Joseph Chartrand, a model of scholarship, eloquence and forces, was listened to with great interest and profit by the large assemblage, a part of the discourse being in English and part in the German tongue, to suit his auditors who were about equally divided between the two nationalities" (Chadwick, 1977, p. 345).

13. The request was made by Unityville's Rev. J Rudolph, nephew to the founder of the order (*Historical sketch of the Convent and Academy of the Sisters of St. Francis*, 1901, p. 148). In the Unity County history, that date is different. The authors state the sisters founded two schools, St. Vincent in 1860 and St. Joseph in 1875. There is no mention of classes being conducted in German (Unity County Historical Society, 1992, p. 69).

14. In fact, the German-born pastor of Unityville German Evangelical Protestant Church taught German, Latin and Greek at the high school, and became the principal in 1885 (Fleming, n.d., "Zion United Church of Christ").

15. The tension between retaining the community's fluency in the German language and culture and giving it up to become "American" was undoubtedly present well before World War

I. This tension must have been palpable to the Unityville audience of the 1912 Unity County Chautauqua Fair who after enjoying the gypsy music of the Austro-Hungarian Orchestra and Bavarian and other German folk songs sung by the Tyrolean Alpine Singers listened to Miss Ruth Hemenway's reading of "The Melting Pot." Isreal Zangwill's (1906) "great immigration problem play," which as the program described it, tells the story of a Russian aristocrat, Russian Jew and German conductor who come together to embody a symphony of immigrants who choose the path of Americanization and leave Europe, with "her pomp and chivalry built on a morass of crime and misery."

16. According to the U.S. census "2013–2017 American Community Survey 5-Year Estimates," 24.4 percent of Unityville residents are of German ancestry. Very few of them (0.1%) speak an Indo-European language other than English at home. At least until the 1990s, Unityville boasted German clubs and celebrated German festivals. For example, one local newspaper advertises "German Heritage Sunday" where they have "German foods prepared from old recipes" and where "everyone is invited to wear old-fashioned or pioneer type attire." There is also a "German Band." (German Heritage Sunday, 1976). According to Unity County History (1992), there was an annual "German dinner" or "Germanfest" held at the Presbyterian Church or elsewhere from 1988 to 1991. This event is sponsored by the society.

17. The authors also mention that in 1918, the German Evangelical Church changed their name to the First Evangelical Church.

18. This is true even in places heavily populated with people of German ancestry. According to 2000 census data, less than 1% of the population of Wisconsin speaks German at home, while over 42% claim German ancestry.

19. He states, "Perhaps it is not a pleasant thought for the German to contemplate: that he is being digested by American institutions. Nor, on the other hand, is it any more agreeable to the Anglo-American to see his peculiar idiosyncrasy digested by a different national spirit. Nevertheless, a mutual process of digestion goes on, and that, too very rapidly. It does not need the mind of a philosopher to perceive great mutual advantages arising therefrom. Both races are originally Teutonic, and both are renowned for industry. But there is an antithesis in their characters. The German is internally rich, theoretical, inventor of methods, scientific. The Anglo-Saxon is the practical-will character, the creator of legal forms, the inventor of useful appliances. From such a broad basis, as these opposite characteristics give, what a super-structure will arise from their fusion (Schlossman, 1983, p. 151)!

20. The law states that if "twenty-five or more children in attendance at any school of a township, town or city, shall so demand it shall be the duty of the School Trustee or Trustees of said township, town or city, to procure efficient teachers, and introduce the German language, as a branch of study, into such schools and the tuition in said schools shall be without charge" (Ramsey, 2002, p. 291).

21. For instance, on In May of 1916, a letter was sent to the school board of trustees for public schools in Indianapolis stating that "We have been reliably informed that the children in at least some of the public schools in the City of Indianapolis have been and are being permitted and required to sing the 'Star Spangled Banner' and other patriotic songs in the German language. The language of the United States of America is the English language. The 'Star Spangled Banner' and 'America' are national songs and should be invested with the same high quality of affection and respect that is paid to the flag." This was just the beginning of the end of German language instruction in the city (Ellis, 1954a, p. 372).

22. In 1923, the Supreme Court of the United States determined, in Meyer v. Nebraska, that it was unconstitutional to prohibit the use of foreign languages in parochial and private schools (Ross, 1994, p. 130).
23. To protect the identity of the town, I have changed the name of the athletes, school mascot, name of the school for African American students, and other details of the event.
24. There are plenty of other examples as well. Even in the 20th century, there was not so uncommon to find language that reinforces racial divisions and stereotypes. The following story found in the *Unity Republican* in 1933 is a particularly offensive example: Mrs. Lulu Sanders, colored, is going to take up the study of the Chinese language in her spare time. Recently, she had an experience which, in her opinion, makes knowledge of the language imperative. She went to the laundry here to get a parcel of collars. She told the clerk, a young Chinese, but she couldn't make him understand. "Collahs, Collahs" she kept shouting, and demonstrated with a handkerchief about her neck, which she kept tightening until she was in imminent danger of choking herself. The young Chinese, apparently under the impression she was not exactly accountable, led her politely to the door in an effort to get her out of his place before she met with an untimely end. Finally, however, she saw a bunch of collars and succeeded in making him understand (Miss Lulu Sanders, 1933).
25. In one history book, there is mention of rumors that one house in Unityville served as a station for the underground railroad.
26. The steep decline in membership came in 1925 when David Curtiss Stephenson, the grand dragon of the KKK in Indiana, was convicted of raping and killing a young white woman. The governor of Indiana, a KKK member who relied on the political support of the organization, refused to pardon him.
27. Known as the "Shock Troops of Klandom," businessmen and women who advertised in the Fiery Cross were routinely thanked for their support in the newspaper, with the added gesture "They expect and deserve the patronage of all Protestant Americans."
28. Not surprisingly, there are some notable differences in interpretation of motivation of the movement. Some emphasize class and modernization, while others anti-communism and national socialist trends that lead to fascism of the European variety (Blee, 1991; MacLean, 1994; Moore, 1991).
29. While researching this case in the archives, a woman there told me, matter-of-factly, that it was the KKK and everyone in town knew it. In fact, she added, her uncle was one of them.
30. Despite its clear bigotry and frequent intimidation against minority groups, the Indianan Klan was not particularly violent. In fact, there were no recorded lynchings in Indiana during the 1920s (Madison, 2001, pp. 37–42).
31. In fact, there was talk of building a new school but that never materialized. On May 10, 1930 a reporter for the *Indianapolis Recorder* complains: "Just as the writer predicted colored children would get no school building this year, the superintendent of the school board (Unityville) told parents and teachers they would erect them a school building next year. The writer told them it was hot air and now shows that it was right ... our taxpayers and colored citizens deserve better treatment" (News of the State of Indiana, 1930).
32. Apparently, no park alternative was suitable until after the integration of schools when it was decided that the old Frederick Douglas school would become the new recreation center.
33. The yearbooks were a useful source of information on both the possible ambitions for black high school students as well as the interpretations of them by the white yearbook editors. The profile of Ophelia P., included the description "a brilliant student and an honor to her race." She later

went on to become a teacher at Frederick Douglas and taught there, until her death in 1945. The profiles of the two black high school students in 1914 are also revealing:

Clarence C.:	Member of debating society, "some" orator
Character:	Queer
Manner:	Eloquent
How Comes to School:	On his feet
Ambitions:	A second Booker T.
Maria W.:	One who praises Public Speaking
Known as:	Woolie
Character:	"loveable"
Manner:	"Stylish"
How Comes to School:	"With Mabel"
Ambition:	Tuskeegee

34. The protest was eventually successful as the black students were transferred out of the school (Thornbrough, 1961, p. 606).
35. For a detailed discussion of the controversy in Indianapolis, see Warren's "The Evolution of Secondary Schooling for Black in Indianapolis" (Gibbs, 1993).
36. To give one example, the night before the semi-finals game, the black players were forced to stay in a small house behind the hotel. This event, according to Graham's and Cody's account, bothered the coach more than it did the black players who were used to such treatment (Graham & Cody, 2006, p. 56).
37. In fact, in the 1970s the high school gym was named after this player and he is routinely included in lists of the greatest and most popular residents of Unityville today.
38. Some references were fictionalized in order to protect the confidentiality of participants.

References[38]

1892–1893 Unityville City Directory and County Gazetteer: Colored Inhabitants Listed. (1893). Retrieved from website not included to protect participant confidentiality.

Blee, K.M. (1991). *Women of the Klan*. Berkeley, CA: University of California Press.

Chadwick, E.H. (1977). *Chadwick's history of Unity county, Indiana*. Indianapolis, IN: B.F. Bowen. (Original work published 1909)

Catholic Church Records. (1982). Retrieved from Unityville archives.

The Colored Orator. (1870, March 17). *National Volunteer*. Retrieved from Unityville archives.

Deák, I. (1997). Holocaust views: The Goldhagen controversy in retrospect. *Central European History, 30*(2), 295–307.

Ellis, F. (1954a). German instruction in the public schools of Indianapolis, 1869–1919, III. *Indiana Magazine of History, 50*(4), 357–380.

Ellis, F. (1954b). Historical account of German instruction in the public schools of Indianapolis, 1869–1919, II. *Indiana Magazine of History, 50*(3), 251–276.

First German Evangelical Zion Church Records. (n.d.). Retrieved from Unityville archives.

Fleming, P. (n.d.). Zion United Church of Christ. Retrieved from website not included to protect confidentiality.

German Benevolent Society. (1870, March 9). *Unity Republican*. Retrieved from Unityville archives.

German Heritage Sunday. (1976, September 28). *Unityville News*. Retrieved from Unityville archives.

Gibbs, W.L. (1993). *Indiana's African-American heritage*. Indianapolis: Indiana Historical Society.

Goldhagen, D. (1996). *Hitler's willing executioners: Ordinary Germans and the Holocaust*. New York, NY: Alfred A. Knopf.

Graham, T., & Cody, R.G. (2006). *Getting open*. New York, NY: Atria Books.

Habermas, J. (1988). Concerning the public use of history. *New German Critique, 44*, 40–50.

Habermas, J. (2001a). On the public use of history. In Pensky (Ed., Trans.), *The postnational constellation: Political essays* (pp. 26–37). Boston, MA: MIT Press.

Habermas, J. (2001b). What is people? The Frankfurt "Germanists' Assembly" of 1846 and the self-understanding of the humanities in the *Vormarz*. In Pensky (Ed., Trans.), *The postnational constellation: Political essays* (pp. 1–25). Boston, MA: MIT Press.

History of Unity County, Indiana. (1887). Brant & Fuller.

Hitler is dead, but not Hitlerism. (1945, May 12). ProQuest Historical Newspapers: *Chicago Defender (National Edition), 12*.

Karmire, P. (2006). *Black history, Unity County, Indiana*. Unityville, IN: P. Karmire.

Körner, A. (2000). "The arrogance of youth" A metaphor for social change?: The Goldhagen-Debate in Germany as generational conflict. *New German Critique, 80*, 59–76.

McFadden, M. (1968). *Biography of a town: Unityville, Indiana 1822–1962* (1st ed.). Unityville, IN: Tippecanoe Press.

MacLean, N. (1994). *Behind the mask of chivalry*. Oxford, England: Oxford University Press.

Madison, J.H. (2001). *A lynching in the heartland: Race and memory in America*. New York, NY: Palgrave Macmillan.

Miss Lulu Sanders. (1933, June 10). *Unity Republican*. Retrieved from Unityville archives.

Moore, L.J. (1996). Good old-fashioned new social history and the twentieth-century American right. *Reviews in American History, 24*(4), 555–573.

Moore, L.J. (1991). *Citizen Klansmen: The Ku Klux Klan in Indiana, 1921–1928*. Chapel Hill: University of North Carolina Press.

News of the State of Indiana. (1930, May 10). *Indianapolis Recorder, 5*.

Oliver, B. (1996). *Unityville: A Pictorial History*. St. Louis, MO: G. Bradley.

Open Letter. (1947, April 2). *Unity Democrat*. Retrieved from Unityville archives.

Probst, G.T. (1989). *The Germans in Indianapolis, 1840–1918*. Indianapolis: German-American Center & Indiana German Heritage Society.

Ramsey, P.J. (2002). The war against German-American culture: The removal of German-language instruction from the Indianapolis schools, 1917–1919. *Indiana Magazine of History, 98*(4), 285–303.

Ramsey, P.J. (2009). In the region of Babel: Public bilingual schooling in the Midwest, 1840s–1880s. *History of Education Quarterly, 49*(3), 267–290.

Ross, W.G. (1994). *Forging new freedoms: Nativism, education and the constitution, 1917–1927*. Lincoln: University of Nebraska Press.

Schlossman, S.L. (1983). Is there an American tradition of bilingual education? German in the public elementary schools, 1840–1919. *American Journal of Education 91*(2), 139–186.

The Sisters of St. Francis Community. (1901). *Historical sketch of the Convent and Academy of the Sisters of St. Francis in Oldenburg, Indiana: And of the work of their community in the United States.*

Sloane, P. (Director). (1929). *Hearts in Dixie* [Motion Picture]. United States: Fox Film Corporation.

Spalding, R., & Parker, C. (2007). *Historiography: An introduction*. New York, NY: Manchester University Press.

Thornbrough, E.L. (1987). Breaking racial barriers to public accommodations in Indiana, 1935 to 1963. *Indiana Magazine of History, 83*(4), 301–343.

Thornbrough, E.L. (1961). Segregation in Indiana during the Klan era of the 1920's. *The Mississippi Valley Historical Review, 47*(4), 594–618.

Unity County Chautauqua Fair official program. (1912). Retrieved from the website not included to protect participant confidentiality.

Unity County Historical Society. (1992). *Unity County, Indiana History and Families* (limited ed.). Paducah, KY: Turner.

Unity County Interim Report: Indiana Historic Sites and Structures Inventory. (1992). Historic Landmarks Foundation of Indiana.

Unity Republican. (1870, April 13). Retrieved from Unityville archives.

Unity Republican. (1942, July 30). Retrieved from Unityville archives.

Unityville, IN has Big Meeting. (1923, March 23). *Fiery Cross.*

Wetnight, J.R. (1971). *Unity county, riled up!* Unityville, IN: Tippecanoe Press.

Zangwill, I. (1906). *The melting pot*. Retrieved from http://www.vdare.com/fulford/melting_pot_play.htm

"Hispanics are the New Niggers" and Other Monocultural Myths: Narrative Reconstructions[1]

A cultural history of homogenization remains yet to be written, but its historical impact is so overwhelming that its key features need to be studied on their own.

(Daniele Conversi, 2007, p. 156)

The (predominantly white middle-class) educators in Unityville thought that assimilation was a worthwhile goal for both practical and ethical reasons. The American assimilation story was ideologically grounding for them and gave them a sense of purpose with respect to the im/migrant, transnational students. I remember a time in my own life when this was also the case. I thought of how success in the United States seemed dependent upon doing things the "American way"—speaking English, understanding American mores and taking up American values, though these ideas were never totalizing for me. I was living in South Texas and I was aware that to say people should do it "our" way was complicated. The "American" way was not monolithic and certainly did not mean ONLY speak English or only have one set of (middle-class white) values. When I encountered assimilationism in Unityville, I was no stranger to its logic. I remember teachers asking me, "Shouldn't they [the "newcomer" students] have to speak English in schools? Isn't that the *right* thing to do?" I remembered feeling some moral under-current myself about American assimilationism, the fought-after melting pot. A white middle class youngster, I remembered the message that assimilation was a moral, personal, and strategic "choice" people made. But, in fact, it was not a choice I had made. I was born into the community to which everyone else was expected to assimilate. As I began to interact with Unityville expectations for assimilation, I found their arguments and stories in support of assimilation resonated with my own sociocultural background, distanced from my thinking by decades at that point. Their stories were constituted of cultural frames of reference to which I had been exposed. I know that they are not unique to Unityville.

One day, Ed was talking with one of the administrators at Junction High School. Somewhat out of the blue, but knowing they were talking with a IU-Unityville team member, the administrator said,

> Mexican-American, African-American—that doesn't matter. We're all Americans" (with hand gesture and emotion behind the words). The administrator continued on to say that when African-Americans use "the African," "they are separating themselves from us." "We're all Americans, that's *it* [stresses "it", pauses briefly]. Don't tack that on" [said with emotion, meaning don't tack "African" on to "American"].[2]

The "us" mentioned by the administrator above was not an inclusive us. This monocultural frame of reference is perilous. It's threat is intensified as the U.S. government put "other people's" children in cages at the southern border (Long, 2019) while the U.S. Department of Justice (August 2019) simultaneously argued to the Supreme Court that the Trump administration had the right to end Obama era DACA benefits for Dreamers (Bernal, 2019). The administration's protectionist attitudes toward southern im/migrants brandishes heinous cultural myths of monocultural patriotism and allows white nationalism to reign unchecked. We as a society need a better understanding how such myths are culturally anchored and retained. We need to understand how these myths contribute to racism and white privilege. About the time Donald Trump was elected president, I published an article articulating how monocultural myths were at work in Unityville (Dennis, 2016), but it was over a decade before the election of Donald Trump that our work in Unityville brought out these myths and their meanings in this local context. It was the high schoolers of our Project who have become the "Dreamers" of today, whose very existence in the U.S. is under attack.

Members of the Unityville School District lived out their monocultural tales. Tales that begged to be more fully articulated. This chapter details the reconstruction of underlying narratives, organizing them into different types of monocultural narratives. The narratives were not the direct tellings of participants but were instead pointed towards as explanations for the storytellers' educational perspectives and decisions regarding the transnational, border-crossing students. News headlines that captured the nation's attention during the 2016 presidential election paralleled the vacuous "stories" we heard the decade before. In both cases, storytellers did not own responsibilities for bearing out the facticity of those tales. Critical ethnography is particularly well-suited to the application of narrative inquiry that I develop here—whereby stories are reconstructed from the lived activities and vocalized platitudes planted into ordinary conversations.

The narrative reconstructions explicated socially acceptable stories and corresponding identities and their meaningful ramifications for sustaining monocultural myths. I used the concept "story seeds" (Dennis, 2016) to indicate that these stories were not told in full. Instead the story seeds were reference points, contested to some extent, that participants used to indicate who they were in the ongoing monocultural "story" of the school. The seeds corresponded with activities and educational decisions. They implied whole narratives but lacked the factual detail that would be necessary to actually tell the story as a whole or, and even more importantly, to challenge the story.

> Throughout the ethnographic period and in an attempt to locate themselves in the challenges they were experiencing, teachers narrated a set of monocultural story myths using common story seeds. These story seeds simultaneously contrasted a presumed, collective white/we/educators position with a presumed newcomer, non-white, student position—as if both positions were unified and homogeneous. I used the word 'presumed' because the facticity of the stories was not really at stake. Through these story seeds, educators positioned themselves as people whose families had overcome the challenges of being newcomers by doing things like giving up their native country's language. Yet, people who voiced the story seeds were not able to fill in the factual blanks for their families—they had no idea when their ancestors came to the country, how they experienced the language shift, what schooling was like for them, and so forth. (Dennis, 2016, p. 1070)

As Noble (2018) wrote, "Our possessive investment in whiteness creates an inability to recognize how white hegemonic ideas about race and privilege mask the ability to see real social problems" (p. 168). Critical ethnographic work must contribute to the unmasking. In this chapter, I describe the ways in which narrative reconstructions indicated cultural structures and engaged us in a dialogue over culturally instantiated identities of privilege and marginalization. The reconstructed stories illustrate the power of unspoken expectations and communal silences. Since the full stories were neither articulated nor questioned, their cultural wielding stifled reflection, self-awareness, and liberation.

Narrative Performances: A Brief Methodological Exploration

If you want to know me, then you must know my story, for my story defines who I am. And if I want to know *myself*, and gain insight into the meaning of my own life, then I, too, must come to know my own story.

(McAdams, 1993, p. 11)

While I don't believe that stories define us, I do expect that they articulate aspects of who we are and resource our self-thinking. By making stories of ourselves more explicit, we learn things about ourselves—who we "other," what we desire, how our sense of self is culturally structured, and so on. Because our subjectivity is never completely knowable or expressable (by either ourselves or others), recognition is the means by which our selves are validated by others. That is, who we are is constituted in part by how we are recognized. Social recognition relies on social expectations, norms, and values. All of these are expressable in the form of stories. In this way, narratives can serve a praxis function—they can provide opportunities for others to recognize our validity, our worthwhileness.[3] Narratives are not representations of life; they are performative reconstructions of doing and being which are socially and contextually meaningful. Performance here means that they are active doings that imply interpretive possibilities. Implicit narratives can be reconstructed from verbal aspects of our interactions and from ongoing activities through which participants are regularly engaged.

[Gough] argues that the ways we give meaning to ourselves and others and the world at large sometimes happens through stories, of which we are largely unaware or which are taken for granted. Reflecting critically on the stories that we read, hear, live and tell may help us to understand how we can use them more responsibly and creatively and free ourselves from their constraints. (Webster & Mertova, 2007, p. 7)

As ethnographers, we watched and listened closely to the ways in which monoculturalism was being sustained. The educators in Unityville often dropped references ("story seeds") to social archetypical stories as a way to justify things they were doing in the school relative to the transnational students. These story seeds were different from the richly personal accounts that have become the hallmark of good quality narrative research (Kim, 2015). As seeds they were not easily refuted or substantiated with any level of precision. The most important part of the meaning of the seeded stories for the storytellers was the way it positioned them in relation to others.

In this section, I describe the methodological approaches I used in the analysis of the story seeds. Specifically, I describe how I reconstructed the narratives from seeds, articulated deep structural contexts, and claimed critical insights.

Reconstructing the Narratives

Reconstructing the stories involved using the seeds to write out the referenced story in very bare terms. This was followed with an articulation of identity claims as we/self/other configurations. Each of those configurations indicated an historical "we" that acted as validator for the current perspective. Storytellers identified themselves with the "we," but did not precisely locate themselves within it. Analyzing narratives helps to bring into discourse any hidden biases/interests, contradictory values, and minoritizing discourses (Webster & Mertova, 2007, p. 9). To do this analysis, I began by reconstructing meaning fields and validity horizons. I briefly describe how to do those analyses below. I deepened the initial analyses by focusing on backgrounded claims. Then I discuss the reconstruction of the narratives themselves.

Meaning Fields and Reconstructive Horizon Analyses. These basic forms of reconstructing meaning are intuitive to the work that qualitative researchers do, just as they are intuitive to our everyday efforts to understand one another. I demonstrated a meaning field in Chapter 3 when I wrote about the ethical argumentation for separating families at the U.S. border. But here I will describe the process in more detail. Then I will follow that with a description of a reconstructive horizon analysis.[4]

To write out a meaning field, one assumes the perspective of the actor. It is important to remember that the first person position involves an awareness of how others would interpret one's actions so the meaning field, though written in first person language, is an articulation of the plausible and varied field of possible interpretations or meanings social others and the self might infer from the action (action here includes talk, silences, and so on). Usually we do not have to write these out, because we intuit the field of meaning. It is bounded, which is important to notice because some critics of qualitative inquiry make a basic error when they argue that an act could meaning anything, that there is no way to winnow down a plausible interpretation. Actually, the meaning of acts are socially bounded and contextual, thus the articulation of meaning fields helps to make that point in very specific ways.

One day, while out on the playground at an elementary school, I was talking with one of the (white) teachers about what she expected in the future for "newcomer" students in Unityville schools. She turned to me and said, "Well, you know, Hispanics are the new the niggers." We IU-Unityville team members heard this statement repeated multiple times, either in this way or as "Hispanics are the new blacks." As awful as it is for me to write that phrase as said, it would be wrong to hide it. This became one of our story seeds. Let's begin by writing out a possible meaning field.

"Hispanics and blacks are different from us." AND "We didn't always have Hispanic students." AND "We didn't always have black students." AND "Using the word 'Niggers' is an okay way to refer to black people" AND "You and I are both white." AND "I know that you are interested in the newcomers." AND "I am not that worried about what will happen with them" Because "We've been through this before and it seems to have worked out just fine with the black kids." OR "I am worried" Because "We've been through this before." (Actually, because of the tone of speech I could tell the teacher wasn't worried so we will cross out this second possibility.) AND "I expect you not to be offended by my use of the word 'nigger'." AND "These kids are different from you and me."

The meaning field is an articulation of the range of inferences to which we might respond when acting in relation to what has just transpired. In this case, I might have said, "Oh, tell me about when you started having black kids in the schools." Or I could have responded by saying, "I would like to reflect on why you used the 'n-word' in your description of black kids." Or I could have expressed my own personal feelings, letting the teacher know that I was offended by the use of the n-word. You can see that there are a variety of ways one might respond. In the first example, I am largely acting in acceptance of the range of inferences and moving forward into the possible story. In the second response I would have been actually challenging several of the possible inferences—namely, I would be challenging that the speaker and I were the same, that the n-word was an appropriate word for a white person to use in this context, and that perhaps I was offended by its use. The third articulation of possible responses moves the conversation toward my own need to distinguish myself from the teacher identifying us as the same and seeds judgement of the speaker.

A reconstructive validity horizon takes an even closer look at the meaning and articulates the various validity assumptions that must be made if the act is to be interpreted as meaningful. The validity categories are drawn primarily from Habermas's TCA (1985, 1987), with Carspecken's (1996) developments. Recall the validity distinctions presented in Chapter 1 between objectivity, subjectivity, and normativity. Carspecken added identity claims to this list and argued that the category of normativity also included evaluative type claims. In addition to these four categories of validity claiming, a reconstructive horizon also expresses the horizon nature of meaning by locating reconstructed validity claims in background and foreground relations. The backgrounded claims help make the foregrounded claim understandable, but they are almost always tacit. As with a horizon, the background can be shifted to the foreground, producing a new background. This is one way of pointing out the contextualization of meaning. Here is an example of an overly simplified version of a reconstructive horizon analysis.

We holistically grasp the meaning of actions in our everyday contexts, but when we are conducting analyses, we take a more refined, precise, detailed look at the meaning, we write out a lot of the subtlety. These reconstructions help us to grasp both the types of validity claims in the meaning and the levels of potential explicitness. The reconstruction in Table 5.1, explicates the ways in which the teacher made assumptions about me. In my response I could have called those assumptions into question—for example, I might have said, "I don't like it when I hear white people use racially offensive language." If my inferences misunderstood her, then she would be able to clarify. Clarifications, misunderstandings, and disagreements will usually make some aspect of the validity horizon more explicit (or foregrounded). One other point to make is that it is possible that there were backgrounded validity claims that both the teacher and I took for granted about our whiteness that are not articulated because of some limitations in my own critical awareness or conscientização. This is where having a peer to review the horizon analyses would be helpful. Working on a diverse team afforded easy and rich opportunities for such reviews. Both meaning field and validity reconstructions were implicit to the narrative reconstructions that I performed on each of the story seeds.

Narrative Reconstruction. Like all narratives, there are minimally two layers—the interactive storytelling layer and the narrative layer referred to in the storytelling. The seedings that I analyzed were set within interactive scenes, leaving traces of social narratives that I was able to reconstruct from those articulated seeds. The reconstructive link between the seed and the narrative was a generative one. Even if the whole story had been told, we would find the seed inherently constitutive of the story's meaning. The social narratives that I reconstructed were weak on fact and rich in moral-imperative and identity positionings. In some instances, the stories were told as if they were personal: The personal details were missing, but the personal identifications with the stories were intact.

By reconstructing narratives from bits given repeatedly over time, critical ethnographers are able to meaningfully articulate more of the story substance in general terms, as a story typification.[5] This is only possible if the researchers share enough cultural understanding since the reconstructions are grounded in what would make sense for participants. Because ethnographers are typically in the field a long time and draw on their own field-based interpersonal relationships, they are particularly well equipped for such analyses. Certainly, this was true for our work in Unityville.

In general, the validity of the reconstructions themselves depends on how well those interpretations resonate or are recognizable to both insiders and relative outsiders and how consistent they are with observations over time. Educational ethnographer Geoffrey Walford (2007) argued that it is not good practice to write fiction and call it research. Reconstructive work is creative in that it requires position-taking with storytellers and broader intersubjective inferencing, but it is, all the while, tethered to what we claim was said, what we witnessed happening, and what we participated in. That is, one aspect of the interpretive process involves making objective inferences. Even so, the meaning of the story is best not thought of as an account of facts, but rather as an interactive moment whose meaning must first be understood within the context of the storytelling itself. In this way, the stories here are not made up, they are developed through reconstructions inferred as stories, just as the tellers might have anticipated of the listeners.

Across all of the interview and observation data, I reconstructed six story seeds associated with monoculturalism that were repetitively voiced by the white educators (and the white high school students) at all of the schools involved in our study. These seeds also represented points of disagreement among educators. The monocultural myth was something that educators in the district believed, in general, about their own schools. That is, they acted and talked *as if* they believed that the schools should be (and had been) monocultural. These story seeds both promoted that grand myth and provided an opportunity to argue against it. I have named the six seeds (1) "When my grandfather came here …"; (2) "Latinos are the new blacks"; (3) "Sink or swim"; (4) "Go home"; (5) "Speak English if you're gonna come here"; and (6) "I read it in the crime section." Even these reconstructed stories are not meant to be taken as whole in their own right. Rather, they indicated a normalized story substance that was drawn on and referenced in socially meaningful ways without it being wholly developed or specified. As such, they provided actors with typified assumptions through which to connect with one another as members of the Unityville community.

Through the reconstruction of story seeds it was, also, possible to reconstruct the identity claims of the narrators in relation to the transnational student "others" as was depicted in Table 5.1. There is a lot written about the idea that people narrate coherent identities for themselves. Drawing on George Herbert Mead's (1934) work, we can think of the self as ongoing activity having two dialogically connected processes—one is the construction of a "me" through actions that form recognizable claims to an identity within given social contexts. The other is the process of knowing one is authoring the self for others to understand and recognize. This second aspect of the self is not tangible and, yet, it is "responsible for human feelings of agency or 'the degree to which an action is unreflectively grasped as one's own and oneself is grasped as its source' (Blasi, 1988, p. 229)" (Blasi as referenced by McAdams, 1993, p. 302). This "always-already-gone-by" sense of self can, at best, be reconstructed through the actions that point toward it. Our basic desires to know ourselves are always thwarted by this inevitable inability to

Table 5.1 Reconstructive Horizon Analysis. "Well, you know, Hispanics are the new the n-words."

Horizon	Possible Objective Validity Claims	Possible Subjective Validity Claims	Possible Normative-Evaluative Validity Claims	Possible Identity Claims
Foregrounded Inferences	"Hispanics are new here." "We've had new students here before." "We know what we are doing," "You are interested in the Hispanic students." "I have been around this school long enough to know its history."	"I feel confident in my own knowledge."	"It's okay to use the word 'nigger' *with you*." Teachers should know the race of their students. Teachers should know the history of racial demographics in their school.	"I identify you and I as the same, *racially*" "We are not like Hispanics or Blacks." "We are different than those students."
Mid-Grounded Inferences	"Blacks were new here once." "Black students are fine." "Neither you nor I are Hispanic or Black." "Race is an important distinction across people." "Race makes a person different." "Being new is a mark of your time in an area."	"I do not feel an affinity with either Hispanics or Blacks." "I accept the presence of Hispanics and Blacks in our school." "I feel ambivalent about *them* being here."	"The race of a person is important to knowing how to act with the person."	"We both identify as White—we are white people, *you and I*."
Backgrounded Inferences	"*White* is a monoculture." "White people like me have been here a long time." "Minorities are new to our community." "If you are not white you are different." "If you are not white you are in the minority." "If you are not white you are A minority." "I can speak authoritatively on the racial history of the school *as a white person*." "Whites are ideal, supreme." "Being (like) white is best." "It is manifest that others would need to be like whites."	"I'm not that committed to worrying about this."	"It is important that I am a white person." "One should act according to one's race." "White supremacy is a legitimate recognition of the goodness of whites."	"We white people stick together." Maybe highly backgrounded: "I am a proud to be white."

capture the "I." Derrida's trace (1973) and mourning (2003) might be most deeply encountered here in the space where the "I" chronically slips away (Carspecken, 2003). Simply put, Derrida (1973) argued that words and signs are always different from and in deference to the substance to which they refer. They leave a trace of the sign itself—a tracing of an absence of the substance to which the sign refers. Derrida also wrote of a mourning (or longing) for that which is missing (Derrida, 2003). Anchoring our identities in stories is a way to have our "I" recognized by social others and it is a way to soothe the human condition of mourning around only being able to identify ourselves through ever vanishing "mes" (the sign of the self so to speak).

Articulating the Deep Structural Contexts

Narratives give us access to the deep structures of social life, "private constructions of identity must mesh with a community of life stories, or 'deep structures' about the nature of life itself in a particular culture [metanarratives] making it possible to connect biography with society" (Riessman, 2008, p. 10).

> Participants construct stories that support their interpretation of themselves, excluding experiences and events that undermine the identities they currently claim. Whether or not they believe the stories they tell is relatively unimportant because the inquiry goes beyond the specific stories to explore the assumptions inherent in the shaping of those stories. No matter how fictionalized, all stories rest on and illustrate the story structures a person holds. As such they provide a window into people's beliefs and experiences. (Bell, 2002, p. 209).

We can, on the one hand, hold the validity of the story for the storyteller, while, on the other hand, refrain from taking the story at face value. Thus, to further our critical aims, I intended to confront the given metanarratives with incredulity (Lyotard, 1979, p. 71). I approached this in two ways. First, I identified structures involved in making sense of the myths, namely historical legitimation and moral legitimation. Secondly, I examined the distribution of the myths in relation to self-other structures.

Claiming the Critical Insights

Drawing on narrative approaches within the context of ethnography affords at least three opportunities for cultural critique. The first is one that emerges from within the dialogically internal contestations that riddle the participants' own interactive awarenesses. The second is one that is articulated in the way structures that are being drawn upon for social action either reproduce, contradict, silence, or oppress the community's self-understanding. The third critique is one that invokes the value of equity as a concern for any unequal distribution or effects enabled by the structures of the myths themselves. I pushed the analysis through these critical possibilities, which you will find articulated toward the end of the chapter.

The Story Seeds of Monocultural Myths

Many of the white people in the school offered somewhat nebulous advice for the "newcomers" in their schools. This advice assumed a couple of points right off the bat. First, white people established themselves as experts on what transnational students should do to succeed. Second, they established that everyone in the school should or would want to be like them—like the white people. These assumptions were part of how they enacted monocultural assimilation. Through each of the story seeds a "we/us" was referenced. The "we" was always inclusive of the speaker and listener (a member of our research team) with an unspoken white American person as the ideal "we." This was articulated in the horizon analysis depicted in Table 5.1.

Each of the story seeds reported on here were offered up within the context of this critical ethnographic project. Perceived language barriers were the most persistent concern teachers expressed regarding their relationships with "newcomer" students and the story seeds reflected this.

Figure 5.1[6] illustrates components of the story reconstructions. Story seeds were recognized in the talk and then reconstructed in terms of stories, counter stories, and implied purposes (in other words, what was the point of dropping this particular seed into this particular conversation or set of activities). From those reconstructions, a "story to self-relation" was recognized. A story to self-relation indicated how the self was located through the story as part of the "we." I took the reconstruction deeper by articulating how the story was positioned in terms of time and identity claims, as well as how the stories posited the existence of particular others (or assumptions about who the "others" were) and what the presumed relationship was between the self and those others (posited relation of self to other). Taking the reconstruction further, it was possible to articulate a self to not-self relationship. I called this a "Positing Self to Shadow" relationship. It helped me locate both shadow identities and erased or unacknowledged others. I am using the word shadow to mean that which one would want to keep hidden because of how those identities compromise the primary identity assertions. The complexities, incoherencies, and partialnesses of our selves can be articulated through this structure. This description illustrates the layered possibilities available to us as we orient toward reconstructing narratives. You will notice that in a deep

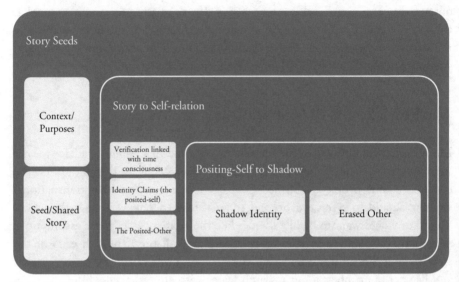

Figure 5.1 The Structure of Story Seeds. Source: Originally published in an article from which, in part, this chapter is derived, *International journal of qualitative studies of education, 29*(9), 1069–1085, published on June 27, 2016. Available online: https://www.tandfonline.com/doi/full/10.1080/09518 398.2016.1201161

way white supremacy and its offspring manifest destiny are the historically-anchored attitudes are reproduced through the particular story seed "Hispanics are the new blacks."

In this section of the chapter, I organize the primary reconstruction of the narratives into two categories: Historical Legitimation and Moral Legitimation. Historically legitimized stories implied validation through objective claims because they anchored what WAS (is) in the world or HOW things worked through objective authority. Morally legitimized stories implied validation through normative-evaluative claims as they indicated ethical authority.

Historical Legitimation

Three of the six monocultural myths were legitimized through an historical anchoring that held up a conceptually ideal "immigrant" who "assimilates" from one "homogenous" group into another. The identity assertions of the narrator involved the person claiming to have transcended time while being anchored in historical knowledge. Such a person can claim a particular kind of third person perspective and locate their identity claim as that third person observer. This form of legitimation showed up as objective validity claims such as:

- "My ancestors used to speak a different language."
- "Everyone in my family speaks only English now."
- "It is possible to assimilate in both language and deed."
- "Assimilation, here, means becoming indistinguishable from white people."

Remember that objective validity claims are those that presuppose an external world which would take into account what was and what worked in the world, including how things were defined. Actors assume that there is multiple access to making and validating these claims; specifically that multiple others could make and validate the claim using the same evidence, definitions, and so forth.

In these particular historical narratives, other groups were imagined in homogenous ways. We know from social psychological research, that this is typical of "othering" processes. What differentiated the storytellers (appearing here as "us") from the transnational students (appearing in the stories as "them") was the ability to just take-for-granted whiteness in the school. Historical legitimation also served to justify a "just wait and it will get better" attitude. The stories implied a natural passivity on the part of the people who (according to the story) did not need to change—namely the white educators. Historical legitimation linked presumed past experiences with anticipations for the future and supplied *authority* to the one who knows the past, locates the present in the past, and anticipates the future. As you read about these three myths you will notice that they contained no substantively helpful details about how one might even succeed with the monocultural aims. Instead, the stories proffered *pre-emptive exoneration* of responsibility for change for the educators.

"When my grandfather came here …." In the previous chapter you were briefly introduced to the history of Unityville. You have also learned through this book that longevity in the town afforded belongingness in the community. Dini's historical analysis of the German immigrant history provided more details than our participants were able to provide when referencing their ancestral migrations.

White educators regularly said (to the IU contingent of the project), "When my grandfather came here" implying, but not explicating a whole story. This is what I am referring to as a *story seed*. The implied story went something like this: *When my grandfather (or great grandparents) came here from Germany he (or they) gave up speaking German and insisted that everyone learn English. They wanted us to be part of America. They assimilated.* The factually historical anchors are two-fold—someone from my (the speaker's) family immigrated to the United States from a non-English speaking country (particularly Germany) and now no one in the family speaks that original language. Plus, "I" am the result of an assimilation process and therefore "I" have the right to speak on the reasonableness of this expectation for "newcomers."

But, the seed-planters could not *really* tell the story. They didn't know when their ancestors had arrived in the U.S., much less Unityville. They didn't know how the shift in culture happened. They didn't know what was lost. And so on. We typically asked, but the stories were never forthcoming. This story seed (and its implied narrative) released the educators' collective responsibility for im/migrant student success in schools because it suggested that the "newcomers" were responsible for their own successful integration—implying that since "my" ancestors did it, the kids, too, could be expected to do it. The tellers reinforced a sense of certainty about their European-heritage identifying completely as AMERICANS through some nebulous immigration process. The basic message had to do both with this outcome (becoming an English-speaking American) being an appropriate goal for all "newcomers" AND with a presumed, but not actually known-about, process. The implied process was vacuous in substance. Nonetheless, this story seed relied on historical legitimation to suggest that successful assimilation outcomes were the responsibility of the "newcomers," not the schools.

"Hispanics are the new blacks." This story seed (also voiced in its even more offensive form, articulated as the title of this chapter) was offered up more often than we as a team could count. It singled out Latino/a/x im/migrants and clearly indicated that Black students were not really the same as white students, in contradiction with the belilef that they had assimilated. This brought some clarity to their use of the phrase "traditional students." (Remember "traditional" was the phrase white educators used to describe the racially unmarked "students" who were in the schools prior to the new transnational students, though it was never used with reference to Black students.) We learned from the previous chapter that white people in Unityville grew to appreciate Black students, especially athletes, and they counted these good feelings on their own parts as the equivalent of "we're the same." The use of the n-word and the basis for this story, however, belied those seemingly good feelings. The story I reconstructed from this seed was:

> Hispanics, they are like the new blacks. Once upon a time there were only white people in Unityville. Then some blacks moved here. And it was hard, at first. No one really knew how to interact with them. They were not really part of the community. It was hard. But now, when you look at the school, there's no black, there's no white. There are just kids. Someday it will be like that with the Hispanics. Eventually, they will blend in and we won't even notice them. They will be like us.

One educator told us, "We don't have a large African-American population; and before the Hispanics, there was a bit of prejudice [toward those African-American students], but now it has truly shifted—there is a lot of prejudice toward Hispanics." Once when we asked an administrator to explain what they meant (just after the person had said, yet again, "Well, Hispanics are *like* the new blacks"). This was the response: "Well, we used to have problems. The Black kids didn't fit in, but now you can't even tell they are here." Nearly bragging about their "colorblindness" indicated the strong monocultural idealism held by many of the educators in Unityville. The racial tones of this historical narration was about blacks becoming more like white people at the school. There was an indication that "not being a problem" meant being more assimilated into "our" white ways. White, American, and "us" were synonyms. This is not new news for social justice educators and activists, but it certainly begged for deeper analysis. At the heart of this story was the historical invocation of white supremacy.

Most of the transnational and Black students were assigned to MJ, a counselor at Junction High School, who was multi-racial (claiming Hispanic heritage). MJ was responsible for her students' scheduling. MJ believed that the school district systematically devalued its Black students. For example, she told us, "Martin Luther King Jr. Day is a [district-wide] holiday for us, but it's also a snow day. So if it snows and we have to miss school one day, then we make it up on Martin Luther King Jr. Day and that right there shows that you don't really—you sort of value that holiday, but not necessarily cuz if we need to—to come to school that day, we will. You know what I mean, so that kind of bothers them [the black students]." She said that the African American students were unhappy about this and interpreted it to mean that the school did not appreciate them or their cultural heritage/values. We can see in MJ's report that assimilation was the mechanism through which the school was interpreting what it meant to be black: They don't see a difference between white and Black students and consequently don't recognize that African American students might place more value on Martin Luther King Jr. Day than their white counterparts. This further cemented the idea that celebrating Martin Luther King Day was not important to whites in the community. The holiday was treated as if it was FOR blacks, not for Americans/"traditional" students/whites. It was deemed unimportant enough, even for "assimilated" blacks, that it could be taken away presumedly without harm. Moreover, it revealed a contradiction between the claim that there were no differences between white and Black students AND the implicit devaluing of black heritage which institutionalized a discriminatory difference between white and Black students.

The seed anchored a festering racialness that simultaneously defied the presumed assimilation goals of the overarching monocultural myth while making that assimilation wholly unavailable. The historical legitimation falsely established that the district had succeeded in its assimilation/promotion of monoculturalism with Black students and therefore, educators have the ability to succeed with Latino/a/x students—failure would not be the school's fault, but rather the fault of the students. The belief went something like this: We did it right with Black students and we can do it with Brown students. Though it is interesting that the action orientation of "did/do" in this sense was passive as in "it was done." Race was both foregrounded and erased by the storyteller as if the historical trajectory bended *naturally* toward monoculturalism. Again, this story seed exonerated the story tellers from responsibility for failures.

"Sink or swim." There was a commonly held belief that if you threw people into the deep end of the cultural/linguistic swimming pool, they would sink or swim, ultimately swimming to survive. People literally said sink or swim, believing it to be a proven way to succeed in learning a new language, culture, or situation. It was an historically legitimized story because it assumed objective verification over time with universal generalizability. The reconstructed story went something like this:

> It's a fact, isn't it, that if you throw people in the deep end, just toss them in, they will find a way to swim because otherwise they will sink. They can't just let themselves perish. This is the spirit of being alive, that when someone has to face something new, the best way to learn is to just be thrown in so you have to make a go of it. We've all had to do that at some time in our lives.

This story seed, was a way to erase any individual or contextual struggles while at the same time, lodging the responsibility for figuring out "how to swim" on the learning "swimmer." The myth was anchored in an idea that throwing someone in the deep end was proven to work. The story depended on definitions of work, survival, and success, that were left vacuous in the story and its seed. Though, admittedly, many of us have been in situations that we might have described as sink or swim, it hardly sufficed as one's best pedagogical plan. Project team members would ask questions like, "Is there a safety net?" or "What do you do when the person sinks?" and there would be no answers. The story allowed for a lack of precision in terms of what it would have meant for the students to have actually "swam" or "sank." The story made it difficult to construct ideas around what would be helpful for the transnational students. And the tale lodged the responsibility for being able to swim on one's innate ability to survive without acknowledging that, in this case, "swimming" was a complicated set of skills that the educators themselves could not articulate. In fact, many of the educators did not have the skills they were expecting the students to have in order to "swim"—most notably the dual-language skills.

This myth provided no clear role for educators in their work with students, and, yet, it justified, letting the students flounder without support on the chance that they would survive. And, if they didn't? During the first year, we heard from many students who told us (in their home languages) how difficult it was for them;

so difficult, in fact, that several thought of death. They didn't want their parents to know how hard it was for them or that they lacked hope that things would get better. In the beginning, they were sinking and the educators were not expressing much empathy in their talk about the transnational students nor were they positioning themselves as having a role in improving things for these students of theirs. Who was the lifeguard?

Moral Legitimation

Three of the story seeds were based on moral legitimation. That is, they were anchored through presupposed shared community values and moral norms. Consistent with post-colonial critiques, we found that the white educators assumed their values and moral judgments were correct and were worthy of upholding (Spivak, 1999). In the story seeds those values and moral norms were not questioned. Each of the stories raised strong "shoulds" as the bases for their validity. Some examples of the reconstructed values/morals of moral story seeds included:

- If you are here, you *should* speak English. We value English as OUR language.
- You *should* not be here. We value our community as OURS.
- We are morally right and if you are not like us, you are *bad*.

In the above reconstructions the use of "we", "our," and "us" indicated the communal nature of the claims as well as harkening that insider/outsider dialectic I wrote about in Chapter 2. Moral legitimation exonerated educators from responsibility on moral grounds.

"Go home." This was a story of "You don't belong here" and "This isn't your home. Go back to your own home." In our early interviews, members of all white subgroups in the community vocalized this story seed—including high school students, parents, educators, support staff such as on-duty police, and community members. Even the transnational students reported this story seed. They told us, "They [members of the Unityville community] don't want us here" and "They [people in the schools] say to us, Beano, go home." Several community members independently described the recent history of immigration into the community using the words "infiltration" and "invasion." In a focus group of white high school students, kids said directly to me that they thought the "Hispanics" should "go home." Latino/a/x students frequently reported to us that their high school classmates would tell them to "Go back to Mexico" (even when they did not know where the particular student really came from). Several of the Latino/a/x students *were from* California, for example—their families long-time citizens of the United States.

White people in Unityville believed that Latino/a/x people arrived in Unityville in order to take white peoples' jobs. A sophomore, affirmed by her classmates, told us that working people with more seniority were bring fired and Hispanics were hired in their place for less pay. In the early days of our ethnography, Latino/a/x students were often verbally bullied, being called "wetback" (a U.S. euphemism that referred to Mexicans illegally crossing into the United States by swimming across the Rio Grande River). When Ed reported the jeering to one of the district administrators, the administrator admitted to also feeling that the students should assimilate or go home. Though he referred to his sentiments as prejudice, he was not apologetic and assumed a moral high ground for holding this belief.

These bits and pieces referenced a consistent story that the [Latino/a] transnational students had come into a place that the long-timers considered home. This myth was only told in reference to Latino/as. This was, in part, because the fathers of the Japanese transnational students came to Unityville with ready-made jobs at nearby Japanese-owned plants for defined periods of time. Other groups of students arrived in such small numbers and seemed, according to the local educators, to assimilate more quickly to the expectations of the local community. Thus, the language of invasion was only used in reference to the Latino/a/x communities.

> They ["Hispanics"] have invaded and infiltrated our town. They [those Hispanics] have taken local jobs away from us, from our people. They ["Hispanics"] have changed the face of the community—going so far as to paint a downtown building in bright colors. My family has lived here since forever and I can tell you that things are not the same with them here. They should go back to where they belong. They live with way too many people in small apartments. They drink a lot of beer. They don't fit in. If they really want to be here, they should become like us. Unityville is not one for change. We don't take kindly to a lot of change. We like the status quo. Most of us don't want them here.

The idea of the place (Unityville) as "home" was a central part of this story. Sometimes specifics were offered that involved things like, "my mom grew up here and then my parents raised us here." Moreover, the town did have a contemporary reputation amongst outsiders as being unwelcoming. Here the stories of "we" "us/them" and "our" reflected a possessiveness and a sense of stability. The im/migrants were interpreted as a threat to that proprietorship and permanence. Words like "infiltrate" and "invade" suggested a lack of control over the influx with a desire to protect oneself. These story seeds positioned the narrators as passive victims of this infiltration. Years later, we saw this attitude toward im/migrants expressed politically by the U.S. President and others.

In the counter story, narrators emphasized the idea that the "newcomers" brought change to the community. According to these not-quite-Unityville-insiders, change was not wanted by most of the long-timers. A guidance counselor at the high school was asked about teacher's classroom accommodations for ENL students: "I think you're always going to have people who are, um, who just don't want to change. Um, aren't willing to change." The counter story went like this:

> They [most of the Unityville educators] don't really want to change. They don't like the idea that the town could be different somehow. These new people threaten their way of doing things. They are so comfortable with how things are that they just do not want to change.

Here you can see that the "they" are people in the town who are not open to change, but the narrators of the counter stories were people who were open to change and who did not resist the "newcomers" on these grounds. There were several such educators in Unityville, but none of them considered themselves Unityville insiders. The counter story kept the following objective claim intact: Im/migrants were changing things (as if that would not have happened without their arrival).

Together the counter story and the "Go Home" story seed indicated the possibility that being "the passive victims" of this unwelcomed change bespoke the way change was experienced as menacing. Change threatened the identity security of the narrators as they associated themselves with the status quo of Unityville. In the story seed, change was perceived as a force thrust upon passive citizens, while for counter storytellers, one's resistance to the change process was active not passive.

The moral injunction had to do with the immorality of invading one's home and the right of the homeowner to protect her home from that invasion. The simple equating of the perceived intrusion with change was entailed in the injunction.

"Speak English if you're gonna come here." This common story seed was frequently articulated as a moral imperative—as if it was not really a story at all, but rather a clear principle for living. For example, Ed was talking with a top district administrator, the top district administrator told Ed, in an informal interview, "I have a prejudiced view there. (pauses) I think they need to learn to speak English. If you come to a country, learn English." He added, "That's important." In the flow of this conversation he mentioned that "I don't say it (stresses say it) like some of the kids though." (Albeit, obviously, he had just said this to Ed.) Of the monocultural myths, this one was the most thoroughly articulated:

> When people immigrate to a place, they need to learn to speak the language of the place and fit in. It doesn't really make sense to move somewhere if you don't want to try to fit in and live the life that is available to you in that new place. I don't think people should move to Unityville if they are not going to learn English. They need to be speaking English in the home and doing their best to be sure that their kids learn English. You can't just come here and then separate yourself out and not speak English. In school, the kids are supposed to only speak English. When I hear them speaking Spanish, I reprimand them. They could be cheating or talking badly about me or who knows what else. They need to be speaking in English.

Dini asked MJ, a guidance counselor at the high school, about teachers' classroom accommodations for ENL students: "I mean it's sad to state, but some people still have that mindset that if you're in America you should speak English and I mean, you just have to be careful around them and let them know that they *have to do* these accommodations, um, but realizing their inflexibility." MJ, herself, thought that the home language should be used when needed. She said, "You don't want to penalize a student who doesn't know English when they still have thoughts and ideas and opinions, you know. You don't want to say 'unless it's in English we're not going to validate you'."

Unfortunately for the transnational students, MJ's attitude was not widely held amongst the educators. Most of the educators believed that the families should even be speaking English at home (despite the fact that there were few fluent speakers of English in the families). In a focus group of white high school students, I was told that they didn't like it when "newcomer" students had bad attitudes, which they said was indicated by a "refusal" on the transnational students' parts to speak English. Many teachers expressed a similar view. Thus, the story provided rationale for assuming that the students were responsible for learning English (rather than that educators were responsible for teaching English) and that the failure/"refusal" to learn English was a moral one. The "sink or swim" myth was closely linked with the moral argument that "newcomers" should speak English.

"I read it in the crime section." This story seed criminalized Latino/a/x "newcomers." Literally keeping personal knowledge of transnational students at an arm's length, teachers formed beliefs about the Latino/a/x communities in Unityville by stereotypically linking all members of the community with crime. The reconstructed story was:

> There it is, again. Another Hispanic name listed in the police report. They are just here to cause trouble. They cannot be trusted and their families are basically criminals. They are bringing crime to our town.

This myth is easily seen in contemporary rhetoric all these years later. President Trump's anti-immigration propaganda propelled this story seed into national news. Trump's politics of vilifying southern border im/migrants marketed the criminalization story seed as worthy of American fear. In October 29, 2018, President Trump tweeted, "Many Gang Members and some very bad people are mixed into the Caravan heading to our Southern Border. Please go back, you will not be admitted into the United States unless you go through the legal process. This is an invasion of our Country and our Military is waiting for you!" Soon after, November 18, 2018, he tweeted, "The Mayor of Tijuana, Mexico, just stated that 'the City is ill-prepared to handle this many migrants, the backlog could last 6 months.' Likewise, the U.S. is ill-prepared for this invasion, and will not stand for it. They are causing crime and big problems in Mexico. Go home!" He expressly linked the "Go home" story seed with the criminalization seed, much like we saw a decade earlier in Unityville. He has consistently accentuated criminalization rhetoric in his references to im/migrants, especially singling out Muslim and Latino/a/x peoples. He has used words like "terrorists," "rapists," and "murderers" to both dehumanize and spread fear of violence. The result has been a documented rise in aggression. In an executive summary of a study on anti-immigration views in the U.S., the Anti-Defamation League (ADL) wrote, "Anti-immigrant fervor, once relegated to more extreme quarters, has been increasingly mainstreamed over the last ten years. Over the last two years, with the advent of a new administration focused on much stricter immigration policies and complementary executive actions, anti-immigrant and anti-refugee sentiment has made life substantially more difficult for all immigrants" (Anti-Defamation League, 2018). The UN High Commissioner for Human Rights decried the U.S. border camps where children have been separated from their families and detained in unacceptable conditions (Wyatt, 2019). That same report also raised alarm about the violent outcomes of vicious hate speech by political authorities like Trump, whose words have been used to incite brutality, for example in El Paso, Texas on August 3, 2019 where 22 people were killed and 24 people were injured.

The criminal story seed peddled several claims that were counter-factual. For example, there was an implied comparison that somehow the crime rates of Latino/a/x and/or im/migrants were higher than those of white U.S. citizens and that those crimes were more often violent. Neither of these claims were true—that is, these implicit objective claims were factually inaccurate. Nevertheless, by only planting the seeds, these implicit assumptions were allowed to stand unchallenged. As such, they likely played into burgeoning fear and fear mongering as described earlier. Moreover, the story seed of criminalization was one that vilified individuals across an entire population and erased the sociocultural contexts of im/migration on a world-scale as if individually bad people became migrants in order to foster their individual badness, most specifically their bad intentions, toward the "citizens" of Unityville whose town they were "invading." This *as if* myth became so prominent in the recent politics of the United States that policies such as publicizing the names of "undocumented" people accused of committing crimes were considered in the common good by some people. Such policies were analogous to this story seed. Establishing the criminality of "the other" gave solace and permission to a group of educators who had not succeeded in orienting relationally toward their new students. Through the criminalization story, we saw educators who believed they *should not* engage with criminals/im/migrants. The catch 22 of this story resulted in the teachers "learning" more about the im/migrant community in

Unityville by reading the "crime" section of the newspaper than through interactions with their students and families. Worries that the transnational students and their families were potential criminals served as rationale for not getting too close to them and for distrusting them within the schools.

The Structure of These Monocultural Myths

These myths of monoculturalism, planted as they were in the form of seeds, relied on the assumption that research team members were part of the white "us" through whom narrators tended to orient (even though we were not all white). Perhaps one reason why narrative details were fairly nonexistent is because the storytellers were not telling of their own experiences. Reconstruction of the myths from seeds provided us with an opportunity to identify structures on which the stories depended and were reproduced.

Implicit Structure to Narrating Story Seeds

In Figure 5.2, I introduce you to the reconstructed structure of the monocultural stories. I want to make those structures more explicit here. Generally, there was an implicit "as if" structure, an implicit contrast structure, and an implicit pointing-toward structure. These structures situated the narrator in the act of narrating.

As If Structure. Once the stories were reconstructed from the seeds, I reconstructed the relations that were obtained between a posited self (the self/we identity claimed at least implicitly by the narrator) and posited others. The "posited" nature of this

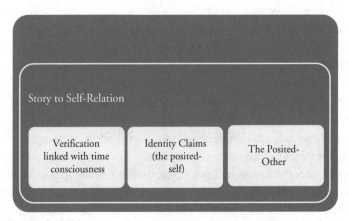

Figure 5.2 Story to Self-Relation

self/other contrast reflected an imagined self(ves) and other(s)—which I referred to through the phrase "as if" structures. An "as if" relation took the place of actually having to fill in with historical objective claims. In other words, the absence of substantive story facts left this imagined/as if self/other contrast to stand in the place of claims about "what was." I used Figure 5.2 to illustrate that the three components (posited self, posited other, and historical time consciousness) established how the story was related to the identity of the narrator. Across each of the myths, this structure was used to elaborate claims about the narrator and the other which were implied through the story seeds. This layer was further peeled back to articulate what was deeply hidden in the stories as fear. No story fully described or captured self-knowledge.

Contrast Structure. Stories don't only posit selves, they hide shadows. Reconstruction allowed us to understand how a posited self relates to a shadow. The shadow was composed of a negative reflection (shadow) self and an erased other. These referenced, but not explicated aspects of one's identity could be raised for dialogue in a deeply healing and non-threatening, accepting interactive circle. Shadow selves and erased others provide us with important insights about the cultures within which we are recognized and come to know ourselves. Think back to the "When my grandfather came here ..." story seed, through the reconstructive analysis I articulated a shadow self that posited a not-knowing of the history: "I really don't know myself. I wish I did." AND "My knowledge of my self is partial." In other words, the shadow in this story is a self who stands on privilege without really being able to substantively recount achieving its merits.

Such reconstructions complicated the idea of a coherently whole self and demonstrated how stories posited coherence while simultaneously muddying that performed coherence through the shadow (not self). The implicit structure of narrating suggested a parallelism between the way both stories and identities were germinated (see Figure 5.3).

Pointing-Toward Structure. Identity claims (even when implicit) established an identification with a recognizable, verifiable "me," while indicating or referencing a person who was doing the claiming, a person who was always more-than, and, already-beyond the claims themselves. The claims must be understood as contingent and partial. At best, they pointed toward something that could not be fully explicated, but, yet, was provisionally recognized. Thus, the best we could do was indicate an "I" who was responsible for and accountable to the claims it enacted. That "I" could not be known directly or with certainty, but pointing toward that "I" through tangible, historically verifiable, observable actions was one way to establish self-knowledge and simultaneously obtain recognition and understanding of

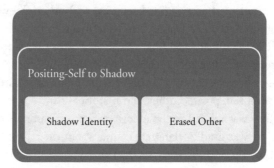

Figure 5.3 Positing-Self to Shadow Relation

ourselves by others (Frankl, 1992). There is a dilemma: we have an existential need to know ourselves, but we are, also, stuck with the incapability of meeting that need in practical ways. Narrating our identities often involves telling or invoking stories about ourselves that function to help us cope with this dilemma and mediate it for practical purposes (McAdams, 1993). The practical terms involve being able to engage interactively with social others who are able to recognize us as worthy, coherent individuals able and expected to justify our actions. By reconstructing these myths, I was able to recognize varying identity claims/contrasts relevant to those stories in structure and substance, acknowledging that the stories served purposes related to identity praxis needs (Frankl, 1992; McAdams, 1993; Mischler, 2004).

Structures Implicit in the Myths

In this section of the chapter, I name two types of configurations that I reconstructed from the implicated substance of the myths themselves: As if structures and binary structures. We were introduced to "as if" structures above in terms of how the narrator structured her relationship with the narrative. "As if" structures were a dependent imaginary that was inferred through typifications (those shared expectations for how to interact meaningful given the particulars of a social setting). Binarial structures were formed of two non-overlapping, oppositional contrasts. Reconstructed binaries were composed of one explicit side and one merely implied (and therefore must be inferred) side. The binaries formed homologous chains.

As If Structures. As if structures of both stories and identities afforded a presumed, shared imaginary. This imaginary was the inferential baggage we carried along when we recognized validity claims as worthy of our assent. The substance carried through the *as if* structure suggested opportunities for cultural reflection and critique. The three examples presented here are illustrative of a host of others.

For example, the seed of the story assumed an *as if* relation to the implied story itself—as if we white people would all tell the same stories. This particular *as if* structure established an imaginary, unquestioned "we." The "we" was white, educated, and "traditional" that functioned to unite the educators with the ethnographers. We put this "we" at risk when we raised questions that suggested we did not claim the stories as our own. For example, with the seed "Hispanics are the new blacks," I said, "I don't understand what you mean. Can you explain that to me?" Through such breaking of the "we" it was possible to encourage consciousness-raising for all of us.

Another prominent *as if* structure involved the relation between doing what was right as educators and a presumed intentionality on their parts—as if good intentions were a bottom-line assumption. The stories situated particular ways of acting with what was the right thing to do—this positioning always carried the assumption that the educators held good intentions for their work with transnational students and/or im/migrant communities. We broke into this inferred "good/right" intention by asking questions like, "What makes that the right thing to do?" For example, with the sink or swim story, I asked, "Help me understand what would be the right thing to do if the child is sinking?" followed by, "How would I know when the child is sinking so I would know to jump in?" These questions poked into the as if structure through which the assumption of good intentions was juxtaposed with being a willing bystander to a potential "drowning." Also, it is important to note that bad intentions and moral badness was imbued on Latinx youth and their families.

There was an *as if* relation established between the imagined conditions and the conditions as they were. That is, the imaginary was *as if* it had been factually established, when it had not (sometimes the imaginary was, indeed, counterfactual). This was most obvious in the "when my grandfather came here" seed. We burst into this structure by asking for the implied facts: "When did your grandfather immigrate?" "What was the experience like for him?" "How has this history resulted in you being who you are?" For our team, we did not take this lack of historical knowledge as an ending place. As you know from Chapter 4, Dini got busy learning about the history from documents. Freire (1970/2000) astutely argued that descriptions of oppression can and must include its facts—its observable patterns. As criticalists, we don't want to take the facticity for granted.

Binaries. Social justice researchers have long argued that binarial thinking is problematic. Deconstructing binaries was important for our critical process (Derrida, 1973). The grounding self/other and insider/outsider binaries described in earlier chapters were implicated in both of the binaries articulated below and you will see evidence of these binaries at work throughout all the chapters in this book.

A *passive/active binary* was associated with transnational students/white educators. In these monocultural myths, the narrators of the stories posited themselves as de facto passive (*as if* that was the way it was), while transmigrants were posited as necessarily active (*as if* acting toward changed fates was their responsibility). As narrated, passivity was a state of affairs (the way things were) while activity was a social responsibility. Through this binary, the storytellers were actively exonerated of their own culpability and accountability for the educational challenges of im/migrant youth in Unityville.

Another binary structuring the narratives was between *process* and *outcome*. This binary was indicated in the story seeds through an if-then way of thinking. Throw someone in the deep end, and they will either sink or swim. Come to the United States and then speak English. This binary afforded the narrators' claims to expertise through presumed outcomes without having to delineate a process.

There were several homologous relations that could be inferred from these binaries. These relations were noted through stable references within and across the stories.

Us	Them
Passive	Active
White	Non-White
Visible	Invisible
Morally right	Morally suspicious
Expert	Un-knowledgeable
Monocultural	Misfit

It is particularly important to deconstruct binarial thinking in order to mobilize that which becomes immobile through the binaries (St. Pierre, 2000, p. 478).

Distribution of Story Structures and Unintended Consequences of the Stories

Monocultural myths serve to name the other, the stranger. In so doing, they forge a "we." Latino/a/x students were most negatively conceptualized and most prominently invoked through the monocultural myths. There were far more Latino/a/x transnational youth than those from any other conglomerate group or subgroup. Latino/a/x students who were U.S. citizens were treated as if they were, also, im/migrants. Half of the story seeds referred to Latino/a/x students only ("Hispanics are the new blacks," "Go home," and "I read it in the crime section").

An assumed propensity for mistake-making or getting it wrong was targeted at the "newcomers," while that same potential was erased for the white educators. Along with this, the distribution of presumed good intentions was not equal. Teachers did not assume Latino/a/x had good intentions, while their own good intentions were rarely doubted.

As there would always be, there were unintended consequences of these story seeds. One unintended consequence was a bystander effect. By narrating their own passivity/exoneration, teachers allowed themselves to stand by as white kids bullied non-white kids or as transnational students failed to achieve. Similarly, the stories kept the transnational youth at arms' length from the educators. That is, an unintended consequence was to create further barriers rather than to burst through barriers, which of course we all would have claimed as one of the goals of the Project. In the name of monocultural assimilation the teachers promoted distrust and failed to foster opportunities for dialogue/learning against their educationally good intentions. These stories served as rationale for policies (such as the English Only policy) that were harmful to the affected students.

Critical Insights

There were three emergent critical insights that are important to articulate at the end of this chapter. White people's needs were met in the telling of these myths. Among the possible functions of storytelling is healing. (Of course, policing is also a possible function.) Narratives can provide therapeutic opportunities for participants as well as researchers and readers (McAdams, 1993; Riessman, 2008)—"stories may also mend us when we are broken, heal us when we are sick, and even move us toward psychological fulfillment and maturity" (McAdams, 1993, p. 31). By putting contesting dialogues and counter stories into dialogue, we open up this potential.

Secondly, structures that were being drawn upon for social action either reproduce, contradict, silence or oppress the community's self-understanding, including my own complicitness. "Poststructuralism does not allow us to place the blame elsewhere, outside our own daily activities, but demands that we examine our own complicity in the maintenance of social injustice" (St. Pierre, 2000, p. 484). Analyses of story seeds contributed to our abilities to call out our own participation in the narratives of privilege which linked white educators with white researchers (me, in particular). By following through on a deeply reconstructed set of inferences, critical possibilities and insights became available for us. It was crucial that researchers reflected on the extent to which these myths seemed sensible to us so that we could call it into question and move our own thinking toward greater freedom and liberation. (This is further explored in Chapter 8.) The internal contradictions, counter stories, and silences in dialogue with questions that raised aspects of the story seeds to the foreground contributed to the process of transformation and consciousness-raising (Korth, 2002).

The ideal of equity surfaces as a critical touchstone for how naming functioned within the community. By reconstructing the stories in this chapter, we engage with very specific content of the naming of others, while also coming to understand how the story seeds embody claiming the self by claiming the other. We are reminded by Ahmed (2000) that the function of pointing out the stranger is to reproduce the community *as if* it is the same over time; a form of certainty that affords "a sense of belonging and identity unburdened by the task of encountering 'embodied others'" (Ahmed, 2000, p. 148). Such reconstructions can contribute to a healing dialogue, a conscientização, an opportunity to learn about the pointing self and the posited self. We can remember that we are talking about ourselves even as we narrate the other. Ahmed thinks of strangers not as the others within the same, but as representatives of knowledges at risk of being erased, devalued, or unwanted (Karavanta, 2019). Mina Karavanta (2019) reminds us that any monolithic "we" or "universalizing rhetoric that appropriates the stranger as a figure within the same [narrating self] can be deconstructed by transnational strangers" (Karavanta, 2019, p. 455).

Notes

1. This chapter is derived, in part, from an article (Dennis, 2016) published in *International journal of qualitative studies of education* on June 27, 2016, available online: https://www.tandfonline.com/doi/full/10.1080/09518398.2016.1201161
2. Taken from Ed Brantmeier's fieldnotes, September 2, 2005.
3. Using praxis here the way Carspecken (2003) developed it.
4. There are a lot of examples of this in the literature, but a thorough description of the methodology can be found in Carspecken (1996).
5. I introduced this concept in Chapter 1 using it to refer to a socially recognizable opportunity to act meaningfully (Carspecken, 1996).
6. The figures in this chapter were first produced for teaching, then secondly for a conference presentation, and most recently in Dennis (2016).

References

Ahmed, S. (2000). *Strange encounters: Embodied others in post-coloniality*, New York, NY: Routledge.

Anti-Defamation League. (2018). Mainstreaming hate: The anti-immigrant movement in the US [Press release]. Retrieved October 13, 2019, from https://www.adl.org/the-anti-immigrant-movement-in-the-us

Bernal, R. (2019, August 20). DOJ to Supreme Court: Trump decision to end DACA was lawful. Retrieved October 7, 2019, from https://thehill.com/latino/458102-doj-to-supreme-court-trump-decision-to-end-daca-was-lawful

Bell, J.S. (2002). Narrative inquiry: More than just telling stories. *TESOL Quarterly, 36*(2), 207–213.

Carspecken, P. (1996). *Critical ethnography in educational research: A theoretical and practical guide.* New York, NY: Routledge.

Carspecken, P. (2003). Ocularcentrism, phonocentrism, and the counter enlightenment problematic: Clarifying contested terrain in our schools of education. *Teacher's College Record, 105*(6), 978–1047.

Conversi, D. (2007). Democracy, nationalism, and culture: A social critique of liberal monoculturalism. *Sociology Compass, 2*(1), 156–182.

Dennis, B. (2016). Myths of monoculturalism: Narratively claiming the other. *International Journal of Qualitative Studies of Education, 29*(9), 1069–1085.

Derrida, J. (1973). *Speech and phenomena: And other essays on Husserl's theory of signs.* Chicago, IL: Northwestern University Press.

Derrida, J. (2003). *The work of mourning.* Chicago, IL: University of Chicago Press.

Frankl, V. (1992). *Man's search for meaning: An introduction to logotherapy* (4th ed.). Boston, MA: Beacon Press.

Freire, P. (2000). *Pedagogy of the oppressed* (30th anniversary ed.). New York, NY: Continuum. (Original work published 1970)

Habermas, J. (1985). *The theory of communicative action, volume 1: Reason and the rationalization of society* (T. McCarthy, Trans.). Boston, MA: Beacon Press.

Habermas, J. (1987). *The theory of communicative action, volume 2: Lifeworld and system: A critique of functionalist reason* (T. McCarthy, Trans.). Boston, MA: Beacon Press.

Karavanta, M. (2019). Community. In E.T. Goodman (Ed.), *The Bloomsbury handbook of 21st century feminist theory*(pp. 449–462). London: Bloomsbury.

Kim, J.H. (2015). *Understanding narrative inquiry: The crafting and analysis of stories as research.* Thousand Oaks, CA: Sage.

Korth, B. (2002). Critical qualitative research as consciousness-raising: The dialogic texts of researcher/researchee interactions. *Qualitative Inquiry, 8*(3), 381–403.

Long, C. (2019, July 11). Kids in cages: Inhumane treatment at the border [Written testimony to the US House Committee on Oversight and Reform, Subcommittee on Civil Rights and Civil Liberties]. Retrieved October 7, 2019, from https://www.hrw.org/news/2019/07/11/written-testimony-kids-cages-inhumane-treatment-border

Lyotard, F. (1979). *The postmodern condition: A report on knowledge* (G. Bennington & B. Massumi, Trans.). Minneapolis: University of Minnesota Press.

McAdams, D. (1993). *The stories we live by: Personal myths and the making of the self.* New York, NY and London, England: Guilford Press.

Mead, G. (1934). *Mind, self, and society: From the standpoint of a social behaviorist.* Chicago, IL: University of Chicago Press.

Mishler, E. (2004). Historians of the self: Restorying lives, revising identities. *Research in human development, 1*(1–2), 101–121.

Noble, S.U. (2018). *Algorithms of oppression: How search engines reinforce racism.* New York, NY: NYU Press.

Riessman, C. (2008). *Narrative methods for the human sciences.* Los Angeles, CA: Sage.

St. Pierre, E. (2000). Poststructural feminism in education: An overview. *Qualitative Studies in Education, 13*(5), 477–515.

Spivak, G. (1999). *A critique of postcolonial reason: Toward a history of the vanishing present.* Boston, MA: Harvard University Press.

United States Department of Justice & United States Department of Education. (2014). *Fact sheet: Information on the rights of all children to enroll in school.* Retrieved July 19, 2018, from https://www.justice.gov/sites/default/files/crt/legacy/2014/05/08/plylerfact.pdf

Walford, G. (2007). Classification and framing of interviews in ethnographic interviewing. *Ethnography and Education, 2*(2), 145–157.

Webster, L., & Mertova, P. (2007). *Using narrative inquiry as a research method: An introduction to using critical event narrative analysis in research on learning and teaching.* New York, NY and London, England: Routledge.

Wyatt, T. (2019, September 23). U.N. takes aim at Trump and others over 'dehumanising' hate speech towards immigrants. Accessed October 13, 2019, from https://www.independent.co.uk/news/world/americas/us-politics/un-trump-hate-speech-human-rights-immigrants-minorities-a9116681.html

CHAPTER SIX

Methodologies of Possibility: Theatre of the Oppressed as Transformation[1]

There exist relatively few occasions, in the course of a lifetime, which provide the opportunity to confront processes of radical social transformation.

(Fals-Borda, 1979, p. 33)

What was happening in Unityville seemed radical to those of us working on the Project. Unityville was in flux. The complexities and instabilities of participants' experiences called for a variety of engagements extending beyond observations and interviews. In the beginning, participants were simultaneously novices at talking about their experiences with "newcomer" students. They were, also, guarded in terms of what they felt comfortable saying. In addition to needing methods that could help us explore these complexities, I hoped that the research would contribute positively to the change process already going on in the schools. Fals-Borda (1979) argued that we have a responsibility as members of the research community to interpret and understand social change so that our work might be a catalyst for transformation. Things are always changing, but we think of transformative possibilities as those that expand our opportunities to be fully human and relational in healthy, affirming, dialogically non-violent, non-oppressive ways.

Methodological creativity facilitated our transformational aspirations by opening up spaces for imagining possibilities. For example, we created a migration game to play with elementary school aged kids. This game mimicked the style of play used in the game "Life." As students moved through the board, they were asked various questions and were given multiple choices as they proceeded toward the end of the game board. We also used drawing with the students. As you already know, we engaged a cadre of teachers at Junction in the creation of an interdisciplinary peace curriculum (Brantmeier, 2005). Teachers at Cambio Middle School were involved in creating "Policies of Care" and across the schools, we developed new handbooks for parents that aimed toward creating new prospects for engagement. Each of these creative endeavors ushered in new dialogues. It was not unusual for much needed conversations to be left lurking beneath the day-to-day surfaces of school life. We hoped to open up those buried opportunities through this Project.

In the early days of the collaboration, Junction High administrators asked our team to orchestrate a day of professional development activities that focused on the educational needs of the "newcomer" students, which has already been partially described for you (Chapter 2). Following the opening activities, we offered a series of workshops. Each of those workshops was given twice, once in the morning and once in the afternoon. Educators signed up beforehand to participate in the various workshops—their participation, in general, was required, but they had several options from which to choose. The workshops were varied. For example, some of our transnational high school students taught basic language phrases in Spanish, Japanese, and Taiwanese. Yoko led a workshop on teaching second language learners. The day was full and each of the workshops benefitted from what we were learning ethnographically. One of the workshops involved using Augusto Boal's *Theatre of the Oppressed* (1979) to reflect on the bullying of transnational students at the high school. This chapter focuses on the two Theatre of the Oppressed (TO) workshops in order to show the potential of *methodologies of possibility* (Fierros, 2009).

In our workshop, TO provided participants with opportunities to explore their own experiences in order to better understand their own place in the reproduction of oppression. TO has the potential to democratize the research process and include participants in analyzing and reflecting on the meanings of their own actions. In this chapter, I demonstrate an analytic strategy useful for dramatic data and for understanding the liberation and transformation of oppressive practices. Teachers drew on authentic experiences while they participated in TO, but those experiences were also rendered malleable to actors' imaginations and for unanticipated revolutions. The data generated through TO reflected possibilities of action related to the life of the schools. The transformative activities that emerged did not comport with anything we had actually witnessed up to that point. This methodology blurred the line between articulating what was actually going on and inspiring what was possible. It afforded change at the hands of actors.

High school students poignantly told us that they would choose death over a lifetime of experiences like those they were having at Junction. It took hope on the students' parts to expect things would get better (Freire, 1994/2014). The Latino/a/x students, especially, lamented that their parents had made many sacrifices to bring them to the U.S. and so they felt it necessary to hide their negative experiences from their parents. According to Jean Harvey (1999), civilized oppression involves the deep and pervasive suffering of groups as a result of unconscious assumptions and effects of well-meaning people in ordinary interactions. The unconscious assumptions are backed up by media stereotypes, social hierarchies, and the systems of advantage we can quite easily take for granted. Freire (1970/2000) argued that oppression was relational, objectively verifiable, and changeable. Both Harvey (1999) and Freire (1970/2000) emphasized the way broad, systemic oppression was located in everyday actions and routines, including the activities of people who might find oppression reprehensible. Understanding oppression at the level of everyday lives of well-meaning people often requires a subtle approach. Our interviews provided us with clues, but we needed methods that could reach deeper into the patterns of ordinary routines and meaning making. The Theatre of the Oppressed did that by fostering our understanding of the complexities and mechanisms of oppression at work through school bullying while also providing an opportunity to begin the work of conscientização—critical consciousness-raising—and the transformation of action patterns.

In this chapter, I describe our adaptation of Boal's TO (1979) for critical ethnography. The chapter contributes to a growing scholarship that uses theatre as research (Conrad, 2004; Donmoyer & Yinnie-Donmoyer, 1995; Norris, 2000; Saldaña, 2005). I drew directly and largely on my own paper published through The International Journal of Qualitative Methods, which is an open-source, online publisher (Dennis, 2009a). Carl Bagley, an educational ethnographer, asked, "how well are we equipped, as an educational ethnographic community, to engage with and analyse these complexities and moreover portray them in a way that can capture the sensuous array of sights, sounds, and smells as well as represent the traumas, passions and emotions, of twenty-first century lived experiences?" (2009, p. 251). His own answer was this:

Such a challenge arguably calls for a re-working or shifting of ethnographic methodological boundaries, and a interdisciplinary recognition of the need and potential for embracing more evocative and sensuous arts-based forms of working; a synergy of social science and the arts creating new opportunities which challenge orthodox ethnographic conceptions and practice. (Bagley, 2009, p. 251)

Bagley (2009) called for a cadre of arts-based ethnographers to serve as a critical community of support and reflection. This chapter is a response to that call.

Drama and Critical Methodology: Theatre of the Oppressed

Through TO, participants explored their own awareness in dialogue with each other and in order to imagine new possibilities for acting within a problematic context. Lather (1991) coined the phrase *catalytic validity* to refer to research projects whose validity rests, in part, on the effects they inspire for those involved in the study. I came to think of this as ethical *withness*. Trinh T Min-ha (1982) argued for a social science whose goal is to provide *opportunities for* experience rather than *explanations of* experience. Denzin (2003) described a form of social science methodology aimed at fashioning the "words and stories" of individuals into "performance texts that imagine new worlds, worlds where humans can become who they wish to be, free of prejudice, repression, and discrimination" (p. 105). He called this performance ethnography. Both Min-ha (see especially the film *Reassemblage*, 1982) and Denzin expressed dissatisfaction with and distrust of research that aims only to present things as they supposedly are. Aligned with critical researchers in general, their versions of ethnography emphasized its moral character: fallible, and always involved in the tenuous, but necessary, relation between what is and what ought to be.

Criticalists do not intend to reproduce, depict, or represent the life of a community for outsiders as if taking a photograph (Korth, 2005a, 2005b) but, rather, to engage with and understand the life perspectives of a community for their own sakes in complement with unleashing potential benefits for others. Criticalists hold that once these goals have been met, the sanctity of norms internal to a community can be rationally queried both on their own terms and by putting them in a dialogue with different sets of norms (Habermas, 1985). Thus, critical ethnographers aim to engage community members in democratic dialogue with multiple possible outcomes, possibilities that allow for the "could be" of social life/social science. Drama and theatre have become part of this critical form of ethnography. For example, Jim Mienczakowski (1995) extended traditions in radio and stage drama with the goal of producing what he called "public voice ethnography for its emancipatory and educational potential" (p. 364). He rightly argued that such potentials could be met by voicing disempowered perspectives for an unknowing audience.

Using theatre as ethnography blurs the line between what is and what could be/ought to be. Furthermore, it challenges uncomplicated notions of "*naturalistic*" and "*observation,*" (Lincoln & Guba, 1985) seeking to find something new and to juxtapose what participants see in their own experiences with what they think about those experiences (Madison, 2005). According to Dwight Conquergood (who moved during his long career from doing traditional ethnography to doing performance ethnography), performance "opened the space between analysis and action" (2002, p. 145). Ethnographic uses of drama necessarily draw from the naturalistic action-repertoires familiar to actors while providing opportunities to experience newness within familiar contexts.

Narratives as Performances

"Stories are social artifacts" (Riessman, 2008, p. 105). Dialogic performance analysis looks at stories from the perspective of performing: who is the audience, when and where is the story told/performed and for what purposes? Catherine Riessman said it like this: "How is the story coproduced in a complex choreography—in spaces between teller and listener, speaker and setting, text and reader, and history and culture?" (p. 105). "What talkers undertake to do is not to provide information to a recipient but to present dramas to an audience. Indeed, it seems that we spend more of our time not engaged in giving information but in giving shows … identities are constructed in 'shows'" and are always social in nature (p. 106). Also, the listener and audience are always implicated/implied in the storytelling itself (p. 106). We saw how this was reconstructed through monocultural mythmaking in Chapter 5.

Riessman (2008) drew on Irving Goffman's ideas about dramaturgy (see Goffman, 1959). Dramaturgy is the presentation of ourselves to social others in a way that is interpretable by them, in a way that makes it possible for them to infer claims about us from the ways in which we are acting. The presentation of self in everyday society (as Goffman titled his book) is intersubjectively structured. Thus, we can monitor ourselves using the same possible interpretations that social others would use to make sense of our actions. Form and meaning emerge *between* people. Social scientists do not have to accept "the narrator as the 'final' authority, the social scientist can interrogate particular words, listen to voices of minor characters, identify hidden discourses speakers take for granted, and locate gaps and indeterminate actions in personal narrative" (Riessman, 2008, p. 107). Audiences/readers/others are an important part of the production of narratives because they are already embedded *with*in the interpretive process. This way of thinking about narratives links them directly with critical performances. We can bring our expectations about others importantly into our reflection through drama. Madeline Fox (2019) conveyed an analysis of adult audience members' responses to youth embodied performances of research. Her insightful work demonstrated the interpretive power of performance and the positioning of audience as potential participants/meaning-makers. The storied link between author/actor and reader/audience can be troubled through drama.

The Use of Theater and Drama as Ethnography

There were some historical developments that led to the juncture we now refer to as performance ethnography/research (Conrad, 2004). As with any history, what converged on any given present moment cannot be simply captured in a detailed account of origins or influences because there will always have been multiple and divergent sets of experiences that were not necessarily linear. In the 1960s and 1970s in the United States, drama and theatre were being used to stir critical consciousness and provoke reflections. When adopted, this form of theatre unsettled the audience and forced them to actively think about what was happening rather than passively experience the vicarious roles as enacted through the script (Brecht, 1964). This was an explicitly political and social way of doing drama. Contemporary scholars developed this further, using drama to resolve conflicts and address social concerns (Salazar, 1991; Saldaña, 1999, 2003, 2005). A variety of alternative forms of theatre that shared these basic ideas gained in popularity through the subsequent decades. For example, in Vancouver, Canada, a group called Theatre of the Living (2008) organized through TO techniques in order to frame/reframe/reimagine participant experiences, transforming them into new possibilities. Taken all together, these efforts in theatre transformed the ostensibly passive theatre experience into an active opportunity to engage in understanding, social change, and personal transformation.

From within the field of qualitative research, the use of TO found synergy with the movement toward participatory action research through which people were engaged in inquiries from and toward their own goals, lives, and social changes (Fals-Borda, 1987; Fine, 2006; McTaggart, 1997). There was some overlap across these two trajectories (the field of drama and the field of research), and that overlap is best marked by a few key references, noted across the major literature on drama and research.

Denzin's (2003) "performance ethnography" was conceptualized as a dialogue through which actors and audiences are engaged reciprocally and democratically in performing common "texts." The idea of performing the texts of ordinary life experiences in order to facilitate such engagements was not new to Denzin, though his work had a particularly powerful impact on the field. Conquergood (1985), Mienczakowski (2001), Smith and Gallo (2007), Jones (2002), and many others developed the use of drama in conjunction with the conduct of research, including thinking of drama an an ethical form of inquiry. Over a decade ago, Mienczakowski (1995) began writing about public-voice ethnography. He was interested in health care policies and practices. He argued that ethnodramas provided emancipatory opportunities for health care community members by putting the reading of data back into their own hands. Mienczakowski (2001) provided clear directions for using ethnodrama as a form of ethnography. First, ethnographers created performance scripts based on observations and interviews. Second, the scripts were distributed to community members who were asked to comment on them. Third, co-performers, who were members of the larger community, read these scripts with the additional commentary. Fourth, the scripts were performed by members of that larger community through reading and staging. Finally, the ethnographers facilitated a post-performance discussion that invited the reworking of texts and understandings associated with the performance. These were the steps we followed in using the scripts we shared in the morning session of the January 2004 professional development workshops in Unityville (see Appendix D for the script).

According to Mienczakowski (2001), ethnodrama involves being fully present in the now—not thinking of the past or the future. His emphasis on the present was particularly insightful. It was not merely a reference to a point in time but more incisively involved an attitude of liminality (Turner, 1969) and a willingness to explore what had not yet come into being by acting in such a way as to bring that very imagined possibility about. Though liminal spaces tend to be regularized through ritual, they always amount to providing a "playground" for becoming new. Ethnodrama keeps the impending nature of the present at play. More specifically, ethnodrama keeps the impending nature of the self-of-the-present at play.

Mienczakowski's (2001) ethnodrama is one example of contemporary convergences between theatre and critical research. His hope for the return to dialogic and democratic, communitarian, and transformative reflection was clearly critical. Dolan (2005) claimed that

... live performance provides a place where people come together, embodied and passionate, to share experiences of meaning making and imagination that can describe or capture fleeting intimations of a better world. (p. 1)

This "place" was fertile for doing research. Analysis of the literature indicated that drama was contemporaneously involved in research on several levels. It was used:

to reflect on data and analysis with broader audiences (Arditti, 2003; Cozart, Gordon, Gunzenhauser, McKinney, & Petterson, 2003; Donmoyer & Yennie-Donmoyer, 1995);

to bring participants and others into dialogues inspired by the data (Jones, 2002);

as a data collection technique (Bowman, 2006; Conrad, 2004; Prentki & Selman, 2003);

as disciplinary critique (Piercy & Benson, 2009; Smith & Gallo, 2007); and

as a participatory form of analysis (Fox, 2019; Korth, 2006; Madison, 2005).

Of course, many of the above scholars/activists used drama in multiple ways.

Through TO, findings were not conceptualized as a final pronouncement of the way things were; instead, they were offered as a point of dialogue for a broader but inclusive audience, juxtaposing what was with what could be. In fact, Mienczakowski (1995) wrote, "Given in the voices of the respondents, there is little need for an ethnographer to academize and rephrase them to obscure their import, as they are already in the public voice" (p. 368). Traditional analysis risks this obscuring. Contrary to more traditional forms of data analysis, the participants were actively engaged in the process, as is shown later in this chapter. As the procedures are described in detail below, I show that at some points the lines between data collection and data analysis were blurred and at other points they were not. This chapter is an opportunity to further the methodological conversation on these blurrings and demonstrate a uniquely critical "public analysis."

Pedagogy and Theatre of the Oppressed

Freire's (1970/2000) *Pedagogy of the Oppressed* fostered the development of consciousness and the transformation of oppressive relationships. Liberation from oppression makes it possible for all of us to engage more authentically and completely in efforts to become most fully human, with one another and with the ecology of the world within which we breathe. Freire wrote, "Dehumanization, which marks not only those whose humanity has been stolen, but also (though in a different way) those who have stolen it, is a *distortion* of the vocation of becoming more fully human" (1970/2000, p. 44, italics in original). There is not a more basic reason for engaging in social science research than to serve the potential of becoming most fully human—for all of us and in conjunction with our environments. It seems to me that all other endeavors make sense with this at heart, even those developing through post-humanist thought.

Freire (1970/2000) located the Pedagogy's critical and liberating potential in the active involvement of oppressors and oppressed in conscious exploration of what binds, legitimizes, and reproduces their oppressive relationships. Theatre of the Oppressed is a form of Pedagogy of the Oppressed, the principles of which are completely compatible with a critical qualitative approach to inquiry (Boal, 1979). For a nice history of TO and related approaches in theatre see Conrad (2004).

Critical methodology, Pedagogy of the Oppressed, and TO share both an underlying critical epistemology that is pragmatic in nature AND a set of social values that work toward a more egalitarian, mutually respectful, communicatively liberal society capable of supporting its members in their quests to be fully human and rightly situated in the world. The objective conditions of oppression have psychological and communicative effects that create space for the oppression to enter our dialogue and our analyses. "In performance ethnography, the performance spills from the stage into 'real' life" (Conrad, 2004, p. 9). And performances can be used to resolve conflicts and to change the ways in which real life is enacted. "Each performance event becomes an occasion for the imagination of a world where things can be different, a radical utopian space where a politics of hope can be experienced" (Denzin, 2003, p. 41). Toward this way of thinking we use the word performative and its derivatives to indicate sincere (rather than disingenuous) imagining of possibilities.

Creating the Performance: A Description of Methodological Process

Following a provocative opening session, Maura PereiraDeLeon and I co-facilitated the two sessions of TO with 12 participants in both the morning and afternoon sessions. Maura and I made a good team. She had worked with Freire directly and I has engaged extensively with his ideas through a variety of institutional positions. I, on the other hand, had experiences facilitating TO. We had been actively involved with the IU-Unityville Outreach Project since its inception and had both witnessed and heard about the ongoing bullying in Unityville. Together we selected the scenario we drew on for the TO activities. Both of us had experiences as teachers and, also, as new language learners in countries not of our origin. Our TO sessions engaged participants in acting out scenes and analyzing those scenes (a kind of pubic analysis). The sessions were audio recorded, and Maura and I took field notes as we co-facilitated.

Each session began with a warm-up activity, following which we shared a bullying scene taken from our data. We then used a modified version of TO's "Forum Theatre" to work with the scene. Using Forum Theatre, we asked participants to continue reenacting the bullying scene, slowly and believably altering it as awareness and understanding of the scene shifted. The transformations drew participants into imagining what could be different in terms of how the scene was played out and what their own possibilities for action were within that scene. For our purposes, each reenactment was considered an iteration that I numbered chronologically in the thick record. Between the different iterations, we spent some time talking about and reflecting on the scenes. I called these "interscene dialogues." The interscene dialogues produced a public analysis. *Public analysis* is my term for the publicly collaborative, open explorations into the meaning and identity constructions implicit in the scenes. These strategies are all common in performance ethnography (Conrad, 2004), but interscene conversations are not typically encouraged in TO. I say a bit more about that below.

Following the workshop, the data were transcribed and field notes were added in to the transcription to produce a thick record. I used hermeneutic analyses, specifically reconstructive horizon analysis (introduced in Chapter 5) and interactive sequence analyses (Carspecken, 1996), to probe more deeply into the scenes, the interscene dialogues, and the facilitated public analysis. Doing this allowed for a more comprehensive exploration. It also honored the involvement of participants in the analysis process.

Discourse analysis is commonly used when examining data outside of the theatre space. Rymes, Cahnmann-Taylor, and Souto-Manning (2008) provided a thorough description of their use of discourse analysis with performative data. Their study illustrated movement from monologue to dialogue across the different performances of various scenes. These findings would not have been generated by participants because they involved a form of analysis and set of concepts that participants did not have. By conducting discourse analysis, researchers were able to make broader sociocultural connections related to habits of language and to step outside the conscious enactments of the participants. In contrast, I used hermeneutic, pragmatic analytic techniques, which allowed me to explicate the implicit patterns of meaning internal to the meaning-making shifts that happened through our work with TO. This approach treated the data as interactive. Rather than going outside the meaning-making intuitions of participants, this approach goes radically internal to those intuitions (Habermas, 1985). Social science benefits from both orientations to analysis.

Thick records and analytic outcomes were shared with participants, and the findings presented in this chapter reflect what emerged following the conversations with participants. Other validity techniques were used to be sure that the meaning-engagements of the participants were interpreted in ways that honored their understandings and in ways that encouraged dialogue around their values and sociocultural commitments. To buttress the validity of our TO methodology, I used audio-recording and photographic records, negative case analysis and strip analysis to check interpretations, as well as key informants and participants to assess the plausibility/quality of the data interpretations (Carspecken, 1996).

Theatre of the Oppressed: Setting the Stage

Maura and I waited on the stage in the auditorium for our 12 participants to convene—12 in the morning and another 12 in the afternoon. We had arranged chairs in a circle on the auditorium stage and had prepared a handout for participants to take with them when we were finished. The teachers looked nervous, which matched the feelings Maura and I shared. Below I report the details of our use of TO in the context of this professional development day for teachers.

Introducing the Guidelines. The success of TO depends on a couple of principles. We articulated these with the teachers and then promised to encourage their use. First, it was important for the acting be authentic. The guideline of authenticity asked participants to enact parts that they could imagine and would consider realistic for themselves personally. In this sense, the ethnographic principle of naturalistic engagement is followed. Furthermore, this principle belies the alternative interporetation of the word "performative" to mean disingenuous and strategic. A second principle asked that all contributions in the form of actions or words be considered confidential and welcome. We maintained the space as shared and safe, vowing to be personally respectful.

Warming Up. As a warm-up, we invited participants to take turns striking a pose in the center of the group. This is a significant modification of "Image Theatre" (Boal, 1979), which allows people to act as sculptors on static images formed with their bodies. We specifically asked people to assume a position with their own bodies that felt personally empowering. The most common postures were stern, stiff, authoritarian poses. Although we had not asked participants to think specifically about the school context, nearly all the stances depicted the teachers in relation to students with the teachers as having power-over the students. For example, a couple of teachers looked at an imagined audience of students over which they expressed power by glaring over the tops of their glasses, pointing their finger, or looking down. The resounding theme was an interpretation of "empowerment" as teacher "power-over" students. This was interesting, given our directions to strike a pose of personal empowerment. Only one person posed himself in a way that did not depict him as a teacher in relation to students; he got down on his knees, bowed his head and held his hands in a prayer position.

This warm-up activity intuitively located a nexus of power and agency for each participant. The rituals of doing school overshadowed responses that might have surfaced for these same participants in different contexts. The limited range of positions expressed a confinement of agentic teacher empowerment which, also, showed itself later in the workshop in the ways that teachers struggled to imagine themselves as part of the bullying scenes we reenacted.

Introducing the Process. Following the warm-up activity, I described the specific procedures we would be using to dramatize a scene from our data. With "Forum Theatre" (Boal, 1979) participants were required to repeatedly re/enact the original scene. There was no script, just a scene description from our observation notes, so the acting was improvisational. The structure of the drama required that there be actors (those actively engaged in performing a scene) and "spectactors" (those who were temporarily audience, but with a readiness to take over a role or add a character to the performance). Repetitions were specifically altered by spectactors who assumed roles in the ongoing performance and subsequently changed the execution by acting the parts differently. The decision to use a bullying scene from the data (while masking the identities of the students) was made as a team. Maura and I chose this particular scene because an increasing number of the ENL high school students were being victimized by bullies during passing periods and because we had heard from both teachers and students that they (the teachers themselves) were aware that the bullying was going on. That awareness had not translated into meaningful disruption of the bullying practices.

Curtains Up

Our grand opening session with all teachers was aimed at creating empathetic responses for our transnational students. We hoped that our creative use of TO would nourish the potential for empathy, while also pushing toward transformative awareness and practices.

After the warm-up activity (where teachers struck poses that reflected "empowerment" for them) teachers reclaimed their seats, faced one another in the circle, and listened as I read the bullying scene to them. I informed them that this scene was taken from our data. I expected it to disturb them.

> This scene takes place in the hallway during the change of classes. A teacher is standing in the hallway. Two Latino kids are walking together down the hall and three Euro-American kids are calling the Latino youth names and basically making them feel unwelcome, saying things like 'Speak English or go home.' 'Get out of here, you dirty Mexican.' The teacher is witness to the activities because the teacher is standing in the hallway monitoring students as they move from room to room.

The scene did not surprise anyone. After listening, we asked people to volunteer for parts. We planned to begin with six actors (playing the parts of 1 white teacher, 2 Latino/a/x kids, and 3 white kids) with six spectactors. Actors moved to the center of the circle and spectactors remained in their seats. I had a soft bell I used to begin, interrupt, and shift action. We started by enacting the scene as it was represented in the description I had read. In what follows, the iterative scenes are described according to roles, but remember that all the participants were white Unityville teachers who inhabited the roles for purposes of our workshop.

Staging the Originating Scene. The beginning scenes were enacted differently by participants across the two TO workshop sessions. In the morning, we had 5 actors (playing the roles of 1 teacher, 2 Latinas and 2 white students—one male and one female). The two Latina students (L1 and L2) began walking down the hallway as they pretended to move between classes. The hallway was staged as going through the middle of our circle. They were speaking Spanish to one another (actors were somewhat pretending, somewhat drawing on what little they knew of Spanish). Two white students (E1 male and E2 female) approached them. A white female teacher was standing nearby grading papers, rarely looking up. E1 and E2 bashed into L1 and L2. E1 said, "Outta my way, mesican." L1 said, "Sorry." Both Latinas continued to walk, but with their heads dropped down. They stopped talking and made eye contact with each other. The two white students walked off in an opposite direction laughing and pointing their fingers at the two Latinas.

The afternoon session performed the originating scene differently. Two Latinas walked down the imagined hall. Two white students **bashed fully into the bodies** of the Latinas and said, "Beano" in a mean-spirited way. The male teacher, who was standing in his imaginary doorway, immediately stepped into the interaction. He turned to the Latinas and he said, "Why don't you guys go ahead and go to class." Then he turned to the white students and said, "Apparently you have some rude comments. [Note that he did not mention the body bashing.] I don't really like the way you are talking. Would you like to go to the administration?"

I stopped the action (uncharacteristic for TO) at this point to ask the teacher, "Why did you say, 'Do you want to go to the administration?' to the students?" His response to me was,

> Everything is sly in the hallway, and generally it is so subtle that you cannot say anything [you cannot accuse students if you do not actually see or hear what has happened]. Unless it's really obvious, then of course I would say something. Let's go talk about it with the administration and see what they think and then they [the students] will [usually] back down. But usually you can't really say anything.

Then I said, "Okay, let the scene continue and see what happens." Actually, the teachers who were pretending to be white students hung their heads in front of the teacher and then went on to class. Again, I stopped the action to ask those role-played students how they felt, how they were affected by the experience. E1 said it was not a big deal, and E2 replied, "No big deal, just make sure next time he doesn't see us." The Latina students walked off. They did not talk with each other or make eye contact with one another. They had been forgotten, even to themselves, through the remainder of the scene.

During the morning group, it took several transformations before the teacher actually DID anything other than stand with a set of papers in the scene. In the afternoon group, the acting teacher presented a limited response—limited primarily by assumptions about who had the authority to confront the white students and what evidence was required to warrant the confrontation.

Reflecting on the Originating Scene: The First Interscene Dialogues. After the scenes were enacted for the first time, participants in each of the groups wanted to take a moment to reflect on the scenes, which brought them in dialogue with the roles they had just played or witnessed. Typically, Boal encouraged participants to stay out of their heads and stay in their bodies. The idea in TO is that our bodies have habits which enable oppression (Boal, 1979). Though I tried to stay with the no-talking guidelines, I failed. Consequently, Maura and I engaged in reflective dialogue practices with the teachers that aimed at enabling consciousness-raising which was followed with a return to activating our bodies in the scenes. As previously mentioned, I called the reflective conversations "interscene dialogues."

In the first of many interscene dialogues, the teachers made four key points. First, "You have to pick your battles." To this way of thinking, teaching behavior was the outcome of weighing priorities, resources, and oppositions. The first "teacher" in the morning group did not pick the "battle," but the first teacher in the afternoon group did, albeit in a constrained fashion. In both cases, the potential for physical violence was the most prominent characteristic in the battle-picking. In the afternoon session the white kids were more physically confrontational, making the possibility for physical violence more probable. With this way of thinking, verbal bullying, for example, was not attended to simply because teachers had to pick their battles and justify their choices. Second, teachers believed they needed to be able to prove the bullying happened before any sort of administrative action toward the bully could be taken. Of course, bullying research (Payne & Smith, 2013; Stockdalet et al., 2002) has indicated that bullies are especially good at not getting caught. Third, the teachers did not originally think of themselves as part of the oppressive relationship. In both groups, from the perspectives of the teacher, the bystanding teacher was not considered a significant actor in the oppression; the oppression was what was going on between the students. Lastly, teachers in neither group initially assumed that the white students were capable of empathizing with the Latino/a/x students.

Our critical endeavors were enhanced because these points were made explicit. When they were first articulated, I had internal reactions that I did not make transparent in those moments. Instead, I listened deeply and rephrased the points so that we could draw on them as we moved along with the TO process. The four points marked possibilities for transformation and they linked precisely with the majority conception of empowerment (as power over) exposed through the warm-up activity. They were, also, problematic in that they were precisely the kind of conceptualizations that have kept bullying practices in place, demonstrating that bullying seems to police conformity rather than reflect anti-social norms (Payne & Smith, 2013). In this case the bullies were effectively policing for language use, assimilation, nationalism, and racial homogeneity.

Reenactments. A succession of reenacted iterations and interscene dialogues followed the first set. With each new iteration spectactors and actors swapped roles. New characters were introduced, and new possibilities were imagined. Every iteration was followed by another interscene dialogue. Maura and I facilitated by stopping action, asking questions of characters, listening, and encouraging dialogue. We refrained from taking their assumptions for granted. The findings to follow are a result of an analysis of these iterative reenactments and interscene dialogues, drawing on any public analysis that resulted from those dialogues.

Later in the chapter, I describe the transformative aspects of the reenactments and interscene dialogues. Suffice to say, it took quite a few iterations before any of the teacher roles were transformatively different in the scene. In the morning group, changes to the scene first involved asking the Latinas to stick up for themselves. When this idea was enacted, it was an utter failure. Of course, the Latino/a/x students did not have the cultural capital or resources to defend themselves and in the end their attempts became fodder for the bullies. It was most noticeable that the teachers in the morning group began the transformation process by proposing changes to the victims' behavior. Next, the teachers enacted a change by adding in a character—a white high school student who defended the Latino/a/x students. This, also, was not very successful. In both the morning and afternoon sessions, the first move to change the teacher was a somewhat passive authoritative move—a threat to the "probable" bullies that if they persisted, they would be turned over to the administration. Interestingly, during the actual ethnographic period, according to official records no teachers ever reported a bully to the administrators unless a physical fight ensued. In the cases of a physical altercation, both the transnational and the white students were reprimanded. You will see, at last, that there were transformative changes, but these did not happen until the teachers began to locate themselves as culpable actors in the bullying scenarios, rather than as external, innocent "bystanders" to it.

Public Analysis. During the interscenes, when participants engaged in reflective, out-of-character conversations, opportunities for public analysis emerged. The public analysis moments of the interscenes were recognizably different from the brainstorming, reflection, and synthesis that also went on through those same interscene dialogues specifically because participants articulated underlying assumptions to the enactments and then looked at relations across those underlying assumptions. One example of our public analysis was grasping how lack of care for and investment in transnational students functioned to maintain oppressive relationships through bullying. One of the participants suggested that the bullies might not be affected by what the teachers or "newcomer" students were feeling because the bullies presumedly did not care what those two groups of people thought about them. Our actors/spectactors began to collectively reconstruct assumptions about caring/ not caring in the dramatic examples that had immediately preceded the particular interscene conversation. The analysis was then applied to why "newcomer" students might feel helpless in the context of bullying; perhaps they did not feel cared for by teachers or white students, and perhaps they did not have the cultural resources to understand or seek caring in the schooling context. Participants found that in the scene, teachers and students inferred care (or its absence) from the activities of those around. Such analyses were collaboratively and pubic achieved through one of the interscene dialogues and it fed into the dramatic reenactments that followed.

Blurring the Lines: The Acting and Reacting Intra-actions

Through our use of TO, we blurred the lines that typically distinguish between data and analysis, the real and the imagined, participants and researchers. Looking closely at each of those blurrings revealed the intricacies of using drama as research including tensions specifically linked to the blurrings themselves.

Data and Analysis. One of the exciting strengths of both the Pedagogy and the Theatre of the Oppressed is that substantive analyses evolved by working collaboratively with the data. The improvisational scenes and the unplanned moments of reflection demonstrated the way drama compelled dialogue. Each enactment, interscene dialogue, and public analysis doubled as a source of both data and analyses. In other words, both the iterative enactment of scenes and the interscene dialogues were products of participants' interpretive analyses of previous scenes.

Explicit public analyses gave form and substance to any subsequent analyses and reenactments. Thus, by paying attention to the elements through which each new interpretation emerged and by looking across iterative transformations, the intuitive interpretations of participants guided all additional analytic processes. Moreover, contradictions and multiple analytic perspectives were kept alive: If interpretations were unresolved in the iterations, then they remained unresolved in the analyses. To the best of our abilities we avoided faulty erasure of the complexities.

Through interscene dialogues, participants actively entered conversations about opportunities for reframing and transforming the drama, but they did so by stepping out of character and back into their own experiences as teachers and members of the community. From their lived vantage points, the white participants interrogated the scenes within which they found themselves playing and/or observing familiar roles. The dialogues included issues and experiences that both reached beyond and were provoked by the scenes. For example, at one point a discussion ensued about the possibility of having other white students enter the scene as advocates for and defenders of the "newcomer" students. This idea surfaced because the bullies did not seem to "care" about what the Latinas or teachers thought of them. It was suggested that perhaps they would care about what their white peers thought of them. Moreover, it was assumed that there were probably some white kids who did care about the Latino/a/x kids not being bullied, even if they did not specifically know the victims. Such interscenes contributed to blurring the line between data and analysis because they were opportunities to reflect analytically on the scenes by discussing multiple interpretations (meaning fields), and they were also moments of data worthy in themselves of further understanding and analysis.

The line was not totally blurred because I did conduct analyses independent of the other participants, treating all of the workshop material as data, even the public analyses. Generally, there is no distinct analysis phase separated in time and space from the dramatic activities in performance research (Mienczakowski, 2001) and the emergent interscene dialogues are not typical of TO. However, Rymes et al. (2008) provided a detailed account of their use of discourse analysis applied to a single scene and its reenactments. They were able to explore sociocultural concepts that would not have emerged otherwise. Their paper was unique in its use of and reporting on researcher-engaged analyses. Similarly, analyses across enactments, interscene dialogues and public analyses were useful for a few reasons:

1. They further complicated the articulations, perspectives, and assumptions of participants.
2. They produced a larger set of data transcending individual episodes or scene.
3. They fostered differentiated expertise/experiences across roles and life experiences which benefitted from our various insider/outsider relationships.

We used a recursive process in all our ethnographic work, so I brought all analyses back to the group. My analyses were tethered quite purposefully to the interpretive accomplishments of the participants while they, also, afforded a critical reflection on the interpretations and the intuitions that had guided participation in the scene reenactments, interscene dialogues and public analyses.

The Real and the Imagined. What about role-playing was real? For example, when teachers were acting the parts of "students," what about that role-playing was real-*istic*? Sometimes, as facilitator, I interrupted the acting to create an opportunity to better understand the experiences of characters in their roles. Whenever I did this, it proved difficult for the teacher-actors to keep themselves in their roles. For example, when I stopped a scene to ask a question of a "Latina student," it was difficult for the teacher who was playing that part to talk in the first person, as that particular Latina student. This was true for all the roles except, of course, when a person was playing the part of the teacher. The perspective-taking capabilities transformed throughout the workshop. By the end of the theatre sessions, teachers were able to stay in character more authentically with gentle reminders to speak in the first person. One aspect of their reality involved the already-noticed difficulties teachers had empathizing with the transnational students. Another aspect of their reality manifested as the stark, practial separation between witnessing the scene and being within the scene.

To treat these role-playing activities as ethnographic data blurred the line between real and imagined. It welcomed into research something that was not exactly "real" in terms of a history of happenings. The acting was clearly an imag-ined play off an observation of something that really happened. The dramatic reenactments were intended to be different than the observation, but nonetheless *realistic*. It was not in every case confidently realistic because the teachers could not know that they were acting the parts of Latinas with much accuracy, but they could try to understand the experiences Latinas might have with bullying by acting out such encounters. The enacted parts were more or less realistic (plausible) to the extent that the actors could position-take with the characters.

There was one extreme example of resistance to position-taking that is worth sharing. A teacher in the afternoon session sat in the spectactor circle with his arms crossed over his chest. He stared at me. I think he wanted me to feel uncom-fortable. He did not say a word and even refused to introduce himself. Refused to do the warm-up activity. Refused to engage with his colleagues. He resisted par-ticipating and in so doing kept himself as an "observer." He did not participate in the ways we intended, but his presence was a form of meaningful engagement—a refusal to accept the starting scene as valid, a refusal to care about the well-being of the characters, a refusal to position-take, even with the role of the teacher in the scene, a refusal of the professional development opportunity for which he had signed up and a refusal of Maura's and my legitimacy, perhaps even the legiti-macy of the Project. Throughout the workshop, he remained tightly in his seat. In the context of our workshop, he had ostensibly assumed the role of the non-in-teracting/witnessing teacher bystander of our starting scene. Neither the real nor the imagined were actively articulated through his presence in our workshop, but his role nonetheless embodied a recognizable set of perspectives in our Unityville community.

For the rest of us, using TO with interscenes created the potential for democratic critique as an effect of a dialectic space between the imagined and the real. In order for the teacher-actors to take on the various roles (including an ultimately transformed teacher role), they authentically engaged their imaginations toward what could be, toward real possibility. Thus, the research was an opportunity not only to describe how the teachers conceptualized the bullying situations, but also to examine how the reality of those situations was conceptually structured, how it could be transformed/revolutionized, or how it pointed toward something other than what it was. This particular blurring allowed us to explicate the juxtaposition between is and ought. Ultimately, we moved toward a belief that teachers ought to actively change the bullying scenes themselves.

Participants and Researchers. Throughout the reenactments, neither Maura nor I engaged as actors. There was as clear line between us as researchers/facilitators and them as participants. Maura took observational notes and managed the audio-recording and photography, while I facilitated the activities. We assisted the unanticipated interscene dialogues by encouraging conversation and asking questions.

In our roles as facilitators, Maura and I committed ourselves to authentic dialogue with the teachers; thus, we did not hide our perspectives (very much). However, we did not want to risk the teachers feeling alienated through differences between their perspectives and ours. With this caution in mind, we primarily sought to understand their perspectives. We intended to engage in our roles as facilitators with the same respect, authenticity, openness, and fallibility that we expected participants to bring to their roles (Bagley, 2009a). At times, I had strong feelings about the things that were said during the interscenes, but for the most part I took up a listening mode which was, also, authentic for me. The following example displays my most intrusive response to participant reflections during the interscenes. I risked being interpreted as an "expert" in the dialogue, yet I, also, expected that the teacher was searching for another way to understand the situation, and I empathized with that.

T1 *(female):*   I believe you hear things like that, [that people should go back to a "home country" if they don't speak English]. I feel it myself. It is our culture. I think they should speak English and maybe that's because I don't understand. Maybe that's why people [American students and teachers] act that way [resentful of newcomer students who don't seem to be learning English]. I know that I DEFINITELY [spoken more forcefully and louder] think that if they ["newcomer" students] are here they should be speaking English. And if you don't, go home. That's the way I feel about it.

Me: It doesn't take a very long history in this country to discover that languages other than English have been around. It isn't like it is immoral to speak a language other than English, is it? I think it would be very hard to go into a new place. It might not be that the students are choosing **not** to speak English, but also "newcomers" probably need to hear their language, they need a language they can express themselves through. At least that is the way I experienced being in Germany without knowing German. I needed to talk English, too, sometimes—but, especially in the early months when I really couldn't talk German. What we hear is that it feels terrible to students to come to a new place to not be able to communicate in the new language and then have the language you are good at disallowed. I know people don't wish these bad feelings on the kids. There is a pedagogical issue; a lot of the kids want to learn English. But it doesn't just happen that quickly. In the meanwhile really bad feelings get generated.

T1:   It's the message that if you throw them in the water, that then they will swim. Isn't that the attitude? Doesn't that work?

T2 (female):   It seems like it just doubles the problem to expect them to learn a content class when they don't know English.

Me: That's how it seems to me.

T1:   So maybe this isn't the best way?

The dilemma of allowing myself to participate "equally" in the idea sharing, was that I couldn't be sure that what I had to say would not have one of two possible negative consequences, namely that it could either carry MORE weight in their minds or shut them down. The other side of the dilemma involved the problem of silencing my own perspective and not giving it an opportunity to be corrected or engaged as well as refraining from being the advocate I had committed myself to being for the transnational students.

With traditional ethnography, the involvement of the researcher in the lives of participants is greater than for most other social science methods. We maximized that involvement in the overall Project. We were participants in many senses of the word. We were open to understanding our collaborators/partners and to being understood by them. We were with them in their desires for change and in our commitments to change processes and possibilities and we reflected on the many expressions of resistance to those changes. We sought egalitarian critical consciousness-raising for ourselves and with them. We had ordinary relationships with them, and we participated in the work that they were doing.

The participants were also researchers. This was evidenced in the public analysis, for example. It was further evidenced in the sense that teachers raised authentic points of inquiry, created and carried out plans, and so forth. Most of the participants were active in the process. As such, they were investigating their own experiences and situations. Moreover, they knew that they were doing this. One teacher said, "I don't know what to do. I can see that this [ignoring the bullying] doesn't work. I want to see other possibilities. I want to have things to try out." Other teachers acknowledged when insightful discoveries were voiced. There were many such examples of participants engaged in the theatre through genuine inquiry.

The tension for me in this blurring involved navigating the balance of role differentiation. Our distinct roles carried external value that we had to work against. For example, the tendency to value researchers' skills more than teachers' skills inspired me to publicly voice my perspectives less often and bare my errors more often. Role differentiation also meant that my time was actually designated to do research business (transcribe, coordinate, analyze, track data, write, and so on) while this was not true for the Unityville folks by and large. This role differentiation necessarily instantiated the researcher-participant distinction.

Summary. The potential for deconstructing traditional research dichotomies between data and analysis, real and imagined, participants and researchers was approached, but not maximized. The tensions involved in fully doing away with the lines reflected limitations of the study and critiques of the conditions within which we conducted this piece of performance ethnography.

Critical Findings: Performative Emergings

Analysis of/during the workshop produced a set of interesting substantive findings related to two questions: (1) How was oppression conceptualized and recognized by the participants with respect to bullying? More specifically, to what extent and in what ways were participants aware of the inner workings of transnational student oppression? (2) What transformations in acting were evidenced through TO? I used the analyses to respond to those questions.

The Questions of Oppression

As mentioned earlier, one of our discoveries involved revealing the difficulty teachers had recognizing themselves as part of this specific oppressive relationship. Freire (1970/2000) encouraged people to discover the mechanisms that keep their involvement in the oppression hidden from view. His theory suggested that the oppression might seem sensible and legitimate to those involved with it. Likewise, it might be difficult for the participants to recognize the extent to which they are complicit with the oppression and/or active oppressors. Thus, in analyzing the data, it was especially important to see how the oppressions were conceptualized by the teachers, how the teachers were positioning themselves in the oppressive relationship/scene, and the extent to which those conceptualizations manifested their own collusive participation in the oppression.

At the beginning of each of the two workshop sessions, participants tended to alter the scenes by changing the way the "students" were acting. When doing this, they almost always began by proposing the suggested change in the second person (even when they were playing the part of the character whose action would change). For example, one of the women playing the role of a Latina student said, "Don't you think that non-traditional students [referring to the Latinas] should stick up for themselves?" and I responded with, "Well, let's *say* that in character from the first person and then we can try it out and see how it goes. But first, how does the idea of sticking up for yourself feel to you? What would it look like?" Another participant (also playing the part of a Latina) said, "Do you think we could get the non-traditional students to tell a teacher?" All the changes proposed by the participants in the morning session initially focused on having the transnational students act differently, yet the participants had a difficult time taking the first-person perspective of those students. At that point, the participants were conceptualizing the oppressive scene as something that involved only the students. Moreover, they were conceptualizing the victimized students from a non-empathetic perspective—failing to imagine the perspectives of the transnational students.

Here is an example of the scene where "students" were blamed for not getting along. We pick up this scene just after the "bullies" called the Latinas names and shoved them a bit. I stopped the acting to probe the scene.

Me: *(to the "bullies")* How do you feel right now? Why did you do that?

E2:   The kids are really passive aggressive. *[Not responding in character]*

Me: Okay, can you try talking in the first person?

E1:   *(jumping in to answer for E2)*. I think, I had a couple of students *[here referring to Latino/as]* and they don't want to talk to Americans *(sounds a little angry)*. They just want to talk to themselves; they don't want to talk to Americans. *[Not responding in character.]*

Me: *(turning to L1 and L2)* So in this scene do you feel like talking to an American? Would you want to talk to an American?

L1:   Well, no because they are being mean to me. *[Responding in character.]*

Me: *(to E1)* Do you want to talk to the Latina students? *[E2 shakes her head to indicate no.]*

E2:   Well, no.

Me: *(to E2)* What might change your mind?

E2:   I don't know. I suppose if they *[Latinas]* talked English.

Me: What might they say to you in English?

E1: Just maybe even, "hi."

Me: Okay, but did you hear her? *[Referring back to L1's response to my question]* She doesn't really want to talk to you because you were mean. What do you think about that?

E2: Well, they just moved here to take our jobs.

Me: We can ask them why they moved here in just a minute, but can you say more about her not wanting to talk with you because you have been mean? Do you think of what you are doing as mean?

In Table 6.1 I enumerated the list of insights because their specificity is important to the progression of critical consciousness-raising according to Freire (1970/2000). By untangling them and looking starkly at them, it was easier to see the precise mechanisms that were entailed in the oppressive conditions and relations. It helped participants to envision their own place in those conditions and relations. It was this kind of awareness that moves us along in the transformational process.

The understandings listed in Table 6.1 emerged as insights that were expressed through TO. They are meant to be read not as facts about the situations but, rather, as articulations of Aha! moments emerging from the white teacher participants' experiences. These articulations were the result of reconstructing implicit aspects of their performances, interscene dialogues, and public analyses.

These varied insights all led to better awarenesses of how the oppression of transmigrant/transnational students in the schools was being stabilized through bullying and how teacher action (even what might have originally been described as inaction) functioned in ongoing bullying events. The role of beliefs in sustaining that oppression was evidenced as each of the insights reflected an interrogation of previously held convictions.

Questions of Transformations

Transformations were also experienced. The transformations were built from the understanding of oppression that emerged through the TO activities. I begin this section by sharing two of the transformations that emerged during the interscenes. Following that, I report on the emerging transformations. These transformations are organized into two domains, those related to understanding transnational students' experiences and those related to understanding the teacher's role in perpetuating oppression.

Dialogue, brainstorming, and general responses to the scene between spec-actors and actors made these organic interscenes ripe for collective transformation. The evolving ideas were often integrated into the next iterations of the scene. For example, "teachers" used Spanish greetings in the hall following an interscene

Table 6.1 Emergent Insights Regarding Oppression

Insights Related to Context	Insights related to Student Experiences	Insights Related to Teacher Roles
Bullying occurred in the context of hostility where there was little opportunity for friendship.	Latinos had fewer resources for dealing with bullying than did Euro-Americans. This rendered them more vulnerable to it. They lacked the English words to explain to teachers what was happening and they lacked the trust that teachers would support them.	Passive teachers were inadvertently supporting the bullies. The dramatization also suggested the possibility that "newcomer" students and Euro-American students knew that teacher-inaction was a tacit go-ahead for bullies.
Authoritarian responses might not be the only ways to respond and might not be the most effective overall.	Not speaking English did not mean "newcomer" students did not like Americans, nor did it mean that "newcomer" students did not *deserve* to be in U.S. schools. Transnational students might have been afraid, unhappy, and bewildered.	Teachers who failed to respond to the bullying set a climate in the school for how transnational students could be treated by their peers—namely, that in this particular school it was okay to bully "newcomers." Transnational students were more visible to teachers when they acted against the bullying than the bullies were in the first place. Thus, if teachers waited to "see" something, they were more likely to catch Latino retaliation movement than bullying activity. In other words, teachers began to realize there was a skill of not getting caught involved in successful bullying that the "newcomer" students did not share. Some teachers really did not want "newcomers" in the school. As long as teachers did not acknowledge that this was the case, there was no way to know if this was a majority or minority of the teachers.

dialogue that questioned the teachers' connections with Latino/a/x students. As one teacher first enacted this idea, they demonstrated a reformed alliance with the transnational youth. This new way of enacting the scene gave the teachers an opportunity to attend to the Latinx students in ways the white students in the scene, also, noticed. The teacher modeled the value of languages other than English and made it less likely that the bullies could victimize the Latinas. They broke the English-only policy. And they centered the transnational students as their own. Another example involved introducing "white students" into the scene as allies for the transnational students. This transformation was instigated when one of the teachers said,

> I think that somewhat, like, how did the other students react? We did not have non-Caucasian students when I was in school. But there were always a few kids like myself who felt confident enough in their positions. The teachers didn't see it, but we as other students did. So we would say like, 'Hey, why are you doing that.' It almost always stopped it. So, not teachers, but other students who these kids want to be liked by, said something. What about that? Is anything like that happening?

Then I said, "Let's try it out. Why don't you be that student?" At first, the teacher-role was not changed through the scene, but then the "student" and the "teacher" found ways to support each other. For example, the teacher noticed the white student supporter and found ways to enable that support. This resulted ultimately in the teacher behaving more proactively to develop allies among the white students in the school. The innovative aspect for the teachers was imagining a way to both be and build allies for the transnational students. Previously, they had not assumed the roles of allies for either themselves or the white students. For the most part, what had been happening in the schools was that white teacher and white student alliances worked against caring for transnational students rather than in service to that caring.

Transformations Regarding an Understanding of Transnational Student Experiences. As the scene iterations progressed, so did the teachers' explorations into "student" feelings. Exploring Latinx student feelings was radical for this group of teachers because at the start they did not actively position-take or engage empathetically with the "newcomer" students. The iterations began to depict the im/migrant students more holistically and empathetically. For example, in Iteration 4 one of the "Latina students" hung her head after being teased. I stopped the action and asked her how she felt.

L1: I feel helpless and abused. *[Notice the immediate use of the first person.]*
Me: So if you are helpless, let's start with how the scene might look different and then see what you can do to help get the scene there.
L1: Well I don't really think I can get them to stop.

Me: *(to E1)* Is there anything she can do to get you to stop?

E1: I don't know. Probably not. *[Not said in character]*

Me: Why is that? Don't you care that she wants you to stop?

E1: No not really, they probably just care about being popular with their friends.

Me: Can you say that in the first person?

E1: No, I don't really care what that Latina thinks about me.

Me: How did it feel to say that?

L1: *(in response to E1)* I knew that.

E1: Well that felt terrible.

Me: How do you feel when you are bullying?

E1: Powerful *[I interpreted this use of the word "power" in light of how teachers enacted the word "empowerment" at the start of the workshop.]*

L1: I never feel powerful. I only feel lucky when I finally get away.

The iterations brought the teachers into the position of having to voice feelings, experiences, and hopes from the perspective of Latino/a children as well as put their bodies into the direct action of bullies. The key transformations in their thinking involved shifting (a) from thinking of the bullying as benign to thinking of the bullying as hurtful and violent (even when only verbal) and (b) from thinking of the transnational students as problems to thinking about the transnational students empathetically. The "power" that was felt by the bully-character was undone by the emergent empathy for the Latina student-character.

Teachers as Oppressors. The teachers were able to identify mechanisms and myths that seemed to keep the oppressive relationships in place. They, also, began to identify what their roles in the oppressive relationships were. The following examples reflect beliefs and behaviors commonly shared amongst the teachers at the start of the workshop. These beliefs were critically examined and understood through the context of oppression and thus, the beliefs became malleable.

Participants believed in the promotion of English-only practices and policies. Many of the teachers bragged about the district's English-Only policy as a strong feature of their approach to transnational students. The TO participants discovered that an English-only ideology made it seem reasonable to blame and target non-English speakers and treat them as outsiders not worthy of the same respect as those who did spoke English. Through TO, teachers noticed ways in which students' home languages could be considered a resource and they experimented with using small amounts of Spanish themselves. The idea of building the linguistic expertise of the teachers had not occurred to them before and they had not previously recognized that their own penchant for English-as-the-only-language was oppressive. For example, even the teachers who taught Spanish and Japanese were not thought of resources for either students OR other teachers in the effort to educate the transnational students.

The participants recognized that they routinely acted with a detached sense of responsibility toward their "newcomer" students. This detached sense of responsibility had been evident in three ways. First, teachers did not talk about transnational students as their own students, as worthwhile members of the Unityville school community. Second, the practice of detaching from responsibility in bullying and other intercultural scenarios was part of the pattern of either teacher non-involvement or teacher use of heteronomous responses, which we saw evidenced in the initiating scenes. After several iterations, participants identified such forms of detachment as mechanisms of oppression and of the maintenance of the oppressive status quo. According to the teachers' analysis, this detachment had previously made sense to them, but through TO it seemed questionable. They queried assigning responsibility for the bullying (oppression) to the students themselves without providing the resources and facilitation necessary for students to change the bullying on their own. They saw their own detachment as an active part of the bullying scene.

At first, the participants believed that they were not calling attention to race and ethnicity and therefore were not racists. They considered color blindness to be a fair-minded way to treat students. As you know, transnational Latino/a/x, Japanese, Taiwanese, and Palestinian students were most often referred to as "non-traditional students" or "newcomers," while the white students were referred to as traditional students. Such naming hid racial and ethnic identifications associated with not being white. Teachers in the workshop identified this as a problem because there were important social class and racial differences across the groups that affected the students' experiences in unacknowledged ways. In addition, such conflation of all transnational students into a homogeneous category of "newcomers" despite important differences (such as the Latino children being most strongly and openly discriminated against) resulted in ignoring key aspects of the oppression. Our TO participants discovered that there were racialized ways of thinking about the transnational students that implicitly supported bullying and negative attitudes toward our "newcomers," particularly Latino/a/x children. To not talk about race or ethnicity, meant that racially motivated discrimination was not fully acknowledged—and this itself had racial implications and racist outcomes. Though TO did not provide teachers with enough skills to fluently include race as part of their conversations, they clearly acknowledged that to not include race was problematic and that such erasures contributed to racialized oppression. The teachers owned responsibility for this. Through TO some of our Unityville teachers recognized the link between the bullying scenes at the high school and racial policing.

Finally, participants realized that they had been conceptualizing potential solutions to difficult situations in noncommunicative terms. For example, they realized that the plan to send white students episodically to the office for bullying was not going to have any systematic effect on creating positive feelings among students or on decreasing oppression because it stunted and inhibited dialogue. In fact, this idea of sending perpetrators to the administrators was not successful in our reenactments (and, plainly speaking, it was not actually used anyway). Participants saw that any dramatic effort that furthered the disjuncture across kids did not ultimately contribute to undoing the oppression. Additionally, this approach did nothing to foster positive teacher-student relationships. They realized that promoting non-communicative, or authoritative solutions to oppression only reproduced oppression.

Across each of these transformations, participants were eager to link their dramatic representations and experiences with their imagined future engagements. As reported on elsewhere (Korth, Martin, Sotoo., 2007), these participants did engage in changes that brought the issue of bullying and its oppressive mechanisms into dialogue throughout the school.

Concluding Thoughts and Reflections

"A commitment to nonviolence structures struggles of liberation, and these struggles always occur within contested terrains. In turn, the permanent struggle for freedom and liberation gives to 'all equally the power to seek self-determined hopes and dreams'" (Denzin, 2003, p. 23). "Performance ethnography performs these struggles and becomes, in the process, the practice of freedom itself" (Denzin, 2003, pp. 228–229). Freire (1970/2000) used the word *conscientizacão* to describe the moment in consciousness when one becomes aware of oppression but is not yet fully able to articulate it or transform it. Our emerging understandings provided evidence of just that: Participants, including me, were beginning to see how the oppression worked through a restriction of communicative understanding among school community members. Our initial focus groups' interviews suggested that oppression was at work, but analysis of those interviews did not provide a deeper understanding of its workings. Using Theatre of the Oppressed in this workshop scenario gave us some precision through which to further our local understanding.

The potential for transformation was not just imaginable through TO, it became actionable. For example, teachers' uses of Spanish in the reenactments took hold in new, previously unimagined, ways. Below is an excerpt of a conversation between Ed and one of the high school teachers that took place a year after this TO workshop.

Math Teacher: And I—yeah. But I was able to learn enough that the basic math, uh, phrases, adding and subtracting.

Ed: In Spanish?

Math Teacher: Yeah, in Spanish. And with this one student in particular. I mean the first time I used it he was like "whoa, what's going on?" But it—it helped.

Ed: So he was more attentive afterwards?

Math Teacher: Yeah. I mean he was more attentive. Um. I mean he wouldn't be afraid, necessarily, to ask questions. Uh. And I'd come over and do a lot of pointing. And began to use a little Spanish. And uh … it's helped him, I mean now his English skills have improved quite a bit. Um.. so it's still not there. I mean *[he doesn't need as much support as he did].*

The math teacher no longer characterized the responsibility for learning as resting primarily on the child's ability (or presumed willingness) to speak English. He expressed empathy as he recognized the child's propensity for fear. Outward engagement with Spanish speakers using Spanish (a) contradicted teachers' earlier claims to be monolingual, (b) complicated their views of assimilation and monoculturalism, and (c) altered their relationships with students. Mind you, these teachers were not fluent in Spanish—so using the language, also, enacted vulnerability on their parts. More and more Spanish was used by the adults across all the schools and eventually educators' use of Spanish rendered the English-Only policy a semi-moot point.

Theatre of the Oppressed was used as an example of bringing open-ended transformative possibilities into critical ethnographic practices through artistic expression. Lydia Degarrod (2013), who conducted what they referred to as an arts-based public ethnography wrote,

> … the use of the methods of collaboration and art made the social and dialogical process of knowledge visible, promoted the creation of embodied knowledge, and strengthened the understanding or empathy among the participants through the mutual sharing of memories, images, and sentiments. Furthermore, these methods facilitated instances for the exiles to contemplate and reflect on themselves. (p. 406)

Degarrod concluded, "Arts-based ethnographies have the potential of expanding ethnographic research, and of providing new means of transmitting ethnographic information, and have the potential to create social change" (p. 410). Critical ethnographic potential through art encourages praxis and self-reflection while opening the door for transformation (Faulkner, 2016). Using artistic opportunities to open dialogic space for reflecting and practicing change is aligned with critical ethnographic goals as it actively entertains *what could be.* Through art, theatre, and critical ethnography, participants necessarily translate an "as if" orientation into a "what if" orientation.

Note

1. This chapter draws extensively on a previously published open-access article, whose copyright belongs to me. The article was originally published in a Sage journal. Dennis, B. (2009). Acting up: Theatre of the Oppressed as critical qualitative research. *International Journal for Qualitative Methods, 8*(2), 65–96. Though changes were made, these were minimal and related primarily to framing the text as a chapter in the larger book.

References

Arditti, J. (2003). Locked doors and glass walls. Family visiting at a local jail. *Journal of Loss and Trauma, 8*, 1–23.

Bagley, C. (2009). The ethnographer as *impresario-joker* in the (re)presentation of educational research as performance art: Towards a performance ethic. *Ethnography and Education, 4*(3), 283–300.

Bagley, C. (2009) Guest editorial. Shifting boundaries in ethnographic methodology. *Ethnography and Education, 4*(3), 251–254.

Benson, K.E., & Piercy, F.P. (2009). A qualitative study of transgender relationships and therapy. In *Poster at the Annual Meeting of the American Association for Marriage and Family Therapy*. Portland, OR: Intellect Books.

Boal, A. (1979). *Theatre of the oppressed*. New York, NY: Theatre Communications Group.

Bowman, M. (2006). Looking for Stonewall's arm: Tourist performance as research method. In J. Hamera (Ed.), *Opening acts: Performance in/as communication and cultural studies* (pp. 102–134). Thousand Oaks, CA: Sage Press.

Brantmeier, E. (2005). *Constraints and possibilities for intercultural peace curricula: A critical case study of teacher involvement in multicultural change at a U. S. midwestern high school.* Unpublished dissertation.

Brecht, B. (1964). *Brecht on theatre: The development of an aesthetic.* New York, NY: Hill and Wang.

Carspecken, P. (1996). *Critical ethnography in educational research: A theoretical and practical guide.* New York, NY: Routledge.

Conquergood, D. (1985). Performance as a moral act: Ethical dimensions of the ethnography of performance. *Literature in Performance, 5*, 1–14.

Conquergood, D. (2002). Performance studies: Interventions and radical research. *The Drama Review, 46*(2), 145–156.

Conrad, D (2004). Exploring risky youth experiences: Popular theatre as a participatory, performative research method. *International Journal of Qualitative Methods, 3*(1). Article 2. Retrieved February 10, 2009, from http://www.ualberta.ca/~iiqm/backissues/3_1/pdf/conrad.pdf

Cozart, S., Gordon, J., Gunzenhauser, M., McKinney, M., & Petterson, J. (2003). Disrupting dialogue: Envisioning performance ethnography for research and evaluation. *Educational Foundations*, Spring, 1–23.

Degarrod, L. (2013). Making the unfamiliar personal: Arts-based ethnographies as public-engaged ethnographies. *Qualitative Research, 13*(4), 402–413.

Dennis, B. (2009). Acting up: Theatre of the oppressed as critical qualitative research. *International Journal for Qualitative Methods, 8*(2), 65–96.

Denzin, N. (2003). *Performance ethnography: Critical pedagogy and the politics of culture.* Thousand Oaks, CA: Sage.

Dolan, J. (2005). *Utopia in performance: Finding hope at the theatre.* Ann Arbor: University of Michigan Press.

Donmoyer, R., & Yennie-Donmoyer, J. (1995). Data as drama: Reflections on the use of readers theatre as a mode of qualitative data display. *Qualitative Inquiry, 1*(4), 402–428.

Fals-Borda, O. (1979). Investigating reality in order to transform it: The Colombian experience. *Dialectical Anthropology, 4*(1), 33–55.

Fals-Borda, O. (1987). The application of participatory action research in Latin America. *International Sociology, 2*(4), 329–347.

Faulkner, S. (2016). TEN (The promise of arts-based, ethnographic, and narrative research in critical family communication research and praxis). *Journal of Family Communication, 16*(1), 9–15.

Fierros, E. (2009). Using performance ethnography to confront issues of privilege, race, and institutional racism: An account of an arts-based teacher education project. *Multicultural Perspectives, 11*(1), 3–11.

Fine, M. (2006). Bearing witness: Methods for researching oppression and resistance—A textbook for critical research. *Social Justice Research, 19*(1), 83–108.

Fox, M. (2019). In the space between us: Reflections for audience members of youth-centered participatory research. *International Journal of Qualitative Studies in Education*, 1–19 online first version.

Freire, P. (2000). *Pedagogy of the oppressed* (30th anniversary ed.). New York, NY: Continuum. (Original work published 1970)

Freire, P. (2014). *Pedagogy of hope: Reliving Pedagogy of the Oppressed.* New York, NY: Bloomsbury. (First published in Portuguese in 1992 and translated to English in 1994 by Robert Barr.)

Goffman, E. (1959). *The presentation of self in everyday life* (1st ed.). New York, NY: Anchor Books.

Habermas, J. (1985). *The theory of communicative action, volume 1: Reason and the rationalization of society* (T. McCarthy, Trans.). Boston, MA: Beacon Press.

Harvey, J. (1999). *Civilized oppression.* Lanham, MD: Littlefield and Rowan.

Jones, J.L. (2002). Performance ethnography: The role of embodiment in cultural authenticity. *Theatre Topics, 12*(1), 1–15.

Korth, B. (2005a). Choice, necessity, or narcissism. A feminist does feminist ethnography. In G. Troman et al. (Eds.), Methodological issues and practices in ethnography. Studies in educational ethnography (Vol. 11, pp. 131–167). Oxford, England and London, England: Elsevier.

Korth, B. (2005b). A reply to Martin Hammersley. In G. Troman, R. Jeffries, & G. Walford (Eds.), *Methodological issues and practices in ethnography: Studies in educational ethnography* (Vol. 11, pp. 175–181). Oxford, England: Elsevier.

Korth, B. (2006, September). *Acting the part: Naturalistic versus contrived data—Using theatre of the oppressed in a long term ethnography.* Paper presented at the Oxford Education and Ethnography Conference, Department of Educational Studies, Oxford University, Oxford, England.

Korth, B., Martin, Y., & Sotoo, N. (2007). Little things that make a big difference: Trust and empathy on the path to multiculturalism. *Scholarlypartnershipsedu, 1*(2), 25–44.

Lather, P. (1991). *Getting smart: Feminist research and pedagogy with/in the postmodern.* New York, NY: Routledge.

Lincoln, Y., & Guba, E. (1985). *Naturalistic inquiry.* Thousand Oaks, CA: Sage.

McTaggart, R. (Ed.) (1997). *Participatory action research: International contexts and consequences.* Albany: State University of New York Press.

Madison, D.S. (2005). *Critical ethnography: Methods, ethics, and performance.* Thousand Oaks, CA: Sage.

Mienczakowaski, J. (1995). The theatre of ethnography: The reconstruction of ethnography into theatre with emancipatory potential. *Qualitative Inquiry, 1,* 360–375.

Mienczakowski, J. (2001). Ethnodrama: Performed research—Limitations and potential. In P. Atkinson, S. Delamont, A. Coffey, J. Lofland, & L. Lofland (Eds.), *Handbook of ethnography* (pp. 468–476). London, England: Sage.

Minh-Ha, T.T. (1982). *Reassemblage: From the firelight to the screen.* Wychoff, NJ: Women Make Movies.

Norris, J. (2000). Drama as research: Realizing the potential of drama in education as a research methodology. *Youth Theatre Journal, 14,* 40–51.

Payne, E., & Smith, M. (2013). LGBTQ kids, school safety, and missing the big picture: How the dominant bullying discourse prevents school professionals from thinking about systemic marginalization or … why we need to rethink LGBTQ bullying. *QED: A Journal in GLBTQ Worldmaking,* 1–36.

Prentki, T., & Sleman, S. (2003). *Popular theatre in political culture: Britain and Canada in focus.* Bristol, UK: Intellect Books.

Riessman, C. (2008). *Narrative methods for the human sciences.* Los Angeles, CA: Sage.

Rymes, B., Cahnmann, M., & Souto-Manning, M. (2008). Bilingual teachers' performances of power and conflict. *Teaching Education, 19*(2), 93–107.

Salazar, M. (1991). Young laborers in Bogotá: Breaking authoritarian ramparts. In O. Fals-Borda & M. Rahman (Eds.), *Action and knowledge: Breaking the monopoly with participatory action-research* (pp. 54–63). New York, NY: Apex.

Saldaña, J. (1999). Playwriting with data: Ethnographic performance tests. *Youth Theatre Journal, 13,* 60–71.

Saldaña, J. (2003). Dramatizing data: A primer. *Qualitative Inquiry, 9*(2), 218–236.

Saldaña, J. (2005). *Ethnodrama: An anthology of reality theatre.* Toronto, ON: Alta Mira.

Smith, C., & Gallo, A. (2007). Application of performance ethnography in nursing. *Qualitative Health Research, 17*(4), 521–528.

Stockdalet, M., Hangaduambo, S.,Duys, D., Larson, K., & Sarvela, P. (2002). Rural elementary students', parents', and teachers' perceptions of bullying. *American Journal of Health Behavior, 26,* 266–277.

Theatre of the Living. [Home page]. Retrieved March 10, 2008, from http://www.headlines-theatre.com/

Turner, V. (1969). *The ritual process: Structure and anti-structure.* Chicago, IL: Aldine Press.

CHAPTER SEVEN

"The times they are a-changin'" (Bob Dylan, 1963)

They always say time changes things, but you actually have to change them yourself.
(Andy Warhol, 1975, p. 115)

The previous chapter explicated the possibility for transformation through ethnographic practice. Transformation was desired. Change was both inevitable and sought.

One morning, following a regular Teacher Inquiry group meeting, I was talking with Ed who began describing a conversation that had ensued in the group. In the conversation, the teacher inquirers distinguished themselves from other teachers in the school who they thought were more reticent to change. In fact, it was not at all uncommon for all of the teachers who aligned themselves with IU-Unityville Outreach Project to characterize their peers as resistant to difference, to change. Change was an ever-present part of the conversation and an implicit part of the trajectory of understanding what we were developing in Unityville. Because the IU-Unityville Outreach Project was born of a recognition that the district's demographic changes meant that something in the school needed to be altered, the Project itself would be at odds with those among us who dug their heels into the sand. The transnational students brought opportunities for newness—but, this was not easily embraced in the Unityville schools.

With a focus on change, time was always a feature of our work. "A universe in which nothing whatever changed would be a timeless universe" (McTaggart, 1908, p. 459). In long ethnographies, "it will become impossible to ignore social change and processes as it becomes impossible to ignore the fact that life never stands still" (O'Reilly, 2012, p. 521). Thus, taking time into account would be especially important for ethnographies, in general, but perhaps even more salient for those that specifically deal with change. Chronological markings of difference and/or patterns of similarity are the most straightforward way to think about documenting change, but because ethnographers are not controlling variables, this approach is not as uncomplicated as it might be for other research designs. One of the enduring characteristics of ethnography is its claim of longevity in the field (Jeffrey & Troman, 2004), yet, there is a paucity of published ethnographies of change and even fewer methodological articles on ethnographic analyses of change or time.

Our initial interviews with Unityville faculty produced over 30 hours of talk about shifts in the district's demographics and corresponding demands. For the transnational students, change involved the differences between Unityville and the places they used to live (including changes in culture and language) as well as hopes for better experiences and brighter futures. Those of us who started the Project together shared a hope in a better future—hopes that were both specific and amorphous. Change and time intimately and explicitly structured our Project, but in complex and uneven ways.

A single illustration demonstrates the time complexities that were salient to our ethnography. During the first two years, we implemented weekly, hour long "Socialization Connections" that consisted of small-group video-conferences with transnational students (no teachers) conducted in the home languages of the students. I mentioned these earlier in the book. These focus group sessions were aimed at exploring cross-cultural experiences, encouraging emotional well-being, and providing various kinds of support. Socialization Connections had an internal trajectory related to time within and across sessions: meeting weekly for an hour with particularly developing agendas, an assigned IU facilitator, and a stable group of transnational student peers. Moreover, these socialization connections were specifically designed for the newest of "newcomers"—those students in their first two years at either the high school or the middle school who demonstrated little English proficiency. Thus, participation in the connections was directly linked to a time-dependent construct—*newness*. The Socialization Connections themselves changed over time independently, but these connections were, also, expected to have an effect on the larger school culture. Namely, the aim was to facilitate an easier cultural transition for the new students. Lastly, it is interesting to remember that the district was espousing strong ideological and practical support for its "English Only" policy during school hours, and yet, this policy was ignored during the times of the Socialization Connections where students used their home languages. We wanted to ethnographically recognize and understand time as it related to changes in the district.

Barbara Adam, a British sociologist, spent much of her later academic career wrestling with the meaning and analysis of time. She (1995) argued that social research intending to critique and facilitate change ought to "unravel the dominant representations of time, show them to be sociohistorical constructions and acknowledge their hidden role as guides to seeing and understanding" (p. 60). Others have also suggested that deeply taken-for-granted aspects of time have been largely ignored in ethnography (including educational studies) (Scheller, 2020; Willis, 2010; Roseberry, 1982; Wolf, 1974). Pierre Bourdieu (1977) criticized the de-temporalizing practices of ethnography noting that time is constitutive of meaning. Johannes Fabian (1983, 2006) similarly opposed "time-distancing" techniques often employed by ethnographers. When ethnographies do not take account of change and time, they are more likely to reproduce the status quo or leave the status quo unquestioned. He made the important point that by freezing ethnographic time, ethnographers contributed to the othering of their participants.

In a 2020 issue of the online journal *Forum: Qualitative Social Research*, Elisabeth Shilling and Alexandra König (2020) introduced four time-relevant aspects of doing qualitative research: time concerns as pertinent across diverse types of qualitative inquiry, time as methodologically relevant (not just of topical importance), time as a theoretical orientation with corresponding sensitivities, and time as a bounded feature in both human and material phenomena. This chapter focuses on the third aspect, that researchers can draw across various theoretical perspectives to establish corresponding time sensitive methodologies. Other researchers, like tempographer Vibeke Scheller (2020), argued that researchers need to consider how they "understand" time as well as how a thematic analysis of substantive time references can be established. Relatedly, Tor Hernes (2017) proposed that temporal trajectories constitute opportunities to articulate the ever-changing, becoming nature of how we think and organize. Such conceptualizing would interest ethnographers, but especially ethnographers expressly interested in change over time.

Adam (1995) began with common philosophical conceptions of time and tried to render these useful for ethnography. My effort takes a similar path. I drew on the work of David Wood (1989/2001), a philosopher of time. He explicated philosophical conceptions of time and its analyses, with the goal of more comprehensively understanding how philosophers conceptualize time as an aspect of their philosophies. He resolved philosophical incompatibilities by implicitly suggesting that the philosophical approaches were reflections of hermeneutic ways of experiencing and conceptualizing time and, therefore, should all be manifest in any comprehensive attempt to organize our ways of thinking about time. In other words, each of the philosophical conceptions of time has merit because they are all relevant to varying aspects of our lived experiences. This is clarified below. I built on his work to produce examples of time analyses useful for ethnographies that are oriented toward change.

The time analytics that I developed offer opportunities to analyze the hermeneutics of time in a site going through rapid demographic changes and to explore the practicalities of time in ethnographies of change. This chapter proposes a way to analyze changes as an aspect of ethnographic inquiry which seem particularly important when the ethnographic work is concerned with being apart of a change process.

Ethnography, Change, and Time

In a recent conference paper, Jan Nespor (2019) concluded that many important aspects of time are ignored by educational ethnographers, including changing sociohistorical, political times as context for ethnographic endeavors. He was specifically interested in how contemporary climate change and other geopolitical concerns function in ethnography. His concerns are relevant to the question of how ethnographic practices can both embody and contribute toward the changes it wants to see in the world. In 1985, Jean Shensul, Maria Borrero, and Roberto Garcia published an article arguing that educational ethnographers have not been successful at contributing to educational change. In the article, the authors were interested in the political possibilities for ethnographers to affect educational practice. They concluded, "The challenge for applied educational anthropologists is to find ways to use applied research methods to bring all sectors together to assess, develop, and utilize new approaches in education that bear on the interests of the communities in which they carry out their research (Lindquist, 1973)" (Shensul, Borrero, & Garcia, 1985, p. 160). Focused on outcomes, their helpful paper did not address the ways in which time was to be understood in relation to ethnographers' commitments to educational changes. There is still a need for more published accounts of ethnographies of change through which the notion of time is analytically taken up (Buroway & Verdery, 1999), particularly for those of us concerned about what our research *does* in the world.

Kathrin Hörschelmann and Alison Stenning (2008) contended that ethnography would be a good tool for understanding "the historical and geographical work dimensions of change" evident in postsocialist transformations (Hörschelmann

& Stenning, 2008, p. 340). In concert with my own ideas that research is primarily constituted of a dialogue, Hörschelmann and Stenning (2008) maintained that ethnographic engagements can change both the participants and researchers involved in the process. They identified a need to

> ... face the challenges of finding methodological approaches that are able to trace and to 'keep up' with often quite speedy transformations, while on the other hand in places where new routines and structures are becoming established the task is to find ways of identifying after the event what caused change, how it occurred and who has been affected. (Hörschelmann & Stenning, 2008, p. 352)

Hörschelmann and Stenning (2008) suggested that in research situations where cultural assumptions were to be questioned, the researcher's focus *should* include change. They concluded with the claim that there are validity problems when the ethnographic site is undergoing rapid transformations because there are no means to analyze change in contemporary analysis (p. 353). In fact, their proposal was to use archival data for this aspect. Certainly, Dini's historical work (Chapter 4) fits this recommendation. Additionally, I intend for this chapter to begin to fill this need for ethnographic analysis strategies of change and time. Beginning modestly, I focus in this chapter on articulating attitudes toward change and changes in attitudes toward change. I draw specifically on David's Woods model of time seriation. Doing this illustrates the potential for creating time analytics that are amenable to the complexities of educational ethnography and account for the hermeneutics of time at play amongst ethnographic participants. David Wood's different cases of time (based on leading philosophical concepts) helped to capture the myriad of findings and ongoing activities relevant to the Project's transformative goals. I use his insights to create an analytic scheme capable of articulating relevant cultural themes regarding attitudes toward changes and ways of noticing how those attitudes themselves changed.

David Wood's Philosophy of the Future

In his 1989/2001 book *The Deconstruction of Time*, Wood examined the philosophical texts of Nietzsche, Husserl, Heidegger, and Derrida. Through his analysis, Wood proposed an integrative philosophy of the future which he built by fashioning these various philosophies of time into "hermeneutic models" of time (p. 332). His hermeneutic models are systematized descriptions of how people ordinarily interpret "time." The models take their place as reconstructions of the various ways people tend to experience time in their intuitive understandings of themselves and their lives. The models do not describe the nature of "time" itself, which is what the philosophers were intending to do (p. 332). Wood created the possibility for a complex conception of time, a possibility just barely introduced and pointed towards in his book. Such philosophical explorations can be made useful for ethnographic practices.

Wood came to the conclusion that a positive philosophy of the future (a philosophy capable of orienting hopefully toward the future) can and should be forged. Wood took seriously West's (1981) criticism that "Post-modern American philosophers ... have failed to project a new world view, a counter movement, a 'new gospel' of the future" (p. 265). Wood proposed two ways in which a positive account of the value of the future might be developed—hermeneutically and ethically. Both the hermeneutical and ethical accounts of time are relevant for critical ethnographers.

According to Wood, the hermeneutic point was best articulated by Heidegger who argued that the future is the horizon of possibility for intelligibility, meaning, and truth. As Wood put it, "Understanding is never a mere grasping of the present, or the presence of something, but always occurs within a triple ekstatic horizonality—of past, present, and future" (p. 364). Ekstatic is a Greek-derived that Wood word takes from Heidegger who used it to indicate that our senses of temporality were based on difference rather than on sameness. Ekstases are primitive breaks from stable identity or sameness evidenced through the use of words like "to," "towards," "alongside," and "being," among others. This is an important point as it directly links to how change is typically linked with time as a break in what has been thought of as "the same" over time.

Wood proposed that the ethical account was best articulated by Thomas McCarthy (1978/1994) who argued that the ethical significance of any critical endeavor involved a positing of the future in the move from the real to the ideal (McCarthy, 1978/1994). Wood wrote, that "no account of an ideal state of human affairs, no account of basic human values, and indeed no prescriptions as to how things ought to be, or what ought to be done, are complete without a projection of the future as the condition of their realization" (p. 365). For this reason, Wood did not assume that this basic attitude toward the future was "western" or relativistically biased. It was toward these hermeneutic and ethical values of the future that Wood's deconstruction of time provokes philosophy. Wood's philosophy of the future is backgrounded in the details I present in this chapter. It's justification in hermeneutics and ethics made it a good fit for a critical participatory ethnography oriented toward change.

Wood's careful critique of varying philosophies integrated seemingly disparate views because the competing assumptions across the approaches were shown to be either invalid or unnecessary. Furthermore, Wood situated the divergent philosophical approaches in a broader hermeneutical context which took the pressure off any one of the approaches to serve as ground for the full investigation. My aim in this section of the chapter is to describe two main contributions Wood made to the philosophy of time which he directly transposed to methodological theory and practice for the field of biography. I took up his ideas for ethnography as I analyzed the Unityville data. This section is divided into two parts: (1) Hermeneutic Models of Time, and (2) What Language Structures Reveal About Time Structures.

Hermeneutic Models of Time

One of the strengths of Wood's philosophy is the way he relocated central and general questions of time from various perspectives into a bigger picture and, in so doing, demonstrated the merits of multiple notions of time overlapping and at play. Wood carefully synthesized, developed and critiqued the philosophical description and assumptions of each of the five approaches he relocated as models for understanding and interpreting time. These models were not intended to supply an adequate metaphysics of time and were instead, as the label suggests, intended to create a descriptive "hermeneutics of time." By hermeneutics of time, Wood meant modes of understanding time in the everyday interpretive contexts of our lives. The five models are Cosmic Time, Dialectical Time, Phenomenological time, Existential Time, and the Time of the Sign. For a more detailed description of each coupled with an explanation of their ethnographic relevancies, see Appendix E "A Short Course on Wood's Hermeneutic Models of Time."

Wood defined time, in general, as difference. Difference is not unidimensional[1] and thus, must conceptually include momentum as an aspect of time. Momentum captures both the movement of difference and the dialectic between sameness and difference. Table 7.1 summarizes the ways in which Wood's hermeneutic models of time are already embedded in the practice of doing critical ethnography.

Wood posited a "structural hermeneutics" through the five models because he wanted to reap the analytic power of structuralism without taking any one of these various interpretations of time as complete in and of themselves. This is why each of the five models reflect interpretations of time rather than natural grounds of "Time." Correspondingly, I was able to articulate the practical relevancies of the models for ethnography. As hermeneutic models, they should be thought of as nodes of interpreting time which we would find within the cultural lifeworld of actors. I expected that they could facilitate the analysis of the lifeworld or culture as well as inform the processes of ethnographic practices themselves.

Table 7.1 Wood's Hermeneutic Models of Time and Critical Ethnography

Hermeneutic Models of Time	Hermeneutic Character	Aspects of Critical Ethnography Sensible Through the Particular Model
Cosmic Time (McTaggert)	The intuitive sense of order related to understanding the world's experiences through the relations of earlier than/ simultaneously with/later than. EXAMPLE: Before humans walked on the moon/after humans walked on the moon	Telling the ethnographic story from the first person perspective of participants
Dialectical Time (Hegel)	Time is qualitative transformation through which the process of opposition, conflict, struggle, contradiction, resolution, reflection, realization, and development, are foregrounded. EXAMPLE: Understanding myself now as a more mature person in contrast with earlier times	Conceptualizing and practicing critical ethnography overall
Phenomenological Time (Husserl)	This model of time emphasizes the first person experience with time and the horizon of anticipation involved in acting meaningfully. EXAMPLE: Being aware of one's potential for acting in a situation	Reconstructing validity horizons and articulating meaning fields
Existential Time (Heidegger)	The future is privileged because we understand ourselves in terms of possibility. EXAMPLE: Expecting to feel sad at a funeral and organizing my presence in light of that expectation	Reconstructing identity claims and identifying normative commitments for actors
Time of the Sign (Derrida)	A pluridimentional model of time through which any form of unification of these multiple dimensions is understood as an act of desire or power. EXAMPLE: Recognizing the co-existence of multiple desires that seem in contrast or conflict with one another, as in, "Part of me wishes x, while the other part of me wishes y	Honoring the complexity and difference of time through the relations across participants' perspectives, text choices, which authentically ensue through the overall endeavor of critical ethnography

What Language Structures Reveal About Time Structures

Wood noted that time and language are co-structured. Explicit structuring includes modifying verb tenses, for example. Implicit structuring involves higher levels of inferencing, for example, repetition, simple progression, or syntactic connection. Wood demonstrated the complexity of language/time structures by closely analyzing seriation. Toward an analysis of seriation, Wood created a typology of temporal cases which reflected ways time was used to unify the order or progression of things. The four cases offer a careful delineation of seriation as dependent on conceptions of time.

Wood claimed that the following temporal cases were modulations of temporal seriality which serve to create order. They include (p. 345):

- Reflective case—projecting order onto phenomenon after the fact;
- Generative case—drawing on underlying formative principle to give order to the phenomenon;
- Participatory case—unrolling the order of phenomenon through successive confirmation or denial of anticipations and the birth of new anticipations; and
- Active case—determining order, at least partially, through active plans that are forward looking.

The implicit layers of repetition, simple progression, and syntactic connection, such as, can be juxtaposed with these cases because time is itself hermeneutically linked to phenomenon. While these are not the only philosophical or methodological possibilities for an analysis of time, they provide a starting place that I found useful for wrestling with how to understand attitudes toward change and changes in those attitudes.

These very specific tools analyze conceptions of time which are both explicit and implicit in everyday communication and action. There is an intersubjective basis for the hermeneutics of each of these tools. The tools are compatible with critical ethnography, however, they need to be expanded from tools for understanding time to tools for understanding culture.

A sameness/difference dialectic is at work across all these analyses and conceptualizations of time. The way time configures unity across differences is one side of the dialectic. Inherently, difference compels our recognition and understanding of time in ordinary contexts. The sameness/difference dialectic is best left unresolved in the analysis of time because it can be used to refine our understanding of the hermeneutics of time and of the momentum through which time ensues.

Transposing Philosophical Insights into Methodological Practice

As a preliminary attempt at transposing David Wood's philosophical analysis of time into methodological practice, I specifically try out two possible applications. The first application, Time Cases in the Analysis of Cultural Themes, involves transposing the cases of time analysis into an ethnographic analysis of cultural themes. The second application, Time Cases as Ethnographic Process, involves using this same set of cases to discuss the ethnographic process.

Time Cases in the Analysis of Cultural Themes

Wood's analysis of time according to its seriation (reflective, generative, participatory, and active cases) facilitated making cultural themes explicit. By thinking of the four cases as categories of ways people culturally conceptualized time, it was possible to articulate varying cultural themes linked to reconstructing peoples' senses of change. To do this, I reviewed the reconstructive horizon analyses looking for indicators of the time cases in the way people were interpreting what was going on in Unityville during the Project.

Reflective Case. The reflective case involves putting events or phenomena in order by looking back at the past and using the order of things (at least implicitly) to construct interpretations of the cultural situation/actors. When analyzing acts, references to the reflective case appeared through words that juxtaposed an implication about the past with the current situation. This was noticed in the use of words like "now" when there was an implied "then" or "would have been like this" when the past was compared to the future. Cultural themes were articulated as what constituted the reflection with the current situation. Through the reflective case, the actor's action-orientation appears agentically passive.

For example, one of the Latinx transnational high school girls interviewed early in the process said what many of her peers had also told us, "My parents left home, and came here to make a better world for us. *And, things are getting better.* But I can't tell them how difficult things are because they sacrificed for us, for this vision"[2] (emphasis added). This particular reflection had to do with looking back at the order of things and projecting a progressive conception of time on how experiences, even the bad ones, fit into an overall expectation that as time progresses, things will get better. This cultural theme, which repeatedly emerged through a reflective case analysis of transnational students' and parents' talk/activities, was the idea of the past being worse and the future being better. The reflective order of things, then, was through the theme "improvement." Here is another example. A Japanese transnational high school female[3] said, "It is much better here, because then [in Japan] I was under too much pressure. There is not as much pressure now." One of the parents told interviewers that she was glad her son was in this [Unityville] school now because he had better [material] things at this school then he did at his other school. When interpreted as an effect of reflective time, the improvement theme was more precisely labeled, "Time Brings Improvement." This was true when one was looking forward from the present or backward from the present. By the end of the Project we were able to analyze the "Time Brings Improvement" theme as a way of putting into record what had been improved and what had not been improved from various perspectives—teachers, administrators, parents or students. It's not that we asked each of the groups what they thought had improved, it's that we were able to analytically track improvements as well as reconstruct desires for improvement. Educators obscurely expressed this theme with respect to how Black students had assimilated because they conceived of assimilation as positive movement into the future: "time bringing improvement."

This theme of improvement contrasted with the white folks' generalized ideas that things had been better in the past. This predominant attitude articulated a reflective order of things expressed through the theme of "Maintaining the Status Quo" (as an active resistance to perceived changes). Over time, the reflective case themes changed for the majority of Unityville educators from "Maintaining the Status Quo" to "Time Brings Improvement." The reflective case analysis helped to recognize this shift.

Generative Case. In generative time, order is constituted of underlying principles that can be reconstructed. Exploring the data for generative conceptions of time involved looking for something akin to deep structures in grammar at work in the background beliefs about change itself. When the principles are articulated, they reflect cultural themes. The actors as agents are decentered in this conceptualization of time as the structures of thought are presupposed to function regardless of actors' orientations. The principles functioned conceptually as implicit organizers for thinking about what was happening over time. I articulate two themes through this analysis.

There was a strong "principle of addition" that was initially involved in the cultural conceptions of change and time. This principle worked across a variety of domains. Here are some simple examples: The changes to Unityville demographics was the result of the "addition" of "newcomers" to the district's schools; the needs of the students involved "adding" ENL classes to the curriculum; as well as "adding" responsibilities to already existing positions—the special programs coordinator "added" ENL programs to the list of those for which she was responsible, one of the high school English teachers "added" ENL classes to the list of those she taught, the schools "added" ENL aides; and the addition of criminality and particular kinds of "problems" thought to have never before been experienced by the schools, like the intrusion of gangs into the community.

This cultural theme of addition carried several particular assumptions that were consequential for how educators engaged with our Project. For example, this theme expressed an assumption that "more *of* us/more *like us* is better" along with the idea that "nothing we are already doing needs to be transformed." Such assumptions meant that teachers and administrators could think of what they were doing as more or less fine for their transnational students. In terms of pedagogy and policy, this theme was evidenced by the extent to which educators' own practices remained somewhat unchanged. On the constructive side of things, it also afforded an opportunity for our team to imagine additive ways of improving the situation for the transnational students and their families. For example, we translated the school handbook into Spanish and Japanese. There were teachers who added new pedagogies to their repertoire of teaching abilities. Eventually, the schools even added new activities as within its general approach to education, for example, allowing high school students to miss school in order to participate in a DACA activitist rally at the state's capitol.

By the end of the Project, another prominent theme emerged through the generative case analysis: "Contrasting Alternatives." Here are some of the examples through which we came to recognize this theme. I referred earlier to a math teacher who used Spanish to explain simple ideas (which contrasted with the English Only policy and with the reigning idea that one should not teach differently just for the sake of the transnational students). There was another teacher who purposefully used body gestures in parallel with words to communicate expectations for the transnational kids (which contrasted with the non-empathetic orientation taken by most teachers at the beginning of the project). The note from Jerry Changer (Chapter 2) contrasted with the status quo and asked for alternative ways to confront racism in the school. We created welcoming books for students and families when students from other countries entered the schools. These were culturally and linguistically specific and drew on the things we were learning through the study. These books were a contrastive alternative to the idea that equity and fairness meant doing the same thing for every student/family as the white students/families did not need these books, but for "newcomers" they proved quite helpful and sent an alternative message ("You are welcome here" rather than "go home").

The use of this principle (contrasting alternatives) indicated an important shift because it afforded a sense of more than one way to think about, respond to, and engage with the various complexities of the moment. In some ways, this principle cut against the idea of monoculturalism and the corresponding desire for maintaining the status quo. This theme of Contrasting Alternatives was largely not functioning as a conceptual organizer for people at the beginning of the Project. It's emergence in the life of the Project sets up its own sense of contrast with the theme of addition that was prevalent from the start.

Participatory Time. Wood referred to participatory time as the case whereby the ordering of events and phenomena was described as an unfolding—an unfolding in which the participants were involved through the acts of confirming, denying, or creating anticipations. Cultural themes were articulated as both the unity of anticipations and as the contrast of confirming, denying, and creating. The sense of agency involved in interpreting time this way had to do with a reacting awareness to what one learned to anticipate. Wood used the imagery of watching a skywriter spelling out words to illustrate participatory time. I was able to analyze the participatory case by reconstructing the sense of anticipation in how participants talked about their experiences. For example, I paid attention to mentions of cues that helped the students figure out what was expected or how they might recognize or anticipate what would happen next and how they should act in relation to those happenings.

For our transnational students this was the way they thought of learning the rules at their new school. They would say things like, "I don't understand why my teacher yells at me" or "I tried to figure out what the teacher was talking about, but it was too hard." Through this participatory case of time, our "newcomer" students envisioned their learning about the school as time passing by through which they must continually anticipate what was going to happen next. Poignantly, they did not know the rules that were useful for anticipating in this new cultural context. The cultural theme that emerged through this analysis of the transmigrant student experiences was "Cultural Interloper as Detective."

Participatory time was also evidenced through positive events. For example, a student said that she thought her teacher was trying to help her by pulling a protractor out of the desk while using the word "protractor" in class. The student implicitly interpreted the teacher's help through the participatory time case. The teacher had understood what the student needed in order to successfully anticipate what would happen next, and the teacher provided the information on the sly so that other students did not catch what she was doing to help the struggling student. The Socialization Connections were used, in part, to help the transnational students "figure out" the culture and how to act within it. The purposes and outcomes of those focus group meetings was understood through participatory time and that same theme "Cultural Interloper as Detective." The theme indicated that transnational student anticipations were linked to a process of figuring things out.

Another theme I articulated through an analysis of participatory time was "Toward ~~Monoculturalism~~/Whiteness." Early on, this theme was more implicit than explicit. Our awareness of its prevalence and link to participatory time developed through conversation and reflection. While monoculturalism was openly talked about, especially through the language of assimilation, its racialized structure did not get fully articulated during the life of the project. For many, the theme "Toward ~~Monoculturalism~~/Whiteness" served as implicit justification and confirmation of project activities even so. An example of this was the time-based comparison of Latino/as with African Americans. The theme itself demonstrated not only white privilege, but the deep-seated nature of racism entailed in the temporal conceptualizations of the Project. Monoculturalism as racially motivated momentum was an important understanding across our work in Unityville.

Active Time. Active time was the case where planning modes were effectively implied, at least partially, in determining the ordering of events/phenomena. As the name suggests, actors are positioned as agentically active through this analysis. Our transnational Dreamers talked about learning English, getting better grades, passing their classes, graduating from high school, and going to college as a large sequential plan within which the pressure of learning English was the first order of business. This sense of time was used to organize their priorities. On a smaller scale, our transnational students talked about how to make it through the day (like sitting together at the cafeteria which they looked forward to doing). Both the large and small versions of active time were part of the cultural theme I called "I Will Survive." Understanding survival as it was conceived through active time helped us to develop priorities for the project. The teacher's planning was not actively focused on transnational student survival, so we worked to bring them into this orientation and its concommitant set of priorities. In Chapter 6 I described a shift in teachers' view of bullying from having to authoritatively manage the bullies to developing interactive opportunities with transnational students. The latter was more directly connected with the minoritized student's survival and the former was more directly connected with maintaining school control (another theme that was articulated through the reflective time case). Thus, the Project facilitated a shift in the subtle time conceptualizations for teachers from reflective to active which encouraged teachers' understanding of the theme "I will Survive."

Summary. These analyses of time cases facilitated the articulation of particular cultural themes associated with Project activities and participants' experiences. The

Table 7.2 Themes Emergent from Time Case Analytics

Time Case	Theme
Reflective Case	Time Brings Improvement
Generative Case	Principle of Addition
	Principle of Contrasting Alternatives
Participatory Case	Cultural Interloper as Detective
	Toward ~~monoculturalism/~~Whiteness
Active Case	I Will Survive

elements of time embedded in the themes were part of their senses of the themes themselves. See Table 7.2.

Time Cases as Ethnographic Practice

Further, I used Wood's Time Cases to characterize different aspects of ethnographic practices. Remember that Wood's time cases magnify the serial aspects of time. The time features of doing ethnography and writing it up are always more complicated than is adequately addressed by a simple linear conception of time. Wood's re-interpreted philosophy of time provided the framework from which to describe multiple dimensions of seriality involved in the conduct of the ethnography and in the production of findings.

Reflective Case is taken up in most ethnographic writing—it is when ethnographic stories are constructed after the fact. Ethnographers look back over sets of events and phenomena and develop order which results in a pieced together story. It is the reflective case in analysis that is often directly translated into ethnographies, but on another level, it is the reflective case which is used to organize the written reports/papers into ethnographic texts. When ethnographers write their ethnographic texts, this time case is often foregrounded in the way the stories are told. The reflective case in this text has foregrounded methodological insights and innovations. Knowing what to write required a reflective case orientation toward time. At the start of the project, I could not have known what these themes would be nor would I have known their salience for the Project.

Generative Case is typically used to articulate the principles underlying a particular order to things. Sometimes the generative case in ethnography is emergent, that is, the ethnographer articulates the principles of time that underlie the ordering of things and practices *for* participants (from various participant perspectives). The ethnographer may also engage generative principles in orienting her research with respect to time. For example, the generative principle of development may be involved in the way the ethnographer thinks of him or herself in the field in relation to pre-engagement, engagement, and disengagement. Identifying generative cases locates the underlying assumptions of time that the ethnographic practice embodies. This is another way of telling the ethnographic story. In other words, the generative case can be made explicit and, also, be used in the telling of the story. You might recall the start of this book where I told the story about getting involved with Unityville and the project of change. The Generative Case I used was that of "making progress toward a collective goal." There were strong principles involving a belief in the potential for progress that shaped our conceptions of the ethnographic project. As you have been reading this text, you are, no doubt, experiencing the Project through this "making progress" conception of time. Even the subtitle of the book indicates this sense of momentum.

Participatory Case is involved from the early phases of ethnography, where the ethnographer is developing anticipations about the site, confirming and rejecting these and creating new ones. The ethnographer is having an impact on the unfolding and ordering of events and phenomena, not in a planned way, but rather just through the acts involved in coming to understand and be part of the cultural life of the ethnographic site. This same case is mirrored in the early phases of data analysis where the ethnographer is beginning to create the unfolding order of things through the analytic process. Even activities such as informal conversations, audio-recording, and participating in decisions that occur as part of the everyday life at the site involve this participatory case. Phrases like "participant observation" indicate an orientation toward this case, however, the effects of this time case in the conduct of ethnography are often left out of ethnographic texts. Patti Lather and Chris Smithies' (1997) *Troubling the Angels* is an example of how to bring in the Participatory Case in a final write up. In that book, Patti Lather and Chris Smithies wrote both subtly and explicitly about their own involvement in bringing order to the events and experiences of the women's groups they studied. They even visually separated some of the writing into top and bottom hemispheres to illustrate the unfolding nature of their work together with the women in the groups.

More or less, Active Case is involved in ethnography in direct relation to the design of the study. The use of interviews at strategic times, for example beginning, middle, and end interviews, affects the order of things gleaned, assessed, and so on from the interviews themselves. The issues of timing are often explicit aspects of the design of ethnography, but then these are seldom rigorously accounted for in the analyses. For example, if we interview at the beginning, middle, and end and then we report changes from beginning to the middle to the end, then we have perhaps been too simplistic in our basic assumptions about time. Taking this into account might involve analyzing the data for the active time case as an effect of the ethnographic process.

In the Unityville project, we started with efforts to understand the transnational students' experiences because we were most concerned about them and knew the least about them. The early focus group interviews were opportunities for us to hear more about their experiences so as to guide the change process. As mentioned earlier in the book, many of the educators in Unityville were not expressing much empathy toward their transnational students and the Project collaborators hoped that that we could build empathetic connections between teachers and students if we had a way to share students' experiences.

Our regular focus group meetings with students had multiple purposes, but the weighting of those purposes shifted over time. Moreover, the focus groups served as our initial resistance to the district's English Only policy. These meetings established not only a school safe zone for students speaking in their home languages, they also gave researchers a chance to engage in home language interactions with students outside the boundaries of the focus groups, for example, when greeting one of the students in the hallway. By now you know that over time, we were able to bring more normalcy to informal uses of home languages in the school buildings. The focus groups also provided the research team with opportunities to build trust with the students and this translated to their families. Trust opened the door for us to become a resource for parents, accompanying them when they were meeting with teachers and so on. In summary, conceptualizing the ethnographic process from these more complicated perspectives on time contributed to richer opportunities for understanding ethnography itself.

A Critical Educational Ethnography of Change and the Use of Time Analytics

In this last section of the chapter, I first demonstrate how I used time analytics to articulate cultural themes related specifically to change and then I discuss the complexities of doing ethnographies of change through the same set of analytics with some adaptations. I focused on change in attitudes among high school teachers with respect to educating their transnational students. As criticalists, we wanted to reap what we learned from our work for the benefits of both our own self-awareness and the liberatory potential others might recognize for themselves.

When we first interviewed people at Junction High School in Unityville, the very depressed voices of the youngsters juxtaposed with the educators' lack of awareness of students' emotional needs inspired a commitment from our team members to be involved in a critical change process at the school. We submitted a lengthy report to administrators (Korth et al., 2004) that endeavored to answer Unityville's own call for educationally salient guidance around their shifting

212 | WALKING WITH STRANGERS

demographics while, simultaneously, integrating our own scholarly and ethical views of change potential. In that report, we organized needs and possibilities along a timeline—immediate to long-term. We did this rather unreflectively with respect to time, taking for granted the role of time in change. Though the first semester's data was about locating the potential for change, relevant change was already happening merely through the activities of the Project itself. Never before had Junction High School pooled together educators concerned about the learning situation of transnational students. Never before had they solicited the support of outsiders for these purposes. People described the ethnographic efforts of the fall 2003 semester as "new," as "a positive response to new challenges," and as "a first step." However, these positive attitudes toward the Project (by some) were directly connected with the attitude that the demographic shifts themselves were negative and challenging: "Unityville's never seen anything like this;" "We've never had so many non-traditional students;" "We've had a good school district [as if that might now be in jeopardy];" and "We didn't have non-Caucasians in school [as if things might have been better that way and as if Black students were not already present in the schools]."

Some school administrators, with a cadre of involved teachers, both recognized and chose change—change that was intricately linked to the ethnographic inquiry process. This change potential was something this cadre was choosing. Their choice implied a critique of the present and the potential for positive futures. It existed right alongside educators and community members who were reluctant to change. We recognized the critique emerging within the Unityville community itself through the contrast between those who actively sought out this opportunity for changing school practices and those that resisted such changes. The IU-Unityville Outreach Project was a joining in a critical change process *with* and *across* Unityville community members.

Time Analytics and the Hermeneutics of Change

The analysis of change in teachers attitudes regarding their racially and linguistically diverse students involved hermeneutically reconstructing cultural themes as exemplified earlier in the chapter. The case analyses gave a richer exploration than one might have gotten without it, but these analyses were in sync with other analyses. Moreover, as alluded to, attitudes about change also changed. This required a second level analysis of the change in attitudes. These shifts were marked more by participation in various activities then by objective time, though objective time was not a moot point. I focused below on the transformation of specific teacher attitudes and attitudes toward change itself.

Choosing to look at changes in teacher attitudes already indicates a shift in both the questions and the priorities of the project. So much of the beginning efforts focused on creating tangible structures to support students. Changing the attitudes of teachers was a complicated and emergent priority. We saw evidence of it early in the Project specifically through the IU contingent's concern to foster empathy for students amongst the teachers and through teachers who suggested that some of their colleagues were resisting change (and that perhaps that specific attitude itself needed to change if transformation was to occur in the school).

I analyzed insights through two iterations of each of the four case analytics described in the section above. The first set of iterations (labeled 1 below) was early in the ethnographic period and the second one (labeled 2 below) reports analysis of data later in the ethnographic period. I end with a subsection titled "Meta-Time Analytics" which looks across the two sets of case analyses.

Reflective Analytics (1). An analysis of the reflective case in teacher attitudes toward change[4] initially involved two main themes: "Hispanics are the new Blacks"[5] and "My grandparents …." These themes were used by most of the teachers to put order to the events which they linked to their current attitudes toward demographic changes in diversity with conceptualizations of those changes. These themes emerged through reflective analytics because they were linked to the way teachers retold history (put order to events) to support their current attitudes. I noticed that time's sense of difference came across through insider/outsider dynamics. Blacks were unacknowledged as outsiders while Latinos were unapologetically noticed as outsiders. Unityville educators considered themselves insiders because their grandparents, for example, learned English or assimilated. Story after story was linked to these two common cultural themes of change. In an interview, a white male educator said, "Yeah, well, Unityville has kind of been in transition. I think historically Unityville has always had a small, ah, minority population, mostly African American, very few others. I mean, we'll get some Japanese kids, but overall it's predominantly, our minority group has been African American, which is a little unique to some areas, because it's not really been a suitcase community [suitcase community is a group that does not stay in one place very long] … Compared to the Mexican population or the Hispanic population probably over about the last 5 or 6 years because of industry." He went on to say, "Even kids who speak FAIRLY good English will continue to speak Spanish and that kind of shuts them out, but from the other populations." Comments like "The Mexican population, for instance, they have their own lunch tables" could also have been said about white kids but wasn't. Instead, the educator compared the Mexican students with Black students by saying, "You don't see that with the African American kids [at least not anymore]." Other teachers said things like, "It is a racial thing, I think" meaning, "*they like* to stick with their own race." The teachers persistently said that it wasn't a racial thing for them, the teachers. This way of ordering events and phenomena by comparing Latinx with Blacks as the new minority, the new racially defined group, was a significant and persistent theme of teacher interviews and disciplinary actions.

One white male educator told a story about a French Canadian Indian student. This story fits the "My grandparents …" theme because it was a vague story about a certain version of American history from the perspective of his own racial/ethnic group. He said, "There was a Canadian Indian [pronounced injun]" who came to the school. They [Indigenous Indian Americans] had *only* been around the White Man for a hundred years. … She only spoke French (which is of course associated with whiteness, too) or something (all languages other than English lumped together here)." After a while, "this student got absorbed and she learned a great deal of English."[6] Many interviewees expressed this sentiment. This obviously harmful attitude when talking about those who have been colonized or enslaved was presented by white educators as a positive form of manifest destiny. Often within the same breath, as was the case with this interviewee, English language learning was immediately linked to assimilation. That such beliefs were implicitly connected with the myth "my grandparents …" was substantiated by many teachers simplistically tacking on, "This is what my ancestors had to do."

Critically, both of these themes emphasized change related to the Latino/a/x transnational student population. Japanese "newcomers" were different because their fathers were all executives employed by local Japanese factories with limited plans to stay in Unityville (albeit longer than children of migrant workers planned to stay in the district). Japanese fathers were not considered migrant workers. Japanese children were, for the most part, learning English and some American culture, but were expressly only strategically assimilating. Through the Japanese Saturday School in Indianapolis, they stayed connected with Japanese culture and schooling expectations, and even prepared for required exams they would take after returning. They retained strong connections with friends back home through the internet. Students from Taiwan were smaller in number with undeclared aspirations to stay in the United States, though assimilation aspirations were loosely held for them. Latino/a/x were also not necessarily determined to stay, and, yet, it was the Latinx group to which strong expectations of assimilation were held. In fact, a white male educator told us something that many educators expressed, "Their [the Japanese students] situation is a little different. In that, I think that the type of kids that we get from Japan … come from fairly wealthy families … I mean almost all the parents who, almost all of them are here because of Japanese plants in Unityville. And they're usually upper management. They're sent here from Japan so they come from wealthy families who REALLY cherish education, and the kids usually have some English skills … and they flow right into the population [said as if their entrance into the school did not result in change]."

Change itself was racialized and change was thought of as a normalization process (comparing Latino/as with what white immigrant grandparents did which narratively established that my grandparents constituted what is normal) through the educators' conceptions.

Reflective Analytics (2). As the Project persisted, there were differences in the cultural themes associated with reflective time and teacher attitudes. The earlier themes were still present, though with less force and fewer who enacted them, and there were a few new themes that were expressed. The new themes were still dominated by an insider/outsider dynamic.

The talk amongst the cadre of teachers involved as collaborators in developing peace curriculum as well as others around the district who were active members of our team could be understood through the theme "These Teachers Aren't Gonna Wanna Change." Several of the teacher inquirers made the point that "Some of them [but not me, a teacher inquirer] are just stuck in their ways." This particular teacher attitude targeted teacher colleagues. It emerged through an analysis of the reflective case because teachers would put events and experiences in order by reflecting on the difference between teachers (like themselves) who were open and welcoming of change and teachers who refused and resisted change. One of the teachers involved in the inquiry group said, "If I were one of the typical teachers that you know got this [referring to the note by Jerry Changer presented in Chapter 2], I'd be like 'Why the hell did they give this to me?' Throw it in the trash." Another teacher involved with this inquiry group was talking about "other teachers in the school" as she reported on a conversation she had with a veteran educator.

> I heard these negative things [about some professional development activities related to ENL learners]. And I said, 'I think these situations need to be addressed.' And that's when a veteran teacher said, 'We have many, many, many, many more AMERICAN kids that need to be taken care of, that we shouldn't have to spend half a day on this.

You can see that the teacher inquirer (who was also a veteran teacher) was differentiating herself from a veteran teacher who was resistant to putting time into the needs of the transnational students. This reflective case theme "These Teachers Aren't Gonna Wanna Change" developed after some activities were initiated, specifically activities organized through the Teacher Inquiry group.

Generative Time Analytics (1). Generative time analysis articulates the implicit, underlying principles associated with how events/things are put into order through time. There were three principles at work regarding attitudes toward change that were expressed through a generative time analysis. These three principles included "Act Normal" and "Change is Disruptive." These principles unified various teacher attitudes toward change. These principles were at work through both positive and negative conceptualizations of change.

Many teachers talked about and enacted attitudes toward change in relation to a sense of normalcy. What this meant is that normalcy served as a principle in the way Unityville people conceptualized the order of change: Acting normal. In most instances the normalcy was positively attributed to white (called "American") practices and people as being "normal." For example, remember this, "Mexican-American, African-American—that doesn't matter. We're all Americans ... [when African-Americans use the African,] they separate themselves from us [white people as normal people]. We're all Americans. That's it. Don't tack that on." The attitude here was indicative of the generative principle normalcy—that change (having African and Mexican Americans) was seen, in part, as ordered through its difference to normalcy or doing things as they normally would. A teacher in the inquiry group said, "I don't think they [some of the teachers in the building] are AS sensitive (pauses) to the needs of (pauses) those kids that, you know, are not English speaking and, um, so I think it would be more of a challenge for them to be (pause) willing to do different things to try to accommodate that."[7]

This sense of doing what was normal included a view that change would be easier for teachers to support if it wasn't seen as primarily for the transnational students and if all teachers were required to make the same kinds of changes. One teacher inquirer told the team that she thought it would be easier to gain participation from other teachers to try new curriculum if consistency (normalcy) were invoked: "I THINK it would be what's the word? More tolerated amongst the whole if everyone has to do the same thing, I think, I think you're going to. I think it would be less, uh, of, ah, an issue with them."[8] "Normalcy" showed up as a generative principle (change departs from normalcy) because it was one of the tenets through which change over time was negatively construed. Change happened and things were not normal. To respond to the change, things needed to return to normal. This theme of normalcy connected with the reflective case "Maintaining the Status Quo" and showed up in concerns that it would not be fair to do things special (change how one does things) just to help the "newcomers" succeed.

The theme "Change is Disruptive" was primarily (though not exclusively) construed as negative. Through this principle the "newcomer" students were described as disruptors. This was especially true for Latinx students who were regularly thought of as troublemakers and criminals. "You know the Hispanics seem to be always in constant turmoil and conflict with themselves." "[With them] ... there's conflict all the time." "They are here today, gone tomorrow." One educator reported, "Yeah, and then we had, you know, there was a rape and attempted murder at one of the hotels and it ended being a Hispanic kid, you know. Um, so they saw a couple big crimes that the community just hadn't seen. Uh, and then you know with the, a few of the, Hispanic kids at the high school age that come in, they obviously try to wear like gang colors and do stuff like that you know." This attitude toward change posited change as a disruption to what was considered normal, safe, and "ours." This particular educator, however, subsumed his point that change was linked to disruption within the theme of normalcy by saying, "Everybody's prejudiced about something, you know. And so it's just a cultural [normal] thing."

There was a positive twist. Educators more directly engaged in the Project talked about the role of the ethnography to *disrupt* negative patterns. Transformation, even by those Unityville educators who wanted it, was thought of as a disruption to practices that were negative for the students.

Generative Analytics (2). The above principles remained intact over the years, but we began witnessing a positive aspect to the addition/increase generative principle described earlier in the chapter. For example, teachers talked about **an increase** in positive attitudes, in understanding students, and in basic success for the students. This positive tone was predominantly voiced by teachers who were directly involved in the education of the transnational students. Another principle of change in teacher attitudes (as articulated through generative analytics) involved conceiving of change as progress. Early on, most teachers did not see change as progressive in the positive sense. Even reluctant teachers began saying things like, "I didn't know what they needed [but now I do]." One not-very–involved teacher told me[9] "Sometimes I work with students who are from Israel. ... I asked him [an Arabic student] to talk in class and Arabic sounded so beautiful. I think after that my relationship with him was much better."[10] You can hear the theme of progression in the way this teacher talked about that incident as signaling change.

Participatory Analytics (1). Participatory analytics located attitudes toward change that engaged the actors in anticipating differences. The attitudes were oriented toward anticipations and expectations which positioned the educators' attitudes toward change more generally. The major theme that emerged through a participatory analysis related to attitudes about change was "I Have to Pick My Battles." This theme was related to change because its sense of differences had to do with accepting or rejecting anticipations about the order of things and their potential effects. I reported on this theme in Chapter 5, but I did not make the connection with time or with attitudes toward change until I employed these time analytics. Such an articulated link between the theme and attitudes toward change indicated that requests or opportunities for participation in change efforts would be construed through the "Pick My Battle" theme and changes over time would be considered calculations related to which battles were worth picking.

Other themes that I named through this analysis included: Criminalizing Latino/as; Control; Being Open; and Problem-solving. There was an interesting relation of agency with the hermeneutics of time for this case. The actual change was largely conceived as outside the agent, but with responsive and interpretive shifts that would affect the order of things as they were impending. Participatory analysis involved locating this interesting relation in one's conception of time as impending. I wrote about two of these themes to illustrate the fruits of the analysis: "Picking my battles" and "Criminalizing Latino/as."

Both teachers and administrators featured the challenge of having to choose when to fight in their attitudes toward change. Picking one's battles was a rationale for not acting on behalf of their transnational students. To this way of thinking, change seemed be construed as battles ignored, battles won, or battles lost (note that the battles were thought to already exist with the teacher's only sense of agency a responsive one). "Picking My Battles" resulted in ignoring negative white student/teacher activities toward transnational students whilst negatively attending to "newcomer" reactions to the negativity. For example, teachers and administrators routinely did not intervene in bullying situations unless transnational students physically fought back (which rarely happened). Indeed, the battles educators picked gave away their implicit values.

Another strong theme was the expectation that Latinx students would eventually engage in various kinds of criminal or unseemingly activity—that Latinx students could not be trusted. Again, this theme had already emerged through reconstructive analyses, but time analytics helped us understand how attitudes toward change and time were connected with this as an expectation. From many teachers' perspectives criminal activity composed an unfolding set of expectations to which these teachers would be accountable. The criminalized expectations ranged from "they may be cheating," to "they bring knives to school—we've never had that before" to "maybe they are illegal aliens,"[11] and "they will bring gang activity to our school." There was a mix of verb tenses evidenced in this analysis that illustrated the unfolding progression of time that structured this theme. When teachers were first interviewed they thought that they knew a lot about crime in the Latinx community because it was reported on in the paper (and they were avid readers of the local paper). They were forthright in wanting to make sure that I knew how criminal the Hispanic community was. They even treated such reports as "They drink way too much" or "They live with a lot of people in one small apartment" as if these belonged in a trajectory headed toward criminal outcomes. Some policy changes were instituted in direct relation to these unfolding teacher attitudes. For example, Latinos were routinely frisked for weapons by an armed policeman. Teachers expected the worst from members of the Latinx community and they only expected this worseness to expand over time and to require increased surveillance, monitoring and protection in response. The teachers did not express this same attitude of change toward other transnational student groups.

Participatory (2). Through the analysis of participatory time, I noticed that the teacher inquirers largely (but not totally) began responding to changes through conceptions of peace and non-peace. This way of conceptualizing change was a shift in attitude that was an explicit effect of their work on creating peace curriculum. Early on, they had also engaged in thinking about change as "Picking Battles." The teacher inquirers began to talk about impending opportunities to respond to change through the notion that a peaceful response would bring about a particular order of things and a non-peaceful response would bring about another order of things. These attitudes toward change were uniquely expressed from teacher inquierers.

Another transformed attitude toward change was engaged through these analytics, namely the attitude that "These are My Kids—Our Students," This attitude toward change was brought out through the participatory time case where I was able to notice that teachers had begun thinking of the impending educational opportunities as opportunities to change their work with their students—"How can I do this better, what can I do differently?" And "I did 'X' and it really worked." These responses engaged the notion that the teacher thought of herself as a teacher *for* the "newcomer" transnational students. Through this thinking, there was a recognition that an attitude of connectiveness with and accountability for transnational students would result in change. "We felt like we did something at least." The time aspect was the momentum of teachers transforming the way they thought of their relationships with transnational students over time.

Active Analytics (1). Active analytics involved examining teacher attitudes toward change where they expected that their own active efforts to *make change* through planning and engaging in specific activities (whether those were personal or collective) would be responsible for bringing about change: I Can Make a Difference. Collaborators who were directly involved in the Project conceived of Project activities through this active time case. Uninvolved teachers tended to interpret changes that came about as a result of these activities from the reflective case. As members of the Project we thought, "I can make a difference."[12] We reconstructed only positive attitudes toward the education of transnational students through this theme. Interestingly, negative attitudes toward change (the preference for no change) were all linked to the analyses using other time cases.[13]

Some teachers talked about change as an opportunity to make a difference in very tangible ways. One educator, speaking on changes in her teaching, said,

> Um, well, you know. I, I. You can see from my classes, you know, I do have quite a few non-English speaking students ... I figured since I have THESE students, I might as well be involved in figuring out ways to have a more inclusive (pauses) learning environment for 'em all.[14]

One teacher described her interventions in the context of trying to make changes in the overall culture of the school. She said,

> If I'm in the hall like yesterday, this, I don't know how old he is. He's no taller than I [am], so I'm very sensitive to that, that whole short thing. And he's with these two-foot taller guys punching on him, and you know. And I have no clue who any of them were. And I said, "Knock it off." And they said, "You don't know me." And I said, "I don't have to know you. Leave him alone." And they said, "Oh, ok." You know, but a lot of teachers don't do that. If it's not, if it doesn't happen in THEIR room, if it's not somebody THEY know. Then it's kind of, you know just kind of overlooked.[15]

This was in the context of describing her own active sense of change, but it was set in contrast with the theme discussed earlier of "Pick Your Battles."

Remember that a math teacher talked about being able to learn Spanish to help particular Spanish-speaking students in his class. Several teachers made concerted efforts to learn some Spanish. One of those teachers told us,

> ... it helped ... I mean he was more attentive. Um. I mean he wouldn't be afraid necessarily, to ask questions. Uh. And I'd come over and do a lot of pointing. And began to use a little Spanish. And, uh, it's helped him ... He doesn't necessarily understand everything I'm saying, but the repetition and kind of how I run the class, I mean it— you kind of guess what's going to happen ... He begins to see the work on the board. And he knows the type of questions to ask and he's able to.

He went on to say that this has an impact on other ENL students who are not as limited in their English language use:

> I mean they're [the other ENL students] able to see that and it just makes them catch on too that the teacher's trying to help out and, um, I think this semester has helped the relationship with those students.[16]

The inquiry teachers talked about the peace curricula they developed and implemented in very direct active-case. They specifically created the curricula and other pedagogical modifications in order to change the learning situation for "newcomer" students. These attitudes were expressed in very forward looking and evaluative ways, by, for example, talking about what they would alter in order to bring about more adjustments next year. These teachers felt isolated in the school through these particular attitudes. The themes I articulated through the active time case were very student focused, but the themes involving their relationships to their colleagues with respect to attitudes toward change surfaced most often through reflective or generative time cases.

You probably noticed the complexity: Most of the analysis that resulted from these active time analytics were complicated by relations to other attitudes about change that did not emerging through these analytics. This is one reason why a meta-analytics of time was necessary.

Meta-Time Analytics. In the above section I mentioned that there were some differences in how various teachers interpreted particular activities and underlying or potential changes. For example, teachers who were more directly involved in the work of the Project thought of Project activities through an active time case whereas teachers not very involved in the project interpreted those same activities through a reflective case. It was differences like this one that showed up when a meta-analytics was pursued. Moreover, the shifts in attitudes toward change involving differences across time hermeneutics could, also, be explicated through a meta-time analysis.

Some new attitudes toward change emerged across time. One of those was a shift from thinking of "newcomer" students as "those kids" to thinking of "newcomer" students as "my kids" and "our kids." There were a few people for whom this shift was part of how they interpreted change, even though most teachers at the high school were still thinking of the transnational youth as "those kids," as outsiders even after the first two years of the project. I described the shift in teacher attitudes from "those" to "my" kids through participatory analytics whereas I described the attitude that embodied stable conceptions of the students as "those kids" through reflective analytics. This difference suggests that certain attitudes are constituted through specific time-relations.[17] In the early interviews (Fall 2003), one teacher expressed the point that the "newcomer" kids didn't belong and didn't really want to be in Unityville anyway. That same teacher, also, said, "I have a lot of students, American students, who I need to teach." However, there were changes in the teacher's talk. They said, at some point during our second year, "Isn't this the right way to do it?" [referring to the sink or swim method of teaching kids English]?

222 | WALKING WITH STRANGERS

Further on in the Project, the same teacher said, "What do we need to do to bridge that gap [in rapport] with "newcomer" students?" These last two questions indicate that the teacher's attitudes toward change had shifted from reflective case toward active case with respect to whose students these transnational kids were.

A meta-time analysis also facilitated an examination of our team's direct involvement in change attitudes at the school. Our team had an effect on attitudes toward changes most directly because we were involved in the creating and implementing of plans. We made proposals and we offered suggestions and sometimes we intervened very directly in order to make changes. Most of our work in this regard was to facilitate changes that the Unityville educators themselves planned and identified. However, there are a few instances where our own university contingent's efforts were somewhat in contention with school personnel. The most significant example of this was action I took on behalf of one of the Taiwanese students, Ms. Tu (whose negative situation with a teacher at the high school was described in an earlier chapter). In addition to calling on Ms. Tu when she was not prepared, our data indicated that the teacher said things in class in front of students that embarrassed and humiliated her. Ms. Tu reported a lot of anxiety during her conversations with Yu-Ting (one of our graduate students who was working on a Ph.D. in counseling psychology). Ms. Tu also talked with her ENL teacher about the situation. The school officials did not want to confront the offending teacher ("Pick My Battles" theme at work), but I was able to have Ms. Tu removed from that teacher's class. Two of our IU researchers interviewed the particular teacher later and their attitude toward the change and toward the changing classroom climate as a result of "newcomer" students was linked to the reflective time case. The teacher explained both the specific class change (moving the student out the class) and his unwillingness to change teaching strategies to benefit ENL students through themes linked to the reflective case.[18]

Conclusion: Time Analytics and Doing an Ethnography of Change

Judith Butler (2015) refers to a community that doesn't ground its self-certainty through its presumed similar desires and concepts of sameness as "polity-in-the-making." We have explored time's challenge to conceptions of sameness in community identity as a move that takes us closer to community as an always ongoing polity-in-the-making. Complicated. More diverse than it might think. The time case analytics applied to ethnographic practice conceptually complexifies the notion of time in our research. Narrative ethnographic text could benefit from these analytics because they magnify the time characteristic o seriation. However, to confront some of the time-related problems mentioned at the start of the chapter it becomes necessary to diversify the analysis across units, events, and phenomena in a more layered way. Though seriation characteristics are not the only time-characteristics important to an ethnography of change, it is reasonable to begin with those.

With respect to teacher attitudes toward change itself, the following aspects made it difficult to tell one chronological story so to speak. There was a core group of teachers who contacted me in the beginning and who were active collaborators through the life of the Project. This cadre expressed the most complex views of the situation in those early focus group interviews. During the second year, there was a different configuration of high school teachers who were involved in a Teacher Inquiry group developing peace curricula. Of course, an even larger number of teachers were involved in the actual education of transnational students during the second year we were in the schools. We facilitated teacher professional development activities to which teachers were more or less open. The point here is that the opportunities to engage one's attitudes toward change shifted and included different people over time. Perhaps most importantly, change in attitude did not seem to conform to simple linear seriation. These characteristics indicate why it is best, if there is an alternative, not to flatten collective cultural change to descriptions of something unified across objective time.

I devote the final paragraph of the chapter to a brief indication of how I have reflected on this chapter itself through my own rereadings of it. First, I am self-consciously aware of the extent to which metaphors for and references to time are strewn throughout these pages. They suggest the complicated nature of the nexus of time and mind. For me there are deep spiritual insights relevant to such explorations, the stopping of thought, and so forth. Of course, I have not included those ideas here, but it troubles me to have avoided them. I also want to acknowledge that my thinking through analyses of time is not as developed as I imagine it could be. Lastly, there is a potential unintended consequence of this particular analysis, namely assuming a higher value on active time cases over reflective time as if active time reflects a more advanced developmental stage. Yet, clearly our thinking through time is more complicated than that. In this particular project, the transformative goals we held benefitted from shifts in conceiving of change through an active case rather than through a reflective case, primarily because of how agency is situated for actors' senses of who they were in the change process. Nevertheless, I would not want anyone to walk away from this chapter with an inclination to establish time conceptualizations as a basis for evaluating participants or the ways they hermeneutically make sense of their lives through references to time. Rather, understanding hermeneutic conceptions of time reveal understandings of culture, not judgements of individuals.

Notes

1. Time can be the patterns of difference, difference from the patterns of difference, and so on.
2. The interview, conducted November 2003, was in Spanish. This quote was translated to English.
3. Interviewed in Mandarin November 2003. The quote was translated to English.
4. In this chapter, I will always be referring to change related to the education of transnational students.
5. This exact phrase was uttered by over half of the teachers interviewed in focus groups and individually during the period between the fall 2003 and the spring 2004.
6. Interview, Mr. Sander 2/9/05 conducted by Ed Brantmeier.
7. Science Teacher interview 12/02/04.
8. Teacher Inquiry Group 1/26/05.
9. Theatre of the Oppressed. Group 1. 2/3/05.
10. Theater of the Oppressed. Group 1. 2/3/05.
11. A U.S. designation for people living in the U.S. without official paperwork.
12. One of the ENL teachers drew on the theme "I love my children" as the basis for explaining her attitudes toward change. This theme was conceptualized through the active time case and emerged through this analysis. But because she was the only one through which this theme was expressed, it is not discussed in this chapter.
13. A counter interpretation is possible. A few teachers described taking the "sink or swim approach with newcomer students" as something that might have a positive effect on language learning. It was articulated as if it had a positive future orientation, but actually it was in the context of talk or action that justified teachers not having a plan, not actively trying out things. In other words, it justified apathy and inaction and seems more attune with the teachers own needs then what they regarded as a good educational plan of action.
14. Interview with science teacher 12/2/04.
15. Teacher Inquiry meeting 3/16/05.
16. Teacher Interview, math teacher, 5/20/05.
17. This statement is intended more to describe the way it works than to offer surprise. Wood (and I agree with him) argued that the hermeneutics of these time cases render them as primarily substantive aspects of the interpretive processes of actors and secondarily as methodological analytics.
18. In some instances an "unwillingness to change" attitude was linked to the participatory case, but for this particular teacher, the attitude was indicative of the reflective case.

References

Adam, B. (1995). *Timewatch: The social analysis of time.* Cambridge, MA: Polity Press.

Bourdieu, P. (1977). *Outline of a theory of practice.* Cambridge, England: Cambridge University Press.

Burowoy, M., & Verdery, K. (Eds.). (1999). *Uncertain transition: Ethnographies of change in the postsocialist world.* Lanham, MD: Roman and Littlefield.

Butler, J. (2015). *Notes toward a performative theory of assembly.* Cambridge, MA: Harvard University Press.

Carspecken, P. (1996). *Critical ethnography in educational research: A theoretical and practical guide.* New York, NY: Routledge.

Dylan, B. (1963). The times they are a-changin'. On *The times they are a-changin'* [Song and record title]. Retrieved from https://www.bobdylan.com/songs/times-they-are-changin

Fabian, J. (1983). Time and the other: How anthropology makes its object. New York, NY: Colombia University Press.

Fabian, J. (2006). The other revisited: Critical afterthoughts. *Anthropological Theory, 6*(2), 139–152.

Hernes, T. (2017). Process as the becoming of temporal trajectory. In A. Langley & H. Tsoukas (Eds.), *The Sage handbook of process organizational studies* (pp. 601–607). Thousand Oaks, CA: Sage.

Hörschelmann, K., & Stenning, A. (2008). Ethnographies of postsocialist change. *Progress in Human Geography, 32*(8), 339–361.

Jeffrey, B., & Troman, G. (2004). Time for ethnography. *British Educational Research Journal, 30*(4), 535–548.

Korth, B., Frey, C., Hasbun, M., Nakamichi, Y., Pereira, M., Soto, N., Sotoo, N., & Su, Y. (2004). *Report of Unityville Outreach Project*. Unpublished report to school corporation.

Lather, P., & Smithies, C. (1997). *Troubling the angels: Women living with HIV/AIDS*. Oxford, England: Westview Press.

McCarthy, T. (1994). *The critical theory of Jürgen Habermas*. Cambridge, MA and London, England: MIT Press. (Original work published 1978)

McTaggert, J.M.E. (1908). The unreality of time. *Mind, 17*, 457–474.

Nespor, J. (2019, September). Ethnographic possibilities and changing times. Presentaton at the Oxford Ethnography and Education Conference, Department of Educational Studies, Oxford University, Oxford, England.

O'Reilly, K. (2012). Ethnographic returning, qualitative longitudinal research and the reflexive analysis of social practice. *The Sociological Review, 60*(3), 518–536.

Roseberry, W. (1982). Balinese cockfights and the seduction of anthropology. *Social Research, 49*(4), 1013.

Scheller, V. (2020). Understanding, seeing and representing time in tempography. *FQS. Forum: Qualitative Social Research, 21*(2), Art. 18.

Schilling, E., & König, A. (2020). Challenging times—methods and methodological approaches to qualitative research on time. *FQS. Forum: Qualitative Social Research, 21*(2), Art. 27.

Shensul, J., Borrero, G., & Garcia, R. (1985). Applying ethnography in educational change. *Anthropology and Education Quarterly, 16*(2), 149–164.

Warhol, A. (1975). *The philosophy of Andy Warhol: From A to B and back again* (1st ed.). New York, NY: Harcourt Brace Jovanovich.

West, C. (1981). Nietzsche's prefiguration of postmodern American philosophy. *Boundary, 2*, 241–269.

Willis, E. (2010). The problem of time in ethnographic healthcare research. *Qualitative Health Research, 20*(4), 556–564.

Wolf, M. (1974). Chinese women: Old skills in a new context. *Woman, Culture, and Society, 133*, 157.

Wood, D. (2001). *The Deconstruction of Time*. Evanston, IL: Northwestern University Press. (Original work published 1989)

CHAPTER EIGHT

Walking With Strangers

Accompañamiento is an attitude of "walking with" that incorporates dialogues and relationships, combats power imbalances and refuses to erase the strangeness of being a stranger.

Enrique Sepúlveda III

For decades now, cadres of scholars across a swath of disciplines have argued that social scientists should not only study the unequal and unjust arrangements of social life but should also fiercely engage in the transformation of those arrangements through their research. Fine (2018) made that point uniquely personal:

> Those of us who are White researchers walk in a long and shameful history of story-lifting, hawking stories of Black/Brown pain and pocketing the profits. We must be exquisitely careful about over-borrowing and under-crediting—stealing—the words, stories, or metaphors of others, especially people of color. Those of us who are White have an obligation to excavate critically our own her/his/their stories of privilege to understand how we sit in tragic dialectics with structures of oppression, and how we might replace ourselves within solidarity movements of resistance. (p. xiv).

Thompson (2019) said it like this, "Whites combat racialized violence in all forms by breaking from racial convention to address the relative power they hold in its perpetuation" (Chapter 5, Kindle Edition).

How might I, a white middle-class cisgender woman, hollow out my own stories of privilege so that I might explore the structures of oppression through which

I have been complicit? How might I join as an accomplice in the "resistance" to injustice (Indigenous Action, 2014)? How do I manifest a walking *with* the Black and Brown youngsters whose lives continue to be en/dangered? "The new human is one who commits his or her life to the eradication of all forces—like racialized violence, sexism and men's violence against women, economic exploitation, hetero-sexism—that adversely affect growth, relationship, community building, and life" (Thompson, 2019, Chapter 5, Kindle Edition).

In the IU-Unityville Project we engaged with the transnational students in order to learn how to create better schooling institutions. We did not conduct a *study on* the transnational youth or their experiences except in the sense of laboring with their wisdom toward our common concerns.

> [T]ransnational communities of affective relations rooted in the figure of the migrant who keeps coming represent community as an intercultural and hybrid pol-ity-in-the-making, whose common cause 'is not merely the condition of passively inhabiting or even participating in/with [the] culture of a given mass or collectivity. It is, rather, an acutely individuated dedication to becoming common' (Ghandi, 2014, p. 152). (Karavanta, 2019, p. 458)

The bases of their common cause are persistent affective demands of their rights to live well, their right to human rights.

This chapter, as a whole, is intended to follow Fine's (2018) lead to locate our methodological practices within the tasks of both "excavating" our own stories of privilege as they squirm in the dialectics of ongoing oppression and "replacing" ourselves within the resistances of our transnational youth. I organized the writing through the following subsections: (1) How did the transnational youth guide our methodological practices through their resistances and despite limits that were structured to control them? (2) How was our research part of a transformation process? (3) How was our research complicit with the status quo? (4) What might critical research in education hope to contribute?

The questioning orientation of these sections is meant to signal a reflective posture through which both privilege and possibility can be entertained. It fur-ther indicates the ongoing nature of this important dialogue, even these many years later.

How Did the Transnational Youth Guide Our Methodological Practices?

Guadalupe Pimentel-Solano has been called Indiana's most famous dreamer (King, 2018). According to Robert King (2018), DACA covered over 690,00(

youth caught in this web of not-quite-belonging. Pimentel-Solano and others like her have said, "Even though I was raised here ... I feel like I am not fully able to claim it" (King, 2018). Pimentel-Solano told King that even though it is hard, this is home (referring to Indiana). Unlike Pimental-Solano, I cannot draw on my own life experiences to understand what it means for home to be a place where you are under the threat of removal, constant and unmitigated surveillance, surrounded by rhetoric calling your very existence "illegal." Black and Brown resistances to oppression and annihilation (symbolic and material) are the stories to be told and heard. Their stories include being exiled in our schools. The youth in Unityville lived the doubled life/doubled consciousness of being outsiders within, simultaneously resisting and allowing, in both small and big ways. Their stories connect with the broader social dialogue around our collective responsibilities to Dreamers. Any efforts engaged in their name must coincide with and benefit from their experiences, desires and goals.

In this subsection, I identify how the activities and experiences of the transnational youth guided our methodological process. The specific activities I highlight include self-advocating, creating friendship networks, refusing cultural/linguistic defection, and enlightening others. I briefly describe the students' activities and then link those activities with the work of the IU-Unityville Outreach Project.

Self-Advocating

The transnational youth, marginalized through their Unityville schooling experiences, were wise. They understood that the school was failing to include them and they recognized that there was little they could do individually to change that. They recognized that the failures were largely not of their making. Nevertheless, they accepted a burden of private anguish in order to spare their parents. Their parents believed their kids were happy at the schools, and the parents were grateful to the country that was educating their children. Initially, the students' struggles were not apparent to their teachers either, as the students sought to hide how difficult things were. Their lack of hope was an outcome and reflection of their marginalized social position within the schools, but it was not an indicator of the value they placed on their own lives or their education. The youth were desperate to be educated and make good on both the sacrifices of their parents and the richness of their own potential. Student self-advocacy was nestled into, and emergent from, this complicated social positioning.

Collective student experiences guided the goals of the project from our very first focus groups. We listened to their stories and followed their leads. Our continued Socialization Connections provided us with the ongoing means to hear what they wanted us to know and how they wanted us to be supportive. The students advocated for their collective social-emotional needs and their strong desire to get a good education and prepare themselves for college.

Personal self-advocacy, also, influenced our ethnographic engagements. In Chapter 2 I described Ms. Tu's response to feeling mistreated by one of her teachers. She expressed her concerns and initiated the need to act by talking with Yu-Ting (our Taiwanese team member) and her ENL teacher. Together a response was forged. Since the response was not successful in the way we had hoped, I took the responsibility to maneuver a change that reflected what Ms. Tu thought was best for herself and, also, what seemed best for her transnational peers. Thus, her self-advocacy involved strategic negotiations and sometimes settling for second best in the moment. The youth were in the best positions to establish the goals of such negotiations while, as team members, we knew generally how to navigate school hierarchies, parameters, and structures. And we had the cultural capital to do so.

Additionally, our transnational students took advantage of formalized advocacy opportunities and we were alongside them. For example, in 2006 Unityville transnational high school students were released from attending school one day in order to participate in a DACA rally at the state capital. Students were accompanied by the ENL teacher, MJ (one of the counselors), and some other members of our IU-Unityville Outreach Project team. Getting ourselves visibly involved in political rallies and movements was one way our Project benefitted from the guidance of the youth. We brought a group of ENL students to the IU campus, also, to participate in a recruitment venture. It was a full day of activities with students from all over the state. The guest speaker at the luncheon was Dr. Gerardo Gonzalez, Dean of the IU School of Education at the time and Cuban child immigrant. These formal opportunities to advocate for the educational needs of our transnational students reflected a confluence of their own self-advocacy and social opportunity.

My point here is that transnational student self-advocy guided our Project. Student self-advocacy also increased and strengthened throughout the life of the Project. The students, in general, comprise the politically motivated group we call Dreamers and those of us who were active in this Unityville Project continue to listen to them writ large and follow their lead.

Creating Friendship Networks

Popularity among their U.S. peers was considered one path to surviving. Living out one's home cultural practices as a transnational student was not easy. Transnational students whose national group numbers were small sough friendships with the white kids, which included learning what it meant to be popular. Ms. Tu was in Unityville with her brother, living at her aunt's house. They were both high school students. She often used the Socialization Connection with Yu-Ting to learn more about American social life for teens and was concerned with making American friends. Small disagreements between her and her brother emerged as Ms. Tu let go of her home culture gendered expectations for modesty and meekness. Her brother was concerned that she was becoming too American. He even spoke with his parents about his sister, garnering their support in chastising her. Sarah, an Israeli Arab student whose brother was also in the school, faced similar dynamics—social life depended upon a certain amount of assimilating and friend-making. The path to friendship with white kids at the high school was culturally precarious. A handful of Latino high school students made friends with white kids through their athletic efforts. These kinds of friendships were reminiscent of the acceptance of Black athletes in the school's earlier history (see Chapter 4). In all cases, being friends with the white high school students required doing it in English through taken-for-granted norms held by the white kids. This cost was not acknowledged by the white community (either adults or students). Moreover, having friends did not entirely protect one from harm in the school community, as we noticed through the note that Jerry Changer wrote to school administrators. Nevertheless, having American friends mattered to our transnational kids.

Unfortunately, within-transnational group friendships were frowned upon by white students and educators (this changed for our project collaborators, but in general the school personnel retained a negative interpretation of such friendships). Of course in-group friendships among white students was totally taken-for-granted. Actually, in-group white friendship groups were so deeply normalized that a comparison of attitudes toward within-group friendships did not penetrate prevailing Unityville awareness. For our transnational students, within-group friendships were crucial to their socio-emotional survival in the schools across every level, but high schoolers considered these friendships vital to their persistence. Even across disagreements and personality differences, there was solidarity that was structured through within-group friendship networks.

At the high school Project collaborators acted in opposition to the negative attitudes toward transnational within-group friendships and we promoted within-group conflict resolution and opportunities for them to garner time and space together outside the surveillance of whites. We created mentoring partnerships that facilitated cross-group friendships and allyships. We centered on the survival and advocacy effects of friendship. All of our Project efforts that focused on friendships followed the guidance of our transnational youth.

Refusing Cultural/Linguistic Deflection

From the beginning of our Project's timeline, most of our transnational students actively retained their home languages and cultures despite the school's insistent and systematic push toward assimilation. Particularly for the Latinx students, active engagement with their home cultures and languages was considered a "bad attitude" or "disrespectful," but our students refused to give in to the school community's misinterpretation of their linguistic and cultural connections with families and friends. For example, many of the white educators and students at the high school called attention to the fact that Latinx students sat together in the cafeteria. They misinterpreted this as a rejection of their white peers, as a bad attitude, as an unwillingness to participate in the school life. But, for our transnational high school youth, their time together in the cafeteria was important for their solidarity and for maintaining their cultural and linguistic connections within the school walls. Though some of the Latino parents participated in community-based English lessons, the students' families retained the use of their home languages in their own homes despite the persistent admonishment from school district personnel to speak English at home for the sake of developing language proficiency.

Japanese students of all ages participated in a Saturday Japanese School in Indianapolis sponsored by the Japanese government. Students, especially high school ones, were worried that they would not be prepared for the difficult exams they would be expected to take in Japan upon their return from the United States. At the Saturday Japanese School, families would spend the day with other Japanese families from around the state. Japanese students also retained close connections with their friends back home via the internet.

Following the leadership of students, our team promoted the meaningful and authentic inclusion of cultural and linguistic diversity across the schools. Like them, we wanted home languages to be used in supportive ways for students, but we also did not want the students to be saddled with the burdens of translating. Moreover, we did our best to use their home languages when we interacted with them. Following the students' leads, we engaged with them in ways that respected their cultural and linguistic commitments and reached out toward them on their own terms. For example, I am not/was not very proficient with Spanish and I didn't (at the start of the project) know any Japanese, Taiwanese, or Arabic. I committed myself to learning from both our project teammates and our students some simple spoken phrases. I fumbled, but I didn't give up. Both Ed and Yoko significantly increased their use of Spanish during their time at the high school. We actively ignored the English Only policy under the guidance of our students.

Enlightening Others

Felipe Vargas spent the first half of 2010 with the "Trail of Dreams," a planned action of undocumented youth who walked from Miami to D.C. in an effort to advocate for im/migrant youth. Vargas (2018) wrote that in D.C., after being warned that arrests were impending, the four immigrant youth he had accompanied for the full 1500 miles left their shoes and walked away from arrest and watched on the sidelines as their allies were taken away. Vargas did not tell this as a story of accompliceship. It was a story of allies once again taking the youth's "power and voice" by completing the action on their own (p. 72). In the spirit of protection, the allies had insisted that the youth step aside and avoid arrest. It was dangerous from the perspectives of their adult allies. Youth in the movement disagreed with the strategies of those elite allies, but their voices were not honored. In resistance, and as an act of asserting their own self-worth, even in relationship with well-intended allies, the youth wanted to "... stop the other folks from speaking for" them (p. 73). Vargas (2018) made it clear that in the movement, tensions around who was speaking for whom mattered. The goals of the movement could not ethically be distinguished from its corresponding means.

Being informed by transnational student experiences guided what we did through the Project, not just in terms of content, but also in terms of form. That is, we sought to not speak out in front of, or in place of, the students when students were able to advocate for themselves. We sought to create opportunities for speaking as part of the Project. Nevertheless, sometimes speaking out from their own bodies was a risk too great. It was usually their decision. In Chapter 5, I wrote about the dialogue script of students' voices (see Appendix D) that our IU contingent performed for the district's teachers and administrators. Though students participated in the activities of that professional development day, they did not want to read their words from their own voices and bodies in that opening assembly. They did not even want to mix it up, for example, Juan reading the part of Sarah. They did, however, help us decide what aspects of the interviews to share, how we should organize the voices, how to reflect the diversity of the group, and how to make sure the voices were used to connect rather than further divide teachers from transnational students.

We stayed continually in touch with the transnational students and we used their experiences as a barometer of how the project was going. We trusted their wisdom, but also put it into dialogue with its own contradictions, diversities, and so forth. For example, our two Taiwanese students, brother and sister, diverged in their own desires for fitting into the American mores. They were conflicted and their relationships with their parents were affected. Their divergent experiences were understood, not only as their personal proclivities for cultural maintenance, but as responses to strong assimilationist structures within the cultural milieu. The response to either hold tightly or let go are both reactions to a similar context. We endeavored to deconstruct the context through which their different orientations emerged. By understanding the larger sociocultural picture, the two students were able to reflect on their own positionalities within it. Their Socialization Connections with Yu-Ting were occasions for this dialogue.

One aspect of the education of white people involves listening to people of color and following their lead—standing beside and behind the efforts of people of color to advocate for themselves. But in institutions, like schools, the power structures work to debilitate, thwart, and expel such advocacy opportunities. Democratizing the research project and centering the voices of the marginalized and minoritized youth kept our ethnographic projects open to being enlightened by them. While our work was animated by and central to the experiences of the transnational students and their own self-advocacy, we believe that the responsibility for educating white people is predominantly a white one. Our advocating required us to self-educate as Project team members and to be accountable for promoting the education of our white peers abetted by our colleagues of varying cultural and linguistic backgrounds and expertises.

How Was Our Research Part of a Transformation/ Resistance Process?

Throughout the book, I reported on links between our methodological processes and the goal of transformation and resistance. Here, I focus on what it meant methodologically to assume a resistance and transformational orientation. I specifically highlight some ways in which our methodology was transformative and resistant: (1) centering the margins; (2) taking risks, imagining futures, enacting values; (3) caring broadly; and (4) resisting monoculturalism. I still imagine, desire, and commit to public schooling (including public universities), as Fine (2018) wrote, owning "… concerns of the common good" and responsibilities for "… carving with others delicate spaces of collective criticality and public science where we interrogate privilege and argue through differences, forging what Audre Lorde called 'meaningful coalitions' and designing research collectives drunk on a wide range of expertise and experience" (p. 117). Our institutions are tangled up in perpetuating oppression. We must do everything we can within, through, and against institutions and the force they bear in maintaining oppressive hierarchies.

Centering the Margins

The IU-Unityville Outreach Project began its transformation as soon as team members shifted the focus of concern from changing students to changing schools. This important shift in orientation relocated accountabilities for the education of transnational students back with school personnel, at least ostensibly. We moved student experiences from the margins to the center so that educators could be asked to face them. The teachers' deficit interpretations of their transnational students were supplanted with relational tales connecting students and teachers. Right from the start, we team members called into question the way "the problem" was framed by the school. We displaced the status quo, including local interpretations as well as routines and practices, with a complicated reimaging of the margins.

Challenging the status quo established a structure for our methodological relationships and orientations. As mentioned in Chapter 1, as a team we prioritized the needs of the transnational students and we oriented toward them as our top priority. In practical terms, this meant we stayed in close contact with students and forged relationships with them that transcended the project itself. Though we also did develop important relationships with educators, our relationships with students were uniquely privileged in the choices we made ethnographically. More importantly, the project was *for* them and never without them. Centering the marginalized students and related goals was an important touchpoint for us as the pull of the status quo was formidable. Methods that moved the margins to the center transformed the school's and university's "business as usual." From the university end of things, we engaged with existing scholarship as the Project developed and as we located needs. We were able to bring that scholarship into the dialogues. Centering the margins meant engaging in atypical methodologies, drawing on typical methodologies in atypical ways, and letting go of institutional modes of doing business even as we, also, benefitted from the university and Unityville monies.

Taking Risks, Imagining Futures, and Enacting Values

'Sometimes, the transformative ethnographic perspective is frightfully ambiguous—a view into the blank space of the unknown" (Cammarota, p. 346). We took methodological risks, while we retained a commitment to our values. The risks transformed our methodological process into collaboratively open dialogue and creative action. For example, when we created a game for playing with elementary school transnational students, we were able to play together with possible futures and ideal selves. We brought these imaginaries into our fieldwork, focusing not just on what was, but what could be. When we entered the field we had no idea what variety of methods we would ultimately use to generate and analyze the data. We were steadfastly committed to social justice values, but we remained wide open in terms of the how and what unfolded.

I thought of risk as a transformative aspect of our methodology because it meant that we as researchers and team members had to let go of some control. We didn't know whether or not the Theatre of the Oppressed would work with teachers who by and large had not established empathetic relationships with the transnational students. The Teacher Inquiry group was another open-ended effort, with a vision of imagined futures. We planned to develop an interdisciplinary peace curriculum, but its shape and specifics were developed collaboratively with teacher inquirers. We necessarily creatively adapted what we were doing as the Project progressed. Both the risks of the unknown and the risks of trying new methods kept us in dialogue, attentive (in formative ways) to what we were doing and how things were working.

Caring Broadly

We bonded with the transnational students, with Project team members, and with educators across the Unityville schools. We cared about them. This care, even love, was an orientation toward how we made sense of one another. At this point, readers will have noticed that not all of the Unityville educators agreed with our team's perspectives and goals. Some of the teachers seemingly worked against those goals, resisted changes, and were angry at the upheavals, disruptions, and distractions they experienced. Even in these cases, our abilities to care for one another were fostered by orienting toward one another's best intentions without falsely accepting harmful aims. As we cared, we faced the challenges of our differences and disagreements.

Methodological caring meant that we resisted the urge to give up on conversations and to caricature one another or oversimplify the perspective of another in the service of our own points of view. We insisted on methodologies that were honoring and that nurtured dialogue. We did not use the research as a means to establish walls or boundaries, but rather as opportunities to maximize our care.

Our caring was transformative because it allowed us to remain open to one another, not foreclosing on expectations or outcomes. Not standing firm in a desire to remain unmoved. Care stood as a critique of the aloof social scientist of traditional authority. Care was the fuel of our *withness*. Care is not understood here as a feeling that comes and goes. Rather it is an *active commitment* to doing what best serves those in need. It is an *active recognition* of the worthwhileness of each person. It is an *active cooperation* across difference toward the common good—as both debatable and imaginable (see Dennis, 2013b; Korth, 2003).

Resisting Monoculturalism

The pedagogical and methodological tendency toward a belief in monoculturalism was powerful. We actively resisted this tendency by complementing our white Unityville teammates with a multilingual, multicultural, IU contingent. We refused the English Only policy from the beginning, by using home languages, alongside our transnational youth, without apology. We queried the myths of monoculturalism in our interviews, focus groups, and analyses. Many of our IU-Unityville Outreach Project activities were specifically multicultural—we created welcome booklets and school information guides in multiple languages; liaisoned with transnational parents; participated in pro-immigrant political rallies; conducted student-led language lessons for teachers; and so on. These methodological engagements actively resisted both the assumption of and the drive toward monoculturalism.

We conducted interviews and focus groups in languages other than English. We transcribed, analyzed and translated across cultural and linguistic differences. And we collaborated, knowing that we both needed and wanted the diversity. As we reconstructed and interpreted across languages and cultures, we depended upon one another to review those interpretations and check for understanding. We worked carefully not to reduce either our ethnographic process and critique or our recommendations and outcomes to a monocultural perspective.

How Was Our Research Complicit with the Status Quo?

Research, like other organized social activities, will have unintended consequences and will reproduce unintended patterns. Though democratizing the research process is one way to mitigate against such unintentional intrusions (Carspecken, 1996; Harding, 1987), I would be remiss if I did not acknowledge that our ethnography resulted in some unintended patterns of reproduction and consequences. One of the benefits of looking back after these years is that is a little easier to recognize the patterns that sustained the status quo. As I said at the outset, there is nothing neutral about doing research. To reproduce the status quo was to contribute to the ongoing oppression and violence of the white supremacy and the racial and cultural oppression of children and communities of color. I will point out three significant ways in which our research was complicit with the status quo, though I imagine that there are others. First of all our methodology suffered the silence of white privilege in the school's assimilationist attitude without transforming it entirely. We methodologically reproduced this privilege through many of our Project activities. Secondly, gendered violence was dealt with interpersonally, but not methodologically. By not taking up gender discrimination as momentum within the Project we reinstated the status quo. Lastly, we were methodologically complicit in the erasure of Blackness. Though racialized assimilation was acknowledged and analyzed, Black students themselves were not invited into the conversation despite some attempts to remedy this problem.

Each of these three aspects of complicity related to a muting of important experiences and divergencies in our understandings of how the educational dynamics of race and gender were inextricably linked with the oppression of transnational students in schools that were actively trying to change. The three areas of complicity were connected. Our methodological collusion was not divorced from our team's (including my own) consciousness, social location, and acceptance of white privilege as normal.

The Silent Power and Presence of White Privilege

White privilege was explicitly talked about among Project team members and within school-Project conversations. White privilege was a perspective from which we analyzed the data. However, white privilege is a layered phenomenon. We did not dig deep. Methodologically, we allowed white privilege to work through its normal channels even when we were using it to benefit the transnational students. For example, in the story of Ms. Tu, I approached an administrator about removing Ms. Tu from class. My privilege played a role in doing that and in bringing about its less-than-satisfying conclusion. Unfortunately, experiences like this did not lead us to reflect on the role of white privilege in the shuffling around of students and the power that whiteness wielded in a predominantly white school district.

For example, recall from Chapter 6 that teachers who participated in the Theatre of the Oppressed workshop engaged in examining bullying incidents. While, at last we experienced a collective noticing of the way teachers and researchers were implicated in the bullying scene, we never got to a conversation about how white privilege was part of the scene. Though the idea that the bullies were white students was raised, the overall context of white privilege was not directly articulated. We did not get to a point of recognizing the manner in which white privilege was inextricably linked with the failure of teachers to both catch and report bullies. Teachers standing up to bullies meant teachers standing up to white kids. If both white and Brown transnational students were involved in a conflict, the teacher did intervene authoritatively. Clearly, there was an unacknowledged racialness in the white teacher/white student interactions.

There are things we could have done to decrease our methodological perpetuation of white privilege. In order for whites to effectively engage in social justice research, according to Karin Case (2004), they must generate awareness of the structures of white supremacy. For example, we could have included readings on white privilege in our work with teachers and organized some sessions and Teacher Inquiry meetings on this topic. We could have engaged in TO on the topic of white privilege taking the example of the lunchroom and the ways in which transnational students were interpreted differently than white students. Systematically speaking, we could have included and encouraged more readings by writers of color. The intercultural peace curriculum developed by the teacher inquirers touched on white privilege but did not center its violent force. A liberatory understanding of peace would require the rejection of white privilege and power (Thompson, 2019).

The Hidden Gendered Violence

The female transnational students experienced life in Unityville schools differently than the males, especially from middle school on. Across the schools we witnessed differential treatment of all students by gender—including for our transnational students. The differences were roughly aligned with what we see internationally (Leech & Humphreys, 2007; Rawlings, 2016). Rawlings (2016) and other scholars drew important links between patriarchy and gender and sexual violence in schools that reproduce the social violence that is prevalent outside of schools.

One day a high school teacher who was actively involved in our project was trying to get two transnational male students to stop playing around during class. She wanted them to get back to the tasks at hand. Ed was in the class observing at that time. He noted that after several failed attempts to get the two boys back on task, the teacher threatened to send the students to the office. But this was not a simple threat. She indicated that she would send a note suggesting that the boys were playing around with one another in a homosexual way. This anti-gay comment assumed and reproduced homophobia in the class. The boys quickly got back on task. Such homophobic micro-aggressions on the part of the teacher were not explicitly considered problematic in Unityville schools. Other taken-for-granted heteronormative activities regularly perpetuated gendered differences. We witnessed boys sticking up for girls, but not for other boys. We did not see girls sticking up for others in public ways. When elementary school Japanese girls began acting "assertive" their teachers and principal described them as being

Americanized in a negative way. Earlier I described the particular challenges Ms. Tu faced, stuck between her school and her family. These challenges were not similarly experienced by her brother. These examples of gendered heteronormativity were deeply embedded in the school culture.

During the time that Yoko was being paid by the school district to work as an ENL aide, she became a confidante to many of the Latinas in the program. She supported the students in ways that were not recorded as part of the research project, including their experiences with gendered oppression. Unfortunately, our orientation toward the commonplace gendered violence took a disturbingly idiosyncratic backseat to the main focus of the Project. Attending to gender violence in such ways reproduced/s gender oppression (Payne & Smith, 2012). Though we acted person to person in ways that called out gender violence and offered support to those victimized through it, we missed lodging a systematic critique that was undoubtedly possible through such a long ethnographic project.

Methodologically speaking, some of this systematization can be analytically accomplished. It is my intention to return to the data to do this in the future. Certainly, we did offer relevant recommendations to the schools. However, the Project would have been improved had we not been as complicit systematically as we were. There was a distinction between the gender awareness of our university team members and the Unityville team members. This would have been a good place to start. For example, we could have talked about our own schooling experiences as gendered beings. We could have read research on gender violence in schools from other ethnographies as way to begin the discussion. We could have worked with the transnational students to identity methodologies capable of understanding the gendered dynamics. Then, we could have used those data/analyses in dialogue with our Unityville team members. Rawlings (2016) found that focus groups with secondary students were successful at enabling participants to talk about sensitive gender issues. We could have also worked with the educators to articulate gender norms and then locate those in the context of violence.

The Erasure of Blackness.

As Thompson (2019) argued throughout her book, the pervasiveness of racism and racist ideology permeates all sectors of U.S. life through which the lies of Black inferiority—white superiority are propagated. Perhaps, as Dini described in Chapter 4, white people in Unityville have established an inclusive story about their relationships with Black people in the community. What they seem to no have articulated through that story is an explicit acknowledgment of racist ideology that must be stopped. They still indicate that their experiences speak fo everyone. Moreover, the use of the n-word and the comparison of Black childrer with Hispanic children in the schools suggested that, in fact, the community had retained an unacknowledged racialized notion of assimilation. This was noted particularly in Chapter 5. This problem was/is not unique to Unityville, though its ubiquity did not/does not excuse it. Neither did it excuse our complicity in it. Complicity in maintaining a racialized status quo is complicity in the perpetuation of racialized violence. This complicated erasure, was an erasure nonetheless. It was a form of hostility and we did not effectively dismantle it as Project collaborators.

While we pointed out the way storying in Unityville erased blackness as it simultaneously re-inscribed race, we did not overcome the erasure that hindsight would foreground. We engaged with Black students at the high school, but we did not systematically include them in the study. Black community members were not invited in for focus group interviews by our school collaborators. There were no Black teachers. Of course, we cannot accept the white story of blackness in the community as the de facto Black story. We are only free to interpret those as stories of how white people in the community imagined their relationships with Black people in the community. It would be inaccurate to interpret what was happening with the transnational students as independent of the relationships of inferiority/superiority that defined the Black/white dynamics of racism both institutionally and interpersonally. The stories of assimilation as synonymous with an implicit idea of becoming more "white" ignored the proliferated racism of the prevailing assimilationist expectations.

Unfortunately, our overall engagement with blackness was superficial. We could have done things differently. Despite the diverse make-up of the team, we could have had more Black members of the team to strengthen the visibility of our alliance with Black students. We could have conducted focus group meetings with combined middle and high school Black students. Then if we were unable to report on those interviews (in order not to risk confidentiality), we could have used them analytically and proactively in Project efforts and programs. More importantly, we could have woven in a deeper understanding of race. We could have more tightly connected white privilege with blackness through shared readings and engaged dialogue. This would have brought both better into focus for us. We also could have met with Black community members. The erasure of blackness in our work meant that we told the story of "newcomers" and traditional stories as if Black students were either fully assimilated or absent all together from the schools. These are common outcomes of white supremacy.

Summary

Our complicitness in the ongoing social inequity and oppression of the society writ large and the microcosm of Unityville involved a failure to significantly include white privilege, gender violence, or blackness as primary interests in our work. We were overwhelmed with the needs of the transnational students and we did not scope in and out to the degree needed. There is a risk in being this transparent, and I don't mean that in a sentimental way. My reason for reflecting on these complicities is to illustrate the role of unintended consequences and under-acknowledged advantage. Fundamentally, transforming society is not an easy task and each step is just that, a step. Never pure. Never unproblematic. Never beyond critique, most especially with respect to its own goals and values and their inescapable challenges.

What Might Critical Research Hope to Contribute?

In this final section of the book I want to briefly return to thinking about what this critical research can do in the world through three aspects: (1) how it might speak into the metatheory, (2) how might this study contribute to methodological thinking, and (3) how the study might contribute substantively. Then, I conclude with a subsection on the social relevance of critical research.

What does the research have to offer the metatheory? This Project drew heavily on the metatheoretical principles of Habermas's comprehensive Theory of Communicative Action. The study contributes to the metatheory by raising the link between empathy and position-taking and by linking this with a form of identity praxis, the development of a polity-in-the-making seems dependent on locating one's self empathetically in a community of/with others. Habermas describes position-taking as a communicatively complex decentering. Being oriented toward understanding, while deeply assumed in any attempt to communicate, seems to reach practical challenges if empathy and good will or at least benign intentions are not drawn on to motivate a more nuanced engagement. Our findings suggest that an increasingly nuanced and empathetic position-taking fosters one's ability to position take more critically and differently with one's own sense of self and that this might enable a praxis orientation that thrives on the *we* of a polity-in-the-making. While this does not contradict the metaheoretical principles, the points here locate opportunities to add to a refined thinking about subjectivity and community.

What contributions can the study offer to critical methodology? It was my intention to draw in complementary methodologies as a way of illustrating that one can draw on a multiplicity of approaches and still engage synergistically with metatheoretical principles. The emergent and collaborative nature of the methodology in this Project emphasizes an openness to a variety of possibilities, including artisti-

and narrative ones which work to deepen the called-for democratization of the research process and allow for researchers and participants to collaboratively and inclusively put themselves into the work, to be wounded. Again, I would say that empathy emerges here as a methodological concept.

We also included a local-historical element to the study (conducted by Dini Metro-Roland). This local historical work adds to critical ethnographic efforts in several ways. First of all, it takes seriously the hermeneutic references to history that participants themselves offer up. Secondly, it opens the door for systemic opportunities of analysis because it helps researchers locate themes and disjunctures over time. The interesting juxtaposition between the vacuous narrative claims of white European immigration, the historical record of migration in the community, and the distribution of white monocultural ideals could be further analyzed in ways that would not have been possible without the historical investigation. The historical analysis can be connected with the hermeneutic analysis to foster an articulation of cultural structures indicative of potential system phenomena (Carspecken, 1996).

What substantive differences can this study offer? Just in summary, though the substantive richness of the study was not the focus of this book, it is possible to see how the methodological orientation was tightly connected with the emergence of substantive insights. Most specifically, we were able to locate the role of empathy in the transformation toward a more inclusively thriving school community. However, we also noted the ways in which white privilege and white supremacy constrained the teachers' empathetic orientations. The very heart of a public schooling promise is put at risk by white privilege and white (colonial) nationalist idealism. In Unityville (as with many places across the U.S.), assimilationism was an idealism of white monoculturalism and a denial of in-group diversity. This is not new news, but we were able to notice its subtle work in Unityville and the manner in which white identity and the aims of inclusive education were at odds with one another. Transforming educational spaces into inclusive transnational polities-in-the-making require(d), at least in Unityville, the transformation of white identity and the anchors of privilege both personally and politically. My complicity in some aspects of white privilege limited the possibilities of our Project.

Can critical research contribute to making the world a better place? A study's methodological, metatheoretical and substantive aspects have specific effects on the social world which indicate the potential for research, more generally, to make the world better place through its conceptualizing, methods and outcomes. The social relevance of educational research has been largely assessed according to the extent to which the research has determined discrete attributions of causation or stable models of relationships. According to Carspecken (2005) the big questions of educational research are not of that sort. The big questions in education are values questions—for whom and given what values should teachers accommodate transnational students, for example. The institutional context of schools constrains the doing of research within them. And we know that schools, as instutions, are slow to change. The wide ranging outcomes of educational research have, so it seems, done little to alter the inequities and systematic consequences of schooling despite the robustness of the research work itself. The big picture can seem bleak for those of us trying to rupture through the status quo in our roles as teachers, administrators, parents, community members, policymakers, or researchers.

Payne (2013) created the methodological practice "Walk with me" to describe how he engaged with people on the streets of Wilmington, Delaware in a Participatory Action Research (PAR) project known as "The People's Report." In this large-scale study, Payne used a social justice analysis with street collaborators to make sense of resiliency and street life. Thompson (2019) used Payne's (2014) work to illustrate a transformative methodological approach useful for liberation and peace work. She argued that the involvement of street people in every phase of the research effort created an opportunity for liberation and peace (Thompson, 2019). The public dialogue was broadly inclusive. Payne's primary audiences were not academic. As Thompson (2019) clearly articulated, the disenfranchisement of Black and Brown people in U.S. cities and institutions demands a return, a reconnection, and a *walking with*. Payne's TEDTalk (Payne, 2014) reached out beyond the academic community with the hope that such dissemination can have effects for critical consciousness-raising and policy making. Payne (2013) was quite literally, *walking with strangers*. It was our hope, as strangers for one another, to walk together forging liberation and peace, uneasily and fallibly. Our methodological practices were necessarily involved in this aim. Our methodological decisions and structures were not neutral. They had consequences.

In the preface, I clearly aligned my own ambitions for critical participatory ethnographic practices with a desire to make the world (including me) better. "Better" is rather ambiguous, open, imprecise, and contentious. Of course, the primary story of this book is that methodological decisions and processes stand alongside "findings" as opportunities for bettering the world. I have promoted the idea that *being with* others opens occasions for transformations that are inclusive and layered. I take seriously the role of consciousness-raising as potential contributions (Korth, 2003). However, systemic change is needed and the process of consciousness-raising is slow. We must couple any efforts toward consciousness-raising with simultaneous resistances to the status quo and actions to end sociopolitical, structural violence. Changes in the public sphere, as many, including Carspecken (2005) have suggested, "… involve ideas about how collective will-formation can take place freely and without distortion, so that [diverse] communities of people may together work out the forms of life that best meet their deepest needs and potentialities" (p. 27). Contributing to public dialogue and public science is crucial to this endeavor, but always alongside those whose lives hang most preciously in the balance.

In the United States at a time when lies are touted as alternative truths, and the phrase "fake news" is bandied about as some form of legitimate way to criticize claims without having to justify the criticism, researchers must grapple with the role of truth in the production of knowledge. In addition to (and maybe even prior to) producing things like books, one must engage publicly in the contentious and unresolved political debates of our times even when we must inevitably do this from fallible positions. The heavy march of speaking truth to power is both the possibility and the responsibility of critical inquiry. It's risky because we must also engage on terms that admit the potential fallibility of our own claims to truth.

Yet, with a tenuous willingness to look forward, we move. Pocohantas reportedly said, "If you walk in the footsteps of strangers, you will learn things you never knew you never knew." Such walking is conscientização, a start for the willing toward unraveling privilege—the privilege of being able to thrive and beget power through one's ignorance of their own ignorance. Critical ethnography can be one way of engaging in this unraveling. Let's walk together with our own strangeness in the company of others who, thankfully, keep coming—a coming that crosses the borderlands and leads us toward methodological justice, educational promise, social transformation[1].

Note

1. Payne (2014), Karavanta (2019), Lawrence (1993), Anzaldua (1987), and Fine (2018), respectively.

References

Anzaldua, G. (1987). *Borderlands. La frontera: The new mestiza*. San Francisco, CA: Aunt Lute Books.

Cammarota, J. (2007). A map for social change: Latino students engage a praxis of ethnography. *Children, Youth and Environments, 17*(2), 341–353.

Carspecken, P. (1996). *Critical ethnography in educational research: A theoretical and practical guide*. New York, NY and London, England: Routledge.

Carspecken, P. (2005). The social relevance of critical ethnography. *What Difference Does Research Make? Counterpoints, 275*, 11–28. New York, NY: Peter Lang.

Case, K. (2004). Claiming White social location as a site of resistance to White supremacy. In J. Harvey, K.A. Case, & R.H. Gorsline (Eds.), *Disrupting White supremacy from within: White people on what we need to do* (pp. 63–90). Cleveland, OH: Pilgrim Press.

Dennis, B. (2013b). No so obvious? The structural elements of caring: An example for critical qualitative studies. In B. Dennis, L. Carspecken, & P. Carspecken (Eds.), *Qualitative research: A reader on philosophy, core concepts, and practice. Series—Counter points: Studies in the Postmodern Theory of Education* (pp. 407–437). New York, NY: Peter Lang.

Fine, M. (2018). *Just research in contentious times: Widening the methodological imagination.* New York, NY: Teachers College Press.

Ghandi, L. (2014). *The common cause: Postcolonial ethics and the practice of democracy, 1900–1955.* Chicago, IL: The University of Chicago Press.

Harding, S. (1987). Conclusion: Epistemological questions. In S. Harding (Ed.), *Feminism & methodology* (pp. 181–190). Bloomington: Indiana University Press.

Indigenous Action. (2014, May 4). Accomplices not allies: Abolishing the ally industrial complex. Accessed on June 1, 2020 from http://www.indigenousaction.org/accomplices-not-allies-abolishing-the-ally-industrial-complex/comment-page-1/.

Lawrence, J. (1993). *The great migration: An American story.* New York, NY: The Museum of Modern Art.

Leach, F., & Humphreys, S. (2007). Gender violence in schools: Taking the 'girls-as-victims' discourse forward. *Gender and Development, 15*(2), 51–65.

Karavanta, M. (2019). *Community.* In R.T. Goodman, (Ed.), *The Blooomsbury handbook of 21st century feminist theory* (pp. 449–462). London, UK: Bloomsbury.

King, R. (2018, March 4). Uncertain future for prominent Indiana dreamer. *IndyStar.* Accessed November 14, 2019, from https://www.indystar.com/story/news/2018/03/04/indianas-most-visible-dreamer-future-never-looked-more-uncertain/351670002/

Korth, B. (2003). A critical reconstruction of Care-in-Action: A contribution to care theory and research. *The Qualitative Report, 8*(3), 487–512.

Payne, E., & Smith, M. (2012). Rethinking "safe schools" approaches for LGBTQ students: Changing the questions we ask. *Perspectives in Multicultural Education, 14*(4), 187–193.

Payne, Y.A. (2013). The people's report: The link between structural violence and crime in Wilmington, Delaware (Formal Report). Wilmington HOPE Commission and University of Delaware, Wilmington, DE.

Payne, Y.A. (2014). Walk with me. A community development project [TED Talk]. Wilmington, DE. Retrieved from https://www.youtube.com/watch?v=PXNQ2C_d27A

Rawlings, V. (2016). *Gender regulation, violence and social hierarchies in school: 'Sluts,' 'gays' and 'scrubs.'* London, England: Palgrave Macmillan.

Sepúlveda, E. (2011). Toward a pedagogy of accompañamiento: Mexicanmigrant youth writing from the underside of modernity. *Harvard Educational Review, 8*(3), 550–572.

Thompson, C. (2019). *A psychology of liberation and peace: For the greater good. (Pan-African psychologies)* [Kindle Edition]. London, England: Springer International.

Vargas, F. (2018). The indignation of *cariño*: A comparative analysis of movement making among unapologetic youth. In L. Carspecken (Ed.), *Love in the time of ethnography*. New York, NY: Lexington Books.

Habermas's Theory of Communicative Action as Critical Metatheory

As a way of briefly introducing readers to the substance of what I will address in detail below, there are a few points that can be made. Habermas (e.g., 1985, 1987) argued that intersubjectivity is the basis for meaning, understanding, and truth. He also argued that truth is intimately linked to validity. These compelling insights draw our attention to the uncertainty of meaning, the conditionality of truth claims, the fallibility and consensual nature of truth, and the distinction between a claim and the content to which it points. Moreover, epistemology presupposes ontology with respect to truth and validity. Habermas differentiated between actions oriented toward understanding and actions oriented toward success which is connected to an empirical analytic distinction between what he refers to as "lifeworld" and "system." He also articulated a distinction between different perspectives comprising truth claims and importantly between claims regarding what is and claims regarding what ought to be. I will present these basic ideas beginning with what seems to me to be the most underlying and I will proceed to build on those by presenting the principles in three tiers. My decision to do this is heuristic—third tier principles being more easily understood when buttressed by the first and second tiers of principles.

First, it helps to have the core imagery described (Carspecken, 1999a)—the core imagery for the Theory of Communicative Action (TCA) is two or more people *in dialogue*. This stands in contrast to the core imagery of many other theories of meaning and knowledge that have the lone observer making sense of the world (this is the imagery we find in positivism, for example). At the most basic level of dialogue, when people are engaged in activities oriented toward understanding, whether directly or indirectly, their interactions will imply a scene through which all participants are freely, openly, and equally able to voice their perspectives and hear the perspectives of others. Clearly, in practice, dialogue rarely meets this description, but in all dialogues it is presupposed. Why freely, openly, and equally? Because understanding/meaning-making cannot be coerced. Meaning is a consensual process—you can never force someone to understand you, even when you might force someone to behave a certain way (Carspecken, 1999b). According to McCarthy (1994), "Habermas's argument is, simply, that the goal of critical theory—a form of life free from unnecessary domination in all its forms—is inherent in the notion of truth; it is anticipated in every act of communication" (p. 273). Habermas uses the phrase "Ideal Speech Situation" to refer to this core image where speakers and hearers engage in efforts to understand one another through mutually recognizing the validity of each other's perspectives.

Imagine a scenario that we can use to bring the following metatheoretical principles to life. Let's say you and I are sitting at my house drinking a cup of tea. We are talking about my experiences in Unityville. You are interested in this not only because you are my friend, but also because you have an interest in qualitative research. As the conversation progresses, I find myself talking about ways I feel inadequate for the work. I share with you that I often feel as if I am in over my head and as if the project needs me to have a different set of skills than I seem to accord myself. Then, I tell you that I feel embarrassed, even guilty, about being effectively monolingual. Let's use this example to examine the metatheory more precisely.

Tier One: The Most Basic Underlying Metatheoretical Principles in TCA

According to Habermas (1985), "Participants in argumentation [let's think of this as the more ordinary act of a conversation or a dialogue] have to presuppose in general that the structure of their communication, by virtue of features that can be described in purely formal terms, excludes all force—whether it arises from within the process of reaching understanding itself or influences it from the outside—except the force of the better argument [and thus it also excludes, on their part, all motives except that of a cooperative search for the truth]" (p. 25). If we unpack this core scene, we find two basic metatheoretical principles on which others depend. We will look at these two first: (1) Intersubjectivity is the basis for meaning, understanding, and truth. (2) Truth is internally linked to validity.

Intersubjectivity is the basis for meaning, understanding, and truth. In Habermas's two volume explication of TCA, he took great care to argue this point. Don't take my word for it: If you are skeptical, test this out against other readings or your own experience. Habermas posits an active conception of intersubjectivity—it involves taking positions with respect to communication (utterances, gestures, words, images, and so on) as we make inferences about the meaning of the communications. Meaning, you see is not objectively given in the external world, and must rather be inferred. In order to make inferences, we position-take. There are two interconnected modes of position-taking that constitute "intersubjectivity" for Habermas (which he developed in reference to Mead and others). One has to do with a yes/no/abstention position: "Yes" we understand and assent, "No" we do not fully understand and therefore cannot assent, or "Abstain" where we hold off assenting to a position, though it is likely we understand the position to some extent. This yes/no/abstention position-taking is most often left tacit in our interactions. You might be thinking, "What about when you assent in your words/deeds, but do not *really* agree?" When this happens, according to Habermas, then the original scene described above has been compromised in practice, even though in principle it is still presupposed. In addition to being able to take a yes/no abstention position, Habermas explained that intersubjectivity also involves grasping first, second, and third person speaker positions within the inferences themselves. In fact, intersubjectivity is thought to be "always-already presupposed" (Carspecken, 2003, pp. 1016, 1017) for the very process of inferencing to be possible. This definition of intersubjectivity is radically different from the notion that intersubjectivity connotes either a perfect moment of understanding said to unify two subjects (some metaphysical oneness between subjects) or an experience of total transparency between subjects. Habermas drew particularly on George Herbert Mead when he contended that truth/validity and understanding are structured through intersubjective position-taking.

Imagine, if you will, that I tell you, "I feel guilty that I am effectively monolingual." For me to offer up such a comment, I have to already, at least intuitively, understand that I have a special, privileged access to my own feelings. Whereas, in contrast, I will also understand that you and I might share the values I am promoting and the implied measure of my language ability. I must also be able to anticipate, in a general way, how you might interpret and respond to my point. In order for you to understand what I mean, you must make inferences related to the status of my linguistic ability as monolingual (which will be associated with the third person speaker position), the sincerity and honesty of my expression of feeling (which will be associated with the first person speaker position), the implied value of knowing multiple languages in the context within which I am speaking (which will be associated with the second person speaker position), what it means to be a monolingual person (which will be associated later with identity claims), and you and I must assume that we speak the same language and that the basic symbols I am using to communicate with you are shared with you. You might respond by saying, "Barbara, I know you have studied Spanish for a lot of years. Are you sure you are monolingual?" You would be saying "no" to one aspect of the meaning of my utterance—but not "no" in the overall sense because you would be tacitly saying "yes" to the implied value of knowing multiple languages. I would at least tacitly understand your response as one of several sensible possibilities. Intersubjectivity explains how particular responses are both plausible and anticipate-able. Your response has called into question something most explicitly associated with the third person perspective because you are asking about the status of my language ability, something that could be objectively verified from a third person point of view. As we understand each other, we rely on intersubjectivity through which these two modes of position-taking are at play. Position-taking itself is intersubjective and inferential.

Truth Is Internally Linked to Validity. Habermas demonstrated that whenever we claim something to be true we do so within an interlocking set of assumptions that must be understood and accepted as valid if the claim to truth is to be accepted as valid. The assumptions are *internal* to the truth claims themselves. That is, truth is immediately understood in the context of what validates it. In this way, truth is located in the realm of communicative, intersubjective action. The test for truthfulness is a matter of validity and not solely a matter of match between the claim and the external world as is often the way the concept "truth" is applied to research (Carspecken, 2003). We can look more concretely at this point, by further examining my claim that "I feel embarrassed that I am effectively monolingual." The truth of this utterance is directly linked to its assumptions of validity. Those validity issues come to the forefront when the meaning of an utterance is questioned. Here are some questions that might be asked:

- Is it valid that I call myself monolingual when, in fact, I have studied Spanish? What level of language proficiency would move one out of the category of monolingualism? What is the definition of monolingualism here? [We will come to associate questions like these with the third person speaker position.]
- Do I really feel embarrassed about this? Can we assume I know my own feelings? Is there something more subtle going on at the feeling level? Can we also assume that I would be free to be honest with you about this? Can

you believe me? [We will come to associate questions like these with the first person speaker position.]

- Is multilingualism a value we should support? If monolingualism is the norm amongst white U.S. teachers, what counter norms am I proposing? Do I think all of us, including you, should be multilingual? [We will come to associate questions like these with the second person speaker position.]

These questions indicate validity conditions that are presupposed in any sensible interpretation of my statement. Habermas categorizes the validity conditions according to epistemological premises associated with first, second, and third person speaker positions—we get more details on this in the next tier. You cannot fail to have validity conditions at work in understanding something to be true.

There has been a long tradition in social science of using the word truth only when referring to a correspondence with something in the objective world and thinking of validity as something externally appropriated as a measure of the correspondence even as philosophy has abandoned this. Habermas was one of many who criticized correspondence theories of truth. He argued that intersubjectivity structured our interpretations while simultaneously providing the ground for accepting that one's inferences were true to the extent that they met the internally required validity conditions. For Habermas (1985), then, truth is quickly turned over to validity. "A *validity* claim is equivalent to the assertion that the *conditions for the validity* of an utterance are fulfilled. Whether the speaker raises a validity claim implicitly or explicitly, the hearer has only the choice of accepting or rejecting the validity claim (taking a yes/no position on it and potentially examining it) or leaving it undecided for the time being" (p. 38). He goes on to say "[Y]es/no positions on validity claims mean that the hearer agrees or does not agree with a criticizable expression and does so *in light of reasons or grounds;* such positions are the expression of *insight or understanding*" (p. 38). Validity claims are the implicit grasp of the work of intersubjectivity—taking yes/no/abstention and perspectival positions to understand an utterance or communicative experience. Habermas was not the first to suggest this link between truth and validity ... it shows up other places to be sure. Basically the argument is that when we understand something we understand what it takes to verify its truthfulness or falsity and we hold the speaker, at least implicitly, accountable to this verification process. Even when none of this is made explicit in the conversation, validity is structured into how we assume truth, such that the validity can always be potentially redeemed and queried.

These two principles (specifically that intersubjectivity is the basis for meaning, understanding, and truth AND that truth is intimately linked to validity) serve as metatheoretical bases for the next tier of principles. The next tier addresses issues of truth and validity directly.

Tier Two: Metatheoretical Principles on Truth and Validity

This second tier comprises metatheoretical insights specifically related to truth and validity. These six insights distinguish Habermas, in important ways, from his critics and from other critical theorists.

Meaning Is Uncertain. Firstly, given Habermas's definition of intersubjectivity, we must assume that *meaning is uncertain.* We can never know for sure, what another person means. This uncertainty is not just a practical aspect of the work of understanding, rather uncertainty is built into the very structure of meaning. When we understand what something means, we immediately grasp the uncertainty in three ways—we get both (1) that the act could have been otherwise (that there is freedom in agency which has implications for interpreting intentionality); (2) that the act could mean a myriad of things for multiple participants, including both speakers and hearers; and (3) that we can only infer but never achieve ultimate, eternal agreement on meaning. This uncertainty principle constitutes an impetus for openness to others' experiences and interpretations which is at the heart of the ideal speech situation.

Truth Is Conditional. Secondly, because meaning is intersubjectively structured and truth rests inherently on its assumptions of validity, another metatheoretical principle of TCA is that *truth is conditional.* What this implies is that all meaningful utterances are meaningful precisely as they are conditioned by the assumptions of validity entailed in them, including the social conditions within which they are meaningful. Toward this end, "Habermas expands the idea of truth-conditional semantics [examining the semantic conditions that render and utterance true or false] to what we might call validity-conditional pragmatics"[1] (Carspecken, 2003, p. 1023). The pragmatic conditions are those "promissory notes" (Carspecken, 2003, p. 1023) that we offer our interacting partners when we act meaningfully (including, but not limited to, speech acts or utterances). This is a way of specifying the social nature of truth and validity without uncoupling the two and without suggesting that truth is relativistic in the extreme. Truth as validity will always be held accountable through its pragmatic conditions. This is one aspect of the way Habermas conceptualizes truth as socially constituted.

Truth Is Consensual. Thirdly, *truth is consensual,* at least tacitly. This principle proceeds logically from the notion that intersubjectivity involves taking a yes/no abstention position with respect to the validity of a truth claim. As such, there is space for establishing consensus via the redemption of validity claims. The space is not always beckoned and in many interactions, consensus is assumed and inferred in the absence of direct questioning validity. Validity claims are presupposed with the limit case of ultimate, eternal consensus in the background, though such consensus can never be known. This principle is evidence that TCA promotes a very specific social view of truth. It also speaks to the characteristics of openness and equality ascribed to the ideal speech situation

Truth Is Fallible. That leads us to a fourth principle: *Truth is fallible.* Because we can never secure ultimate consensus, we must acknowledge that there is always some sense in which the fallibility of our truth claims might be just beyond the consensus we have been able to achieve. We must remain open to the potential fallibility of our claims to truth, even if in practical terms such fallibility has not been articulated. This fallibility means that at any moment in time we must assert our claims with an openness to having their potential fallibility articulated—again linked to the characteristics of openness we find in the ideal speech situation.

There Is a Difference Between the Claim and What It References. Fifthly, a claim must be understood as *different* from that to which it refers—the two are not ontologically the same. This insight was well-developed by Derrida (1975), but is also important to Habermas's TCA. According to Habermas, our claims are speech acts. As such, they are involved in the coordination of social life and as expressions of meaning in that social life. Claims always point beyond themselves. While claims presuppose ontological existences, for example, of the external world, the claim itself is examined within a validity web—a dialogue—which will require more than establishing a simple correspondence between the claim and that about which the claim is being made. We can easily imagine this if we think of the basic scene—the dialogue. We, also, can imagine two people are talking about, perhaps, my concern over being effectively monolingual. Though the claims we make refer to my monolingualism and to me, the meaning of the claim is not as simple as pointing to my language skill or to me. There is no simple correspondence between claim and thing that would provide a satisfying description of the meaning. "Truth [and meaning] belongs categorically to the world of thoughts and not to perceptions [not to that thing perceived]" (Habermas translated and cited by McCarthy, 1994, p. 307). Truth and validity are communicative rather than merely technical achievements.

Epistemology Presupposes Ontology. One last metatheoretical principle that I would locate on this tier is Habermas's subtle way of thinking about the relationship between epistemology and ontology for validity and truth. Ontology is the study of the nature of existence or things as they exist. Ontological theories always posit a world of things. In social science we refer to social ontologies—theories about the nature of social life as it exists. Epistemology is the study of the nature of knowledge and its validity. For Habermas, ontological suppositions coincide with epistemological orientations. That is, *an epistemological orientation will presuppose ontological assumptions.* Not the other way around. This is a pragmatic view of the relationship between epistemology and ontology—namely, that doing/claiming implies being. An ontology-first view often results in limiting one's exploration to defining, describing and identifying some objective thing in the world. Doing social science like this necessarily resorts to a correspondence view of one's research goals. An epistemology-first principle looks, instead, at meaning first and then reconstructs its presuppositions. The distinction here is a corollary of Habermas' argument that intersubjectivity precedes perception. Perception-based social science emphasizes the nature of the being before one's senses. Intersubjectivity-based social science emphasizes the processes of coming to understand, coming to know.

Let's take the example of my claim that "I feel embarrassed that I am effectively monolingual." The error made if ontology is considered most primary, is to limit the scope of knowledge to tests of my linguistic skills through which it might be determined if, in fact, I am monolingual. The only THING one can easily grab hold of in the traditional objectivist ontological way is my existence (which is so obvious as to be unworthy of investigation objectively speaking) and the status of my linguistic production/ability. Here language ability gets treated like a thing in the external world—something we can define and measure with more or less agreement. To put it simply, Habermas's epistemology-first approach allows us to ask, "how can we know:

- that Barbara feels embarrassed?
- that Barbara is effectively monolingual?
- that there is something wrong with being monolingual?"

For each of those questions there are ontological assumptions which would be presupposed in our investigation.

- When we ask how we can know Barbara feels embarrassed we are presupposing an external, objective world to which we can associate Barbara's existence as verifiable by objective means, but we are also presupposing an internal world to which Barbara has privileged access—the world of her feelings, intentions, states of mind, and so on.

- The ontological presuppositions associated with asking how we can know that Barbara is effectively monolingual emphasize the external, objective world which works on the principle of multiple access because in our knowing whether or not Barbara is effectively monolingual, we have to have definitions and measurements (even if these are informal) that we can agree would identify her as monolingual. Being linguistically skilled is an externally verifiable attribute.
- When we ask the question "How can we know that there is something wrong with being monolingual?" we are presupposing the existence of a social world in which members of a community are linked together through norms, values, and regulations.

We will get more into these distinctions and link them to speaker positions in the next section. Here we see how epistemological questions are linked with ontological assumptions. They co-emerge, yet, heuristically, can be best examined by starting with epistemological questions.

Tier Three: Grand Metatheoretical Distinctions

I draw on three fundamental distinctions made in TCA that are typically taken up as metatheoretical principles by criticalists who draw on Habermas. These distinctions are between (a) objectivity, subjectivity, and normativity; (b) acts oriented toward understanding and acts oriented toward success; and (c) lifeworld and system. Below I write briefly about each of these.

Objectivity, Subjectivity, and Normativity. Habermas (1985) identified the limitations and critiqued the obsession with objectivity that was prevalent in the social sciences of Europe and the Americas in the twentieth century. TCA promoted an expansion of our conceptualizations of both reason and social science. His critique will make sense to our intuitions if we think about how he explains objectivity, subjectivity, and normativity. Basically, what Habermas proposed is that the meaning of our activities has to do with the reasons we would give to validate what we are claiming through the activity. The demands for validation, that is—what it takes to verify a claim—can be differentiated into three epistemological categories objective, subjective, and normative) which are correspondingly associated with third, first, and second person speaker positions. I have been building toward this description all along. Each of the three epistemological categories presupposes distinct communicative ontologies. These will be discussed below using the word world" to refer to the different ontological presuppositions. "[T]he idea is not that there are three ways in which things exist but rather that communication requires *existence* claims pertaining to three categories" (Carspecken, 2003, p. 1018). Habermas's contributions here cannot be overstated. Most social science literature uses rather imprecise distinctions across objectivity and subjectivity (locating them on a continuum, rather than as distinct categories) while rarely even mentioning normativity. These shortcomings do not have to be retained.

Objective validity implies the onotological world of things existing external to subjects, but available to them primarily through the senses. These claims indicate the status of things in the external world—"what is" and "what works." The validity of these claims depends on the principle of multiple access and involves testing out "what is" and "what works" using specified procedures and definitions. The principle of multiple access means that multiple people can verify the same claim by employing the same methods and definitions. Thus, the epistemology entailed in objectivity is familiar to most westerners in its prototype: the scientific method. In the example of my feeling embarrassed over my monolingualism, I implied that linguistic skill was something that could be validated objectively. This is because we can assess objective features of skills—skills involve "what works" in the external world—in this case, the production of language into the world. Precise definitions would be needed with respect to what constitutes different levels of skill. Measures (or procedures) would need to be identified. The *implied correspondence* of claim to external objective world shows up as a reference point in the inferencing process. We could proceed to verify if, in fact, I am monolingual. Notice that I am describing what must happen to validate an objective claim—I am not describing the eventual outcome of that validity process. It is not the outcome that determines the status, but rather the process of validation that one goes through when justifying the claim in the face of scrutiny. Whatever procedures we use for measuring my linguistic ability will have some fallibility in its objectivity. The test might mismeasure me. It might be poorly administered. Its definition of ability might be limited. But we would recognize errors in our definitions/measurement strategies precisely as failures to the objective expectations for validity. These errors would not result in recategorizing the claim as *not objective*. I argue for a critical path in public scholarship that does not lose its capacity to interrogate the facts as part, but not all, of its labor. In order for me to take up ethical orientations in my work, I must be able to engage with factual claims. Public scholars, like myself, do not engage with facts as if they are sacred, but instead we collectively wrestle with their criticizability.

Subjective validity implies the existence of an ontologically internal world comprised of my feelings, intentions, desires, states of mind, and so on as well as an objective world into which that internal world can be projected. Subjective claims indicate "what is" about experiences internal to me. The validity of these claims involves testing my honesty and sincerity. Subjective claims work off of the principle of privileged access (rather than multiple access). This means that the way I have knowledge of states of affairs/feelings/experiences internal to me is different from the way you would come to acquire that same knowledge about states of affair/feelings/experiences internal *to me*. Subject self-knowledge and subject knowledge of others is distinguished here. Subjective claims *imply a correspondence* between my expression/claim and a presupposed internal "world." The expression is valid if it is honest and sincere. Your understanding of my internal "world" is achieved through these various expressions, but my understanding of my own internal experiences involves more than this—it involves something to which you cannot have direct access with respect *to me*. I told you that I feel embarrassed about my monolingualism. My feelings of embarrassment are of this epistemological type—the way I know I feel embarrassed relies on a privileged access to my feelings. Ultimately you will make an assessment of how honest you think I am being and how authentic (or in touch with my own feelings) you think I am. If you lodge your own assessment of my feelings against my claims about my own feelings, you are basically asking me to provide you with information you can use to assess my honesty and sincerity. For example, you might say, "Well, you don't look embarrassed." You would be suggesting that were you to base your understanding of my feelings on an interpretation of my appearance, you would not see evidence of such feelings. The mismatch causes you to wonder whether I am being honest. In the end, even if we disagree on the definition of embarrassment (deliberating definitions is an aspect of the objective category) or on whether embarrassment is typically warranted in this situation (deliberations indicating the normative category), the question of my feelings must, in the end, be resolved by your believing in my honesty and self-awareness or not. Habermas's way of thinking about subjectivity is highly refined and extremely useful for social science. He does not think of subjectivity as a flawed form of objectivity, but as something categorically distinct.

Normative validity implies a social world for which there is a mutually agreed upon, shared set of norms and values. This social world is ontologically structured via communication. Normative validity does not refer to something that exists outside of communication as we find presupposed in objectivity and subjectivity. Normative validity claims indicate what should be consented to as good/bad AND right/wrong. Norms and values are validated by examining whether or not they should be consented to, based on both the system of norms and values within which they make sense and also based on the extent to which they facilitate the best good for those affected by the claim. Validity is achieved by examining the network of claims within which the questioned claim emerges. The implied correspondence at work here is entirely communicative and involves matching norms and values to a system of norms and values concomitant with a presupposed audience who employs them. We articulate these most easily by using words like should and ought. Whenever you notice yourself using these words to express the meaning of an act, you have most likely reconstructed a norm or a value. The norm most prominent in my point that I feel embarrassed about my monolingualism is that, in this day and age, U.S. Americans *should* make efforts to learn languages other than English. There is another prominent value associated with my claim, namely that linguistic imperialism is wrong (i.e., it is wrong to expect that members of non-English-speaking communities, must acquire English, but members of English-speaking communities need only speak English). If we were going to decide the extent to which the normative claims are valid we would have to do so by looking at their validity within a system of norms and values assented to by a community in both practical and ideal contexts. We would also have to discuss the extent to which the claim facilitated the best good for those affected. The distinction between *is* and *ought* is linked here to the distinction between claims regarding norms to which we *ought* to assent and claims regarding the status of the world as it *is*.

The distinction Habermas articulated between objectivity, subjectivity, and normativity is a reconstruction of the way people understand meaningful acts as evidenced in the way they resolve misunderstandings and query disagreements. In everyday life, these types of validity are tethered in their content to specific communities. That is, we cannot separate the validity of any of the three types of claims from the specific communities within which those claims are sensible. This is most obvious with normative claims and least obvious with subjective claims, but holds across all three. Thus, all validity claims are contextual.

Acts Oriented Toward Understanding and Acts Oriented Toward Success. Habermas stated that, "social actions can be distinguished according to whether the participants adopt either a success-oriented attitude toward one another or one oriented toward understanding. And, under suitable conditions, these attitudes should be identifiable on the basis of the intuitive knowledge of the participants themselves" (Habermas, 1985, p. 286). Habermas suggests that when a person is engaged in actions oriented toward success, the "actor is primarily oriented to attaining an end (which has been rendered sufficiently precise in terms of purposes), that he selects means that seem to him appropriate in the given situation, and that he calculates other foreseeable consequences of action as secondary conditions of success"—success is interpreted as "the appearance in the world of a desired state" of affairs which can be causally produced. "The effects of action comprise the result of action (which the actor foresaw and intended, or made allowance for) and the side effects (which the actor did not foresee)" (Habermas, 1985, p. 285). Given this, I will sometimes refer to actions oriented to success as actions oriented to consequences.

According to Habermas, there are two broad types of actions oriented toward success:

- Instrumental action—"following technical rules of action and assess the efficiency of an intervention into a complex of circumstances and events" (1985, p. 285).
- Strategic action—"following rules of rational choice and assess the efficacy of influencing the decisions of a rational opponent [rational other]" (1985, p. 285).

When a person is engaged in actions oriented toward success, she has minimal interest in winning the assent of others beyond what is necessary to secure the success of the goal. Habermas has argued that one can never solely be socially engaged in actions oriented toward success. He has written that "in communicative action participants are not primarily oriented to their own individual successes; they pursue their individual goals under the condition that they can harmonize their plans of action on the basis of common situation definitions [understandings]" (Habermas, 1985, p. 286). This communicative condition of harmony involves acts oriented toward understanding. For Habermas, understanding is always in play, even in acts oriented toward success, but we see the limits of one's concern for understanding through the boundaries of his or her strategic engagement.

For Habermas (1985), acts oriented toward reaching understanding are the original mode of language use (p. 288). Actions oriented toward understanding acknowledge a communicative relation among actors as subjects. Both speakers and hearers are open to listening to others and voicing their own perspectives and experiences toward a mutually agreeable consensus at some level—even the agreement to disagree. Actions oriented toward understanding always involve the potential of discussing both the validity of claims being offered and the communicative event itself, including the possibility that one's interactive partner is acting strategically. These points reiterate the idea that Habermas is not suggesting we will find an empirical distinction per se between acts oriented toward understanding and acts oriented toward success, but rather that this distinction is a principle that our communicative engagements will presuppose.

Let's see how this relates to the IU-Unityville ethnography. When I first listened to the phone message from Roberta, I interpreted her request for help as emphasizing a success-orientation. Of course, success was foregrounded, but this was just the start of the conversation. Through our early conversations the original request was resituated through our attempts to understand one another. I suggested that I didn't know enough about Unityville to contribute to solving the problem without learning more first and this created the opportunity for a shift which foregrounded understanding. When a success-orientation is taken up through interactions there will be assumed elements of understanding embedded within the success-orientation. In most instances, one can refocus such interactions toward an emphasis on understanding by engaging with those assumed elements. This is what happened in the initial days of my work with Unityville educators.

Lifeworld and System. The distinction between lifeworld and system is as interesting as it is controversial. There has been a tendency for social sciences to branch off from one another by emphasizing as primary either "lifeworld" or "system." Lifeworld, according to Habermas, can most simply be thought of as the milieu through which actors reach understanding and both actively and meaningfully coordinate their life plans with one another. Some people begin to understand "lifeworld" by using "culture" as a synonym. This can be helpful. The concept of "lifeworld" can nuance the concept of "culture." Habermas (1985) said that the concept of lifeworld is a correlate of the processes of reaching understanding (p. 70). "Subjects acting communicatively always come to an understanding in the horizon of a lifeworld. Their lifeworld is formed from more or less diffuse, always unproblematic, background convictions" (p. 70). The lifeworld also collects the interpretive work of preceding generations and in this sense is the conservative "counterweight to the risk of disagreement that arises in every actual process of reaching understanding" (p. 70). The IU-Unityville Outreach Project was born of dialogue and interest in understanding one another. We experienced the borders of our backgrounded lifeworlds through misunderstandings and we experienced limits on our potential for dialogue and understanding. In cross-cultural interactions, our background convictions are often brought to the foreground because those we are interacting with do not interpret our experiences from the same set of convictions. The very heart of being a stranger calls our attention to the limits of assuming, unproblemmatically, that we share interpretive an milieu/lifeworld.

   In complex societies, the burdens for communicatively achieving understanding across all negotiated, coordinated interactions overtaxes the capacities of its individual members. This has happened at the same time that the force of unquestioned beliefs, norms, and even traditions passed along from one generation to the next have been undermined, thus, requiring more communicative effort to establish consensus. Habermas (1985, 1987) used an historical analysis to argue this point. What is important for us is the idea that meaning in the lifeworld can be abstracted from its communicative achievements in systematic ways. Once this happens, the coordination of action can be systematically achieved without the communicative negotiation, at least in principle, that is presupposed through the coordination of activities in the lifeworld. For example, we can have "money" stand in for our "consumer and wage-earning capacity." As a consumer, I do not have to negotiate the fair trade for goods of my labor, money stands in for that negotiation. It might take me 12 hours to earn enough money to buy a coat, but the coat maker and I do not have to come to an agreement about the worth of the coat in terms of my work worth. It is the coordination of that money flow across time and space which stands in as a marker for labor and facilitates my transposing my labor into my consumption. Habermas refers to this level of coordination as the "system." It contrasts from the lifeworld precisely in terms of the way communicative action is entailed. One of the best ways to describe system relations is to describe the conditions and consequences/functions of action—particularly important are the characteristics of distribution.

Systems relations disengage from the lifeworld through actions oriented to success (which you recall are not totally disenfranchised from acts oriented to understanding). The system establishes its own momentum, that is, systemic relations are constructed through conditions and consequences/functions and will be perpetuated through a kind of homeostasis. What the system needs to maintain this homeostasis, we will think of as its "imperatives." Sometimes, imperatives of the system keep it sustained and reproduced without providing the kind of justification we would presuppose in the lifeworld. Money, for example, has become not just a stand-in for labor and consumership, it is also being bought and loaned. Money has become a commodity itself. A whole host of imperatives regulate the flow of money and now some of those imperatives are related to money as a commodity.

One example of system imperatives at work in Unityville had to do with the way a global market economy is involved in the movement of international workers across national borders, bringing workers children into nationally organized schools. If it is profitable to hire workers from south of the border, and the wages one can offer are still higher than wages the laborer would receive in their home country, the wage-earning/consumer power of the worker will draw her across national borders which in turn affects the distribution of labor—production, money, and people in national terms. We can track these distribution patterns using indices like the Gross Domestic Product, employment statistics, and spending.

Summary

To summarize, I presented metatheoretical principles which are important to understanding the ethnographic story I am telling. The concepts introduced here are developed further throughout the book. You can see that these principles say a lot more than the common statements about criticalists sharing a concern for oppression in the world. Seldom do we have the luxury of publishing our findings in a venue that allows us to thoroughly articulate the metatheory so we suffice to say … "Following Habermas, …"

Note

1. Put simply, pragmatic conditions are those that bind us as interactants to provide (and anticipate) reasons aimed at explaining why our actions should be interpreted as sensible. Semantics would be included in this, but pragmatic conditions are broader as they might involve, for example, the mode of utterance as well as the word choice.

References

Carspecken, P. (1999a). *Four scenes for posting the question of meaning and other essays in critical philosophy and critical methodology.* New York, NY and Frankfurt, Germany: Peter Lang.

Carspecken, P. (1999b). There is no such thing as "Critical Ethnography": A historical discussion and an outline of one critical methodological theory. *Studies in Educational Ethnography, 2,* 29–55. Oxford, England: JAI Press.

Carspecken, P. (2003). Ocularcentrism, phonocentrism, and the counter enlightenment problematic: Clarifying contested terrain in our schools of education. *Teacher's College Record, 105*(6), 978–1047.

Derrida, J. (1975). *Speech and phenomena: And other essays on Husserl's theory of signs.* Chicago, IL: Northwestern University Press.

Habermas, J. (1985). *The theory of communicative action, volume 1: Reason and the rationalization of society* (T. McCarthy, Trans.). Boston, MA: Beacon Press.

Habermas, J. (1987). *The theory of communicative action, volume 2: Lifeworld and system: A critique of functionalist reason* (T. McCarthy, Trans.). Boston, MA: Beacon Press.

McCarthy, T. (1994). *The critical theory of Jürgen Habermas.* Cambridge, MA and London, England: MIT Press. (Original work published 1978)

Comparison of Various Critical Orientations

Given the array of critical inquiry projects and methodological endeavors, I thought it might be helpful to provide a few comments about some of the methodological similarities and differences across modes of doing critical qualitative research. The categories I have established are false in the sense that their definitions and boundaries are most certainly blurred, nuanced, and cross-pollinated. In fact, there is a tendency amongst methodological theorists to draw from/expand on a variety of sources, and yet their work is still likely to be aligned more particularly with one metatheoretical perspective over another. Habermas's TCA is just one of several theories that would be considered critical and similarly Phil Carspecken's (1996) critical ethnography is one among several. In order to try to locate the critical methodological underpinnings of my study within the field of critical theories and practices, I must brush over the complexities that riddle the task itself. The following chart is meant to sketch a few broad categories for this purpose (recognizing that many distinctive critical traditions are being left off). I specifically considered the metatheoretical scholarship of Foucault, Derrida, Hartsock, and Habermas. In the subsection to follow, I will draw our attention to Carspecken's methodological theory and do so in part by contrasting it in general terms to those theories which owe more of their metatheoretical principles to Foucault, Derrida, or feminist perspectives like standpoint epistemology (Hartsock and Smith, for example).

Table B.1 Critical Perspectives

Metatheoretical Thinker	Methodological Theorists	Research Examples
Foucault (1972)	Scheurich (1997) Butler (1990)	J. Halberstam (2018)
Derrida (1975)	Lather (2007)	Lather and Smithies (1997) Mazzei (2008)
Hartsock (1987, 1998)	Harding (1987a, 1987b) Haraway (2003)	Avakian and Haber (2005)
Habermas (1985, 1987)	Carspecken (1996)	Winkle Wagner (2009) Ross (2017)

What is it that theorists from these different traditions mean when they use the word "critical"? We can examine this question, for now, by narrowing it to ask: Is what postmodernists, post-structuralists, and feminists mean by the word "critical" similar or different from what Habermas and Carspecken mean when they use the word? Of course there will be many variations in the use of the word "critical" by any one particular person, so we must remember that I am raising this as a point of comparison.

In general, there are a few things that the identified theories have in common with respect to the use of the word "critical." For one thing, "critical" tends to mean *challenging given assumptions about truth with a conditional and relative sense of truth at work*—criticalists intend to *not* take knowledge for granted. Knowledge is understood to be a human production. Also, these theories emerge as critical forms of inquiry in relation to some preceding, enlightenment-way of doing research.

In each case, the very theory itself (Habermasian criticalism, postmodernism, post-structuralism, feminism—as well as queer theory, critical race theory and so on) emerges *as* a critique of social science—a specific critique of very specific social science practices/ideas/concepts. In Table B.2, I presented a very simplistic view, but I hope it illustrates how various critiques bring forward different concerns over modernist social science practices and philosophy.

Just as the critiques of social science differ, so do the methods through which the critiques have been derived (See Table B.3.). Again, please accept the simplicity of these distinctions as a way of demonstrating that there are important contrasts across these critiques which are invoked in the methodological theories that carry them forward.

Table B.2: Critique of Enlightenment and Modernity

Critique of Enlightenment and Modernity

Derrida critiqued, for example, Husserl—a phenomenologist whose modernist ideas depended upon the taken-for-granted concepts of unity, sameness, and presence—the modern foundation for certainty. Derrida's critique drew attention to the distinction between what is signified and the signifying event, object, or experience (in other words the correspondence between the symbol or metaphor and what it symbolizes). He critiqued the modernist tendency to conceptualize this correspondence through a belief in pure presence. His criticisms undo one's capacity to be "certain" about one's knowledge. Derrida also proposed that desire and longing are linked to the belief in pure presence.

Foucault critiqued, for example, Saussure and Levi-Strauss—structuralists whose ideas depended upon a taken-for-granted sense of agency and structural coherence. Foucault criticized the modernist idea that "agency" was the core explanatory mechanism in social science—calling this an effect of the modernist way of thinking and not something that was "true" in the typical way we think of that word. He concluded that the structures of power at work in a given time and place account for what is considered truth and the rules for calling something truth, including what legitimizes a person as a "subject." His critique is a scrutiny of the power structures which underlie any given account of truth reducing truth to the descriptive power structures.

Hartsock (1987, 1998) critiqued mainstream science's notion that truth was most closely approximated through an aloof, disinterested scientific position. Her critiques of science invigorated and reworked Marxist material historicism from the standpoint of women's experience. Feminist critiques, in general, have evolved through a questioning of the core concepts and empirical practices associated with (a) differentiating women from men and (b) perpetuating oppressive and unequal effects through that differentiation. Feminists approach this critical task from a variety of (incongruent and evolving) perspectives and methods. Hartsock's standpoint epistemology (which begins as a translation of Lukacs', 1971, standpoint of the proletariat) suggests that a woman's life experience "under patriarchy allows for the *possibility* of developing an understanding both of the falseness and partiality of the dominant view and a vision that is more complex than that view" (Hartsock, 1998, p. 243, emphasis added, but congruent with emphases she made elsewhere in the same text). In other words, the critique here is one of perspective. By engaging in specifically female perspectives derived of their experiences, the falsities and complications of social story that hides its own dominations can be critiqued and supplanted with a view that is more inclusive and realistic—more truthful. Her main critique is that ahistorical principles of inquiry do not insure more accurate representations of the world.

Habermas critiqued, for examples, Parsons and Weber, to show errors in social science's overemphasis on objectivity with its false sense of neutrality and perception-first, correspondence theories of truth. Related to this, Habermas also critiqued the monological, one-observer assumptions implicit in enlightenment philosophy of social science. He argued that dialogue is implicit in the monological assumptions that were being taken-for-granted—that is the idea of the lone observer as progenitor of knowledge.

Table B.3: Critical Methods or Strategies

Critical Methods or Strategies

"Critical" practices associated with Derrida's work most often involve finding (a) that which is deferred in the act of assuming "pure presence" (deference in the sense of power and deference in the sense of putting off) and (b) that difference which is hidden in the act of claiming unity of presence and experience (the difference between signifying something and experiencing something). Being critical results in finding the difference, finding what is othered internal to what is being claimed as the same. This is a critique of the roots of modernism on self, on identity of meaning/sameness, and on agency. The critical strategy most often talked about is "deconstruction." This strategy results in the articulation of the contingent relations of all internal contradictions, binary oppositions and so forth through which the sense of unity seems given. (See specifically, Derrida, 1973; Lather, 2007.)

Foucault's criticism involves examining underlying artifacts that are implicit in the process of reifying names, concepts, discourses, and other meaning-reifying devices. This critique also involves identifying the power relations that keep the structures of those reifications in place. The critical methods associated with Foucault's work include archeology and genealogy. The critique that emerges through these approaches is structural. At base, the critique begins with what is given as universal and shows its contingent nature and articulates the power relations that keep the contingency buried from view. (See Butler, 1990; Dreyfus & Rabinow; 1983; Foucault, 1972.)

Hartsock's criticism employs an invitation to allow the voices and experiences of women to shed light on patriarchy and its myriad dominating effects by examining those effects from the standpoint of women's experiences. The critical methods associated with Hartsock's theory require researchers to struggle with the problematic and complicated social positions that are historically and materially given in the particular situation under inquiry. She says that first we must "use what we know about our lives as a basis for critique of the dominant culture" and then second "we must create alternatives" (1998, p. 223) The methods require an invested engagement in oppositional and differentiated consciousness toward a more accurate or realistic description of the way things are which in turn opens the space for liberatory endeavors. (See Harding 1987a, 1987b, 2006; Hartsock, 1998).

Habermasian criticalism involves dialoguing with those affected/involved about their life experiences by checking out their validity claims and by considering this life with respect to an ideal. The relative and contextual nature of the critique has to do with putting the specific contingencies of the lives engaged in the study into "dialogue" with other affected voices and universalized ideals (most simply imagined as democratic principles). Agents are empowered to the extent that they are understood and the validity of their claims to worthwhileness (etc.) are recognized. Simultaneously, the critique examines systemic forces which get in the way of this ideal potential for dialogue. Even when examining system phenomena, the researcher must maintain a performative attitude. (See Carspecken, 1999a; 2003; Habermas, 1985, 1987).

Table B.4: Critical Conceptions of Power

Critical Conceptions of Power

Foucault's famous "death to the subject" de-centers/ousts agents from any explanatory power for social outcomes. The subject is thought to be one outcome of a set of social truths and for Foucault, social truths are not really truths in our ordinary way of using that word. Instead social truths are reflections of social power. Accordingly, social power is most directly visible through discourse rules. Truths are artifacts of the structures of power. Truth is reduced to power. And subjects or agents can no longer suffice as the locus of explanation. Agency is supplanted by enforced rules about what is true and how truth is structured. Power is not only external to subjects, it does away with subjects. Butler (1997) critiqued and reworked this using Freud to argue that power and psyche are intertwined.

Derrida's work offered subtle insights about power and subjectivity by drawing our attention to the tacit processes associated with referencing one's identity through experience. Derrida wrote of both a longing and mourning for presence/sameness (identity) through which there is the power to be, to exist (Carspecken, 2003). From this point of view, "Power is the claim to existence of subjects who must live without any certain grounds, without anything but their power" which informs "efforts to gain recognition. ... Power is a feature of human motivation" (Carspecken, 2003, pp. 1010–1011).

Much like Marx, Hartsock's standpoint epistemology emphasized power as the mechanism behind historical materialism. Power, in her view, is masked by ideology, fueled through social relations, and indicative of the distribution of material goods and services. She argued that there must be the possibility of knowledge free from power and she calls for liberation from oppressive relations evidenced both structurally and materially.

Habermas's theory, like Hartsock, treated knowledge and power as separate. "This distinction between knowledge and power is an internal standard for critical ethnographers and all people generally to determine whether a culture is sexist, racist, classist, colonizing, or oppressive in any other way" (Carspecken, 2003, p. 1026). The central explanation for this conception of power has to do with the basic description of meaning we find offered by Habermas—namely that understanding cannot be coerced. Behavior can be coerced. Objects can be controlled. Outcomes can be delivered. But understanding cannot be coerced in terms of people's willingness to assent to what they understand. Recall the description of the Ideal Speech Situation presented in Chapter 1. The idea here is that when two of us come together to understand one another: "Power and its relation to knowledge come into the Habermasian framework ... through the emphasis placed on consensus for supporting validity claims" (Carspecken, 2003, p. 1026). A presupposed consensus is garnered from real or idealized audiences who are *free* to disagree. Power also enters Habermas's description of actions oriented toward success as the capacity to succeed with one's action intentions. Carspecken's methodological theory addressed gaps in this theory of power which will be introduced later.

Harstsock's concern for the liberatory potential of science, which she said is possible through standpoint methods, implicated an agentic tenacity for making things better by unmasking oppressive ideologies. Yet, among these four post-enlightenment critical theories (Carspecken, 2003), it is only with Habermas that we see the explicit engagement of values as linked to provisionally universal ideals such as freedom and egalitarianism. It may seem odd to say "provisionally universal." By this, I mean ideals which we open to query on universal standards of acceptance, that is, with a universal audience in mind, while at the same time acknowledging both the fallibility of such efforts (since we could never *really* anticipate a universal audience) AND an ongoing openness to have this universal audience revised/ made more inclusive as critiques of the presumed universal claims are offered. According to Kincheloe and McLaren (2007), criticalists "become detectives of new theoretical insights, perpetually searching for new and interconnected ways of understanding power and oppression and the ways they shape everyday life and human experience" (p. 407), including examining their own claims and assumptions. What they described is the criticalist's active invitation for broadening the presupposed audiences of work.

It is also important to get a glimpse of role power assumes in theory across these four broad critical streams of thought. In all four cases we must look at the concept of power in terms of its relation to subjects/agents and truth. The ideas of power across these various theories and approaches deserve some serious attention (see Table B.4).

In summary, four major streams of metatheoretical thought have been presented in order to demonstrate substantive differences and similarities in what "critique" means for each stream.

Carspecken's publications advanced a particular post-enlightenment, critical epistemology that moves forward from Habermas's work. (See especially Carspecken's 1999 essay on "Four Scenes for Posing the Question of Meaning" and 2003 paper on "Occularcentrism, Phonocentrism, and the Counter Enlightenment Problematic" which focus expressly on providing detailed explanations of the simple distinctions I presented above.) He not only described the post-enlightenment situation, he contributed to clarifying problems and shaping new possibilities and integrations. All of the specifications in Carspeckens' critical methodology rely on epistemological fine points (which I do not intend to reproduce here).

Phil Carspecken's 1996 book on Critical Ethnography is a popular resource for critical researchers. This and other texts by Carspecken served my work as methodological theory and practical guidance. In this appendix, I want to briefly explain some of the conceptual and practical advances of Phil's work. More detail will surface through the chapters. My descriptions of Carspecken's methodological theory advance the metatheoretical points articulated in the first chapter becaus some key features of his methodology serve to direct our attention toward the metatheoretical principles already identified.

New work in the area of post-qualitative and post-critical studies has emerged. Lather (2017) and St. Pierre (2014) provide important challenges for what it means to produce critique. These challenges encourage critical researchers to think about the limits of their work and to problematize their ongoing use of core imagery and concepts (Lester & Anders 2018).

References

Avakian, A., & Haber, B. (2005). *From Betty Crocker to feminist food studies: Critical perspectives on women and food*. Amherst, MA: The University of Massachusetts Press.

Butler, J. (1990). *Gender trouble: Feminism and the subversion of identity*. New York, NY and London, England: Routledge.

Butler, J. (1997). *The psychic life of power: Theories of subjection*. Stanford, CA: Stanford University Press.

Carspecken, P. (1991). *Community schooling and the nature of power: The battle for Croxteth Comprehensive School*. New York, NY and London, England: Routledge.

Carspecken, P. (1996). *Critical ethnography in educational research: A theoretical and practical guide*. New York, NY and London, England: Routledge.

Carspecken, P. (1999). *Four scenes for posting the question of meaning and other essays in critical philosophy and critical methodology*. New York, NY and Frankfurt, Germany: Peter Lang.

Carspecken, P. (2003). Ocularcentrism, phonocentrism, and the counter enlightenment problematic: Clarifying contested terrain in our schools of education. *Teacher's College Record, 105*(6), 978–1047.

Derrida, J. (1975). *Speech and phenomena: And other essays on Husserl's theory of signs*. Chicago, IL: Northwestern University Press.

Foucault, M. (1972). *Archeology of knowledge* (A. Sheridan Smith, Trans.). New York, NY: Harper Colophon.

Foucault, M. (1988). *Michel Foucault: Politics, philosophy and culture*. New York, NY: Routledge.

Habermas, J. (1985). *The theory of communicative action, Volume 1: Reason and the rationalization of society* (T. McCarthy, Trans.). Boston, MA: Beacon Press.

Habermas, J. (1987). *The theory of communicative action, Volume 2: Lifeworld and system: A critique of functionalist reason* (T. McCarthy, Trans.). Boston, MA: Beacon Press.

Halberstam, J. (2018). *Trans: A quick and quirky account of gender variability*. Oakland, CA: University of California Press.

Haraway, D. (2003). *The Haraway reader*. New York, NY and London, England: Routledge.

Harding, S. (1987a). Introduction: Is there a feminist method. In S. Harding (Ed.), *Feminism & methodology* (pp. 1–14). Bloomington: Indiana University Press.

Harding, S. (1987b). Conclusion: Epistemological questions. In S. Harding (Ed.), *Feminism &* *methodology* (pp. 181–190). Bloomington: Indiana University Press.

Harding, S. (2006). *Science and social inequality. Feminist and postcolonial issues.* Urbana-Champaign: University of Illinois Press.

Hartsock, N. (1987). The feminist standpoint: Developing the ground for a specifically feminist historical materialism. In S. Harding (Ed.), *Feminism & methodology* (pp. 157–180). Bloomington: Indiana University Press.

Hartsock, N. (1998). *The feminist standpoint revisited & other essays.* Oxford, England: Westview Press.

Kincheloe, J., & McLaren, P. (2007). Rethinking critical theory and qualitative research. In N. Denzin & Y. Lincoln (Eds.), *The landscape of qualitative research* (3rd ed., pp. 403–456). Los Angeles, CA: Sage.

Lather, P., & Smithies, C. (1997). *Troubling the angels: Women living with HIV/Aids.* London: Routledge.

Lather, P. (2007). *Getting lost: Feminist efforts toward a double(d) science. (Suny Series in the Philosophy of the Social Sciences) Second Thoughts: New Theoretical Formations.* Albany: State University of New York Press.

Lather, P. (2017).*(Post) critical methodologies: The science possible after the critiques: The selected works of Patti Lather.* London: Routledge.

Lester, J.N., & Anders, A.D. (2018). Engaging ethics in postcritical ethnography: Troubling transparency, trustworthiness, and advocacy. *Forum: Qualitative Social Research, 19*(3), Art. 4.

Lukacs, G. (1971). *History of consciousness.* Boston, MA: Beacon Press.

Mazzei, L. (2008).Silence speaks: Whiteness revealed in the absence of voice. *Teaching and Teacher Education,24*(5), 1125–1136.

Ross, K. (2017). *Youth encounter programs in Israel: Pedagogy, identity, & social change.* Syracuse, NY: Syracuse University Press..

Scheurich, J. (1997). *Research method in the postmodern.* London, England: Routledge Falmer.

St. Pierre, E. (2014). A brief and personal history of post qualitative research: Toward "post inquiry." *Journal of Curriculum Theorizing, 30*(2), 1–19.

Winkle Wagner, R. (2009). *The unchosen me: The creation of race and gender in college.* Baltimore, MA: John Hopkins University Press.

Details of Important Theoretical Ideas in Carspecken's Critical Ethnographic Approach

In this appendix, I provide theoretical explanations for six core ideas:

- Reconstruction is different than representation;
- Typification is a way of describing how we understand situations;
- Praxis is linked to recognition and the capacity for humans to see themselves as known and understood by others;
- The distinction between system and lifeworld has methodological impact;
- Egalitarianism is necessary when doing research WITH others and is central to understanding one another; and
- Facts and values should be distinguished from one another, though certainly they are intertwined.

Reconstructive Sciences and Reconstructive Analysis

The phrase "reconstructive sciences" is used to distinguish a kind of social science whose task involves the articulation of implicit, "pre-theoretical," symbolically structured, practical knowledge as a contrast to the inductive-empirical-analytic practices that were/are prevalent in western social science (Carspecken, 2008). This is a shift in orientation from empirical-analytic to reconstructive is embedded in a broader change in the social sciences from emphasizing sense-perception to emphasizing meaning as the most primary method for understanding human social life. Habermas (1985) said that doing reconstructions require us to go radically inside the everyday understanding of participants rather than to work from an either abstracted point of reference or an externally situated set of meanings. Going radically inside the everyday lives of participants *means that* researchers learn to take the perspectives of participants in the first place—engaging in what participants ordinarily do when making sense of one another. Researchers use reconstructive analysis to put into discourse that which participants would intuitively understand, but not necessarily be able to explicate. I like to use the example of getting a three year old to tell you how she makes sentences. It is unlikely that she would be able to tell you *how* she does it, but she makes lots of sentences and so she *knows how* to do this. If you collect a lot of sentences, you can reconstruct *how* she is doing this on an intuitive level. "The researcher learns the underlying 'structures' (generative rules, interpretative schemes, cognitive or moral schemes, logical relations) intuitively and implicitly in the way her subjects understands them, and then moves the implicit understandings into explicit, reconstructed, formulations" (Carspecken, 2007, p. 3823). There is a significant difference between this approach to inquiry and a strictly speaking inductive-analytic approach or an approach that emphasizes representation.

Here I provide a brief introduction to the details of using reconstructive horizon analysis (Carspecken, 1996). "Every meaningful expression can in principle be reconstructed as a horizon of validity claims falling within the three categories of subjectivity, normativity and objectivity; and arrayed along a continuum of foreground to background relations. This is called 'the validity horizon' and it is the most precise articulation possible for a meaningful expression" (Carspecken, 2008, p. 741). In the background of these validity horizons we often find deep, taken-for-granted worldviews, ideologies, beliefs and identities constitutive of routine cultural practices. According to Carspecken (2008), "[r]econstructive analysis becomes a form of critical qualitative research when it brings to light implicit and/or explicit forms of sociocultural criticism made by cultural members themselves. Internal standards for critique include the relation of norms and identity-repertoires to human needs for self-formation, development and emancipation and the relation of beliefs to actual experiences of an objectivated world" (p. 743). Carspecken (1996) developed a number of insightful substantive and analytic concepts which facilitate reconstructive methods.

Typification

Carspecken refined Habermas's formulations on position-taking and intersubjectivity by appropriating the phenomenological concept of typification to the domain of social life. When we understand others we engage in position-taking, but this position-taking is neither metaphysical nor direct. Instead, according to Carspecken (see especially 2003, pp. 1018–1021), as social actors we recognize a social situation in a holistic way, including a sense about various ways to appropriately engage with social others. We find an interactive place for ourselves and others so to speak in the social situation. Recognizing this social situation and the opportunities it provides for us to act meaningfully is recognizing the "social typification." "Position-taking is taking the position of another person or a group, but only through socially and experientially constructed typifications" (Carspecken & McGillovray, 1998 as referenced in Carspecken, 2003, pp. 1018–1019). What is given through a typification are varying degrees of specificity related to such things as what we might expect of others in an interaction, role structures that might be drawn on, the trajectory of the interaction over time, what kind of a person we can be, the range of possible norms we might reproduce or not, the capacity to articulate validity presuppositions, assumptions about the past, and the extent to which we share all of these with our interactants and the likely limits of our capacity for mutual understanding.

There is a general and a specific nature to typifications. The general nature is that when we grasp a social situation within which we notice we have an opportunity for acting meaningfully, this grasp will always include a general third person perspective associated most broadly with cultural rules and values. Typifications can also include a more specific or intimate third person perspective associated with having a history of experiences interacting with the particular people involved. When you are reading a novel, the author will cue you into the typifications relevant to the characters' actions by describing the interactive setting with the hope that you will recognize what would be expected of the characters by others in the novel and so forth. "In daily life typifications nest, intersect, expand, modify and layer in all sorts of ways that may be captured by the qualitative researcher" (Carspecken, 2003, p. 1019). There are two final points to make here about typifications. One is that they give us a range of ways to act and are structured on the idea that a person could always have acted otherwise. In other words, typifications to do not determine what actors do and say with respect to one another, they are instead resources for recognizing how one might both interpret and be interpreted. Secondly, we assume that we share typifications with our interactants, but we may not. When we are interacting in, what for us might be, an unusual context, we are often keenly aware that we must draw on quite broad social typifications in order to discern the extent to which we share interpretation repertoires and in order to maximize our capacity to act within some boundary of social acceptability.

I can provide an initial illustration with an example of my feeling guilty at the start of the project about my being effectively monolingual. I was talking with our the IU members of our IU-Unityville Outreach Project team and expressing that I felt guilty that I had not become fluent in a language other than English. I was the least fluent in languages other than English than anyone in our IU contingent. Such a claim would seem appropriate in that context. It would be easy to imagine me expressing that same point as a reflection in the context of talking with a friend about my experiences in Unityville or reflecting within a methodological tradition that encourages researcher authenticity. However, imagine if you will, that I walk into a staff lounge at Junction High School in Unityville where a group of female teachers are eating their lunches. I am the ethnographer-outsider. I have a paper and pencil. I don't know anyone in the room by name or job description, but they all know (at least by role) who I am. I sit down at the long table where they are eating. They are talking about how frustrated they feel that the new students do not speak English. In this setting, there is a general understanding all of us probably share that I am an outsider and that it would be most appropriate for me to not intrude in the conversation, not take notes, and not offer claims that expressly challenge the assumptions they are happily taking for granted. Had I spoken up about my own guilt, it would have been inappropriate and easily misunderstood. For example, it could easily have been interpreted as an admonishment against their own monolingualism. Moreover, it would stand as a good indication that I did not understand them or the situation very well. Likewise, if I was part of a policy-level meeting discussing whether or not to make an informal English-only rule more formal, my professional take on monolingualism/multilingualism might be appropriately offered, but not my personal feelings of guilt. This would fall outside the topic expectations for the conversation as well as level of intimacy amongst member participants.

Let's return to the scenario of me walking into the teacher's lounge when the same bunch of teachers are having lunch two years after the Project's inception I know the teachers by name and they know more about me. I carry my lunch instead of a notebook. This time I sit down with them and they are talking about how they feel inadequately prepared to teach non-English-speaking students Here, the typification is something like "mutual reflection and support amongst colleagues." This could be a situation appropriate for me to share my own guilt feelings about being primarily monolingual.

Let's see how a different typification holds a different kind of interpretive possibility for this claim of mine (not as an active articulation of reflection as I have cast it so far). I walk into the teacher's lounge at the high school in Unityville two years after first arriving at the school. The teachers and I are familiar with one another and, in fact, have developed a sense of trust. Roberta mentions that she has started a night class in Spanish primarily in preparation for a trip to Spain she has planned. Others at the table suggest this is a waste of time because "everyone in the world nowadays speaks English." They are not connecting this conversation with their own variously held expectations that when someone comes to the U.S. they should speak English. Then at some point, Roberta says, "Well, it has also helped me interact with our ENL [English as New Language] students." Now heightened awareness of my presence is noticed because Roberta, in trying to dispel the idea that her studying Spanish was a waste of time, has called attention to the something we are "supposed" to share—a desire to support English Language Learners (ELLs). And I am a visceral reminder of that "agreement." I feel the need to say something. … Something that removes the expectation that I might judge them over the extent to which they engage in activities directly related to supporting ELLs, but something that also supports Roberta whose Spanish-learning I actually admire. At this point I say, "I feel guilty about being effectively monolingual." The typification in place could be described as "chit-chatting among friends/equal colleagues," but it has the potential of being transformed into "Let's evaluate, from Barbara's perspective, who is doing their best to support ELLs." The typification of "chit-chatting among friends/equal colleagues" I was not referenced as a relative outsider, however, at the mention of ELLs, the typification could shift—relocating me as a relative outsider. Because I at this point, I had developed trusting relationships with the teachers in the room, I am able to contribute to ruling out that shift and I am also able to claim something that might not others in the group might explicitly disagree with. I would not have been able to do that in the first year. All claims must be interpreted with reference to the typification(s) within which they are comprehensible. The concept of typification is particularly relevant to Chapters 3, 5, and 6.

Praxis

Carspecken (2003) expanded Habermas's use of the concept power to further the very goals Habermas seemed to have in mind. He did this by suggesting, first of all, that when people are engaged in actions oriented toward understanding is a special case of trying to explicate validity claims that might be in dispute there are intrinsic motivations for reaching understanding that stand alongside the satisfaction in resolving disagreements as a means of advancing our knowledge and perspectives. Namely, there is intrinsic value in understanding and being understood by others as well as the pleasure in sharing ideas (Carspecken, 2003, p. 1030). "People feel empowered when they feel understood, recognized, appreciated" (Carspecken, 2003, p. 1030). We can probably all remember experiences that give evidence to this argument. By providing the details that support this point philosophically, Carspecken clarified how actions oriented toward understanding are connected with feelings of self-empowerment and the "self" itself. Given his reformulations of praxis as the production of "self" "through work and interaction with others" (Carspecken, 2003, p. 1036), we learn that "the desire to have one's self recognized, ultimately by one's own self, is a motivational structure core to praxis theory" (p. 1036). Recognition that best meets praxis needs is obtained because one's claims to truth and validity are considered worthwhile by others who are free to dissent. In this way, our worthwhileness as subjects, as selves, is precariously established.

"[F]ew things empower the self more than the experience of expressing a potentiality and then recognizing one's self within and through the expression" (p. 1036). Carspecken's elegant reworking of praxis theory led to the argument that it is self-knowledge which is longed for as presence and self-knowledge to which praxis is oriented. The consent to and recognition of our validity claims, which ultimately involves our claims to be a good person in very particular ways, makes possible the validity of our own self-knowledge. "Our claim is chronically, necessarily, uncertain and dependent on the 'gaze' of others" (Carspecken, 2003, p. 1037). Carspecken's praxis theory linked the social values of critical theory with the dis/empowerment of individuals within the ordinary interactive contexts of their lives. Every social act has some element of self-recognition to it and is, thus, amenable to critical reflection. For example, what is empowering for me in confessing my feelings about being monolingual is that you recognize in my imperfection a contriteness whose intentions you will associate with my "heart." In other words, if you acknowledge that I am a person of good intentions despite feeble capacities, I will feel empowered. If you recognize through my reflections that I am irreducible to those reflections, then I will feel empowered. If you recognize that I am a person willing to allow her imperfections to provide a mirror of appreciation for others, then my feelings of empowerment are strengthened. Lastly, if you recognize that despite my monolingualism, I am a person who brings something of value to this Project specifically and the world more generally, then I will feel empowered—at least in the moment, in a provisional and temporary way. These are things I *want to* recognize in myself.

System and Lifeworld

Carspecken (1996) made use of Habermas's distinction between system and life-world. In his five stage critical ethnography, the first three stages are designated for explicating the lifeworld of participants and the last two are devoted to spelling out systemic relations and the intersection of lifeworld and system in the everyday routines of participants (Carspecken, 1996, p. 189). Analyzing system phenomena extends beyond reconstructive analysis to describe the systematic or structural elements conditioning the coordination of actions across cultural/lifeworld contexts. "Epistemologically, systems analysis foregrounds universalizing claims to multiple access [remember these are associated with objectivity]. These claims approach ... a position that any anonymous person could occupy" (p. 189). The relation of system to lifeworld is not a determinate one because actions always could have been otherwise. Ultimately, across the work of social science, it is important to critical ethnography to include both system and lifeworld phenomena because an articulation of one without the other gives us only a limited explanation, description, and understanding of the phenomena of interest. As Willis (1977) put it, "Though the achievements of counter-school culture are specific, they must be set against the larger pattern of working class culture in order for us to understand their true nature and significance" (p. 52). One of the "central problems" plaguing social theory is the structure/agency dichotomy (Giddens, 1979). In its simplest form, this explanatory problem asks the question: Are humans the authors of their own destiny or are the conditions within which they live out their lives deterministic of their life outcomes? Though Giddens (1979) did not agree with Habermas's hard distinction between lifeworld and system, what he puts forward as a remedy for the structure/agency problematic in social science is methodologically compatible with TCA. Giddens (1979) created the concept "structuration" to reconcile the idea of human agency with structural explanations for action. *Structuration* refers to the theory that "the same structural characteristics participate in the subject (actor) as in the object (society). Structure forms 'the personality' and 'society' simultaneously—but in neither case exhaustively" (Giddens, 1979, p. 70). The concept of structuration effectively linked the actor to conditions of action. Accordingly, all actors have some potential for penetration into the system because they draw upon the very structures that might coalesce as systemic imperatives, including those that effectively oppress them—as was evidenced in Willis's (1977) study of the lads.

Carspecken (1996) drew on the work of Giddens (1979) in developing methodological theory and practices that could help qualitative researchers articulate system/pre-system phenomena in relation to lifeworld phenomena. System analysis moves the research beyond, without negating, what can be reconstructed of the cultural horizons of the lifeworld. Giddens (1979) proposed two principal ways to study system properties and Carspecken made use of them both. First, Giddens (1979) suggested that that social scientists could "examine the constitution of social systems as strategic conduct"—which is "to study the mode in which actors draw upon structural elements—rules and resources" (p. 80) to regularly bring about certain outcomes. Secondly, Giddens (1979) advocated identifying unintended consequences/outcomes of practice which are chronically reproduced through ordinary routines and consequently linking peoples' actions across time and space. Using these methods makes it possible to examine lifeworld data with respect to systematic and pre-systematic imperatives and descriptions. The fourth stage of Carspecken's critical ethnography facilitates the discovery of routine action patterns which are coordinated across time and space (Giddens refers to system integration as actions coordinated across space and time). The fifth stage of Carspecken's critical ethnography encourages the use and refinement of "concepts which aid in building abstractions off of empirical data toward macrosociological theories" (Carspecken, 1996, p. 203). Methods associated with stage four and five involve taking a relative outsider's view toward the more objective patterns visible through routines, outcomes, and functions of lifeworld activities across time and space as well as connecting those patterns with a broader world/literature of findings.

Egalitarianism

Egalitarianism is important to Carspecken's methodological theory in multiple ways. It is not insignificant that he closes his 1996 book with the following: "Remember that, morally, social research will either hurt or help people: it rarely has purely neutral effects with respect to human welfare. Making your research project as democratic as possible, from start to finish, is the best way to help rather than harm" (p. 207). Underneath this moral reminder are two important principles. The first principle is an articulation of the ideal speech situation—that any endeavor to understand others must take, both seriously and equally, those perspectives, experiences, and justifications others' would claim for themselves. Here equality and consensus-seeking are inextricably linked through the practices Carspecken is referring to as "democratic." The second is a principle that involves acknowledging that those who participate in our research are subjects not objects. When we conduct research, we do so WITH people who are subjects, that is with agents who themselves make subjective claims and identity claims, expressing intentions, motivations, proclivities and so on. To treat our research participants as means to an end or as objects in our quest for knowledge is to not really orient toward understanding them. Such an objectivating approach toward participants is deeply non-egalitarian. In agreement with other criticalists, Carspecken asserted that knowledge is never neutral. Knowledge is always a complicated prism of multiple perspectives. Egalitarianism is the best way to insure that the multiplicity of perspectives are voiced and examined.

Facts and Values

Let's look at the distinction between facts and values—the distinction between *is* and *ought*. This distinction was not made through either Derrida's or Foucault's criticalism, though we do find it implicated in Hartsock's (1987) standpoint epistemology and Habermas's TCA. A fact would be something like a claim that such-and-such IS a certain way—a claim about the way things ARE and the way things WORK. It is falsifiable or supportable through primarily objective means and thereby works through the principle of multiple access. Here are some examples: "Barbara speaks English." "Barbara has taken Spanish classes." "Some people speak more than one language." On the other hand, values are a specialized kind of claim emphasizing importance. Here are some examples of value claims: "Being linguistically skilled is important." "Multilingualism is important in our contemporary world." "It is important for language groups to be treated respectfully." Certainly, one's facts might be tangled up with one's values in ways that are not easily recognized. This is something that critical researchers must discern, particularly given that one of the characteristics associated with criticalism is a set of values. Carspecken's methodological theory helps us see what this distinction means for our social science theory, epistemology, and inquiry (see Table C.1).

Martin Hammersley (1998, 2000, 2002) wrote about the role of values in the conduct of qualitative research by posing such questions as "Should ethnography be critical?" His answer was "no" because to do so would involve, from his point of view, researchers extending their claims about the research findings beyond those given, from within the research process itself, as facts. When he asked "Should ethnography be critical?" he was asking about the purposes of research—that is, should a researcher have critical purposes, intentions or outcomes when conducting research which direct the way the findings are implicated, for example, on a policy level? OR should a researcher enter the field without particular purposes vis-à-vis how the findings might change the social world? He was not suggesting that one should not draw on critical theory or epistemology when conducting

Table C.1 Facts and Values in Critical Inquiry

Social Science Theory	Critical Epistemology	Critical Inquiry Practice including aims
The distinction between facts and values is important to Habermasian criticism of empirical social science which has traditionally masked its values as neutrality so that the facts it produced seem free of values. Making this distinction gave critical theory is critical edge over any social science that values neutrality at the same moment it claims not to have values, only facts.	Facts and values emerge from two different epistemological presuppositions. Facts work most directly from objective epistemology and values are most salient through normative epistemology. This means that factual claims must be responsive to a particular set of epistemological standards of validity (questioning what is and what works) while values must submit to epistemological standards of validity that question what should be regarded as good or bad, valuable/important/significant.	Facts are considered relative to values but are not held hostage to values. Researchers should always put their own value claims into the conversation in order to clarify in practice the relation between facts and values and to reveal the extent that the identified values might unwittingly influence the recording of factual findings. Also, researchers invest themselves and their research through values. The distinction helps researchers hold their factual claims transparently accountable to audiences whose values differ from the researcher.

research. Thus, we might agree with Hammersley on the level of ethnographer's held values/aims and still conduct a critical ethnography that instantiates a distinction between facts and values through its use of critical theory and epistemology. Carspecken made the point that you CAN use critical methodology without doing a study that explicitly intersects with typical criticalist aims.

References

Carspecken, P. (1996). *Critical ethnography in educational research: A theoretical and practical guide.* New York, NY: Routledge.

Carspecken, P. (2003). Ocularcentrism, phonocentrism, and the counter enlightenment problematic: Clarifying contested terrain in our schools of education. *Teacher's College Record, 105*(6), 978–1047.

Carspecken, P. (2007). Reconstructive analyses. In G. Ritzer (Ed.), *The Blackwell encyclopedia of sociology, Q–Se, Volume VIII* (pp. 3822–3825). Oxford, England: Blackwell.

Carspecken, P. (2008). Reconstructive analysis. In L. Given (Ed.), *Sage encyclopedia of qualitative research* (pp. 740–743). Thousand Oaks, CA: Sage.

Giddens, A. (1979). *Central problems in social theory: Action, structure, and contradiction in social analysis*. Berkeley and Los Angeles: University of California Press.

Habermas, J. (1985). *The theory of communicative action, volume 1: Reason and the rationalization of society* (T. McCarthy, Trans.). Boston, MA: Beacon Press.

Hammersley, M. (1998). Partisanship and credibility: The case of antiracist research. In P. Connelly & B. Troyna (Eds.), *Researching racism in education*. Buckingham, England: Open University Press.

Hammersley, M. (2000). *Taking sides in social research*. London, England: Routledge.

Hammersly, M. (2002, September). *Should ethnographers be against inequality? On Becker, value neutrality, and researcher partisanship*. Paper presented at the Oxford Ethnography in Education Conference, Department of Educational Studies, Oxford University, Oxford, England. (Revised version published in B. Jeffries & G. Walford (Eds.), *Ethnographies of educational and cultural conflicts: Strategies and resolutions*. Oxford, England: Elsevier)

Hartsock, N. (1987). The feminist standpoint: Developing the ground for a specifically feminist historical materialism. In S. Harding (Ed.), *Feminism & methodology* (pp. 157–180). Bloomington: Indiana University Press.

Willis, P. (1977). *Learning to labor: How working class kids get working class jobs*, New York, NY: Columbia University Press.

Dramatization for Teacher Professional Development

We created this script from interviews we conducted with transnational students in Unityville. The quotes are taken out of the context of the interview, but retain their meaning. We translated them so that all the quotes were in English. IU-Unityville Outreach Project team members read the parts of the students, while seated in the auditorium alongside the educators.

Translating Others: Voicing the Unwelcome Whispers

Actors
Barbara as herself (B)
Spanish speaker student 1 (SS1)
Spanish speaker student 2 (SS2)
Spanish speaker student 3 (SS3)
Spanish speaker student 4 (SS4)
Spanish speaker student 5 (SS5)
Mandarin speaker student 1 (MS1)
Arabic speaker student 1(AS1)
Arabic speaker student 2 (AS2)
Japanese speaker student 1 (JS1)

Japanese speaker student 2 (JS2)
White Teacher 1 (T1)
White Teacher 2 (T2)
White Teacher 3 (T3)

Scene One

T1:	I can't have these students in here. They don't know English?
T2:	What am I supposed to do here? Can't someone tell them how to behave?
T3:	What are they doing here?
Teachers:	Help.
Barbara:	*(To audience)* Initially, only the educators' voices were heard; students and parents were silent.
Barbara:	*(To dramatic actors)* Can you tell us about your experiences here in Unityville?
Then in response:	All participants talk at the same time in the home language.

- *Spanish speakers talking together in Spanish* (about not really understanding the new school, missing home, and family)
- *Mandarin speaker talking in Mandarin* (about living with aunt, how the expectations are different, liking the decreased pressure)
- *Japanese speakers talking together in Japanese* (about Saturday school, family, not understanding what is going on in school)
- *Arabic speaker talking in Arabic* (about job, not wanting to be in the ESL program, demands of family, school, and work)
- *Teachers talking in English* (about the untrustworthiness of students, their failure because their language skills are weak, wondering about why these students are showing up here in Unityville)

Scene 2

Notes for the Scene: Whenever the teachers talk they are talking as an aside to each other and/or me, but not talking with the students. The students are talking with me and not with the teachers.

Barbara:	*(To students)* Let's see if we have this right. It's really great that you are at this school. Do you know that?
SS1:	*(To Barbara)* Naw, we're not welcome here.
SS5:	*(To Barbara)* They don't want us here. They scream at us in the halls.
SS3:	*(To Barbara)* They tell us, "Migrant leave our town."
T2:	*(To other teachers)* Don't you think Hispanics are like the new Blacks

T3: *(In response to T2)* Yeah, I mean eventually they will probably blend in like the Blacks do.

T1: *(In response to T2 and T3)* Blacks and whites are the same here. The Blacks really came to fit in after awhile, the assimilated.

JS1: They don't like us.

SS3: They never call us by our names.

SS4: Sometimes they say to me, "Go back home you dirty Mexican."

SS2: They call me beano. And knock into me in the hall.

T1: *(To Barbara)* The white kids call the Hispanics lots of names.

Barbara: (To T1) How do you know this is happening?

T1: *(To Barbara)* Well, I see it and hear it.

Barbara: (To T1) What happens when the white kids do this?

T1: *(To Barbara)* Then the newcomers just walk off.

Barbara: *(To teachers)* Well, when I asked the white kids (those belonging to the key club and considered advanced by school teachers/administrators) if they wanted to make friends with the newcomer students, they said No. I asked why not and they said because the newcomer students have bad attitudes. I asked them to say more about their bad attitude. Everyone of the students interviewed said that not speaking English was the main indicator of this "bad attitude."

T2: *(To Barbara)* Yes, you see, the newcomers do not make an effort to fit in.

JS2: *(continuing the previous conversation, talking to Barbara)* They don't want us here.

Barbara: *(To the students)* What about the teachers?

AS1: *(To Barbara)* Even the teachers don't want us here.

T3: *(To Barbara)* Why are they here? I've heard there is a sign at the border saying, "Go to Unityville."

T2: I wish they would leave my town. I don't really want them here."

T3: Did you see that brightly colored building down town? It's an eyesore really.

T1: They take attention away from **my** students. That's not fair or right.

Barbara: *(To audience)* Notice that here when the teachers are using the word "they" in this instance, they are referring to Latino students.

SS1: They don't want us to talk in Spanish, but what can we do?

T1: *(To Barbara, said with pride)* I won't let them speak Spanish in my class.

T2: They could be cheating or talking about us. How would we know?

T3: And the best way for them to learn English is to use it exclusively.

T1: I wish we could get their parents to talk to them in English only.

MS1: Some teachers make fun of us in class. I don't know if they know this.

S2: Why is my teacher screaming at me? At the beginning I thought that she was upset. Then I understood she was trying to speak slowly and clear. Still, when she talks to me I'm embarrassed because everybody turns to look at me and I don't like people looking at me like I'm strange.

'S2: There are some teachers that help us, but not most of them.

S4: I like my class but my teacher speaks so fast that most of the time I can't follow him. I can't take notes because I don't understand the idea.

arbara: *(To the students)* Have you made any friends?

SS3:   I won't talk to my classmates. If I say something they will say a bunch. That scares me horribly. If I don't say anything, they won't bother me.

JS1:   We don't have friends.

MS1:   There's nobody close to me.

SS3:   My English is a lot better this year, but I don't have friends because I feel like I'm neglected.

Barbara: What about during times like lunchtime, for example? Can you make friends with local kids then?

T3:   *(To Barbara)* Sometimes, during lunchtime I find newcomer kids hiding in the bathrooms. When this happens I either send them to the office, after all they know they are not supposed to be in there, or I send them back to the cafeteria.

T2:   *(In response to T3)* They sit off by themselves when they are in the cafeteria. They keep themselves separate.

JS2:   I don't like to go to lunch. They see me and start making fun of me.

SS5:   At lunch, if we go to the other tables, the kids say, 'Go back to Mexico' or 'speak English.'

AS2:   They say, "You are in America, speak English."

SS1:   I like to speak Spanish.

SS3:   It feels good to speak in Spanish.

Barbara: Do you want to make friends with the EuroAmerican and local students?

SS4:   They are lazy. Mexicans are hard workers—in school we have to work twice as hard.

JS1:   They think they are better than us … I had to completely change and they still don't accept me.

SS3:   I play soccer. I love it and enjoy playing with them. What I don't like is that they don't call me by my name. They call me Mexican, migrant, or use other terms that I don't even know its meanings. This puts me down. But then, I try not to think about it.

Barbara: This sounds very sad.

SS4:   There is no time when I feel happy here.

Barbara: What about some of the rest of you?

JS1:   When I am sad, I swallow my sadness.

SS5:   I skipped school yesterday. My parents do not even know about it. I can't tell them. I can't make them worried about me.

SS2:   If I thought the rest of my life was going to be like it is here, I would want to kill myself.

MS1:   I don't really want to complain.

Barbara: Have you been able to get some support?

JS2:   My parents think everything is right at school.

SS1:   I don't talk to anyone about how I feel. My parents wouldn't understand me.

SS3:   My family moved here to give me a better chance. How can I tell them how hard it is for me?

Barbara: Do you think you can be successful here?

SS4:   I'm not that smart.

AS1:	Me either.
AS2:	I don't want to be in that ESL class. I think that will just make things worse.
JS1:	I don't know what they say, how am I going to make it in college?
JS2:	It was a thorn in the side that I was forced to write essays in English when I first came.
SS5:	I was so happy when I spelled the word correctly, which was very difficult for me.
SS2:	I cannot make it.
MS1:	We have to go ask questions to teachers on our own. At first, it was very difficult to do that, but if we won't the teachers assumed we understood.
AS1:	School is very different in my country. I don't usually know what to do here.
MS1:	I feel less pressure here, but I'm not passing my classes.
AS2:	Do you think I can pass?

*********** AT THE END OF THE PRESENTATION***********

Barbara:	It is possible to feel hopeful about the multicultural, multinational transformation of Unityville schools.
SS1:	My English is getting better—I understand more of what the teachers say.
MS1:	My teacher was talking about a "protractor" and then got one out of the desk and held it up so I could see what was being talked about. This was done without calling attention to me and it really helped me. The teacher was trying to help me.
JS1:	I made an A in a really hard class because the teacher gives me powerpoint papers to take notes on when there is a lecture. This helps me.
SS4:	We love this school because I'm going to graduate next year. My parents are happy because I'm going to graduate, get my diploma, and be able to work.
T1:	Help me figure out what else I can do?

A Short Course on David Wood's Hermeneutic Models of Time

The five models are Cosmic Time, Dialectical Time, Phenomenological time, Existential Time, and the Time of the Sign.

Cosmic Time

The cosmic model of time is what McTaggart (1908) referred to as b-series of time—a view of time that relates its components to one another through earlier than/simultaneous with/later than formulations. Wood said that cosmic time "[c]an be represented as a sequence of moments characterized by singularity, homogeneity, transitivity, universality, and directionality" (p. 321) whose moments retain constant relations across time (Futch, p. 127). According to Wood, this orientation toward time is important for the actual/real functioning of actors in the context of living out their daily lives, but should not be taken as a description of time itself. For Wood,[1] Cosmic Time can be grounded in the phenomenological model of time (described later).

B-series views of time are in contrast to the A-series with its view of "past, present, and future as mind-independent monadic properties that truly characterize events or times" (Futch, p. 126). In the A-series, time is always moving from the far future to the near future to the present and then to the past. The A-series, tensed distinctions are dependent upon objective time, but according to B-series theorists, truth validity involves the designations of earlier and later (Dorato, 1995, pp. 1–2). Futch (2002) offered this example of an account of change from the perspective of the B-series which I think illustrates the cosmic model of time. "A poker that is hot at some time T^1 and cold at some later time T^2 will have undergone a change from T^1 to T^2. The poker does not change by having its coldness move from the future to the present and then to the past …. This, though, means only that an event's temporal location does not change, not there is no change in the thing itself" (p. 128).

As a hermeneutic model for time, cosmic time refers to the intuitive sense of order related to understanding the world's experiences through the relations of earlier than/simultaneously with/later than—always relational, and never in terms of a progressive movement of time, but with things as they are: for example, humans walked on the moon later than they walked on the earth. This will never change.

If we put this in the language of doing ethnography, this model of time is what we would find when happenings are juxtaposed in relation to each other as opposed to being juxtaposed in terms of their tense relations (past, present, and future). Rituals[2] are a good example of cultural practices which are well-articulated through cosmic time, especially coming of age rituals, like getting a driver's license in the United States. When writing ethnographically about phenomena which are best understood through cosmic time, the necessary use of tenses can seem intuitively inadequate probably precisely because B-series time concepts lose something when they are expressed through A-series formulations. In the Unityville ethnography we can use the model of Cosmic Time to talk about the relations of particular attitudes that come earlier than other attitudes with the tensed point of those relations being moot and uneven. Attitudes of exclusion preceded welcoming attitudes toward transnational students. Also, descriptions of Unityville before "newcomers" and after "newcomers" reflect a cosmic sense of time.

Dialectical Time

The Dialectical Model of Time draws on Hegel's 1807 work (republished and translated in 1977). According to this model, what "the surface sequentiality of events reveals when interrogated is a deeper pattern of qualitative transformations, of development through conflict, the emergence and resolution of contradictions, and so on" (Wood, 1989/2001, p. 324). The principle at work in the dialectic model of time is qualitative transformation through which the process of opposition, conflict, struggle, contradiction, resolution, reflection, realization, and development, for examples, are foregrounded (Wood, p. 324). This dialectic time is essential to the way critical ethnography proceeds methodologically. The recursive nature of the research process is not well depicted through a strictly linear model, but is better captured through a model of dialectical time because it is the to-and-fro relations that mark the way time would be understood. This is usually the source of a misunderstanding amongst students enrolled in my ethnography course. They often begin by using a very linear hermeneutic model of time to make sense of the five-stage critical ethnographic (Carspecken, 1996) approach I teach. The stages are intended recursively so that the method can be described as embodying a Dialectical Model of Time though students tend to initially interpret the stages linearly and this produces some limitations in how they conceptualize the methodology.

Phenomenological Time

Wood identified what he called Phenomenological Time in Husserl's work wherein the temporal capability of consciousness is considered an intentional structure. This idea of intentionality with respect to temporality (and what Wood uses the word "temporability" to describe) is important to Husserl's *time* distinctions.

"How is the unity across time possible (experiencing a melody, itself temporally extended)? The key to this question is his [Husserl's] distinguishing and inter-relating three different aims of temporal intentionality: primal impression, protention and retention" (Wood, p. 325). Temporal intentionality refers to intentions specifically relevant to interpretations/expectations of one's past, present and future. The intentions need not be purposefully explicit (as we commonly think of intentions). Benjamin (1955) proposed a concept of time that introduced affect back into the historical thought (republished in 2019). He suggested that happiness, which is never experienced in the NOW, is, nevertheless, elusively experienced as possibility on the horizon (Hamacher, 2001).

This model of time emphasizes the first person experience with time and the horizon of anticipation involved in acting meaningfully. Phenomenological Time enters the ethnographic field work as part of the horizon of understanding meaningful action in context. Analysis that reconstructs interpretive fields from the perspective of the actor draws implicitly on this model of time by intuiting the way meaning is temporally charged through the three intentional structures of primal impression, protention, and retention. Fields of meaning are bounded, in part, by such a model of time, by what one "gets" of the previous acts (primal impression), by what one projects onto future interpretive possibilities (protention), and by what one retrains interpretively from the flow of interpretations (retention) within which one's act is sensible. The Phenomenological Model of Time is implicit in analyzing fields of meaning (Carspecken, 1996).

Existential time

Existential accounts of time are what Wood referred to as participatory; "participatory in that sense that it claims that we are temporal in our very being and the most basic temporal patterns affecting us are not those that organize the persisting objects around us, but those that involve our actions and our self-understanding as finite beings" (Wood, pp. 326–327). Wood drew on Heidegger's (1927/2008) work to exemplify this orientation toward time. Heidegger privileged this time in that it is the temporality of a subject for whom "being is in question and for whom the temporal dimension [its impending to-be] of its Being is [for itself] a key issue" (p. 327). With existential time, the future is privileged because we understand ourselves in terms of possibility, the possibilities of Being. In the later Heidegger, in *Time and Being*, "presence" is that by which Time gets involved in Being through acts of presencing, opening, giving, bestowing, and so on. Wood used the later Heidegger to speculate that humans' relation to existential time is one of "active receptivity" (Wood, p. 329).

Like Phenomenological Time, this model of Existential Time has relevance for the analysis of ethnographic data. It speaks to the openness of interpretive possibilities and can be linked to intersubjective validity of interpretations. That actors must and are the only ones who can be accountable to their own impending to-be's reveals the temporability of making identity claims and of situating one's self in the normative horizon of the culture (Tugendhat, 1989).

Time of the Sign

Wood referred to Derrida's (1975 translation) work when he wrote of the Time of the Sign. According to Wood, Derrida's work challenged the structuralist idea that the sign was free of temporal determinations. His use of terms like "trace" and "differance" introduced "an essential temporality into the sign, and hence into the whole empire of signs and signification" (Wood, p. 330).

Wood and others have argued that Derrida was treating both the sense and reference of a sign as having the structure of desire. "Meaning and reference always defer completeness. Textuality, in this light, can be seen as the movement of a impossible desire for plentitude, presence" (Wood, p. 330).

Wood's argument suggested that the Time of the Sign posed a pluridimensional model of time inclusive of narrative chronologies of events (even such things as the internal repetition of words, situations and themes) and different types and modes of time (imaginary, symbolic, biographical, historical, for examples) which were mapped onto texts (Wood, p. 31). Time's pluridimensionality is unavoidable in the Time of the Sign where any form of unification of these multiple dimensions is understood as an act of desire or power.

This model of time is relevant for ethnography because it justifies leaving the complexities intact, recognizes that where models of time unify (even in the case of this particular model) there is an interpretation of the relation of time and events at work rather than thinking of the unity of time as a mirror of objective, chronological facts. Woods' accomplishment, however, was to admit this as a model of time without discounting or eliminating the other models and without abandoning the idea that objective time has hermeneutic importance and factual status in life conditions. Lather and Smithies' (1997) *Troubling the Angels* featured this model of time most explicitly in the creation of their text. This text has many dimensions of time woven together. There was the expressive time of the women who were interviewed—talking about their lives in the present. These voices were shared in the text in the present tense through which they were originally articulated. But the analysis involved a dialogue between the past and present of the researchers and the voices of the participants. One really poignant complexity of the time dimensions of the text was the present tense expressions of women who died before the text was completed. Then there were sets of facts about HIV and AIDS which marked very specific knowledge at a given time (statistics from 1990, for example). Lastly, I want to mention Lather and Smithies' use of the metaphor "angel" which worked to transcend notions of objective time all together.

Notes

1. There is controversy about this. For an opposing view, see Futch (2002).
2. I am using the word "ritual" broadly here to indicate even such things as regular school-level practices for the ordering the day or even for ordering the school year.

References

enjamin, W. (2019). *Illuminations: Essays and reflections* (H. Arendt, Ed., H. Zohn, Trans.). New York, NY: Mariner Books. (Original work published 1955)

arspecken, P. (1996). *Critical ethnography in educational research: A theoretical and practical guide.* New York, NY: Routledge.

Dorato, M. (1995). *Time and reality: Spacetime physics and the objectivity of temporal becoming.* Bologna, Spain: Clueb casa editrice.

Futch, M. (2002). Leibniz's non-tensed theory of time. *International Studies in the Philosophy of Science, 16*(2), 125–141.

Hamacher, W. (2001). 'Now': Walter Benjamin on historical time. In H. Friese (Ed.), *The moment: Time and rupture in modern thought* (pp. 161–196). Liverpool, England: Liverpool University Press.

Hegel, G. (1977). *Phenomenology of Spirit* (Revised edited ed., J.N. Findlay, Ed., V.A. Miller, Trans.). Oxford, England: Oxford University Press. (Original work published 1807)

Heidegger, M. (2008). *Being and time* (Reprint ed., Sein & Zeit, Trans.). New York, NY: HarperCollins. (Original work published 1927)

Lather, P., & Smithies, C. (1997). *Troubling the angels: Women living with HIV/AIDS.* Oxford, England: Westview Press.

McTaggert, J.M.E. (1908). The unreality of ime. *Mind, 17*, 457–474.

Tugendhat, E. (1989). *Self-consciousness and self-determination (Studies in contemporary German thought)* (P. Stern, Trans.). Boston, MA: MIT Press.

Wood, D. (2001). *The deconstruction of time.* Evanston, IL: Northwestern University Press. (Original work published 1989)

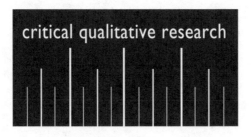

Shirley R. Steinberg, *General Editor*

The Critical Qualitative Research series examines societal structures that oppress and exclude so that transformative actions can be generated. This transformed research is activist in orientation. Because the perspective accepts the notion that nothing is apolitical, research projects themselves are critically examined for power orientations, even as they are used to address curricular, educational, or societal issues.

This methodological work challenges modernist orientations and universalist impositions, asking critical questions like: Who/what is heard? Who/what is silenced? Who is privileged? Who is disqualified? How are forms of inclusion and exclusion being created? How are power relations constructed and managed? How do different forms of privilege and oppression intersect to affect educational, societal, and life possibilities for various individuals and groups?

We are particularly interested in manuscripts that offer critical examinations of curriculum, policy, public communities, and the ways in which language, discourse practices, and power relations prevent more just transformations.

For additional information about this series or for the submission of manuscripts, please contact:

Shirley R. Steinberg | msgramsci@gmail.com

To order other books in this series, please contact our Customer Service Department:

peterlang@presswarehouse.com (within the U.S.)
order@peterlang.com (outside the U.S.)

Or browse online by series:

www.peterlang.com